ROYAL BRITAIN

CONTENTS

Produced by the Publications Division
of the Automobile Association

Editor
MICHAEL BUTTLER

Art Editor
MICHAEL PREEDY MSIAD

Assistant Designer
ROBERT JOHNSON

Tours compiled and researched by the
Publications Research Unit
of the Automobile Association

Tour maps and Special Feature maps by the
Cartographic Services Unit
of the Automobile Association

Maps in this book are based upon the
Ordnance Survey maps, with the sanction of the
Controller of Her Majesty's Stationery Office
Crown Copyright reserved

Photography by
Benmuir Photographic, David Bowen, Outline Photographic

Phototypeset, printed and bound by
Sir Joseph Causton Ltd, London

The contents of this publication are believed
correct at the time of printing, but the current
position can be checked through the AA

Published in England by
The Automobile Association,
Fanum House, Basingstoke, Hampshire RG21 2EA

ROYAL JUBILEE

The Queen and her family –
their lives and work

HER MAJESTY, QUEEN ELIZABETH II
During the last 25 years, Queen Elizabeth II has been a beloved and hard-working monarch, who has contributed enormously to the quality and colour of life in Britain and throughout the world. Her reign has seen great changes in the British way of life and her influence in shaping the role of the monarchy in our society has helped to provide a fixed point in a sea of change.

Childhood in the country
Elizabeth Alexandra Mary (known to her family as Lilibet) was the first daughter of the Duke and Duchess of York, born on 21st April 1926 at 17 Bruton Street, London. In 1931, the family moved to Royal Lodge, Windsor, and led a predominently country existence with dogs and ponies for company. The Queen's love for horses was born at this time, and she spent much time riding with her father in the Windsor parks. King George V died in 1936, and King Edward VIII, after only a few months on the throne, abdicated because of his greater love for Mrs Simpson. Elizabeth's father now became King. Before long the fires of war were starting, and the King and Queen went to Buckingham Palace, but kept their children out of London, at Windsor or Balmoral. Elizabeth's life in the early part of the war was relatively quiet.

After her 18th birthday, Elizabeth was allowed to enter National Service and joined the ATS as a Second Subaltern in 1945. She was posted to No. 1 Mechanical Transport Training Centre. With the end of the war, Elizabeth's public duties increased and she often accompanied her parents on official engagements. Prince Philip was now often in her company and in her conversation, and in 1946 she told her father that they wanted to marry. To give them time to know their own minds, the King and Queen took Elizabeth and her sister on a tour to South Africa in 1947, and it was not until 10th July that year that the engagement was announced. Their wedding on 20th November 1947 was a splendid occasion which did more than anything else to cheer up the post-war nation.

The Princess marries
They spent part of their honeymoon at Broadlands, the Mountbatten's country home at Romsey, and part at Birkall near Balmoral. It was planned that they should live at Clarence House, but it was not ready, so, after a brief spell in Buckingham Palace, they leased Windlesham Moor, a house in Surrey. Prince Philip was away at sea a good deal, and the health of the King was not good, but at least Elizabeth had the joy, during 1948, of expecting a baby. He was born, Charles Philip Arthur George on 14th November 1948, six days before their first wedding anniversary. By July 1949 the family were at last able to move into their London home, Clarence House.

With the King in poor health, Elizabeth and Philip took on a larger and larger share of public duties, although Philip was soon to be stationed in Malta. In August 1950, their second child Anne was born, and it was becoming clear that Philip would soon have to to give up his naval career. He did this in July 1951, and in the autumn of that year a tour of Canada and the United States of America had been arranged. Because of the King's illness, the start of the tour was postponed, so it was necessary to fly across the Atlantic, the first time this had been done on a royal visit. The tour was a great success, and early the following year, they set off on another, this time of East Africa, Australia and New Zealand. However, five days after they arrived

Princess Elizabeth and Prince Philip on their Wedding Day. The photograph was taken in the Throne Room at Buckingham Palace

in Kenya, on 6th February 1952, word arrived that the King had died. They flew home immediately.

The new Queen

The new Queen's accession was publicly declared on 8th February, by the Garter King of Arms at St James's Palace, and at a number of other points in Britain and the Commonwealth. The family moved into Buckingham Palace, and the Queen was instantly immersed in the business of monarchy. The twelve months until June 1953 were filled with activity, which came to a head on 2nd June with the Coronation ceremony. It was a tremendous occasion with full State ceremonial, and attracted enormous interest from the public, even though the weather that day was wet.

After the Coronation, there were a great many engagements to attend to, the domestic arrangements at Buckingham Palace and Windsor Castle to sort out, and Prince Philip's own position to clarify. Although he is the Queen's husband there is no official position of Prince Consort, and his individual role in the life of the nation has been worked out through his personality and interests over the years. Six months after the Coronation, the Queen and Prince Philip set off on their round-the-world Commonwealth tour. Back home they gradually set about modernising the monarchy. Domestic arrangements were streamlined and modernised, anachronistic functions, such as the presentation of debutantes were phased out, and new events like the garden parties and the informal luncheons were brought in.

Elizabeth and Philip were not able to be together as much as they would have liked due to their busy lives. This led to press reports of a rift in their marriage which were not true but which must have caused them considerable distress. Both of them did what they could in their public statements to set the record straight, but it was a long time before the rumours quietened down. During 1968, it was agreed that a television documentary film

The Queen and Prince Philip at Balmoral, on their Silver Wedding Anniversary

should be made about the life of the Royal Family. This was the first time that the details of their family life had been revealed to the public and the film was an enormous success. It also made the system of monarchy and the personalities of the Royal Family seem more approachable, and was undoubtedly one reason why the monarchy in Britain is so popular. The Queen also uses television for her regular Christmas broadcasts, which have almost become a tradition in themselves.

Milestones

1972 saw the Silver Wedding celebrations of the Queen and Prince Philip. By that time they had a family of four fine healthy children, the eldest, Prince Charles, already invested as Prince of Wales. They had made 21 State visits to foreign countries and a great number of Commonwealth tours which included the innovation of the "walkabout" in the Australasian tour of 1970.

They had also entertained many visiting statesmen and leaders from other countries, including most of the major historical figures of the past twenty years. In the years since then this work has increased, and now Prince Charles and Princess Anne can take a larger part in Royal functions, including overseas trips.

In private, the Queen loves the countryside, and is particularly fond of her home in Balmoral. She loves horses and horse racing, being a successful owner and breeder of horses. It is less well known, perhaps, that she is very interested in art. She has built up her own personal collection of paintings which includes several contemporary artists, and is now very valuable.

During the first 25 years of her reign, Queen Elizabeth has evolved a thoroughly modern style of monarchy which preserves the thread of British tradition without allowing it to become stuffy, and which sponsors with critical enthusiasm a wide range of active pursuits which are central to the development of society.

Two Princes

Prince Philip

Prince Philip is descended from the royal houses of Denmark and Greece. He was born on 10th June 1921, in Corfu, the son of Prince Andrew and Princess Alice of Greece. He was 18 months old when his family left Greece, and they made their home in St Cloud, France. He was sent to Cheam School, then near Newbury, where he turned out to be very good at sport. At the age of twelve, in 1933, his family decided he should go to the German school of Salem, run by Kurt Hahn. Hitler was Chancellor of Germany at this time, and when Philip arrived at the school, the headmaster had been arrested by the Gestapo. After one year, Philip was removed from the school, and joined Kurt Hahn at the new school he was encouraged to start in Scotland, Gordonstoun. That school developed much of Philip's character, and also many of his interests, particularly his love for the sea.

Naval Career

At the age of eighteen, he entered the Royal Naval College, Dartmouth. Two months after that he met Princess Elizabeth for the first time, although she was only thirteen, when she visited the college with her father, King George VI. Some years passed before they were to meet again, due to the intervention of the Second World War.

Prince Philip's first position in the Royal Navy was midshipman in the battleship *Ramillies* on escort duty in the Indian Ocean. By 1941 he was seeing considerable action in the Mediterranean on *HMS Valiant*. Philip's next meeting with Princess Elizabeth was later in 1941, when he was back in England studying for Naval exams. They enjoyed each other's company but it was not a serious relationship at that time. Later in the war, Philip attained more senior rank and was serving in the Pacific, celebrating VE day in Melbourne.

Engagement and Marriage

After the war, Philip and Elizabeth saw each other increasingly and rumours of a royal engagement started to fly around. On 10th July 1947 their engagement was officially announced, and from that point on, Philip's popularity with the British public soared. They were married on 20th November 1947, and had to live in a series of temporary homes until Clarence House was ready in July 1949. Prince Philip resumed his career as leader of the First Mediterranean Fleet based in Malta, and started to take on the additional responsibility of acting as a Royal representative. By 1951, it was clear that King George VI was unwell, and Philip decided the time had come to leave the Navy and take up a life with Elizabeth in England. Sadly, the King did not live long after that, and died on 6th February 1952. Elizabeth was to be Queen, and Philip was her husband.

A Modern Consort

He found there was no place in the British constitution for a Prince Consort, and this gap has allowed him to complement the Queen in her regal functions, while still maintaining his

One of Prince Philip's many sporting interests is carriage driving

individual personality. Philip's common-sense approach to life was soon felt in the domestic arrangements of the Royal Family, which he insisted on streamlining. He is not closely involved in affairs of state, preferring the freedom to speak his mind with breezy informality. He has become closely involved with a number of causes, particularly wildlife and conservation, and work with young people, which led to the institution of the Duke of Edinburgh's award.

Prince Charles

Prince Charles, the heir to the throne, was born on 14th November 1948 in Buckingham Palace. He was christened Charles Philip Arthur George. He was four years old when the Queen came to the throne, and he was present for part of the ceremony. He learned to ride young, and was able to swim before he was six. Both these activities have continued to give him a great deal of pleasure.

The Prince's education

His first school was Hill House in Knightsbridge where the Queen was anxious he should be treated like any other boy. His progress was average. He played a good deal of sport and he was developing an interest in drawing and painting.

His next school was Cheam, of which his father was a distinguished old-boy. While he was there, in 1958, the Queen announced that he was to be Prince of Wales. His full title was now His Royal Highness Prince Charles Philip Arthur George of Wales and Earl of Chester, Duke of Cornwall, Duke of Rothesay, Earl of Carrick, Lord of the Isles and Baron of Renfrew, Prince and Great Steward of Scotland, Knight Companion of the Most Noble Order of the Garter, but at school he was a junior boy called Charles. He was not an academic pupil, but one with lively intelligence and wide interests. His love of music was starting, and he enjoyed games, particularly swimming; during the holidays he had learned to shoot.

Many people had expected his next school to be Eton, but Prince Philip pressed for the more unconventional Gordonstoun, his old school. At the school, Charles built up his reserves of self-reliance on different "outward-bound" expeditions. He was also made aware of the extent to which Press interest could cause him embarrassment, when a book of his essays disappeared and was later published. During

Among Prince Charles' qualifications is that of air-sea rescue helicopter pilot

his time at Gordonstoun, he developed a keen interest in archaeology and prehistory. He passed his O-level exams, although mathematics caused him difficulty. He expanded his interests in music and theatre, taking the lead part in *Macbeth* in 1965. The rather shy, withdrawn boy was now becoming a much more confident, mature young prince, and ended up as head boy, or Guardian, of the school. In 1966, he left Gordonstoun to spend two terms at Timbertops, an outpost of Geelong School in Australia. Here he read for his A-levels and took part in all the outdoor activities of the school, including hiking, fishing, camping, and even sheep shearing.

His schooling now ended, it was decided that he should enter a university before going to the Royal Naval College at Dartmouth. The College selected was Trinity College, Cambridge, his grandfather's college and a royal foundation. In 1969, he spent nine weeks at University College, Aberystwyth, where he learned to speak the Welsh language.

A modern Prince

The highlight of Prince Charles' life came on 1st July 1969, when he was presented to the people of Wales at Caernarfon, and installed as their prince. The ceremony involved months of expensive preparation, but was a resounding success, the biggest display of pageantry in Britain since the Coronation.

After Cambridge, Charles had a short term of service in the RAF where he gained his wings. Then he opted for a naval career, entering the Royal Naval College, Dartmouth, in September 1971. In recent years, Charles now plays a fuller part in royal engagements, travelling all over the world for different functions. In 1975 he visited Fiji, Australia, Canada and the Arctic, Nepal and Papua for different royal occasions.

Now, at the age of 28, Charles stands as an elegant, witty, thoughtful person, with a wide range of interests and a busy naval career, who brings his own brand of humour and dignity to the occasions he graces.

The Queen's Family

Princess Anne

Anne, the Queen's second child, was born on 15th August, 1950 at Clarence House. At that time, her father was still serving overseas in the Navy, but he was in England when she was born, and returned for her christening in October. Her first Christmas was spent in the company of her grandparents at Sandringham, as her mother and Prince Philip were in Malta. Her first few years were, like Charles', spent in a fairly conventional way in the nursery. She was an affectionate child, adventurous and quick-tempered, but a born ringleader. When Charles went away to school, she remained at home receiving education from the governess. She grew up with, apparently, more self-confidence than her elder brother, but like him, was very fond of outdoor pursuits. In 1963, at the age of 13, she went away to boarding school at Benenden in Kent. She did well at school and fitted in successfully. She passed six O-levels and two A-levels, but excelled best in sport. She represented the school at lacrosse, but most of all, she enjoyed riding. The training she received at school gave her the grounding for her subsequent successful career in horsemanship.

When she left school and entered public life, Anne found, at first, the restrictions and limitations were irksome. However, she quickly adapted to the situation as it was and made the best of it. She developed a distinctive fashion sense, and increasingly attracted the attention of photographers. At times this attention was not entirely welcome, but Anne learned to tolerate it. She now fulfils a wide variety of engagements, particularly as president of the Save the Children Fund. She has her own office and staff in Buckingham Palace, and takes her public duties very seriously.

Princess Anne riding Goodwill in the 1976 Olympic Games in Montreal

A particularly auspicious event in which many aspects of Princess Anne's public presence were seen to advantage took place in autumn 1971, when she and Prince Philip went to Persia, to the 2,500th anniversary of the founding of Persepolis. It was an international occasion, and Princess Anne, looking radiant, was a glamorous representative of Britain. 1971 also saw her elected Sportswoman of the Year. Anne's love of horses had developed naturally from the Royal Family interest. She rides with enthusiasm and skill, and in 1976 represented Britain in the Olympic Games in Montreal.

During 1973, she was seen frequently with Captain Mark Phillips and rumours started of a royal wedding. To everyone's delight these turned out to be true, and the wedding took place in Westminster Abbey on 14th November 1973. For a while the couple lived at Sandhurst, but in 1976, the Queen gave them their own house at Gatcombe Park in Gloucestershire.

In March 1974, a highly dramatic event took place in which Princess Anne's life was threatened. She was coming home to Buckingham Palace with her husband after an evening at the theatre. Driving down The Mall, their car was stopped by an armed man firing into it, and attempting to kidnap the Princess. The detectives and bodyguards were able to foil the attempt, and were later presented with bravery awards by the Queen.

The Queen Mother

On 4th August 1975, Queen Elizabeth the Queen Mother celebrated her 75th birthday. She married George VI, then Duke of York, in 1923, little realising that he was going to be the next King. She was born Lady Elizabeth Angela Margerite Bowes-Lyon, daughter of the Earl and Countess of Strathmore of Glamis Castle in Angus in Scotland, where she was educated and brought up. Her first child, Princess Elizabeth, Alexandra Mary, our Queen, was born on 21st April 1926, and four years later, Princess Margaret Rose was born. King George V died in 1936 and was succeeded by the Prince of Wales, Edward VIII. Before he was crowned, however, his love for Mrs Wallis Simpson led him, after profound heart-searching, to abdicate the throne in December 1936. Next in line was the Duke of York and he became King George VI. He was a diffident monarch, but was helped immeasurably by the devotion and strength of his wife, Elizabeth.

Much of their life encompassed the tribulations and tragedies of the Second World War, but the resolute cheerfulness of the King and Queen helped sustain the British people. By 1949, concern was starting to grow for the King's health, and many of his duties fell on the Queen. He died on 6th February 1952, and was succeeded by his daughter Elizabeth at the age of twenty-five. At first the Queen Mother intended to withdraw from public life, but the public would not let her. She bought a remote Scottish castle, now called the Castle of Mey, which she has carefully restored. Her public activities still keep her fully occupied, but her greatest pleasures come from her family. She is especially close to Prince Charles, and indeed the two of them are the best fishermen in the Royal Family. She maintains her interest in horse racing, owning several horses. Her life has spanned the whole development of

Queen Elizabeth, the Queen Mother on her 75th birthday

the modern British monarchy, and she has herself contributed to this with her sunny good nature and her informal dignity, endearing herself unforgettably to the British people.

Prince Andrew

The Queen's second son is over eleven years younger than Prince Charles, and is now 16 years of age. He was born on 19th February 1960, Andrew Albert Christian Edward. In his early years he was not much in the public eye except when new photographs of him were released. He is now at Gordonstoun, Prince Charles' old school, and during 1975 was able to spend a few weeks in Toulouse studying French without his presence being revealed by the Press.

Prince Edward

The youngest of the Royal Family, he was born on 10th March 1964, and christened Edward Anthony Richard Louis. Like his brother he has been little in the public eye, but has shown early promise of artistic ability. In July 1976 he flew with his brother Prince Charles to the Olympic Games in Montreal to join his parents watching Princess Anne compete for Britain in the three day equestrian event.

Prince Andrew

Prince Edward

The Grand Occasions

The twenty-five years of the Queen's reign have seen thousands of impressive occasions, but, of all of them, four stand out because of their importance to the Royal Family personally, and also because of the splendour of the pageantry seen at the time.

Coronation—2nd June 1953

The coronation is one of the most ancient ceremonies in Britain. It signifies the re-birth of national life after the death of the previous monarch, and originally took place immediately after the funeral. Today, about a year elapses between the two events because of the complexity of the arrangements which have to be made. The first known coronation was that of King Edgar in Bath in 973. Since the time of William the Conqueror, however, all coronations have taken place in Westminster Abbey.

The planning of the coronation of Elizabeth II was the most complex of any previous ceremony of state. The arrangements were in the hands of the Earl Marshal, the Duke of Norfolk, and presented particular problems because the event was to be shown on television. Many other committees were also actively involved, and Elizabeth herself imposed her own views on how the arrangements should be conducted. After over twelve months of planning, the day dawned, Tuesday 2nd June 1953, and at 10.26am, the Gold State Coach, drawn by eight Windsor greys, left Buckingham Palace *en route* for Westminster Abbey. In spite of the overcast weather, the processional route was thronged with people waving and cheering.

As the Queen entered the nave of Westminster Abbey the choir shouted "*vivat*", and she processed down the aisle to the High Altar for the ceremonial Recognition. The Archbishop of Canterbury presented her to the assembly, asking them to pay her homage. The reply was

Elizabeth II, crowned Queen, holding the Sceptre and the Rod

"God Save Queen Elizabeth". After the Recognition, she took the coronation oaths, and this was followed by Holy Communion. The Annointing was carried out by the Archbishop, with the Queen sitting in King Edward's Coronation Chair, and after this she received the regal ornaments, the gold spurs, the Sword of State, the Robe Royal and the Stole Royal. Seated in the coronation chair, she received the Orb, the Sceptre with the Cross, and the Rod with the Dove. Then the Archbishop placed King Edward's Crown on her head, and the congregation shouted "God Save the Queen". The Queen was then taken to the Throne to receive the acts of Homage, first from the Archbishop, then from Prince Philip, and subsequently from the other royal peers. After receiving communion, the service was concluded, and the Queen retired to be divested of her coronation robes. She changed King Edward's Crown for the Imperial Crown, donned the royal robe of purple velvet, carried the Orb and Sceptre in her hands, and joined the great procession to the west door of the Abbey. The journey back to Buckingham Palace took a longer route than the first, and was concluded with a triumphant appearance on Buckingham Palace balcony.

Investiture of the Prince of Wales— 1st July 1969

This ancient ceremony dating back to the 13th century was the most important Royal event of the last twenty-five years, after the Coronation. It took place in Caernarfon Castle, and was a splendid occasion, which like the Coronation, took months of careful planning. The previous investiture to take place at Caernarfon was of Prince Edward, son of King George V in 1911. Before that, the investiture ceremony was given little prominence, sometimes consisting of a brief ceremony in the House of Lords, and often it was not celebrated at all.

The planning of the investiture of Prince Charles followed the pattern of the previous ceremony of 1911, although there were more difficult security problems and the needs of television had to be catered for. The Earl Marshal was in charge of the arrangements and Lord Snowdon, as Constable of Caernarfon Castle, was also involved in the planning and design. The cost was approximately £200,000, and the event became a mini-coronation, with elaborate ceremonial and pageantry in an historic setting.

Caernarfon 1969, scene of the investiture of Prince Charles as Prince of Wales

For the ceremony, the Queen was seated on a slate throne at one end of the castle. The Garter King of Arms summoned the Prince, who came in procession from the Chamberlain Tower, in the company of heralds and lords bearing the princely insignia. He knelt in front of the throne, and the Letters Patent, the instrument by which he would be created a peer, were read out, first in English, then in Welsh. At the appropriate moment during the reading of the Welsh text, the Queen invested the Prince by girding him with a sword, putting a coronet on his head and a gold ring on his finger, and also delivering a gold rod into his hand, and putting on the mantle. After doing homage, he took his place on the throne, and replied in Welsh to the loyal address.

The fluency of his pronunciation endeared Prince Charles considerably to the Welsh people. After a short religious service, the Queen and Prince Philip went with the Prince of Wales to present him to the people, accompanied by trumpet fanfares.

Silver Wedding Anniversary— 20th November 1972

This particular anniversary marked a significant milestone, not only as a personal celebration of twenty-five years of happy marriage for the Queen and Prince Philip, but also a point in time when the monarchy in Britain could be assessed. The Queen had been on the throne for twenty years, and during that time much had changed. It began to be appreciated that the sovereign had an important role as a focus of stability in the midst of change, and the Queen's success in fulfilling this role was widely recognised. A special service to celebrate the anniversary was held in Westminster Abbey, after which the Queen, Prince Philip, Prince Charles and Princess Anne drove for lunch to the Guildhall in the City of London. Later the Queen visited the new building development in the Barbican for a walkabout, and in the evening held a private party at Buckingham Palace.

Princess Anne and Mark Phillips at their wedding ceremony in Westminster Abbey

Princess Anne's Wedding— 14th November 1973

Princess Anne had come to meet Lieutenant (now Captain) Mark Phillips of the Queen's Dragoon Guards in the early 1970s due to her love of horses. They were seen together increasingly, and when their engagement was announced on 20th May, it delighted the nation. Their wedding took place almost six months later on Prince Charles' 25th birthday, in Westminster Abbey, watched on television by millions. The Princess wore a dress of woven white silk, with a high neck, and Elizabethan sleeves edged with pearls and jewels. She had a train of transparent silk net held in place by a diamond tiara, and was attended by her brother, Prince Edward, and Lady Sarah Armstrong-Jones. Her bouquet was of white roses, lilies of the valley, stephanotis and orchids. Afterwards, when they had returned to Buckingham Palace, they made the traditional appearance on the balcony, alone and also with the Queen, Prince Philip, Captain Phillips' parents, and other members of the Royal Family.

The Queen's family, pictured on her Silver Wedding Anniversary in 1972. Included are The Queen, Prince Philip and their family; The Queen Mother; Princess Margaret, Lord Snowdon and their family; The Duke and Duchess of Kent and their family; Princess Alexandra, Hon. Angus Ogilvy and their family

THE MONARCH'S DUTIES

Very few countries in the world are monarchies, and none of them has a monarchy which combines public esteem and regal dignity in so graceful yet so friendly a manner as the British monarchy. The Queen's full title is Elizabeth the Second by the Grace of God of the United Kingdom of Great Britain and Northern Ireland and of the other realms and Territories Queen, Head of the Commonwealth, Defender of the Faith. This title reveals the complexity of the duties of the Queen as the Head of State, and Supreme Governor of the Anglican Church, and in the role which George VI described as resembling the chairman of an international corporation made up of Britain and the Commonwealth. These duties, handed down by tradition, have not stultified the present monarchy, but rather have been moulded by the characters and interests of both the Queen and Prince Philip into a unique and contemporary version of an active and useful Head of State.

When the Queen came to the throne in 1952, she ushered in a new spirit in Britain. The austerity of the post-war years was just being surmounted, and the drama and spectacle of this beautiful young woman attaining the highest office in the land gave the people of the country a much needed boost. The new Elizabethan age was dawning, and Britain's recovery from the war accelerated.

Neither the Queen nor Prince Philip would allow the position of the monarchy to stagnate. Changes in the style of monarchy were introduced, and continue to be made. The personal lives of the Royal Family have become much better known to most of the British people, and this intimacy has been a marked feature of the Queen's approach to her subjects.

She has broadcast on television nearly every Christmas time, and she has had made a detailed television film about the life of the Royal Family. Many public events in which she takes part appear on television news programmes, and all this makes her a very well-known figure to most of the British people. She abandoned the parties at which debutantes were presented at Court and introduced a system of garden parties which bring together a very wide range of people. She attends assiduously to affairs of state and has now accumulated considerable experience and knowledge of politics and politicians.

Head of State

As Queen she is the head of the constitution, and summons, prorogues or dissolves Parliament. She meets with the Prime Minister every week and retains the function of appointing him. Because she is above party allegiances, and through her wide knowledge of world statesmen and countries, she becomes an increasingly valuable source of advice for her Ministers, and a strong bulwark for the British people against undesirable extremism.

Much of her day-to-day life is spent at an office in Buckingham Palace. She has to deal with parliamentary affairs and Commonwealth matters as well as large amounts of correspondence. Considerable time is spent planning future engagements, overseas visits being planned twelve months in advance, and she avidly reads newspapers and magazines to keep in touch. She may give as many as four or five audiences to different people during one day, and will often be involved in meeting

The Queen, seated on the Throne in the House of Lords, for the State Opening of Parliament

visiting statesmen. Much of her time, however, is spent away from the Palace, on engagements of one kind or another at home or overseas. In these, as in much of her daily work, she is often accompanied by Prince Philip, who has carved out his own individual niche, helping to mould a modern monarchy with his own personal enthusiasm and wit.

The cost of the monarchy
One aspect of the monarchy which always arouses controversy is its cost. In recent years the effects of inflation have been such that it has been necessary to increase the Queen's official income, the Civil List. In 1974 it was increased to £1·4 million. This can be compared to Government spending on Covent Garden Opera House of over £2 million. Out of the Civil List come the salaries of the Royal Household staff, annual sums for five of the Queen's close relatives, the cost of garden parties, and much more. For this relatively small expenditure, the country, and indeed the world, receives the services of the Royal Family at a variety of functions, their work for charities, their involvement in traditional occasions with their array of pageantry, and their work as ambassadors for Britain on their overseas visits.

ROYAL CEREMONIAL
The pomp and majesty of the monarch is best seen in the displays of pageantry which take place regularly in Britain. There are several ceremonial occasions when the Queen is present in State where the power and tradition of the monarchy is strongly felt.

State Opening of Parliament
In October or November every year, the Queen travels in State from Buckingham Palace to the Houses of Parliament to officially open Parliament and to announce the forthcoming government programme. She travels in the Irish State Coach, accompanied by her escort of the Household Cavalry. Inside the Palace of Westminster, she dons the Royal Robe and Imperial State Crown, and processes down the Royal Gallery towards the House of Lords, with the heralds, Kings of Arms, the Lord Great Chamberlain, the Earl Marshal and members of the Royal Household. Inside the House of Lords, peers attired in a breathtaking variety of traditional dress, wait to greet her. Conducted by Black Rod, the members of the House of Commons enter, and the Queen reads the Queen's Speech. At the end of the ceremony, the Queen returns to the robing room, and then back, in State, to Buckingham Palace.

Trooping the Colour
Every year, the sovereign's official birthday (11th June in 1977) is celebrated by the most colourful military parade of the year, Trooping the Colour. It takes place on Horse Guards Parade and consists of the ceremonial trooping of the colour of one of the battalions of footguards. In 1975, Prince Charles in his capacity as Colonel of the Welsh Guards, took part in the ceremony for the first time. Details of the ceremony are given on page 82.

Trooping the Colour, Horse Guards Parade

The Queen and Prince Philip in the Garter procession at Windsor

The Garter Service
The Queen is Sovereign of all the orders of chivalry, the most senior of which is the Most Noble Order of the Garter, founded in 1348. It is reserved for members of the Royal Family and senior statesmen. Every year in June, on Garter Day, any new Knights are invested in the Throne Room at Windsor Castle during the morning, then, after lunch in the Waterloo Chamber, the procession of the Queen and members of the Royal Family, together with the Knights and Officers of the order, the Military Knights of Windsor and the Yeoman of the Guard, all move from the Grand Entrance of the Castle to the West Door of St George's Chapel. In the Chapel, the Knights go to their stalls which have their banners hanging above them, and the traditional service celebrates the founding and continuation of the Order.

The Conferment of Honours
A regular ceremony which the Queen conducts is the conferment of honours. Every year, many honours are awarded, from Knighthoods to the Order of the British Empire, and the investitures are regularly held in the Ball Room at Buckingham Palace.

The Queen at Work

The Queen at Home and Abroad

The lives of the Queen and the Royal Family are full, varied and extremely busy. She has a great many engagements and obligations which bring her in front of almost every person in the country at some time or other, even if only on television. The magnificent ceremonial occasions described on previous pages attract a good deal of attention, but there are many other aspects to the Queen's life and work.

Royal Patronage

As soon as she came to the throne, the Queen was inundated with requests from organisations and societies wanting her to become their patron. Many of them would also want her to come to a forthcoming function, and the business of choosing between organisations which might have conflicting views was unenviable. For example, when the Queen agreed to be patron of the Hunt Servants Benefit Society, she upset the National Society for the Abolition of Cruel Sports. In addition, the Queen regularly receives a large number of requests for her presence at some function, perhaps the opening of a new building, but, in general, she accepts only about one in fifty of these.

Affairs of State

In her position as Head of State, the Queen must keep in continual touch with state affairs. Much of this work involves reading and signing secret and official documents, which are kept in red despatch boxes, securely locked. This work follows her wherever she is, even when she is travelling abroad. She does not attend many government meetings, but regularly presides over meetings of the Privy Council.

The Royal Household

The Queen uses five palaces in carrying out her duties, Buckingham Palace, Windsor Castle, Sandringham, Balmoral and Holyroodhouse, although the Royal Family themselves occupy only modest accommodation in each of them. In addition, the Crown owns a number of other palaces, and the Queen has the disposal of 121 "grace and favour" residences. The staff of the royal household totals nearly 400, although three-quarters of these are honorary positions, often connected with ceremonial occasions. The royal household staff has been cut back quite a lot, however, during the Queen's reign and the Queen herself takes a considerable interest in the running of her households. The Queen, Prince Philip and the Queen Mother own a great many horses, and they have extensive stables for them. The needs of the Royal Family for transport are quite large. The Queen runs 20 cars, of which four are Rolls-Royces, Prince Charles has an Aston Martin DB6, and Princess Anne a Reliant Scimitar GTE. The Royal Train consists of twelve coaches, two of which were extensively modernised last year. The Queen's Flight consists of three Andover planes and two helicopters, often flown by Prince Philip. But the most popular royal transport is probably HMS Britannia, a small liner of 3,990 tons.

The Queen opened The Queen Elizabeth Country Park at Butser, near Winchester, in August 1976

Family Life

Queen Elizabeth is determined to have as full a family life as her position will allow and the Royal Family continually exemplifies the strengths and virtues of family life. Whenever possible they relax together as a family, either walking or riding in the countryside, or enjoying some sporting occasion. The Queen is well known as a lover of the turf, and indeed all the family have a strong love of horses. Princess Anne is an accomplished horse rider, and Prince Philip, although a fine polo player, has given it up in favour of the sport of driving horses. Every summer, the Queen takes a holiday in Balmoral, away from the pressures of her normal life.

The Queen and the World

The Queen is not only Head of State in Britain, she is Head of the Commonwealth, and a world-famous figure. Certainly the size of the Commonwealth has diminished since she came to the throne, but her popularity all over the world has increased. She has travelled extremely widely, has encouraged her family to travel as well, and has also met an enormous number of foreign visitors to Britain.

Receiving the nations of the world

All nations which send ambassadors to Britain have their envoys accredited to Queen Elizabeth. By tradition they are ambassadors to the Court of St James, but nowadays the Queen receives them, on their arrival, in the 1844 room at Buckingham Palace. As Head of State, she also extends hospitality to visiting statesmen and other Heads of State, and during her reign the Queen must have known all the major world figures of the last twenty-five years. This has given her a unique knowledge of political affairs, which enormously increases the value of her advice.

Royal travel

Almost every year of her reign, the Queen has embarked on one or more State Visits or overseas tours. She has travelled more widely than any previous monarch, and has been greeted everywhere with affection and enthusiasm. Very often, a Royal visit has more than a cultural effect, commercial and trading

The Queen entertains many foreign visitors to Britain; this occasion was the visit of the President of Mexico

links often being strengthened in the process. The Royal Family have been especially fond of the Commonwealth countries of Canada and Australia, although their Commonwealth tours have been most extensive. They have travelled widely in Europe, Asia and South America as well, and in 1972 visited a communist country, Yugoslavia, for the first time. Prince Philip has always undertaken tours by himself as well as with the Queen, and Prince Charles and Princess Anne are increasingly travelling by themselves to represent the Queen overseas. Wherever they go, it is always apparent how fascinated they are by what they find, and how pleased they are to meet the peoples of the world. The map overleaf indicates the different places the Queen has visited during the twenty-five years of her reign.

Queen Elizabeth and Prince Philip with President Ford and his wife at the Dedication of the National Cathedral in Washington, DC, in July 1976

The ceremony at which The Queen opened the new London Bridge

Royal visits overseas

Since she became Queen, Elizabeth II has travelled widely all over the world. The map shows the extent of her travels, and we list here a diary of the places she has honoured with Royal Visits.

1953
BERMUDA
JAMAICA
PANAMA
TONGA
FIJI
AUSTRALIA
NEW ZEALAND
CEYLON

1955
NORWAY

1956
NIGERIA
SWEDEN

1957
PORTUGAL
FRANCE
DENMARK
CANADA
UNITED STATES OF AMERICA

1958
NETHERLANDS

1959
CANADA
UNITED STATES OF AMERICA

1961
INDIA
PAKISTAN
NEPAL
PERSIA
ITALY
GHANA
LIBERIA
SIERRA LEONE
THE GAMBIA

1963
FIJI
NEW ZEALAND
AUSTRALIA

1964
CANADA

1965
ETHIOPIA
SUDAN
GERMANY

1966
BRITISH GUIANA
TRINIDAD
TOBAGO
GRANADA
ST VINCENT

BARBADOS
ST LUCIA
DOMINICA
MONTSERRAT
ANTIGUA
ST KITTS AND NEVIS
BRITISH VIRGIN ISLANDS
TURKS AND CAICOS ISLANDS
BAHAMAS
JAMAICA
BELGIUM

1967
CANADA
MALTA

1968
BRAZIL
CHILE

1969
NEW ZEALAND
AUSTRALIA
TONGA
FIJI

1970
CANADA

1971
TURKEY

1972
THAILAND
MALAYSIA
SINGAPORE
BRUNEI
SABAH
SARAWAK
MALDIVE ISLANDS
SEYCHELLES
MAURITIUS
KENYA
FRANCE
YUGOSLAVIA

1973
AUSTRALIA

1974
AUSTRALIA

1975
JAMAICA
JAPAN
HONG KONG

1976
FINLAND
UNITED STATES OF AMERICA
CANADA

CANADA

UNITED STATES OF AMERICA

Ottawa

Washington

BERMUDA

BAHAMA ISLANDS

Tropic of Cancer

JAMAICA

LEEWARD IS

WINDWARD IS

BARBADOS

TRINIDAD

Panama City

PANAMA

GUYANA

Georgetown

BRAZIL

Brasilia

CHILE

Santiago

NORWAY
SWEDEN
FINLAND
Helsinki
Oslo • Stockholm •

GREAT
BRITAIN
DENMARK
Copenhagen •
London • NH BEL Bonn
Brussels • WEST
Paris • GERMANY
FRANCE ITALY Belgrade
Rome • YUGOSLAVIA

PORTUGAL
Lisbon •

MALTA

TURKEY
Ankara •
Tehran • Islamabad •
I R A N
PAKISTAN NEPAL
Delhi • Kathmandu •
I N D I A

JAPAN
Tokyo •

HONG KONG

THE
GAMBIA
njul•
SIERRA
LEONE
eetown•
Monrovia•
LIBERIA
GHANA
Accra •
NIGERIA
Lagos •

Khartoum •
S U D A N
Addis
Ababa•
ETHIOPIA

KENYA
Nairobi •

THAILAND
Bangkok •

SRI LANKA
Colombo •

MALDIVE
ISLANDS

BRUNEI
Kuala
Lumpur • MALAYA SABAH
SINGAPORE SARAWAK

SEYCHELLES

Tropic of Cancer

Equator

MAURITIUS

Tropic of Capricorn

FIJI

TONGA

AUSTRALIA
Canberra •

NEW
ZEALAND
Wellington •

Tropic of Capricorn

19

The Great Events of British History

Edward III groat,
1351–1352.

William the Conqueror penny,
1066–1087.

1066	Harold was killed at the Battle of Hastings
1066–87	Reign of William the Conqueror
1086	The Domesday Survey was begun
1087–1100	Reign of William Rufus
1100–35	Reign of Henry I
1135–54	Reign of Stephen
1153	Treaty of Wallingford brought peace between Stephen and Matilda
1154–89	Reign of Henry II
1170	Thomas Becket was murdered in Canterbury Cathedral
1189–99	Reign of Richard the Lionheart
1199–1216	Reign of John
1215	Magna Carta sealed at Runnymede
1216–1272	Reign of Henry III
1264	Henry III defeated at the Battle of Lewes
1265	Simon de Montfort killed at the Battle of Evesham
1272–1307	Reign of Edward I
1277	Edward invaded Wales
1282	The Edwardian castles in Wales were begun
1301	The future Edward II was created the first Prince of Wales
1306–29	Reign of Robert Bruce in Scotland
1307–27	Reign of Edward II
1327	Queen Isabella and Mortimer had Edward murdered at Berkeley Castle
1327–77	Reign of Edward III
1346	The English defeated the Scots at the Battle of Neville's Cross
1348–9	The Black Death decimated the population
1376	The Black Prince died
1377–99	Reign of Richard II
1399	Richard was deposed and Bolingbroke became Henry IV

Reign of Henry IV	**1399—1413**
Henry IV won the Battle of Shrewsbury	**1403**
Reign of Henry V	**1413—22**
Henry was victorious at the Battle of Agincourt	**1415**
Reign of Henry VI	**1422—61**
The Battle of St Albans began the Wars of the Roses	**1455**
Henry VI was defeated at the Battle of Towton	**1461**
Reign of Edward IV	**1461—83**
Edward was expelled by Richard, Earl of Warwick	**1470**
Edward regained the throne after the Battle of Tewkesbury	**1471**
Reign of Edward V, for three months	**1483**
Reign of Richard III, who usurped the throne from Edward V	**1483—5**
The Battle of Bosworth Field at which Richard was defeated	**1485**
Reign of Henry VII	**1485—1509**
The Battle of Stoke Fields	**1487**
Perkin Warbeck made several attempts to gain the throne	**1492—9**
Reign of Henry VIII	**1509—47**
Henry married Catherine of Aragon	**1509**
The Battle of Flodden Field, where the English defeated the Scots	**1513**
Henry secretly married Anne Boleyn	**1533**
Anne Boleyn was executed and Henry married Jane Seymour	**1536**
Jane Seymour died	**1537**
All monasteries were dissolved	**1539**
Henry married Ann of Cleves, but the marriage was annulled in the same year. Henry married Catherine Howard	**1540**
Catherine Howard was executed	**1542**
Henry married Catherine Parr	**1543**
Reign of Edward VI	**1547—53**
Lady Jane Grey became Queen for nine days	**1553**

Edward IV, second reign, groat,
1471–1483.

Henry IV penny,
1399–1413.

Henry VI, groat,
1427–1430.

Henry VII, groat,
1485–1509.

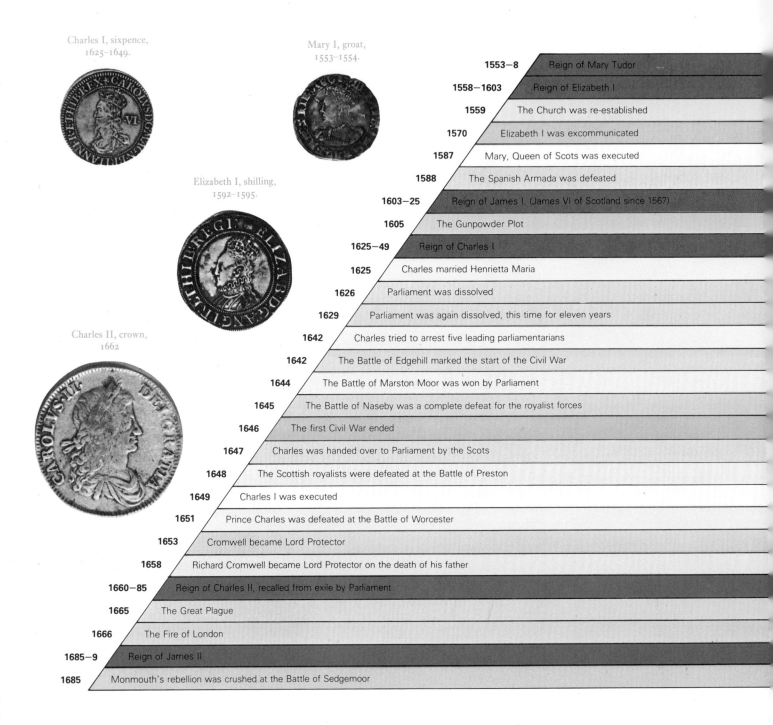

Charles I, sixpence,
1625–1649.

Mary I, groat,
1553–1554.

Elizabeth I, shilling,
1592–1595.

Charles II, crown,
1662

1553–8	Reign of Mary Tudor
1558–1603	Reign of Elizabeth I
1559	The Church was re-established
1570	Elizabeth I was excommunicated
1587	Mary, Queen of Scots was executed
1588	The Spanish Armada was defeated
1603–25	Reign of James I. (James VI of Scotland since 1567)
1605	The Gunpowder Plot
1625–49	Reign of Charles I
1625	Charles married Henrietta Maria
1626	Parliament was dissolved
1629	Parliament was again dissolved, this time for eleven years
1642	Charles tried to arrest five leading parliamentarians
1642	The Battle of Edgehill marked the start of the Civil War
1644	The Battle of Marston Moor was won by Parliament
1645	The Battle of Naseby was a complete defeat for the royalist forces
1646	The first Civil War ended
1647	Charles was handed over to Parliament by the Scots
1648	The Scottish royalists were defeated at the Battle of Preston
1649	Charles I was executed
1651	Prince Charles was defeated at the Battle of Worcester
1653	Cromwell became Lord Protector
1658	Richard Cromwell became Lord Protector on the death of his father
1660–85	Reign of Charles II, recalled from exile by Parliament
1665	The Great Plague
1666	The Fire of London
1685–9	Reign of James II
1685	Monmouth's rebellion was crushed at the Battle of Sedgemoor

Parliament invited William and Mary	**1689**
Reign of William III and Mary II	**1689—94**
The Battle of the Boyne	**1690**
Mary died	**1694**
Reign of Anne	**1702—14**
Union of Scotland and England	**1707**
Reign of George I	**1714—27**
The revolt of James "the Old Pretender" failed	**1715**
Reign of George II	**1727—60**
The rebellion of Charles "The Young Pretender" began in Scotland	**1745**
The Battle of Culloden, at which the Jacobites were crushed	**1746**
Reign of George III	**1760—1820**
The American Declaration of Independence	**1776**
Union of Great Britain and Ireland	**1801**
Reign of George IV	**1820—30**
Reign of William IV	**1830—7**
Reign of Victoria	**1837—1901**
Famine in Ireland	**1845—6**
Victoria was made Empress of India	**1876**
Victoria's Diamond Jubilee	**1897**
Reign of Edward VII	**1901—10**
Reign of George V	**1910—36**
The First World War	**1914—18**
Reign of Edward VIII, who abdicated in the same year	**1936**
Reign of George VI	**1936—52**
The Second World War	**1939—45**
Republic of Ireland founded	**1948**
Reign of Elizabeth II	**1952—to present**

George III, halfcrown, 1817.

Victoria, sovereign, 1894

Anne, halfcrown, 1708.

Elizabeth II, crown, 1953.

Royal Britain

Guided tours through
this historic realm

The Silver Jubilee of Queen Elizabeth II is not only a time to celebrate the achievements of the past twenty-five years, but it is also an opportunity to look at the way the monarchy has shaped the United Kingdom. This country has been a monarchy for over 1,000 years, and the country's history has been, to a great extent, a reflection of the personalities and ambitions of our Kings and Queens. They did not spend their time always in one place, but travelled the length and breadth of the country, either for their own pleasure, or, as was frequently the case, from military necessity. This has meant that all over the country, there are towns, villages, and even isolated houses and castles where monarchs have spent some time, and where the turning points in the history of the country have been enacted. To visit these places is to breathe the air of centuries past, recapturing moments in the lives of Kings and Queens.

This book collects together the places in Britain which have had associations with any of our Kings and Queens from the present day right back to the earliest recorded time. In every area selected for a tour, the place on the tour which is of greatest interest is taken as the starting point, and is described and illustrated in detail. This description brings out the history of the place, gives details of the different sovereigns who have visited it, and what took place while they were there, and in as many ways as possible, brings its background story to life.

Leading out from these central starting points are carefully planned tours round all the places in the vicinity which have been associated with royalty. These tours have been devised so that they can be completed in one day's driving, and are circular tours, returning to the starting point. The route can be followed from the map which accompanies the tour, the road numbers being clearly marked, and distances being seen at a glance from the scale bar marked on each map. The stopping places on the tour are printed in a different colour for emphasis, and each of these places is fully described with an account of its history and its royal associations. The tour is devised to be followed in a clockwise direction, following the arrow from the starting point. Naturally, however, they can be adapted to suit individual requirements where perhaps only two or three of the places can be fitted into the time available.

One place in Britain has had more numerous and more involved connections with monarchs through the centuries than anywhere else, and that is London. There are so many places of royal interest in London that they have been grouped into various categories (see contents page) and described in that way. No attempt at a tour has been possible in these cases.

The lives of our Kings and Queens have touched almost every corner of Britain. Visiting the places with which they have been associated will help to bring their personalities to life, and will create a vivid sense of the history of the country, in which the importance of our present Royal Family can be appreciated.

BATH

According to legend, Bath was founded by Bladud, son of Brutus, King of England in the 8th century BC. The myth relates that Bladud was banished from court when it was discovered that he had contracted leprosy. The prince became a swineherd and very soon his pigs caught the disease. He noticed that after some of the pigs had wallowed in hot springs in the Avon valley they lost all signs of the disease. The prince then leapt into the pool and within a short time he was cured. It was the Romans, however, who fully exploited the springs, building round them a magnificent concourse of baths. After the departure of the Roman legions the baths gradually fell into disuse and disrepair. By the 7th century enough order had been restored to the country for a nunnery to be founded at Bath. This was superseded in importance by St Peter's Monastery, which is thought to have been founded by King Offa of Mercia in about 755. In 973 Edgar was crowned King of all England at Bath. As a symbol of the unity of the country the ceremony was jointly performed by Dunstan, Archbishop of Canterbury, and Oswald, Archbishop of York. Bath came into royal hands when Edward the Confessor confiscated all his wife's property.

Medieval Bath

Throughout the middle ages Bath was closely associated with royalty. William Rufus ordered his court chaplain, John de Villula, to replace the Saxon abbey with a great Norman church. The church gradually fell into ruin, and it was not until the time of Bishop King, a favourite of Henry VII, that considerable repairs and much rebuilding were put in hand. King's rebuilding of the abbey church was inspired by a vision. A representation of this vision (now much restored) can be seen at the western end of the church, as can a Victorian statue of Henry VII.

The West Front of Bath Abbey forms a representation of a dream by Bishop King, inspiring him to rebuild the Abbey, and support the Tudor cause. Over the door is a statue of Henry VII

At the Dissolution, the abbey suffered very badly. All the adjoining lands and properties were sold, and the church itself was stripped. In 1574 Queen Elizabeth I visited Bath and was so appalled by the state of the abbey that she authorised a national collection to raise funds for the repair of the building. Work on the abbey continued intermittently until 1923 when the present cloisters were built.

Elizabeth's visit seems to have encouraged the citizens of Bath, for they began to improve the town and the bathing facilities. Even so the place had no proper drainage or sewage system, accommodation facilities were inadequate, and rogues of every sort abounded.

Queen's Bath

In 1613 Anne of Denmark, queen to James I, visited the baths and greatly enhanced the reputation of the place. She claimed that the waters eased her disease, which was dropsy. New Bath was renamed Queen's Bath in her honour. Anne's son, Charles I, came to Bath in 1628 and persuaded his wife, Henrietta Maria, to take the waters in 1634. Henrietta came only once—put off by rumours of scandal and the appearance of the city.

Charles II came to Bath in 1665, bringing with him his wife Catherine. He hoped that the waters might help her provide him with the heir that he so desperately needed. No heir was forthcoming, but Catherine continued to take the waters in later years. James II and his wife, Mary of Modena, were more fortunate, and after a state visit to the baths in 1687, Mary gave birth to a son.

The future Queen Anne, then a princess, visited Bath in 1692 with her husband George of Denmark. The Mayor and corporation gave the couple a royal reception, but in doing so incurred the ill-favour of Queen Mary, Anne's sister, who at that time was at loggerheads with Anne. Mary sent the Mayor a letter which read: ". . . . that you are not for the future to pay her Highness any such respect of ceremony without lease of her Majesty, who does not doubt of receiving from you and your brethren this public mark of your duty".

The Regency

During the 18th century Bath reached its peak as a place visited by the rich and influential. Two names are principally associated with this time—Beau Nash, who organised the social life, and John Wood, who was responsible for much of the architecture. Monarchs, however, do not seem to have been impressed; George III, a great lover of water cures, could not be enticed here. The banqueting hall in the Guildhall does, however, contain portraits of George III and Queen Charlotte in state robes. There are also paintings of Frederick, Prince of Wales, and his wife Augusta.

In 1830 Princess Victoria came to Bath with her mother, the Duchess of Kent. Victoria asked that the Common Lands of the city, then being turned into a park, should be named the Royal Victoria Park. The Duke of Cambridge opened the extensions to the Pump Room in 1898, Jubilee Year.

The Pulteney Bridge, built in 1770, is the only work of Robert Adam in Bath. The interior has shops on both sides

Royal Crescent, Bath, one of Europe's finest crescents. It consists of 30 houses, and incorporates 114 Ionic columns

Longleat and the Mendips

FARLEIGH CASTLE

The castle was begun in about 1370 by Sir Thomas Hungerford, first recorded speaker of the House of Commons. Eventually it passed into the hands of Richard, Duke of Gloucester, the future Richard III. When Richard ascended the throne he gave the castle to the Duke of Norfolk, and in 1486 it returned to the Hungerford family. Charles II is known to have banqueted at the castle.

The ruins, which are open to the public, consist principally of a gatehouse tower and the chapel which serves as a museum.

LONGLEAT

Home of the Marquess of Bath, the existing Longleat House was built on the site of a 13th century Augustinian priory which was dissolved during the reign of Henry VIII. All that remains of the priory are some fishponds which may be seen to the south west of the house. Most of the house was built in the 16th century, but later additions were made, principally in the 19th century, when the then marquess imported architects and builders from Italy to embellish his home with the craftsmanship he had admired on his travels abroad.

The house has seen many royal visitors, including Elizabeth I, Charles II, and George II. Perhaps the most notorious of all residents in the house was Bishop Ken of Winchester. A man of high principles, he was frequently in conflict with those in authority. He refused to allow Nell Gwynne, mistress of Charles II, within the precinct of his cathedral. Fortunately for Ken the King overlooked the affair. Ken, however, went too far when he refused to give allegiance to William and Mary. He lost his bishopric and accepted the offer of a home at Longleat.

Standing at the foot of the staircase is the state coach in which the 6th Marquess of Bath travelled to the coronation of Elizabeth II. Also of royal interest is the state bedroom, which was last used by the Duke of Windsor. The waistcoat which Charles I wore to his execution is on display, as are several letters written by Elizabeth I.

WELLS

Wells has had a generally quiet history, so its beautiful cathedral and many of its buildings survive virtually unaltered. The building of the present cathedral was begun in the 12th century to replace an earlier foundation. The cathedral had never been a monastery and had always been run by canons, a fact which undoubtedly saved it at the time of the Dissolution.

On the 1st of July 1685 the Duke of Monmouth, at the head of his army of rebels, marched into Wells. The rebels became out of control, and according to a contemporary witness they "profaned the cathedral furniture, almost ruined the organ, and transformed the sacred edifice into stalls for their horses".

A The West Front of Wells Cathedral, providing a setting for nearly 400 statues
B A wooden statue of Queen Elizabeth I, in the church of St Mary Redcliffe, Bristol
C The great early Renaissance house at Longleat
D The west gateway of Farleigh Castle

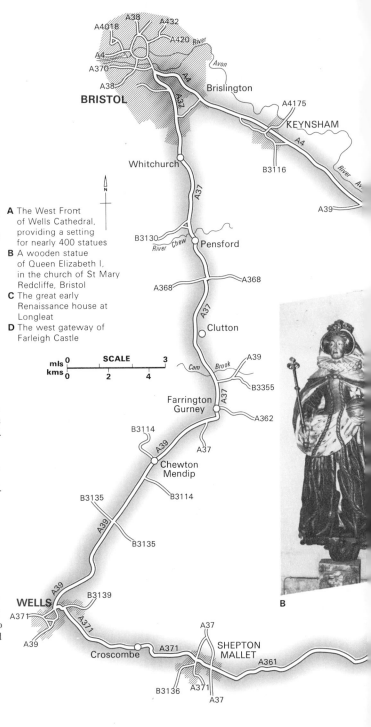

A

B

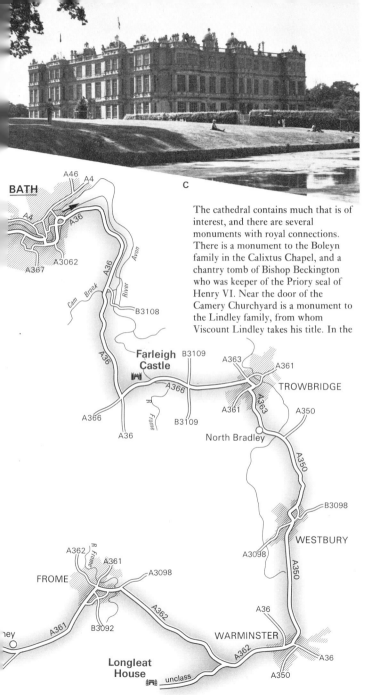

The cathedral contains much that is of interest, and there are several monuments with royal connections. There is a monument to the Boleyn family in the Calixtus Chapel, and a chantry tomb of Bishop Beckington who was keeper of the Priory seal of Henry VI. Near the door of the Camery Churchyard is a monument to the Lindley family, from whom Viscount Lindley takes his title. In the north transept is the grave of Creighton, chaplain to Charles II when the King was in exile. After the Restoration Charles made Creighton bishop.

Paintings of both Charles II and James I are contained in the 18th century town hall. Also in the town hall is a letter from Charles I in which he asks for a loan of £500.

BRISTOL

At the time of the Norman Conquest, Bristol was a small and relatively unimportant place. The construction of a castle shortly after the Conquest vastly increased its importance, and it was soon necessary to enlarge its port facilities. The castle, which no longer exists, was sited at the confluence of the rivers Avon and Frome, and was built in 1126 by Robert, Earl of Gloucester. The Earl's tomb is preserved nearby in the church of St James in Union Street which he founded while working on the great castle keep. According to legend Robert saved every tenth stone from the building of the castle to be used later for the construction of St James'.

Many monarchs past and present have helped build Bristol's history—King Stephen was held prisoner in the castle for nine months during 1141, while in 1208 King John came to spend Christmas here, during which time his second son Richard, Earl of Cornwall, was born. Henry III retained Bristol Castle as one of his string of residences, installing his cousin Eleanor of Brittany here. Henry was a generous man and on one occasion gave food and cloth not only to Eleanor but also to the whole of her household.

Captured by Prince Rupert in 1643, the castle became one of the chief royalist strongholds—but not for long, for in 1655 by order of Cromwell the castle was completely destroyed.

In Queen Square there stands a fine statue of King William III on horseback, while nearby is the church of St Mary Redcliffe, described by Elizabeth I on her visit to the city in 1574 as "the fairest, goodliest and most perfect parish church in England"—a wooden statue of the queen stands in the chapel beneath the church tower.

Once Bristol was a spa town, and St Anne's well at Clifton was visited by many noble visitors including Henry VII. Unfortunately the spa became polluted by river water and the surrounding buildings were demolished. Royal functions have always played an encouraging role in the progress of Bristol. In 1843, Prince Albert arrived to name the ship SS Great Britain before her launching, and some years later in 1899 Victoria herself made a visit. Bristol University was officially opened in 1925 by King George V and Queen Mary.

A later addition to the university, the Queen's Buildings, designed to house the new engineering block, were opened in 1958 by Queen Elizabeth II. The Queen has made three other visits to Bristol, once in 1956 to open the Council House, which houses the municipal offices, again on the 8th September 1966 to open the Severn Bridge between England and Wales and, more recently, in 1973.

29

West of England

The West Country is still considered today as being in some way separate from the bulk of England. The establishment in 1337 of the Duchy of Cornwall for the Black Prince had far reaching effects on Cornwall as a whole, even though the Duchy does not include, as is often mistakenly thought, the entire county.

Loyalty has often meant that the West Country had ended up on the losing side; its adherence to the cause of Charles I and its widespread support of the Duke of Monmouth's rebellion are just two examples of this.

DEVON

Barnstaple

The castle mound here gives a clue as to Barnstaple's history. It was an Anglo Saxon fortified town, and had its own mint by the time of King Athelstan. William the Conqueror probably ordered the construction of the castle. Queen Anne's Walk is so named after the statue of that monarch which looks over it.

Brixham

Brixham is, some might think, a somewhat unusual place for a would-be king of England to make his first footfall on English soil. But such was the case with William of Orange, who landed here in 1688 to claim the throne from James II.

Dartmouth

During the middle ages, Dartmouth was one of the most important ports in England.

The defences of the port were strengthened by Henry VII, who ordered the construction of a chain defence across the estuary, and Henry VIII, who ordered the construction of the fort at Bayard's Cove. Charles II arrived here in 1671 in the yacht *Cleveland* and stayed at one of the houses in the Butterwalk.

In 1905 the Royal Naval College was opened at Dartmouth. Since then almost all the regular officers of the Royal Navy, including George V, George VI, the Duke of Edinburgh and Prince Charles, have begun their service careers at the college.

Exeter

Originally a small, though important town, Exeter was taken over by the Romans and made by them into the capital of the south west, which it has remained ever since.

Edward I held a parliament here in 1285, and Edward IV presented his sword to the city after the Wars of the Roses. On certain occasions this sword is still carried before the mayor. Another sword, and a cap of maintenance, was presented to the city by Henry VII after it had withstood a siege by the imposter Perkin Warbeck.

Prince Maurice captured Exeter for the royalists in the Civil War, and it remained in royalist hands until 1646. Many Exeter men joined the Monmouth rebellion against James II, and after William of Orange had landed at Brixham to take the throne from James, he spent twelve days at Exeter during which time the city pledged its support to his cause.

Honiton

In July 1644 Charles I encamped here with his army on his way west; upon his return in September of the same year he used the site once more. Charles is also said to have stayed at Merwood House, on his way to attend parliaments at Exeter. In 1798 George III stayed here whilst travelling from Weymouth. The famous Honiton lace was worn by Queen Charlotte at her wedding in 1761, and Queen Victoria wore a veil of the same material at her wedding.

Newton Abbot

Forde House was visited twice by Charles I before the Civil War, and William of Orange dined at the house after his arrival on English soil at Brixham.

Okehampton

Most of England submitted to the Norman Conquest, but the south west was one of those areas which resisted the new order. Eventually William crushed the rebellion with characteristic thoroughness and ordered the construction of several castles; one of these was Okehampton. It is now a ruin.

Plymouth

Before its amalgamation by order of Henry VI in 1439, the town of Plymouth in fact consisted of three quite distinct communities. The port for the area had been Plympton, one of the three communities, and it was to Plympton that Edward I came in the spring of 1297. Princess Joan sailed from the port in 1348 escorted by a fleet of 40 ships. This was during the so-called Hundred Years War, and the Black Prince, the principal general in that war, used the port on many occasions. In 1378 Richard II, the Black Prince's son, ordered the construction of defences for the port.

Plymouth held out staunchly for Parliament during the Civil War, and after the Restoration Charles II built the Royal Citadel on the Hoe. Most of its guns faced towards the town as a sign that its anti-royalist sympathies were not forgotten.

CORNWALL

Falmouth

Originally the name of this harbour town was Pennycomequick; it was given its present rather pedestrian title by Charles II. The church of King Charles the Martyr, which was built just after the Restoration, was entirely paid for by Sir Peter Kelligrew. The Kelligrews were constantly loyal to the crown, and Sir Peter's grandson Thomas was a page to Charles I and went into exile with Charles II.

One mile south east of Falmouth is Pendennis Castle. It was built by Henry VIII at a time when invasion from France seemed imminent. The royal arms of Tudor are carved over the entrance gateway. In 1598 the defences were strengthened by Elizabeth I when there were fears of a second Armada. The castle was held by the royalists during the Civil War and withstood a siege of six months in 1646. Queen Henrietta Maria stayed in the castle for a day before embarking for France.

Fowey

Throughout the middle ages Fowey supplied ships for various royal ventures and campaigns. During the Wars of the Roses it sided, as did most of Cornwall, with the Lancastrian faction.

Launceston

Launceston played an important part in Cornwall's early history, it was for long a strategic mainstay, and until 1840 was the county town.

In 1337 the castle was granted to Edward, the first Duke of Cornwall, better known as the Black Prince. During the Civil War the castle was held for the royalists, and Prince Charles, Duke of Cornwall, retired here after the fall of Bridgwater in 1645. The castle was captured by Parliament in 1646 and was slighted.

Lostwithiel

Edmund, Earl of Cornwall, chose Lostwithiel as his capital in the 13th century. A palace was built, parts of which remain, and it became a seat of government. It was used as a prison throughout the middle ages and earned itself a reputation as a place of evil deeds.

One and a half miles north of Lostwithiel is Restormel Castle which is the best example of its kind in Cornwall. It was originally a simple motte-and-bailey castle but it was strengthened by Edmund, Earl of Cornwall, between 1272 and 1299. Edward, 1st Duke of Cornwall, is better known to history as the Black Prince. He visited Restormel several times, but after his death it gradually fell into decay. During the Civil War it was held for the king. On 2nd September 1644 a battle was fought at Lostwithiel at which not only was Charles I present but the royalists won a resounding victory.

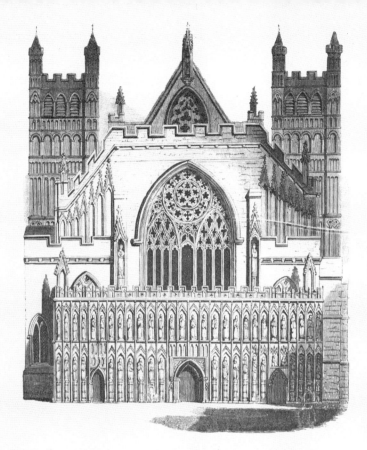

West Front of Exeter Cathedral

St Mawes Castle

Henry VIII ordered the construction of this castle, as he did so many others, when invasion from France seemed inevitable. It was begun in 1540 and completed in 1543.

St Michael's Mount

Edward the Confessor founded a priory for Benedictine monks on the island, but it had been a place of importance long before that. During the reign of Edward IV the mount was seized by the Lancastrian Earl of Oxford. He eventually surrendered. The pretender Perkin Warbeck landed on the mount, and was apparently welcomed. At the time of the Civil War it was at first held by the royalists, but surrendered without a shot being fired. Queen Victoria visited the mount in 1846.

Tintagel

Tintagel is one of the many places in Cornwall which is associated with King Arthur. He is said to have been born in the castle in about 470AD. Whether there was a castle, or indeed a residence of any kind, at Tintagel at that time is uncertain. However it is known that there was a Celt monastery here at about the time of Arthur. The castle ruins to be seen today date, at the earliest, from the late 12th century.

GLASTONBURY

Very probably this is the site of the earliest Christian foundation in Britain. Legend has it that it was founded by Joseph of Arimathea in the 1st century AD, although the story of Glastonbury and its magical tor can be traced back to long before the advent of Christianity and it is said to be one of the entrances to the Celtic Otherworld. One of the names which has become woven into Glastonbury lore is Avalon, the mysterious land to which the dying Arthur was taken.

The myths and legends which surround Glastonbury are so many and so complex that is is hardly possible to explore them without becoming hopelessly lost in a maze of theories, counter theories, crack-pot assertions and serious research. One fact, however, stands high above the morass of controversy; it is that there is something special about Glastonbury and this has been recognised from very early times.

A date for the founding of Glastonbury Abbey is not easy to come by. If the legends are true then it was not many years after Christ's death on the Cross. There was certainly a Christian community of some sort here as early as the beginning of the 6th century. During the 8th century the abbey was much improved by King Ine of Wessex. He built a new church, enriched the older buildings and granted more lands. During the 9th century it was raided, but not totally destroyed, by the Danes and after some sort of order had been restored by King Alfred, the abbey began to recover.

The influence of St. Dunstan
One man brought Glastonbury to its full glory as an abbey of paramount importance throughout England. His name was Dunstan. He was born near Glastonbury in about 909, and by the time he was about 30 he had become the chief advisor to King Edmund, and he was

The Abbot's Kitchen at Glastonbury is the best-preserved relic from the old monastery

made Abbot of Glastonbury. In 946 Edmund was murdered and buried at Glastonbury. Dunstan continued in his position of adviser under King Edred.

After Edred died, his nephew Edwy took the throne. Dunstan and Edwy did not see eye to eye and Dunstan was forced to take refuge in Flanders. Edwy was not a popular monarch, and before long he was usurped by his brother Edgar, who promptly recalled Dunstan and created him Archbishop of Canterbury. Later, when Edgar was crowned King of all England at Bath, Dunstan co-officiated at the ceremony

with the Archbishop of York. Edgar gave generously to the abbey, and under the guidance of Dunstan it became a great centre for learning and the arts. In 975 King Edgar died and was laid to rest in the abbey. Dunstan himself died in 988, and was buried at Canterbury.

In later years an extraordinary dispute arose over Dunstan's remains. The monks of Glastonbury begged that they be returned to the abbey. The then king, Edmund Ironside, agreed to this and four monks set out to retrieve the holy relics. After this the story becomes somewhat confused, the Glastonbury monks insisting that they had collected the relics, while the Canterbury monks claimed that they had not. It seems likely that most of Dunstan's relics stayed at Canterbury, though some may have been taken to Glastonbury.

In 1016 King Edmund Ironside died, and he too was buried at Glastonbury.

King Arthur's burial place
During the succeeding centuries Glastonbury grew from strength to strength. Its ancient sanctity and its associations with King Arthur gave it unparalleled importance.

The story of the "discovery" of King Arthur's bones is one of the enigmas of Glastonbury. Whilst travelling through Wales, King Henry II was told by a bard that the body of Arthur lay at Glastonbury between two pillars or pyramids. This was information Henry could not ignore, for Celtic opposition to the Norman kings was kept alive by the hope that one day Arthur would return. The name of Arthur had come to stand for all that was kingly, so finding the bones of the great king would bring greater glory to the monarchy in England.

However nothing was done for several years. In 1184 the abbey had been all but destroyed by a fire, and during the rebuilding, much that would normally have been considered too holy to disturb came under close scrutiny. In 1190 one of the brothers died, and by coincidence he had asked to be buried between the two strange pillars or pyramids. The whole question of Arthur was revived, and it was decided to dig there.

The area was curtained off and digging began. At a depth of seven feet a slab was discovered into which was set a cross with an inscription. It read: "Here lies buried the renowned King Arthur in the Isle of Avalon". The monks continued digging. Eventually they came upon an immense wooden coffin which contained the bones of a large man whose skull had been cracked by heavy blows, together with the bones of a woman. It was firmly believed at

The beautiful and mysterious ruins of Glastonbury Abbey including the choir

the time that these were the remains of Arthur and Guinevere.

The cross and its tantalizing inscription are now lost, although drawings survive. It seems likely, however, that the cross was a product of the 12th century, placed there as absolute proof that the bones were indeed those of Britain's greatest hero. With great ceremony the bones were put in two coffins and placed in the abbey. When Edward I and his wife Eleanor visited the abbey on 13th April 1278, they were shown the ancient relics, which were then deposited in a new resting place before the high altar at a spot which is still marked by a notice. But no one can say for certain that these were of Arthur and his wife.

Dissolution
The active life of the abbey came to an end in 1539. Henry VIII's commissioners took all that was of value, broke up the estates and had the Abbot, Richard Whiting, imprisoned in the Tower of London under false charges of treason. The buildings fell into ruins, but the legend lived on.

Today the abbey is cared for by the Church of England, and the ruins consist of St Mary's Chapel, the abbey church and monastic buildings.

St Mary's Chapel, which dates from 1186, is now a ruined shell, but retains its magnificent sculptured north doorway. Underground, the crypt dedicated to St Joseph is accessible. On a wall of the chapel is the original inscribed dedication stone, above which may be seen a shower of bullet holes, an abrupt reminder of the Dissolution. East of the chapel is the 13th century Gallilee which leads into the abbey church. Even though the building is in ruins one can imagine the vast size of the original structure; by 1524 it was almost 600ft in length. Near the choir is the site of the high altar where the relics of King Arthur and his queen are believed to be buried. Beyond the end of the choir are the foundations of the Edgar Chapel, the last part of the abbey to be completed.

Of the monastic buildings, undoubtedly the best preserved is the Abbot's Kitchen, which was used to prepare food for guests and pilgrims. It stands intact, complete with domed roof, and contains relics from other parts of the abbey.

Each year sprigs of the famous Glastonbury thorn, said to have been planted by St Joseph, are sent to the Queen and the Queen Mother. The abbey is open daily to the public throughout the year.

Scene of Monmouth's defeat

CADBURY CASTLE

The royal connection with Cadbury lies in the belief that this hill-top fort was the headquarters of the 6th century war leader whom we call King Arthur. "At South Cadbyri standith Camallate . . . . .", so wrote the historian John Leland in 1542. He obviously had no doubts that this hill, fortified by ramparts in the Iron Age, was the site of Camelot, the court of King Arthur.

Excavations to discover just what Cadbury had been were begun in 1966. During the 1967 digging season a great discovery was made. It was proved beyond doubt that the old Iron Age fortifications had been rebuilt on a massive scale in about 500, exactly Arthur's time. Remains of a mighty palace were not discovered, although the foundations of a cruciform church whose shape made it unique in Britain were revealed. The church was never built, even the foundations were incomplete, but it probably dates from about the time of Arthur. Although excavations did not bring to light

any conclusive links with Arthur, they did prove that at the right time a leader of considerable stature made Cadbury his centre of operations.

MONTACUTE

William the Conqueror gave Montacute to his half brother, the Earl of Mortain, who built a hill-top castle here. It was destroyed by Henry I and an 18th century tower now marks the site where the castle once stood. At the bottom of the hill is a fine 15th century gatehouse, the only remains of a priory built by the earl's son.

It is the great Elizabethan mansion, Montacute House, that visitors come to see today. Built in 1580, the house was occupied by the Phelips family for three centuries; it is a superb piece of architecture. Especially notable on the exterior are the ornamental buttresses crowned by carved beasts and statues of warriors—including one of King Arthur. Great fireplaces, sweeping staircases and the magnificent gallery are the highlights of the interior.

ATHELNEY

In the time of Alfred, Athelney was an island. It was here that the King sought refuge whilst planning his campaign against the Danes and here Alfred, lost in thought, allowed the cakes to burn.

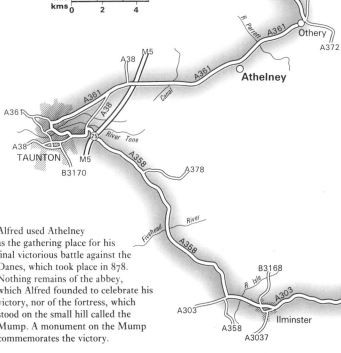

Alfred used Athelney as the gathering place for his final victorious battle against the Danes, which took place in 878. Nothing remains of the abbey, which Alfred founded to celebrate his victory, nor of the fortress, which stood on the small hill called the Mump. A monument on the Mump commemorates the victory.

SEDGEMOOR

It seems likely that a ditch on Sedgemoor changed the course of British history. For it was a drainage ditch called the Bussex Rhine that halted the night offensive which James, Duke of Monmouth, an illegitimate son of Charles II, had hoped would surprise the forces of James II.

Monmouth had landed at Lyme Regis in June 1685 with 300 men and £80 in cash. He claimed that he was the rightful king of England and that James II was a usurper. By 18th June, Monmouth was in Taunton, and there he had himself proclaimed king. He had by now raised a motley army of 4,000 men, most of whom were

poorly armed and untrained. They tried to capture Bristol, but were soundly beaten, and fell back to Taunton.

The evening of 5th July found Monmouth and his army at Bridgwater, whilst three miles away outside the village of Weston Zoyland the army of James II, commanded by Churchill and Feversham, made camp. Monmouth had two alternatives; he could retreat and lead his army into the north of England, or he could make a stand and hope for a swift and decisive victory. He chose the latter course.

From his lookout in St Mary's Church, Monmouth could see that the enemy were not preparing for battle. He decided that the best use he could make of his men would be for them to creep up on the enemy at night and cut them to shreds before they knew what was happening. At 11pm the march began.

Monmouth stood every chance of victory, for the enemy were certainly not expecting him to attack; a mist had come down, and the terrain of Sedgemoor muffled the approach of his troops. The march became a nightmare. Several times the whole army nearly became lost on the moor.

The inevitable happened, a shot was fired, and soon James' army was being called to battle by its drummers. Obviously, surprise was then out of the question. Monmouth's cavalry, commanded by Lord Grey, charged— and came up against the Bussex Rhine. It was not difficult to cross, but they did not know that. All they could see was a water-filled ditch of unknown depth. The cavalry raced back and forth looking for a place to cross. The troops of James' army opened fire, and the cavalry panicked. As the cavalry fell back in total disorder it threw Monmouth's still advancing troops into confusion. They continued to advance, however, and soon they too

came up against the ditch. They halted and began firing haphazardly. Nothing would induce them to cross the ditch, and the steady fire from the enemy shot Monmouth's rebel army to pieces.

By morning it was all over. Monmouth fled the field, leaving his standard behind. Of his army, some 1,400 were killed, and several hundred were taken prisoner. Feversham said that his forces had lost 50 dead and 200 wounded.

It was the last battle to be fought on English soil. A stone monument now marks the site where the rebel victims were buried, and a memorial at Weston Zoyland church recalls that 500 rebels were held in it on the night after the battle.

BRIDGWATER

The Duke of Monmouth proclaimed himself king at Bridgwater Castle in 1685. Two weeks later his hopes were crushed when his army was utterly defeated at the Battle of Sedgemoor. Of the castle only a stone archway, part of the old watergate, remains.

From the tower of St Mary's Church Monmouth watched the arrival of James' army, and it was in the tower that he finalized his plans for a surprise attack. In Silver Street, opposite the church, is the house where Judge Jeffreys sentenced 300 of the defeated Monmouth rebels to death.

A Monument to the Battle of Sedgemoor
B The superb Elizabethan mansion at Montacute
C St Mary's church, Bridgwater, with its fine tower
D The earthworks at Cadbury Castle

BERKELEY CASTLE

Magnificent 12th century
Berkeley Castle, ancestral home of
the Berkeley family for over 800 years

Set high above the little Georgian town of Berkeley is the dominating 12th century castle. It was here that King Stephen came at Easter in 1121, just three years after the castle had been built, and here in 1215 the barons of the west gathered before setting out for Runnymede to witness the sealing of the Magna Carta by King John.

Murder of the King

More than anything else, however, Berkeley Castle is remembered as the place where Edward II was confined for the last months of his life, and where at last he was murdered in a particularly sordid way. Edward was brought to Berkeley Castle in April 1327, and imprisoned in one of the keep towers at the request of his wife Eleanor and her paramour the Earl of Mortimer. Their intentions were to prove the King's incompetence to rule, and to remove him permanently and legally from the throne. The King suffered everything during his captivity short of actual physical violence; semi-starvation, lack of sleep and light, insanitary conditions, in fact anything that might promote his early death. For example, a shaft from the room where he was imprisoned dropped down to a pit into which rotting carcasses of animals were dropped, in the hope that the prisoner might die of asphyxiation from the appalling stench. The King, who was aged 43, hung on to life with a grim tenacity. His love of the outdoor life had kept him in superb physical condition and it became apparent that he would not succumb to filth and deprivation alone.

Two attempts were made to rescue him from Berkeley. Both failed and each time he was returned to his damp and dismal dungeon—until finally on 22nd September of the same year, the intriguers could wait no longer and

Edward II was brutally murdered. There was a story that Edward II left a ghost behind to haunt the castle after his gruesome death; the late Lord Berkeley was so fed up with the ghostly rumours attached to one particular bedroom, and the disturbing effect they were having upon the servants, that he ordered it to be pulled down.

The Castle and the Berkeley family

For many hundreds of years the Berkeley family were involved with affairs of State and with the monarchy. Political involvement began when the family decided to join Simon de Montfort's rebellion; surprisingly the Berkeleys managed to retain their stronghold, probably due to Thomas Berkeley's loyal efforts on behalf of Edward I's northern campaign. It was during this time that King Edward I granted Thomas Berkeley the special privilege of

hunting foxes, hares, badgers and wild cats with his own pack of hounds—probably the beginning of the famous Berkeley Hunt.

The Berkeley family were ousted from the castle during Edward II's confinement in it, and claimed that they were innocent of any of the events which took place in their home. Although the family must, at least, have had their suspicions of the evil goings-on, they were afterwards exonerated from the actual deed.

During the Wars of the Roses, the Berkeleys were waging their own personal battles to determine which branch of the family should retain the family seat. Eventually William, son of James Berkeley, was the victor. Unfortunately he had no heir and rather than allow the other side of the family to get their hands on the castle, he passed it, together with all the attached land, to Henry VII in exchange for the

The cell in Berkeley Castle where Edward II was murdered. The windows were mere slits in the 14th century

The pew with the coat of arms of Henry VII in the Long Drawing Room. It was formerly in the Chapel

title of Earl Marshal. This was in 1486, and the deed earned him the name of William Waste-all. The house remained the property of the crown for the next 61 years, until the time of Edward VI, when, since the King had no heir, the property passed back to the Berkeley family. Queen Elizabeth I was considerably upset that the seat was no longer in royal hands since she had hoped that upon her assumption of the crown it would be hers to give to her court favourite the Earl of Leicester. It is said that on one occasion Queen Elizabeth came to make her royal presence felt at Berkeley, and as she rode in through the front gates of the castle, so Lord Berkeley rode out through the back. In 1810, the direct lineage of the Berkeley estate faltered, and the castle, but not the title of Berkeley, passed into the hands of the illegitimate son of the 5th Earl, William

Fitzhardinge, and in spite of the fact that William's mother, Mary Cole, married his father, the Earl, nine years later, William was never recognised as the legitimate heir. Today, the castle belongs to the Berkeley family.

Mary Cole, the daughter of a Gloucester butcher, was herself an exceptional woman— she designed the Worcester china exhibited now in the china room, to commemorate the birth of her son. After the Earl died, Mary Cole was proposed to by the Duke of Clarence, later William IV. She refused, but had she accepted, she might well have been queen of England.

Berkeley Castle today

The castle stands perfectly preserved today, surrounded by a 14ft buttressed wall overlooking terraced gardens and a deer park.

The interior of the castle is open to the public, and the scene of Edward's confinement and death may be examined. The whole building is of interest, however; particular mention may be made of the 60ft great hall, the kitchens, state apartments and the beer cellar. In the housekeeper's room is the 10th century Godwin chalice, which once belonged to King Harold's father, Earl Godwin, who probably lived in Berkeley Mansion during the 10th century. The legend says that each day it was the habit of the Earl to take communion from the silver cup, until one fateful day when he forgot. Disaster overtook him and all the land that he owned around the Kent coast was washed away by a terrible storm. There are many beautiful tapestries and paintings to be seen in the castle, as well as a fine collection of silver and china.

Edge of the Cotswolds

CIRENCESTER

As the Roman *Corinium*, Cirencester was the largest town in England after London. During the middle ages it was one of the richest wool towns in the Cotswolds; this wealth is reflected in the magnificent 15th century parish church. It contains the Boleyn Chalice which once belonged to Anne Boleyn, wife of Henry VIII and mother of Elizabeth I.

Henry VIII was responsible for the destruction of Cirencester's abbey church. All that can now be seen of what was once a great Christian foundation are the excavated remains of the cloisters and the abbey gateway. In Spitalgate Lane stands the Hospital of St. John which was originally founded by Henry I. The building has been restored but some of the original arches are still to be seen.

A painting of the market place as it appeared in 1642 hangs over the fireplace of the King's Head Hotel. This serves as a reminder of the part that Cirencester played in the Civil War, and of the fact that the first blood of that war was spilt here. Lord Chandos came to Cirencester to recruit men for the royalist cause. He was forced to take refuge in the King's Head when angry pro-Parliament rioters tried to lynch him.

Until February 1643 Cirencester was held by parliamentary supporters. Its capture was essential to the royalists who saw it as a blockage in their line of communication to the south-west. It was also hoped to divert the rich proceeds of the wool trade into the purses of the royalist cause. On the 2nd February Prince Rupert, aided by the forces of the Marquis of Hertford, launched an attack on the town. The defenders of Cirencester were not prepared to give up without a struggle, but the royalist forces were overwhelming in their numbers and energy. Rupert and the main royalist body forced the main gate and in less than two hours the town was taken. Rupert was soon able to send much needed supplies to Charles' growing army.

In 1651 whilst escaping from the parliamentary forces after the defeat of his army at Worcester, Charles II spent the night at an inn at Cirencester.

MALMESBURY

The ancient name of Malmesbury, *Maldelmsburg*, is said to be derived from that of Malmud who, according to legend, was King of all England in

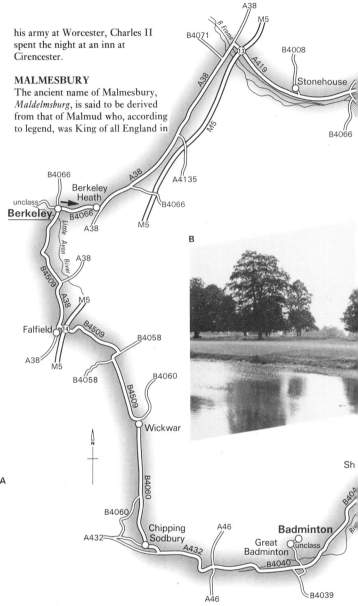

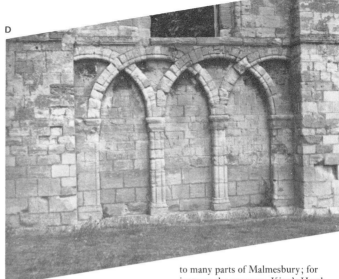

D

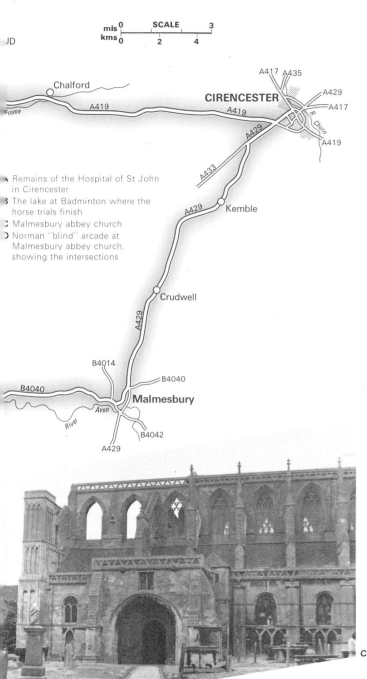

JD

SCALE

mls 0   3
kms 0   2   4

Chalford

A419

Frome

A417 A435

CIRENCESTER

A429

A419   A417

A429

R. Churn

A419

A433

A429

Kemble

A Remains of the Hospital of St John
in Cirencester
B The lake at Badminton where the
horse trials finish
C Malmesbury abbey church
D Norman "blind" arcade at
Malmesbury abbey church,
showing the intersections

Crudwell

A429

B4014

B4040

B4040

Malmesbury

Avon

River

B4042

A429

C

the 4th century BC. Ine, King of Wessex in the 7th century, sent his nephew Aldhelm to a school at Malmesbury which had been founded by an Irish missionary. Aldhelm was obviously a gifted scholar for he grew up to become headmaster of the school, which he later turned into an abbey. King Athelstan, grandson of Alfred the Great, is closely associated with Malmesbury. He won a great victory over the Danes here, and when he died in 940 he was buried at Malmesbury. His now empty tomb can be seen in the abbey church.

The abbey church dates largely from Norman times. It was endowed both by Edward the Confessor and William the Conqueror. At the Dissolution more than half of the church was destroyed and the part that remained was bought by a rich merchant and given to the people of Malmesbury in place of their own wrecked church.

Athelstan also founded the town's Hospital of St. John. A tablet above one of the windows commemorates his generosity in giving £10 each year to the poor of the almshouses and £10 to the school. The King's name is linked to many parts of Malmesbury; for instance the common, King's Heath, is named after him.

BADMINTON

Badminton House has been the home of the Beaufort family since the 17th century, and is famous for the three-day horse trials that take place in the extensive grounds each year, which are very popular with our Royal Family. The title of Beaufort was conferred upon the family in 1682 by Charles II, himself a visitor to the house. On one occasion the King came to dine at Badminton bringing with him his queen and a large retinue of other people. It was probably this event, and a growing dissatisfaction with the facilities that he could offer such noble guests, which prompted the first Duke of Beaufort to plan to enlarge and improve his home over the next thirty years. By the early 18th century work on the house was complete and when Queen Anne came to visit the second Duke was able to entertain her royally. The house has much of beauty, but it is the paintings particularly that demand attention. In the Red Room there is a fine portrait of Charles I by Van Dyck, while in other parts of the house there are family pictures painted by Reynolds, Lawrence and Canaletto.

CORFE CASTLE

Two hundred years ago this small village, dominated by its magnificent castle ruins, was the "capital" of the Isle of Purbeck. It had a charter granted by Elizabeth I which was confirmed and extended by Charles II.

The castle is set on a hill high above the village and overlooks the whole of the Isle of Purbeck. In its completed state it must have presented a formidable appearance. The first building on the site is thought to have been a church built by St Aldhelm, but no trace of this remains, nor of a probable stronghold erected here in the time of King Alfred as defence against the Danes. The fortress was extended by King Edgar, and traces of this castle can be seen in the keep.

Murder of Edward

The murder of King Edward the Martyr supposedly took place here when, in 978, he was hunting in the Royal Chase of the Island of Purbeck. Feeling tired, he called at the castle which was the home of his stepmother Queen Elfride. She desperately wanted to see her own son, Ethelred, on the throne and while Edward was drinking wine she stabbed him in the back. The scene of the murder is supposed to be Martyr's Gateway in the castle.

Before he died the King managed to mount his horse and attempted to ride away, but he fell off and was dragged down the steep hill. His mutilated corpse was hidden by the Queen's servants and later buried in the church of St Mary. Subsequently it was moved to Shaftesbury Abbey.

After the Norman Conquest a strong fortress was built here, and during the war between King Stephen and Queen Matilda, it was held by supporters of the Queen until the end of the war in 1153. The castle was a favourite residence of King John, who kept his treasure

The King's Tower in Corfe Castle was one of the main features of the original castle, before it was demolished after the Civil War

and royal regalia here. He also made it the state prison, in which he imprisoned and starved to death 22 French knights who had supported the claim of the Duke of Brittany to the English throne.

During the reigns of Henry III and Edward I the castle was extended and much of the existing building dates from this period. King Edward II was imprisoned here for a time before his removal to Berkeley Castle, where he was murdered. Richard II granted the castle to the Earl of Kent and it then passed to the Beaufort family. After the death of Margaret, Countess of Richmond, it returned to crown ownership until 1553 when Queen Elizabeth granted it to Sir Christopher Hatton. After his death it was eventually sold to Sir John Bankes.

The dominating position occupied by Corfe Castle above its pretty Dorset village, gave it command of the whole of the Isle of Purbeck

Martyr's Gate at Corfe Castle was probably the main entrance to the castle in 978, the date of Edward's murder

Brave resistance

Sir John was an ardent royalist, and during the Civil War he went with Charles I to Oxford. His wife, left behind, prepared the castle against attack, which it successfully withstood for thirteen weeks in 1643. Royalist fortunes waned during the following year and the castle again came under attack. It held out through 1644 and 1645 and finally surrendered in February 1646. This surrender, however, was only brought about by the treachery of one of its own defenders, who secretly admitted some of the attackers into the castle. This quickly brought about its surrender. Lady Bankes, with her family and dependants, was allowed to

leave the castle unharmed, but her property was confiscated.

Parliament then voted to demolish Corfe Castle. This demolition was carried out so effectively that it is now difficult to imagine what the castle must have looked like. Before its destruction the castle was plundered of its treasures of tapestry, carpets and furniture, some of which were extremely fine. After such a battering, restoration would have been unthinkable and the castle has remained a dramatic ruin ever since.

The village

The village itself is a charming and picturesque place built of local stone, some of it

supposedly from the castle ruins. The existing pedestal and shaft of the Market Cross were placed on the ancient base in 1897 to commemorate the sixtieth year of Queen Victoria's reign.

The church is dedicated to St Edward the Martyr and was badly damaged during the siege of the castle. A modern effigy of the young king stands at the eastern end of the church. The choir wear red cassocks, a sign that the church was a Royal Peculiar, which means that at one time it was subject only to the Crown. Impressions of the seals of the constables of the castle can also be seen in the church.

In the village is a 1/20th scale model of the village and the castle as it appeared more than 300 years ago. The model of the castle shows how it would have looked to Cromwell's soldiers before it was destroyed. The rest of the village is modelled in great detail and demonstrates its former importance.

Dorset Castles and Abbeys

WAREHAM

Once an important port, Wareham can still be described as the gateway to the Isle of Purbeck. Its strategic value was appreciated by the early Britons and the Romans, both of whom had settlements here. The town reached its greatest importance, however, during Saxon times. Its position made it an obvious target for the Danes, who frequently raided the area. In AD800 Beorthric, King of the West Saxons, was buried here. Eventually the Danes captured Wareham and held it until it was relieved by King Alfred in 876. A treaty was signed between Alfred and the Danes, who agreed to leave the country.

During the fighting Wareham had been reduced to ruins. In the next ten years it was rebuilt and enclosed by fortifications, the remains of which can still be seen. The present-day church of Our Lady St Mary stands upon the site of a Saxon nunnery in which the Martyr King, Edward, was buried after his murder at Corfe Castle. The body was later removed to Shaftesbury.

Wareham was besieged again by the Danes in 988, and was devastated by Canute in 1015 during his campaign to gain the crown of Wessex. Once more the town recovered and saw relative peace until wrecked by King Stephen, whose main object was to occupy the castle. Of the castle nothing remains; it occupied a site on high ground overlooking the river and was probably destroyed during the reign of King John.

WEYMOUTH

Weymouth owes its popularity as a seaside resort to George III. For many hundreds of years before that it was important as a port, being the only

safe haven for shipping for many miles. It was George III's doctor who persuaded the Monarch to take to the water at Weymouth. The doctor thought that the cold water would have a curative effect, and George is thought to have been the first British king to take a deliberate sea bathe. In 1789 the King tried out one of the new bathing machines, whilst, concealed in another machine, a band played "God Save Great George Our King". The Monarch, his queen and their three daughters used to stay at Gloucester House, which is now a hotel. It was built by the King's brother, the Duke of Gloucester.

A statue of George was erected in 1809 by the townsfolk of Weymouth in thanks for his patronage of their town. It stands at the southern end of the esplanade. Portraits of the King are hung in the Guildhall. St Mary's Church was rebuilt in 1816 and George presented the church authorities with an organ.

OSMINGTON

Cut into the chalk on a hill north east of Weymouth is the enormous figure of George III upon a horse. The horse was carved first, shortly after the King's first visit to Weymouth. The figure was added as an afterthought, with the horse and rider facing away from Weymouth. George took this as a personal insult and never visited the town again.

ISLE OF PORTLAND

Situated to the south east of Weymouth and connected to the mainland by Chesil Bank is the Isle of Portland, which Hardy referred to as the "Gibraltar of Wessex". It has been a royal manor since the time of William the Conqueror. William Rufus built the first of several fortifications to have

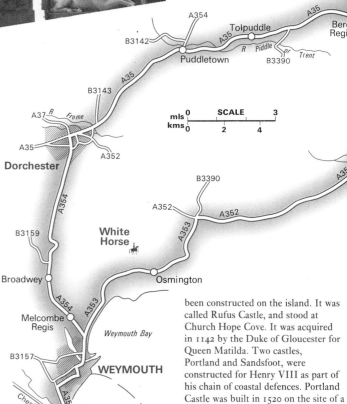

been constructed on the island. It was called Rufus Castle, and stood at Church Hope Cove. It was acquired in 1142 by the Duke of Gloucester for Queen Matilda. Two castles, Portland and Sandsfoot, were constructed for Henry VIII as part of his chain of coastal defences. Portland Castle was built in 1520 on the site of a Saxon fortress and was also occupied at the time of the Armada. During the Civil War it was held by royalist forces. Sandsfoot Castle stands on the opposite shore and incorporates fragments of Norman architecture. Henry VIII leased the island to three of his wives, and it was also leased for a time to Queen Marie of Denmark.

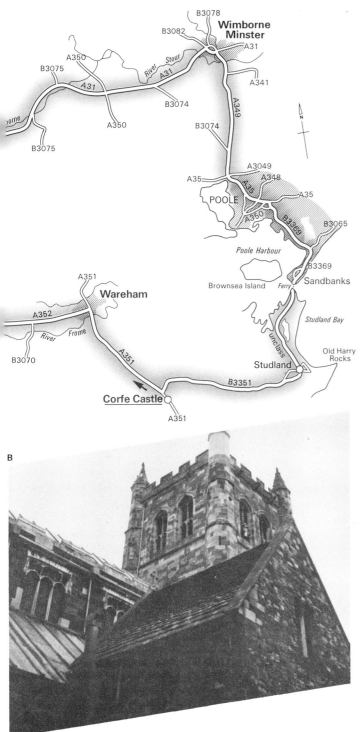

DORCHESTER

This historic town was founded by the Romans in about AD43 after they had captured the major British stronghold of Maiden Castle, situated south west of Dorchester. Dorchester Castle, which was built by the Romans, was probably used as a temporary hunting lodge by King John. During the Civil War it was badly damaged, and was subsequently demolished in 1794. The kings of Wessex, including Alfred the Great, were frequent visitors to the town. Early in the 10th century Alfred's grandson, the son of Edward the Elder, established a mint here. William the Conqueror also visited Dorchester.

After the disastrous Monmouth uprising of 1685, Judge Jeffreys tried about 300 of the rebels at Dorchester, and between 60 and 70 were hung, the rest being deported.

WIMBORNE MINSTER

A monastery was founded at Wimborne in about AD705 by Cuthburgha, a sister of Ine, King of Wessex. She had been married to Aldfrith, the King of Northumbria, but it was not a happy match and eventually the couple separated. Cuthburgha took holy orders and settled at Wimborne. The Danes frequently attacked Wimborne during the 9th and 10th centuries. Whilst fighting the Danes in 871 King Ethelred was killed by them. His body was brought by his brother Alfred to Wimborne for burial. Alfred then assumed the throne and began a reign that has ensured his place in history as the only English king to have the prefix "Great" attached to his name.

In 901 Wimborne was captured and barricaded by Aethelwold. King Edward the Elder prepared to besiege the town, and camped his army at Badbury Rings. Aethelwold declared that he would remain in the town— alive or dead. A truce was drawn up, and under cover of this Aethelwold escaped to join the Danes in Northumbria.

A Inscription on the base of the statue of George III in Weymouth commemorates the King's 50th birthday

B The Collegiate Church of St Cuthburgha, Wimborne Minster

C Henry VIII's castle at Portland

The monastery was destroyed in 1000, possibly during the struggle for power between Edward the Confessor and Earl Godwin. Edward replaced the monastery with a college which was unique in that it was virtually independent of the Church hierarchy. Edward II called it the "Kings Free College" and severed its links with the bishopric altogether, making it directly answerable to the monarch. This state of affairs continued until the Dissolution in 1547.

The church which was attached to the college is familiarly known as the Minster though its official title is still The Collegiate Church of St Cuthburgha. The building as it appears today displays Norman, Decorated, and later architectural styles. Set into the chancel floor is a brass engraved with a medieval portrait of King Ethelred which is inscribed in Latin: "In this place rests the body of Ethelred, King of West Saxons, Martyr, who in the year of Our Lord 873 on the 23rd day of April fell by the hand of the pagan Danes". The inscribed date of the King's death is incorrect, however.

WINCHESTER

The massive medieval cathedral at Winchester. It also shows notable early Norman and early perpendicular work

It is fitting that Winchester's main street should be dominated by a statue of King Alfred, for it was he who ensured that Winchester should have a place in the history of the English nation second to none. Upon his death in 901 Alfred was buried in the New Minster (the site of which is near the present cathedral) but when that building was demolished his remains were moved to Hyde Abbey which stood outside the city's north wall. At the Dissolution this foundation too was demolished and the bones of one of England's greatest kings were lost.

The statue of Alfred, by Hamo Thornycroft, was erected in 1901 to commemorate the 1,000th Anniversary of the death of the King. Alfred looks up the Broadway and up the High Street where stands Godbegot House, a 16th century structure which is built upon the site of the palace of Canute, King of England, Norway, and Denmark; and his wife Emma. Something of the character of Emma may be gleaned from the fact that her subjects called her *Aeilgifu*, which means the gift of the elves. She had previously been married to Ethelred the Unready and was the mother of Edward the Confessor and the great-aunt of William the Conqueror. Canute and Emma ruled from Winchester for 20 years until Canute's death at the age of 40 in 1035. Emma favoured her son Hardicanute (by her marriage to Canute) rather than her son—Edward—by her marriage to Ethelred. In the end both sons wore the crown, and Edward, who came to be called "the Confessor" was the last king to be both crowned and anointed in Winchester.

The importance of Winchester did not fade with the passing of Anglo Saxon England in 1066, for William the Conqueror founded his royal palace in the city. The palace stood near to the colonnaded Pentice in the High Street. The great survey of William's England, the Domesday Book, was compiled at Winchester; hence its real name *Rotulus Wintonienses*, or the Roll of Winchester. William, a man of tremendous political subtlety, knew that his power would be the more consolidated if he ruled his Saxon realm from the old Saxon capital. In order to show that he considered Winchester to be equal in importance to London William underwent a second crowning in the city. The last king to be crowned both in London and Winchester was Richard I.

William the Conqueror also founded a castle at Winchester. Henry III built a strong stone castle on the site of the Conqueror's defences in the 13th century, but all that remains of this is the Great Hall as the structure was demolished by the parliamentary forces in the Civil War. The Great Hall, however, remains and is one of the best examples of its type in the country. It has seen the passing of many kings and queens. Queen Matilda defended the site in the 12th century, Henry III was born in it, and Henry V received the envoys of the French kings here before Agincourt.

Hanging on the west wall of the hall is the famous Round Table of King Arthur. It is certainly very old—it is first mentioned in manuscripts of the 15th century—but as to whether this is the same table round which the knights of a half legendary king sat must remain a subject of romantic conjecture. The appearance of the table as it now is dates from 1522 when it was repainted for the visit of the Emperor Charles V after the Field of the Cloth of Gold. It has been claimed that Winchester is the site of Arthur's "Camelot", and this again is a matter of debate, though many modern scholars would say that if Camelot was anywhere it was at Cadbury Castle in Somerset.

Beyond the castle hall, in Romsey Road, is the site of a palace which was begun, but never completed, for Charles II. The design was by Wren and his architectural drawings for a palace on a truly royal scale may be seen in the City Museum. After Charles' death Wren was called by James II to work at Whitehall and the Winchester palace was abandoned. Later it was used as a barracks, and continued to function as such until its destruction by fire in 1896.

44

More tangible evidence of the association of Winchester with royalty may be seen in Winchester's greatest treasure—the cathedral. It was begun in 1079 to replace the ruinous Old Minster which dated originally from the 7th century and in which Canute had been buried. Recent excavations on the north side of the cathedral revealed parts of the Old Minster, and remains of the New Minster which was founded by King Alfred and completed by his son Edward the Elder.

On either side of the nave doors are bronze sculptures of James I and Charles I. These originally formed part of a nave screen that was designed by Inigo Jones but which was dismantled in the 19th century. It is interesting to note that the west window is made up of

The east end of Winchester High Street is dominated by the statue of King Alfred, who made the city one of the most important places in England

fragments of early glass broken by the forces of Parliament during the Civil War. Indeed, the roundheads wrought so much damage that it is a wonder that anything survived. The windows above the south door, and in the north aisle, commemorate King George V and the coronation of George VI and Queen Elizabeth.

In the centre of the choir stands the tomb of William Rufus, the much maligned monarch who was shot by an arrow in the New Forest. There was considerable opposition to his being buried in the cathedral at all, ostensibly because he was so wicked, although possibly because his religion was not Christianity but something older and more mysterious. The objectors to William's presence in the cathedral must have been delighted when, seven years after the King's death, the tower beneath which he lay collapsed. This was pronounced as being Divine proof of William's wickedness.

On top of the presbytery screens are six 16th century mortuary chests which contain the remains of many Saxon kings. These include Kynegils who died in 640 and who endowed the first church on this site. Here also are the relics of Canute and Emma. The altar books in the presbytery were a gift of Charles II.

The Lady Chapel was rebuilt in the early 16th century through the gift of Elizabeth of York, wife of Henry VII. Her son, Prince Arthur, was born in the Deanery and christened in the cathedral. The east window of the chapel commemorates the Diamond Jubilee of Queen Victoria. Elizabeth of York is depicted in one of the lower panels.

In the Chantry Chapel of Bishop Gardiner is the chair in which Queen Mary sat during her marriage to Philip of Spain which took place in the cathedral in 1554. The couple spent their honeymoon at Wolvesey Palace, the remains of which are situated to the south east of the cathedral. The ruins of the palace date from the time of Bishop Henry de Blois, but the site was occupied originally by a Saxon palace. Henry was brother of King Stephen and a man of

The interior of Winchester cathedral showing the extremely long nave, 556 feet in total. Most of the work here is early perpendicular

ambition. He dearly wished to make Winchester an archbishopric, a plan of which the Pope approved, and in order to make himself more secure he turned his bishop's palace into what amounted to a castle. During the civil strife between Stephen and Matilda, Henry took whichever side seemed best suited to his aims at the time. Because of this Winchester was the scene of sieges and counter-sieges and much of the town was destroyed, including the New Minster and the recently completed Hyde Abbey. When Henry II came to the throne Bishop Henry fell into disgrace and retired into exile. Not many years later he returned to Winchester and spent the rest of his life doing good works.

Winchester has many more reminders of its past associations with royalty, for instance several of the city's churches contain royal arms and the old Guildhall, now a bank, has a figure of Queen Anne upon it. This was given to commemorate the 1713 Treaty of Utrecht. The city's excellent museums also contain mementoes of royalty.

Through the New Forest

SOUTHAMPTON

The history of Southampton is as long as that of Winchester, which at one time it superseded as the capital of Hampshire. Its importance was based largely on its excellent harbourage and double tide. Indeed during medieval times it ranked second only to London as a port.

Southampton's importance has meant that most English sovereigns have taken an interest in it, and many of them have visited the town. Canute was offered the crown here, and Richard the Lionheart spent his only Christmas in England at Southampton Castle. In 1217 King John gave the town its first charter, and made several visits here. Henry V marshalled his forces here before setting off for victory at Agincourt, and Philip of Spain landed at Southampton on his way to marry Mary at Winchester.

Indescribable damage was done to Southampton during the Second World War, and much was lost. Considerable parts of the ancient town walls survive, however, as does the magnificent Tudor House Museum, which though much restored, gives an idea of the lifestyle of Tudor times. Henry VIII and Anne Boleyn are known to have stayed at the house, and may have strolled in the gardens looking upon a view that now includes the great docks where the Cunard liners Queen Mary and Queen Elizabeth used to berth.

LYNDHURST

By long standing Lyndhurst is the capital of the New Forest. Its oldest building is the Queen's House, which was built as a hunting lodge for Charles II. Later it became the official residence of the Lord Wardens of the forest, and today it is still used by the forest verderers.

It is not true that William the Conqueror created the New Forest. Nor is it true that he destroyed many forest villages and evicted many people. The forest had, in fact, been a royal hunting ground for the Saxon kings long before the Norman conquest, and it was always sparsely populated simply because so much of the soil was, and remains, infertile. The term, forest, originally applied to any area of land, irrespective of vegetation, which was subject to forest law. The forest law was principally designed to protect the game although it also governed pasturage and the use of timber. It was William, who, in 1079 drew up these rules to protect his stags and to control the remaining Saxon landowners. In later centuries it was realized that not only could the forest supply pleasure in the form of hunting, but that its vast supply of beech and oak could supply timber for the Royal Navy. Soon, too much timber was being used, and the Tudor kings introduced some controls to encourage the regeneration of timber. It was James I, however, who took effective steps to preserve the forest, enclosing areas of the forest, ploughing them, and planting them with acorns. Charles II continued the traditional enthusiasm which monarchs showed for the forest, as the hunting lodge at Lyndhurst displays. Today the forest is said to cover 92,395 acres, of which 64,737 are crown lands.

THE RUFUS STONE

This simple monument marks the site of one of England's most mysterious events. King William Rufus died here, but doubt exists as to whether it was an accident, murder, or some sort of pagan sacrifice.

The traditional story is that on the 2nd August 1100 William went hunting with one of his favourites, Walter

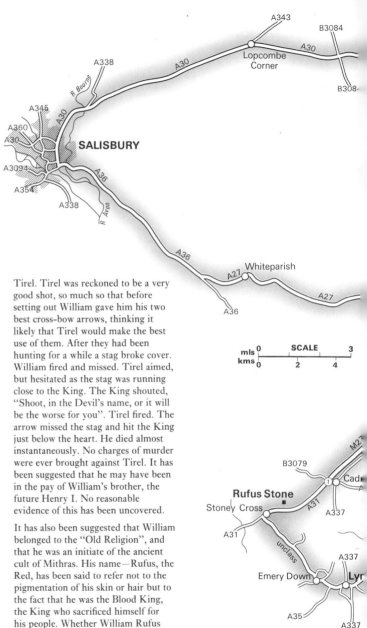

Tirel. Tirel was reckoned to be a very good shot, so much so that before setting out William gave him his two best cross-bow arrows, thinking it likely that Tirel would make the best use of them. After they had been hunting for a while a stag broke cover. William fired and missed. Tirel aimed, but hesitated as the stag was running close to the King. The King shouted, "Shoot, in the Devil's name, or it will be the worse for you". Tirel fired. The arrow missed the stag and hit the King just below the heart. He died almost instantaneously. No charges of murder were ever brought against Tirel. It has been suggested that he may have been in the pay of William's brother, the future Henry I. No reasonable evidence of this has been uncovered.

It has also been suggested that William belonged to the "Old Religion", and that he was an initiate of the ancient cult of Mithras. His name—Rufus, the Red, has been said to refer not to the pigmentation of his skin or hair but to the fact that he was the Blood King, the King who sacrificed himself for his people. Whether William Rufus was a wicked king whose passing was mourned by no one, or whether, albeit unwillingly, he died for his people, this monument recalls an ancient mystery.

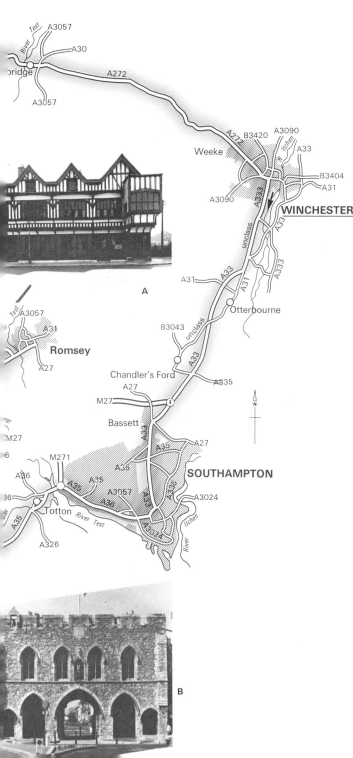

ROMSEY

The entry in the *Anglo-Saxon Chronicle* for the year 971 states that: "In this year Prince Edmund passed away, and his body lies at Romsey". He would have lain in the abbey church, said to have been founded by King Edward the Elder in the 10th century. All that remains of the original Saxon foundation is a crucifix in the choir, as the abbey was largely rebuilt in Norman times. Not far from the abbey is King John's House, which was used as his hunting lodge and, until 1221, served as a royal residence. The building has been restored and now houses a museum.

Romsey is the home of the Mountbatten family. It was at their house—Broadlands—that Queen Elizabeth II and the Duke of Edinburgh spent part of their honeymoon. The royal couple still visit here informally from time to time. The last official visit was in 1957 when the Queen and the Duke attended the 350th Charter Anniversary Celebrations.

SALISBURY

The city of Salisbury was founded in the 13th century after the abandonment of Old Sarum. The new cathedral was started in 1220, using material from the old one. Its magnificent 404 ft spire is the tallest in England. The cathedral houses several items of royal interest, including a statue of a gigantic knight in armour who formed one of the bodyguard of Henry VII during the Battle of Bosworth, as well as an effigy of the Earl of Salisbury, son of Henry III.

In the cathedral library is one of the four original copies of the Magna Carta the famous document signed by King John at Runnymede. It was brought to Salisbury by William Longespee, Earl of Salisbury. He was half-brother to King John and had been one of the witnesses to the signing of the document. In the 14th century,

A The finely-restored Tudor House Museum, Southampton
B Bargate, the major gateway to medieval Southampton
C The old Queen's House, Lyndhurst, is still used for Forest Court sessions
D Salisbury Cathedral has the highest spire in England, rising to 404 feet

Edward III gave permission for a wall to be built round the cathedral and the nearby houses, and much of this wall survives today.

It is said that Charles II hid in the Old King's Arms after the Battle of Worcester.

47

OSBORNE

Queen Victoria was happy with none of her royal homes—Buckingham Palace was too crowded, and both Windsor and Brighton Pavilion lacked privacy. She longed for a quiet retreat where she and her growing family could escape the turmoil of palace life. The Queen remembered her childhood holidays on the Isle of Wight, and so, in 1844 she made enquiries after a property on the island.

A retreat is found

Osborne House seemed the most suitable. Victoria rented it for a trial year from Lady Isabella Blatchford. The house stood on rising ground, east of the Medina estuary, overlooking the Solent. Both Victoria and Albert were enchanted with it. Victoria wrote that "It is impossible to see a prettier place, with woods and valleys and points of view, which would be beautiful anywhere; but when these are combined with the sea (to which the woods grow down) and a beach which is quite private, it really is everything one could wish". Albert said that the view reminded him of the Bay of Naples. In 1845 the house, along with 1,000 acres of land, were bought by the Queen for £26,000. The house as it stood was far too small for the royal family and within weeks of moving in Prince Albert had produced, in collaboration with the builder Thomas Cubitt, plans for a new house.

The inspiration for the new home was the Solent, which so much resembled the Bay of Naples. Obviously the house should be a Neapolitan villa, complete with Italianate campaniles and a loggia.

The completed building including the foregoing features plus mock Renaissance terraces with a fountain and statues, all leading down to the sea. Several new construction methods, including the use of cast-iron beams, were employed. The "Osborne" style rapidly became very popular and smaller versions of it sprang up throughout the country. In the 90ft Clock Tower is a clock mechanism which is an amalgam of pieces from the clock constructed for George III in 1771 for use at Kew, and the mechanism for the clock removed from Brighton Pavilion in 1849.

Prince Albert was able to indulge his tastes for landscaping and forestry in the grounds. He planted much of the farmland with oak, beech and elm and nearer the house he introduced Christmas trees and Monkey Puzzle trees as well as other exotics. The woods around the house were full of birds, and much to Albert's pleasure these included a good many nightingales, which were his favourites. In her memoirs Victoria wrote that she and the Prince frequently walked in the woods and that Albert would make the nightingale's distinctive call, which was invariably answered.

On the beach the Queen had her own bathing machine. In the grounds stands the "Swiss Cottage". This Prince Albert had imported direct from Switzerland as a playroom for the royal children. It is no mere doll's house, but a full-sized house with a kitchen, pantry, dairy, carpenter's workshop and numerous upstairs rooms. In it the royal children not only played, but learnt a variety of skills; the princes being taught carpentry whilst the princesses grappled with the problems of household management. Each of the children had a garden plot near the cottage. These they cultivated themselves and grew not only flowers but vegetables also.

Death of Albert

For the whole family Osborne was a happy, carefree home. In December 1861 tragedy struck—Prince Albert died. Queen Victoria gave instructions that nothing in the house should change; it was to be a mausoleum to the memory of her beloved husband.

Osborne continued to be a centre of life for the royal family. As the children grew up, married, and had children of their own, they brought them here for seaside holidays. Once again the house was considered to be too small. In 1891 the Durbar Room was built. This enabled the Queen to entertain all her relatives at dinner in one sitting, as well as providing a suitable place for state banquets. The Durbar Room is Indian in style, and was decorated by Indian craftsmen.

Queen Victoria died at Osborne on 22nd January 1901. She had previously given instructions that the place of her lying in state should be the Dining Room. The room was draped in white, and the body of the woman who had worn nothing but black for 40 years was likewise dressed in white.

Edward VII was more than happy at Sandringham, and anyway he found the museum-like Osborne depressing. So he presented most of the estate to the nation and turned the household apartments into a convalescent home. The State apartments, with the exception of Victoria's private suite, he opened to the public; Queen Elizabeth II opened the private suite to the public in 1954.

The buildings and much of the furnishings, have remained virtually unchanged since Victoria's day. Everything, down to the smallest detail, is a reminder of the standards and tastes of Victorian England.

Osborne House on the Isle of Wight was Queen Victoria's favourite house. When Prince Albert died, she turned the house into a shrine to his memory

The Isle of Wight

WHIPPINGHAM

The very un-English looking church here was built to designs by Albert, the Prince Consort, in 1860. In fact the whole building, especially the tower, is Germanic in appearance. The royal family worshipped here on numerous occasions, and memorials to some of them may be seen. Opposite the church are the almshouses in which several of Queen Victoria's servants were placed after their retirement.

BRADING

Tourists are much drawn to this attractive village. Its history is long and it had many early charters which were renewed by Edward VI. The church is the oldest on the Isle of Wight. Lying ¾m west of Brading is Nunwell Manor. This has been the home of the Oglander family since they came over with William the Conqueror. The present house dates mainly from early Tudor times, but there are a variety of building styles and periods incorporated in the structure. The Oglanders were one of the principal families on the island and were important enough to have Henry VIII as a guest. Charles I was a visitor to the house during his confinement at Carisbrooke.

NEWPORT

Prince Albert laid the foundation ston of the church of St Thomas, which replaced an earlier structure in 1854. Princess Elizabeth, the 15 year old daughter of Charles I, who died whilst in captivity at Carisbrooke Castle, is buried in front of the altar. The actual spot is marked by a brass plate. A Marochetti memorial in Carrara marble to Elizabeth was placed on the north side of the chancel by Queen Victoria.

Charles I stayed at the old Grammar School, which was founded in 1614, when he was on parole from Carisbrooke Castle. The prominent 19th century Guildhall stands on the site of a building in which Charles I signed the Treaty of Newport with the Parliamentary Commissioners. The nearby Forest of Avington was the scene of hunting expeditions by Henry VIII.

CARISBROOKE CASTLE

Set on a 150 ft plateau, Carisbrooke Castle is principally associated with King Charles I, who spent most of the last year of his life here. The history of Carisbrooke, however, began thousands of years before that. It is thought to have been a neolithic settlement and was certainly a Roman fort. In 1070 a Norman castle was built on the site and during the civil strife between King Stephen and Queen Matilda the castle was held for Matilda.

In 1153 the keep was begun, and during the 13th century considerable alterations were made to the castle. It had been granted by the crown to the Redvers family, and after the line had died out, it once more became royal property. Richard II gave it to the Earl of Salisbury who made many improvements to the structure, including the building of the great hall. Several times during the middle ages the castle became embroiled in warfare. During the Wars of the Roses, three of its lords were beheaded for treason. As fears of a Spanish invasion mounted in the reign of Elizabeth I, the castle was made ready for such an eventuality. The work was carried out by the Italian engineer Genebella whose tremendous curtain wall enclosed the whole 20 acre extent of the grounds. It was a massive, hurried operation which was completed in 245 days. The Armada was a failure for the Spanish, and until the English Civil War, Carisbrooke remained quiet.

By the middle of 1647 Charles I was in the custody of the parliamentary forces and the war had been over for nearly two years. The country, however, was in chaos, with Parliament and the army at loggerheads. Both sides hoped to be able to use the King for their own purposes. Charles saw that this situation was to his advantage, and whilst it continued he negotiated with the Scots, who promised to return him to the throne if he granted their religious wishes. In November 1647, Charles fled to Carisbrooke where he thought he had a friend in the Governor, Colonel Robert Hammond. Hammond, however, was a loyal parliamentarian, and was connected to Cromwell by marriage. Despite this, Charles was able to move about the island quite freely at first. He spent his time riding, hunting, dining with island notables—and continuing secret negotiations with the Scots.

Early in 1648 England was in such a state of confusion and uproar that a second civil war broke out. Charles' dealings with the Scots were uncovered and he was made a prisoner. None-theless Parliament still tried to come to terms with him. Cromwell soon crushed the royalist uprising, which was badly coordinated and ill timed, and returned from the war determined to have the King's head. By now the country had become virtually a military dictatorship. Charles was taken from Carisbrooke to stand trial in London, and at four minutes past two on 30th January 1649 the King of England was executed.

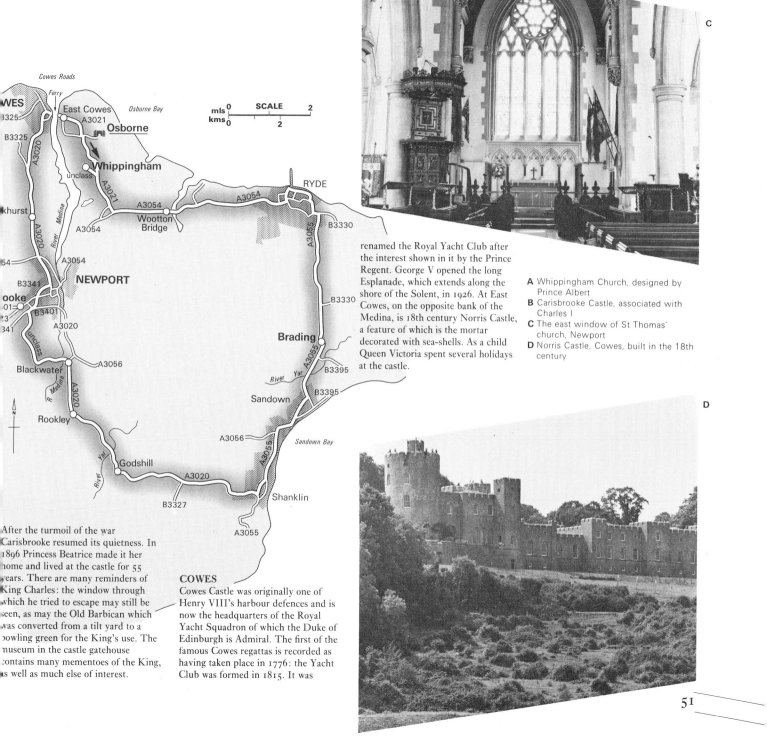

renamed the Royal Yacht Club after the interest shown in it by the Prince Regent. George V opened the long Esplanade, which extends along the shore of the Solent, in 1926. At East Cowes, on the opposite bank of the Medina, is 18th century Norris Castle, a feature of which is the mortar decorated with sea-shells. As a child Queen Victoria spent several holidays at the castle.

A Whippingham Church, designed by Prince Albert
B Carisbrooke Castle, associated with Charles I
C The east window of St Thomas' church, Newport
D Norris Castle, Cowes, built in the 18th century

After the turmoil of the war Carisbrooke resumed its quietness. In 1896 Princess Beatrice made it her home and lived at the castle for 55 years. There are many reminders of King Charles: the window through which he tried to escape may still be seen, as may the Old Barbican which was converted from a tilt yard to a bowling green for the King's use. The museum in the castle gatehouse contains many mementos of the King, as well as much else of interest.

COWES

Cowes Castle was originally one of Henry VIII's harbour defences and is now the headquarters of the Royal Yacht Squadron of which the Duke of Edinburgh is Admiral. The first of the famous Cowes regattas is recorded as having taken place in 1776: the Yacht Club was formed in 1815. It was

BRIGHTON

George, Prince of Wales, son of George III, was secretly married to Mrs Fitzherbert on 15th December 1785. The union had to be clandestine as Mrs Fitzherbert was a Roman Catholic, and all members of the British royal family were legally barred from marriage to Catholics. Indeed, by this act, George was in theory forfeiting his right to the Crown.

Mrs Fitzherbert had at first strongly opposed the advances of the Prince, but George pressed his suit so strongly, even to the extent of stabbing himself and saying that he would die if she did not marry him, that Mrs Fitzherbert was virtually forced to comply. After the marriage the couple behaved with great discretion (never a strong point with George) even though the whole of London society was alive with rumours about the affair.

Early visits
The Prince of Wales had first visited Brighton, or Brighthelmstone as it was then called, in September 1783. He stayed at Grove House with his uncle and aunt, the Duke and Duchess of Cumberland, whose company he found far more convivial than that of his disapproving mother and father. Brighton had begun to be popular in 1753 when Dr Richard Russell, a great advocate of the health-giving properties of sea-water, had built himself a house on the sea-front.

George enjoyed himself so much at Brighton that he returned the following year, partly on the advice of his physicians who told him that the sea-water would help cure the swollen glands in his throat. That year, 1784, was even more enjoyable, and the Prince decided that he would like his own house at Brighton. It was chosen for the Prince by his trusted servant Louis Weltje and was a modest but respectable farmhouse on the east side of the Steine with a view of the sea-front.

In July 1786 George moved from London into his new home and installed Mrs Fitzherbert in a nearby villa. During the summer and autumn of that year George led a very quiet life at Brighton. One of the reasons for this was that he had vowed to economise, after a number of years in which his vast expenditure had become a public scandal.

The farmhouse on the Steine was soon replaced by a far more imposing building which was designed by Henry Holland. This structure, the first version of the Pavilion, was built in the Graeco-Roman style with a domed rotunda as a centrepiece. It was to this handsome building that Mrs Fitzherbert and George, his finances once more secure, came in the summer of 1787. The Prince did not actually purchase the Pavilion site until 1800, when further extensive modifications and extensions were planned.

Fashionable resort
By this time Brighton had become, according to the *Brighton Directory* of 1800 "the most frequented and without exception one of the most fashionable towns in the Kingdom". The completion of the Royal Crescent in 1807 was celebrated by the erection of a statue of Prince George. Unfortunately one of the statue's arms dropped off, leading visitors to believe that it represented Lord Nelson. Mrs Fitzherbert had a new house, next to the imposing structure owned by the Duke of Marlborough.

More changes were made to the Pavilion, and in 1805 the massive stables (now a concert hall) were begun. These took three years to complete and cost a small fortune. The accommodation provided was for 54 horses and their ostlers and

The oriental-style palace at Brighton created by John Nash for George IV

Queen Adelaide. For Queen Victoria it was entirely unsuitable; she did not like Brighton as it was too public, nor did she like the Pavilion. Osborne House on the Isle of Wight was much more to her liking, and after she had settled there she sold the Pavilion to the Brighton Town Commissioners.

Today the Pavilion is restored to its former glory, and due to the generosity of the Royal Family, much of the original furniture is on display. The visitor may wander through a collection of rooms whose richness and colour are breathtaking. The enormous kitchen, whose pillars are made to resemble palm trees, is permanently laid out as if for a banquet. Two of the rooms in the Pavilion serve as special reminders of its great ladies; there is a bedroom reconstructed as George's daughter Princess Charlotte would have known it; and the other is called Mrs Fitzherbert's Drawing Room. In the latter is the ring with which she was married to Prince George.

grooms. The interior of the Pavilion was itself modified and redecorated, including the construction of a Chinese gallery. The Prince was so delighted with this that he moved the contents of his Chinese Room at Carlton House to Brighton. In 1807 plans were completed by Humphrey Repton for a new Pavilion in the Indian style, but even though George thought the plans were perfect and vowed to begin the work straight away, nothing was in fact done until 1815 when John Nash began his great rebuilding of the Pavilion.

The result was not Indian at all, but a conglomeration of oriental styles. The building is so extraordinary that to most people it appears beautiful; not all of Prinnie's contemporaries saw it that way, however, and it was variously described as a "pup of St Paul's" and "an absurd waste of money".

The Pavilion completed

After Nash had completed every detail of his work George, now King, lost interest in the Pavilion and turned his energy to restoring the royal apartments at Windsor Castle. William IV, however, found the Pavilion to his taste, and spent a part of every summer here with

The Banqueting Room in Brighton Pavilion is lavishly decorated in Chinese style

The South Downs

ARUNDEL

Arundel Castle, standing on a hill in the centre of this ancient town, commands magnificent views of the river Arun and the Downs. In 899, Alfred the Great bequeathed the stronghold to his nephew Athelm. Before the Norman Conquest it belonged to King Harold, and William the Conqueror gave it to his commander Montgomery. It was he who built the stone castle on the site of the earlier Saxon fortification. The castle was captured by Henry I after a siege brought about by the treason of Robert de Belesme, who was captured and imprisoned at Wareham. Adeliza, the widowed wife of Henry I, endowed it to her second husband William de Albini.

The castle eventually became the home of John Fitzalan, the lord of the manor. In 1580 it was, once and for all time, endowed by marriage to the now rightful owner—the Earl Marshal of England. During the Civil War the castle was bombarded by parliamentary forces, and the royalist garrison surrendered. Much reconstruction was carried out in the 18th century but the gatehouse and the State rooms, where King John slept and where Queen Matilda made her decision to relinquish the throne to King Stephen, were retained. In 1846 Queen Victoria and Prince Albert visited the castle and the room which they occupied still contains the furniture specially installed for the royal visit.

BOGNOR REGIS

Bognor owes its royal associations to its equable climate and excellent bathing beach. George III frequented the town during the 18th century, and the Dome House (now a training college) was built as a residence for him. It was also used as a holiday home by Princess Charlotte, daughter of George IV. The suffix "Regis" was added to the town's name after George V convalesced here in 1929. Craigwell House, at which he stayed, has been demolished.

CHICHESTER

The cathedral town of Chichester was founded originally by the Romans. The Saxon King Aella captured the settlement in the 5th century and gave it to his son Cissa. The name Chichester is a corruption of *Cissa's Ceaster* (ceaster means camp).

The town's 15th century Market Cross probably carried the arms of Henry VII, although the shields are now so worn that they cannot be read. On the east side of the cross is a bust of Charles I. In the south eastern part of the town is a cottage, bearing an inscribed plaque, which stands on the site of the Hospital of St James and St Mary Magdalene. This was probably founded by Queen Matilda, the wife of Henry I. Lord Lumley is reputed to have entertained Elizabeth I at The Old Punch House. The 16th century interior of this building has

been preserved although the exterior was remodelled during the 18th century. Portraits of Charles I, Charles II, and George I are contained in the Council Chamber of the 17th century and later Council House. Many of the town's treasures are housed in the ante-room to the main Assembly Room and these were inspected in July 1956 by Queen Elizabeth II and the Duke of Edinburgh. The foundation stone of the Festival Theatre, in the north of Chichester, was laid by Princess Alexandra in May 1961.

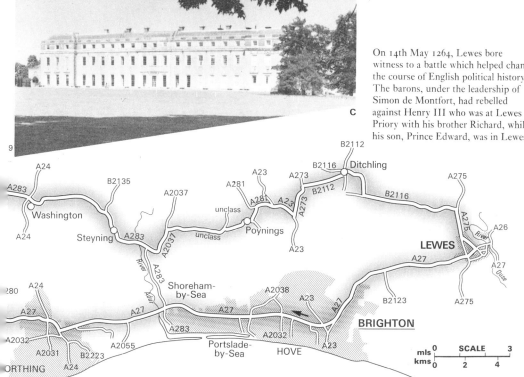

On 14th May 1264, Lewes bore witness to a battle which helped change the course of English political history. The barons, under the leadership of Simon de Montfort, had rebelled against Henry III who was at Lewes Priory with his brother Richard, while his son, Prince Edward, was in Lewes Castle. The rebel army mustered north of Lewes at Fletching and planned an action whereby they would capture first the castle and then the priory. The ensuing battle was a series of attacks and counter attacks, but by the end of the day de Montfort had captured the town and held both Henry and Richard. The subsequent treaty laid the foundations for a democratic system of government, and even though de Montfort was killed at Evesham the following year the principles remained intact.

Anne of Cleves was presented with a house in Southover upon her divorce from Henry VIII in 1540. The house is thought to date from 1499 and now houses a folk museum.

A Arundel Castle, fortress home of the Dukes of Norfolk
B The tower and spire of Chichester Cathedral
C Petworth House, set in magnificent parkland
D The 14th century barbican protecting Lewes Castle

PETWORTH

Standing in the Market Square of this charming old town is the 18th century Town Hall above the doorway of which is a baroque sculpture of William III. Petworth House is an imposing 17th and 19th century mansion which was once a seat of the Percys of Northumberland. It was largely rebuilt by the 6th Duke of Somerset, husband of Elizabeth Percy. The house, which belongs to the National Trust, is especially famous for its collection of paintings which includes, in the state room, an extra large portrait of Henry VIII.

LEWES

A settlement was founded here by the early Saxon invaders, and this was surrounded with defences on the orders of King Alfred in 890. Two mints were in operation in the town during the reign of King Athelstan; that these still functioned during Harold's brief reign is evidenced by the coins that were minted here with his head imprinted on them. Lewes was given by William the Conqueror to his son-in-law William de Warenne. The castle which de Warenne built differed from the usual Norman model in that it had two mottes. The original wooden fortifications of the castle were replaced by stonework at the end of the 11th century. De Warenne also founded St Pancras Priory, which became the most important Cluniac house in Britain. It was dissolved in 1548, but the ruins may still be seen. Both de Warenne and his wife Gundrada were originally buried in the priory, but the bodies were later moved to the Church of St John in the suburb of Southover, where the coffins and a tombstone to Gundrada are still preserved.

55

BATTLE

The most famous, and the most important, battle ever fought in English history, took place here. In a way it is strange that it should be called the Battle of Hastings, for the battle site is some miles from that town; its alternative name, Senlac, is perhaps more appropriate.

Harold as King

On 5th January 1066 Edward the Confessor lay dying; before he did so he nominated Harold, Earl of Wessex, as his successor. The next day this choice was confirmed by the old King's advisers. Harold was brother to Edith, wife of Edward, and his title to the throne was immediately disputed by Duke William of Normandy. William claimed that not only was he related by blood to Edward (they were distant cousins) but that in 1051 Edward had promised him the throne and that Harold when in Normandy in 1064 had sworn to uphold William's right to the throne. William prepared to invade England, but Harold had other worries for, in September, King Harold Hardrada of Norway (who also had a claim to the throne) arrived in the north of England with a mighty force. He was joined by Harold's embittered brother Tostig and an army from Scotland. This combined force defeated Harold's allies on 20th September and occupied York.

Harold had spent the summer months on the south coast waiting for a Norman invasion that never came. When he heard of the northern invasion, he force marched his army up to York and met the invaders at Stamford Bridge on 25th September. The battle was fierce, and both Harold Hardrada and Tostig were killed. Quarter was given to Olaf, the dead Norwegian King's son, who made promises of peace and friendship between his people and the English. On 1st October, Harold learnt that William had landed unopposed at Pevensey.

The Battle of Hastings

Once again Harold made a forced march, or rather gallop, for he can only have been accompanied on the break-neck race back to the south by his mounted housecarls. An infantry was quickly collected together from London and the Sussex countryside, and by 14th October Harold's army was drawn up for action. William had heard that Harold was approaching, so he had set up an advance post on Telham Hill. At that time it guarded the only route into Hastings where William had drawn up his ships and built fortifications. The soldiers on Telham Hill must have been amazed to see Harold's army drawn up on the morning of the 14th, for the Normans had no idea that Harold was so close.

The Normans made the first assault and had the difficult task of attacking uphill, for Harold had placed his army well. Arrows from the Norman crossbowmen made gaps in the English line, but not enough, and the first Norman attack was repulsed. Despite strict orders some of the English broke rank to pursue the Normans. It began to look as if Harold would

Battle Abbey, built by William the Conqueror, celebrating his victory at the Battle of Hastings

win the day, but William himself rode in amongst his wavering men and eventually called them to order. The English who had broken cover were overwhelmed.

A brief pause then followed, for which both leaders must have been glad, then once more William's men attacked. Again they were beaten back, and once more many English broke rank to pursue them. Through the gaps made in the defences William's cavalry charged, followed by the infantry. The English began to retreat, and the final blow came when Harold was struck down by a Norman swordsman (it was not an arrow that killed the King—that legend sprang from a mis-reading of the Bayeux Tapestry).

By now it was evening; the English were on the run and as the light failed William called off the pursuit. Harold's body was buried without ceremony on a cliff above the seashore.

The battlefield where King Harold was slain

William founded Battle Abbey on the site where Harold's standard had flown. The building was not finally consecrated until the reign of William Rufus, who witnessed the ceremony in 1094. The original buildings no longer remain, and the ruins standing today date mainly from the 13th century. In 1903 a memorial was erected to mark the place where Harold was killed; originally the spot was occupied by the high altar of the abbey.

A Mansion for a Princess

The abbey existed as a Benedictine foundation until the Dissolution of the monasteries in 1538 by Henry VIII. The buildings were presented to Sir Anthony Browne, Henry's master of horse. Sir Anthony demolished the church and turned the rest of the buildings into a mansion for himself. Before Henry died in 1547 he made Sir Anthony the guardian of his daughter, Princess Elizabeth. It was intended that Elizabeth should come to live at Battle, but Sir Anthony died in 1547 and his charge never stayed at the home he prepared for her.

Of the abbey church, only foundations remain, but many of the associated buildings still stand. Sir Anthony Browne's mansion, based on the Abbot's Lodge, was rebuilt after a fire and now functions as a boarding school. A small museum houses relics of the battle as well as a reproduction of the Bayeux Tapestry. Queen Elizabeth II stood on the terrace of the school, immediately in front of which ran the line of Harold's forces, and surveyed the battle site in 1966.

Battle's parish church of St Mary contains the tomb of Sir Anthony Browne and his wife Alis. A window in the north aisle depicts Edward the Confessor and the north door is carved with the heads of kings and queens. Also in the church is an unsubstantiated list of the names of all the knights in William's army.

From castles to battlefields

BODIAM

From the outside Bodiam presents every appearance of a perfect castle, right down to the lily-filled moat. Its interior, however, is quite hollow and carpeted with grass. Entering through the gatehouse into the grassy courtyard, the skeleton of the three storeyed bedroom towers, great hall, chapel, kitchens and servants' quarters is still clearly visible.

The castle was built between 1386–8 on the instructions of Richard II by Sir Edward Dalyngrygge, a brilliant and wealthy knight. Richard II granted Sir Edward a royal charter to battlement his home, since Bodiam stood on an unprotected stretch of the River Rother. He hoped that by fortifying Bodiam he might prevent the French from plundering farther into Sussex and Kent. In spite of these preparations, Bodiam with its 6ft thick walls and 6oft towers was never put to the test. Its shell-like condition results from the fact that it was slighted by parliamentary forces during the Civil War.

NORTHIAM

The town of Northiam is famous for a heavily propped and chained tree that stands on the village green, under which Queen Elizabeth I informally picnicked in the summer of 1573, while on a tour of Kent and Sussex. The tree is named Elizabeth's Oak and here it was, so the legend goes, that after being brought food from the nearby Hayes Inn (a building much older than its facade would suggest) she kicked off her green high-heeled shoes and left them as a memento for the villagers of Northiam. The shoes still exist, exhibited occasionally in

Brickwell House, a striking 16th century half timbered house recently adapted to become a boys' school.

CAMBER CASTLE

During the 1530s Henry VIII found himself threatened by the great forces of the French and the Spanish but with an inadequate army of his own. He set to work to provide himself with a coastal defence network of forts which eventually stretched from the coast of Kent to the coast of Cornwall. One of these was Camber Castle. Henry VIII arrived at Camber in 1539 and decided to improve and enlarge what was probably a 12th century structure. The money (and some of the materials) for this and all his other coastal castles came from the monasteries which he had broken up. Camber Castle was no exception, for the building materials used had been stripped from the religious houses of Winchelsea. The castle originally stood in a strategic position guarding a stretch of the River Rother, which subsequently changed course. In 1642 the castle was dismantled, and anything of value, such as lead or timber, was given to the committee of Sussex. At present the castle is in an unsafe condition and is not open to the public.

HASTINGS

The original castle that William the Conqueror built at Hastings was made out of sections of wood brought over from Normandy, as is depicted by one of the scenes on the Bayeux tapestry. Later the wooden castle was replaced by a stone fort, much of which has since crumbled into the sea; fragmentary bits of the curtain wall, arches and the western gatehouse still remain to be seen, while beneath the castle a warren of tunnels with extraordinary acoustics once served as dungeons or storehouses. Hastings was one of the Cinque Ports, which gave allegiance to the crown, supplying ships, fighting the King's enemies and ferrying troops to and from the

Continent in return for certain royal concessions. Hastings continued in prosperity until partially destroyed by a great storm in 1287, followed by two devastating invasions by the French in 1339 and 1377 from which the town never recovered.

Facing the pier, the White Rock Pavilion serves as a reminder of the rocks that continually fell from the cliffs above, frequently blocking the main London to Hastings road. On one occasion the path of Princess Victoria and her mother became blocked en route for a holiday visit to St Leonards, causing extreme royal annoyance and forcing them to make a long detour.

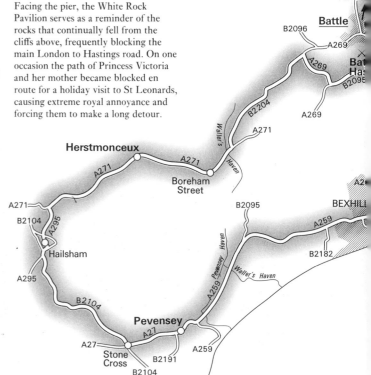

PEVENSEY

William the Conqueror landed at Pevensey on the 28th September 1066. At that time it stood on the coast, but changes in the coastline since then explain why Pevensey now stands a mile from the sea. He enlarged and improved Pevensey Castle, a structure that had stood by the sea since Roman times and which had been occupied by Alfred the Great during the 9th century while he was fighting the Danes. The five-towered castle still stands surrounded by its original Roman walls and a moat. It was besieged on many occasions and was usually captured by being starved into submission by its attackers. William's brother Robert was forced to surrender the castle to William Rufus in 1088; while in 1147 Pevensey fell again, this time to King Stephen.

In the 14th century, the castle was held by the Pelham family for Henry IV against the attacks of Richard II. Henry was victorious and he granted Pevensey to the Pelhams as a mark of his gratitude.

HERSTMONCEUX

Henry III stayed here for one night in 1264 on his way to the Battle of Lewes. At that time Herstmonceux was a Norman manor house, but a licence to crenallate was granted in 1440 which transformed it into a castle. Most of the building was demolished in 1777 and remained in ruins until the early 20th century, when it was rebuilt. The structure was greatly restored and further additions were made to house the Royal Observatory which moved there from Greenwich in 1948. The Observatory contains one of the largest telescopes in the world, and was opened by Queen Elizabeth II on 1st December 1967. The grounds are open to the public.

A Bodiam Castle, in its perfect, moated setting
B Camber Castle, erected by Henry VIII
C Pevensey Castle, originally a Roman sea-fort
D The home of the Royal Observatory at Herstmonceux Castle

59

CANTERBURY

The ancient city of Canterbury has a history stretching back over more than 1,000 years, and has many royal connections. When the County of Kent was an independent kingdom, the city was the capital and seat of the king. The most notable of these monarchs was Ethelbert who reigned during the late 6th and early 7th centuries. Although he had not yet been converted to the Christian faith, he refurbished the Roman built church of St Martin for his Christian wife, Queen Bertha. He continued to worship his gods in a nearby temple which was later to become the Church of St Pancras, the remains of which can be seen in the enclosure of St Augustine's Abbey.

St Augustine's Abbey

In AD 597 St Augustine brought his monks to these shores and had considerable success in converting the people of Kent to Christianity. He baptised King Ethelbert in St Martin's Church, where a stained glass window can be seen depicting the event. Another window shows Queen Bertha with her maids.

In 602, with the support of King Ethelbert, St Augustine founded the abbey, which became the burial place of the Saint and of Ethelbert. In later years various abbots altered and enlarged the building until the year 1538, which saw Henry VIII's Dissolution of the monasteries. From this time the abbey was allowed to fall into disrepair, with the exception of the Fyndon Gateway and the adjoining building which were retained as a royal residence. In 1557, surrounded by her usual pomp and splendour, Queen Elizabeth I spent two weeks here. King Charles I came here in 1625 with his new bride, Queen Henrietta Maria, the sister of the French King Louis XIII. They spent their wedding night in the chamber over the gateway.

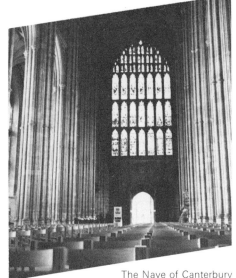

The Nave of Canterbury Cathedral, "one of the greatest masterpieces of art in the world", looking towards the West Window

Canterbury Cathedral, with Bell Harry Tower, seen from the south east corner of the precincts

The castle at Canterbury has the third largest Norman keep in England. It was built by William the Conqueror between 1070 and 1094, but none of the outer fortifications are still in existence. It would appear that these defences were not all that they should have been because every attacking force eventually took possession of the castle. These included the French Dauphin who came to support the barons in their rebellion against King John in 1216, and later Wat Tyler who led the Peasants' Revolt of 1381.

England's oldest Cathedral

Most of the people who visit Canterbury do so to see the magnificent cathedral, the religious centre of England. It is known that a place of worship existed on the site as long ago as the 5th century. The original building was destroyed by fire, but rebuilding started in 1070. Many changes in the fabric of the cathedral have been made throughout the centuries, the last being in 1831 when the Norman north west tower was replaced by the one which exists today.

It was in the Chapel of Martyrdom on the night of 29th December 1170 that Thomas Becket was stabbed to death by four knights. They had been trying to persuade Becket to approve King Henry II's plans to revise the position of the Church in relation to the Crown, but his adamant refusal resulted in his murder. The place where Becket fell became the object of pilgrimage for centuries, further establishing Canterbury as the premier centre of Christianity in England. A priceless jewelled shrine to Becket was erected in 1220, where, it is said, several miracles were performed. Those who were reputedly cured included a leper and a man with toothache, and the stories are related in the famous "Miracle Windows" in the Trinity Chapel. No trace of the shrine remains, as it was plundered during the Dissolution and its jewels were placed in the coffers of Henry VIII. A small stone now marks the place where Becket fell, with a simple inscription on the wall nearby.

The tremendous outcry that followed Becket's murder forced Henry II to agree to the Church's demand that he should do penance for the crime and for this purpose he came to the city. On reaching Canterbury, he dismounted and entered St. Dunstan's church to remove his ordinary clothing before walking barefoot through the gate in the city wall and on to Becket's tomb in the crypt of the cathedral. Here he was scourged by the monks.

In the Trinity Chapel of the cathedral is the tomb of Edward of Woodstock, the famous Black Prince, who was buried here in 1376. Although Edward was the Prince of Wales and heir to the throne, he died before his father, King Edward III, and so never gained the crown.

His tomb takes the form of a brass effigy behind ornate railings. Above the tomb hang replicas of the Prince's helmet, crest, coat of arms, shield, scabbard and gauntlets, as worn no doubt during his great victories at Crecy and Poitiers. The original articles can be seen in a glass case nearby. They are over 600 years old and in an extremely fragile condition.

The Prince always had a special affection for Canterbury Cathedral and in 1336 he endowed a chantry in the crypt and financed the Chapel of our Lady Undercroft. It was here that he wished to be buried, but the people insisted that a grander position would be more appropriate for such a hero. A stained glass window can be seen in St. Anselm's Chapel, adjacent to the choir, portraying the Black Prince and his wife at a feast with the captive King of France.

Not far from the tomb of the Black Prince are the tombs of King Henry IV, who was King of England from 1399 to 1413, and his second wife, Joan of Navarre. Henry, the only monarch buried at the cathedral, usurped the throne from Richard II and was responsible for his death. It is thought that, by being buried close to the shrine of St. Thomas and the tomb of his victim's father, the Black Prince, Henry was trying to ease his troubled conscience. He also endowed the Chantry of Henry IV, sometimes called Edward the Confessor's Chapel, to the cathedral. It is situated off the north aisle of the Trinity Chapel and is said to be the most beautiful of the chapels in the cathedral.

Henry IV is also featured on the ornate choir screen which separates the eastern from the western part of the cathedral. The screen has six carved figures which probably represent Henry V, Richard II, Ethelbert, Edward the Confessor, Henry IV and Henry VI.

Close to the cathedral, just inside the city wall is King's School. Originally a monastic foundation dating from the 7th century, it was installed as a school by Henry VIII to educate 50 boys. There are now around 700 pupils in this, one of the oldest schools in England. An interesting feature of the building is the unique Norman exterior staircase.

In 1607 King James I presented the sword of state to the city. This is now kept in the Guildhall, along with the Mayoral Mace bearing the monogram of Charles II and given by him in 1681.

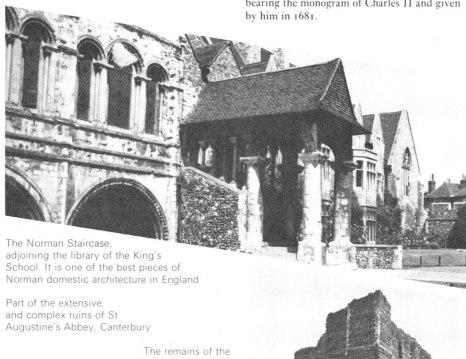

The Norman Staircase, adjoining the library of the King's School. It is one of the best pieces of Norman domestic architecture in England

Part of the extensive and complex ruins of St Augustine's Abbey, Canterbury

The remains of the keep of Canterbury castle, Formerly one of the largest Norman keeps in Britain

Defences against invasion

A

BIRCHINGTON
Quex Park, the home of the Queke family, which lies half a mile south of Birchington was used by William III as an overnight stopping place on his journeys to Holland.

MARGATE
Now a popular seaside resort, Margate's harbour was at one time frequently used by King William IH. It also saw the embarkation of Frederick V (King of Bohemia) with his bride, Elizabeth Stuart.

SANDWICH
During the reign of Edward the Confessor, Sandwich was designated as one of the Cinque Ports, but the silting up of the river made its continued use as a port impracticable. Such has been the extent of the build up of sand that the town now lies nearly two miles from the sea.

It was here that Thomas Becket landed in 1170 shortly before his murder in Canterbury Cathedral after his self imposed exile in France to escape the wrath of Henry II.

King Richard I, who reigned for ten years but who spent only six months of that time in England, re-entered the country through this port in 1194. He had been imprisoned by his enemy, King Leopold of Austria, on his way home from the Holy Land and was only released for a "King's Ransom" of 150,000 marks raised by heavy taxation and by the relinquishing of some of his lands.

The picturesque and well preserved gateway called the Barbican was constructed on the orders of Henry VIII in 1539 to guard the river approaches to the town. The building is now used as a theatre.

The King's House, in Strand Street, once belonged to the monks of Canterbury and was visited by Queen Elizabeth I in 1573. It is said that Henry VIII was also a guest on two occasions. The house is now privately owned and not open to the public.

WALMER
Like Deal, Walmer Castle was built by Henry VIII as part of his coastal defences. The huge stone walls were built from dismantled monasteries and followed the pattern of the Tudor Rose or Clover Leaf constructional technique. The purpose of the curved surfaces of the four semi-circular bastions was to deflect incoming cannonballs without restricting the use of the sixty guns within the castle.

In 1730 the Duke of Dorset considerably altered the castle to transform it from a fortress to the official residence of the Lord Warden of the Cinque Ports, for which purpose it is still used. Among the Lord Wardens to reside here have been William Pitt the Younger, who was also Prime Minister at the time, and the "Iron Duke" of Wellington who spent 23 years here and died at the castle.

DEAL
King William IV donated a unique tablet to the memory of Admiral Lord Nelson in the Church of St. George the Martyr in Deal, the place where Nelson frequently worshipped. It is thought to be the only such memorial by a king to a seaman.

Deal Castle was built by Henry VIII in 1539 as a part of his extensive defence programme to protect the south coast of England. It is in an ideal position to watch over the Downs, the stretch of water between the shore and the treacherous Goodwin Sands. Henry had broken the religious ties with Rome over his divorce and declared himself Head of the Church of England. When the French made an alliance with the Pope, Henry was in fear of an invasion so he began to construct a number of fortifications along the coast. Deal Castle was one of the larger and more stylish of these, but the invading forces that Henry expected did not materialise.

The only fighting that Deal Castle saw was during the Civil War in 1648. Parliamentary supporters occupied the castle until they were driven out by an attack of royalist vessels in the Channel. The King's men held the castle for some time, but it was eventually repossessed by Cromwell's superior army.

In 1941 a bomb demolished a part of the castle, but it has since been restored to its original condition. A museum within the castle houses exhibits from 25 BC to AD 1300 and a display of Henry VIII's defence system.

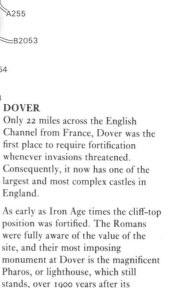

Quex Park, Birchington, housing the Powell-Cotton big game museum

The Barbican, Sandwich, built in the time of Henry VIII

Walmer Castle, official residence of the Lord Warden of the Cinque Ports

Dover Castle, occupying a commanding position on the south east coast of Britain

DOVER

Only 22 miles across the English Channel from France, Dover was the first place to require fortification whenever invasions threatened. Consequently, it now has one of the largest and most complex castles in England.

As early as Iron Age times the cliff-top position was fortified. The Romans were fully aware of the value of the site, and their most imposing monument at Dover is the magnificent Pharos, or lighthouse, which still stands, over 1900 years after its construction, alongside the Saxon church of St. Mary-in-Castro.

After his victory at the Battle of Hastings, William the Conqueror made for Dover where he spent some time strengthening the Saxon fortifications.

It was Henry II, however, who made the greatest contribution to the strength of the castle, spending what was then an enormous sum of money on the building of the three storey keep, the inner bailey and much of the curtain walling.

The cost was well justified in 1216 when, against ferocious attack from the French Dauphin who came in search of the English throne, Hubert de Burgh held the castle for King John. Fortunately for the castle, if not for the monarch, King John died and the Dauphin lost the support of the barons and retreated to France.

Edward I was brought to the castle as a prisoner of the powerful barons, and returned in 1274 in more favourable circumstances on his way home from the Crusade. The port also saw the return of Henry V from Agincourt and the departure of Henry VIII for the Field of the Cloth of Gold.

A relic of Tudor times stands beside the road leading to the castle. Known as "Queen Elizabeth's pocket pistol", it is a gun made in Utrecht in 1544 and presented to the Queen by the States of Holland for her help against the Spanish.

When the Napoleonic wars in the 18th century again threatened our shores, the castle was drastically altered. Walls were cut off to house heavy guns and ditches were dug deeper, so that the castle we see today is vastly different from the one planned by Henry II eight hundred years ago.

ROYAL TUNBRIDGE WELLS

By Kentish standards, Tunbridge Wells is a young town, being less than 350 years old, whereas most towns in the county have at least medieval origins. Its existence stems from the mineral spring which was discovered by chance at the beginning of the 17th century. A local legend tells how the water gained its sulphurous and health giving property. Apparently St Dunstan, then a humble blacksmith, was shaping a horseshoe in his forge when he saw the Devil approaching. He seized the Devil's nose with his red hot tongs, causing him to leap to the spot where Tunbridge Wells now stands, in order to cool his nose in the spring.

The spa is born

The spring was discovered in 1606 by Dudley, Lord North, who had lost his way whilst returning to London from Eridge Castle where he had been staying with friends. The purpose of his visit had been to recuperate from the rigours of life at court. Noticing the stains on the rocks around the spring, which were similar to those he had seen at a health resort, he stopped to taste the water. He also thought it would be a good idea to take a sample back to London with him for analysis, where it was confirmed that this was a chalybeate spring and highly beneficial for a number of conditions.

In 1630 the spring acquired royal patronage when King Charles I brought his queen, Henrietta Maria, to recover after the birth of their first son. It must have been a very strange excursion for the royal couple. Not only did it lack the grandeur of the court, but the place possessed no buildings at all, and a number of tents had to be erected to house the King and Queen and their entourage. It was clear that the spring was going to be a popular resort for

some time and so an extensive building programme was embarked upon to provide more civilised shelter for visitors.

King Charles II was a frequent visitor with his wife Catherine of Braganza, a selection of mistresses and the rest of the nobility. In 1665 when the Great Plague was killing the population of London, the royal family evacuated to Tunbridge Wells. They returned again in the following year when the City of London, and the remains of the disease, were destroyed by fire. By 1678, the town had expanded and was becoming so popular that the people decided the time had come to raise money to build a place of worship. Work was completed in 1696 and the church was named after the first royal visitor to the town, King Charles the Martyr. The plain exterior contrasts with the beautiful ceiling with its plaster cherubs, flowers, leaves and fruit. Here too can be seen the place where the young Princess Victoria sat when she visited the town.

Princess Anne, later to become Queen Anne, came to Tunbridge Wells in 1697 with her young son, the Duke of Gloucester. While visiting the spring the boy slipped and hurt himself. The Princess complained to the town officials and gave them £100 to pay for the paving of the area. For some reason this work had not been done by the time the Princess returned the following year and, greatly offended, she left the town never to return again. Soon afterwards the area around the spring was paved with pantiles and the area is still known by this name, even though few of the original tiles remain today.

During the Civil War, loyalties were divided in Tunbridge Wells. The royalists gathered around Southborough Hill, while supporters of Oliver Cromwell used the Rustal area. Mount Sion and Mount Ephraim were the sites of parliamentarian army camps for about a year following a royalist rebellion near by.

Regency patronage

The town reached the height of its popularity during the 18th century when the "Quality" came to promenade along the Pantiles, to take the waters, but most of all to see and be seen. In 1735 Beau Nash arrived from Bath and declared himself Master of Ceremonies. During the season the town abounded with gossip, scandal and matchmaking. At the end of the season the visitors abandoned the town for the London scene, or to spend the winter at their stately homes in the country. This pattern of life continued until the advent of the bathing machine during the reign of George III, when it was considered more beneficial to breathe sea air and take a dip in the ocean than to take the waters at an inland resort. The popularity of Tunbridge Wells then declined.

In 1825 the Duchess of Kent arrived in the town with her young daughter, Princess Victoria, the child who would become Queen of England at the age of 18 and rule for 63 years. Victoria spent a great deal of time in Tunbridge Wells over the next ten years, staying at Calverley House, now the Calverley Hotel. These visits seem to have stimulated interest in the town again, as evidenced by much Victorian architecture in the town today. The civic dignitaries of Tunbridge Wells applied to the King, Edward VII, in 1909 for permission to use the prefix "Royal" in their town's name. They considered their request justified by the number of kings, queens, princes and princesses who had visited the town during its relatively short history. The King was obviously in agreement because he gave his consent and the town has ever since been known as Royal Tunbridge Wells.

Kent's Stately Homes

PENSHURST

A house has stood on the site of the present Penshurst Place since the 12th century, and sometime during the 14th century the Black Prince spent a Christmas here with Joan, his fair maid of Kent. It was in Tudor times, however, that the house saw its greatest days. It was given in 1552 by the young King Edward VI to Sir William Sidney who had fought at Flodden Field and accompanied Henry VIII to the Field of the Cloth of Gold. He died soon afterwards and the house passed to his son, Henry. Sir Henry served under Edward, Mary, and Elizabeth and his hard work for the crown finally ruined his health. His wife nursed Queen Elizabeth through smallpox, but unfortunately contracted the disease herself and, because of the terrible scars it left, spent the rest of her life in solitude.

Without a doubt the most famous of the Sidneys was Henry's son Philip, named after his godfather, King Philip of Spain. Courtier, soldier and poet, he was exceptionally charming, particularly in the eyes of Queen Elizabeth, who was entertained at Penshurst Place on more than one occasion. The Queen Elizabeth Room still contains the chair and table she used, and a portrait of the Queen which she gave to Sir Philip hangs in the house today. After a brilliant career, Sir Philip died as a result of wounds received in battle, a heroic death as famous as the life he led.

James I is known to have visited the house, and the children of Charles I were looked after here by Dorothy Sidney after the death of their father.

HEVER CASTLE

Hever Castle, with its origins in the 13th century, was more of a fortified manor house than a castle. It was bought by a former Lord Mayor of London, Sir Geoffrey Boleyn, in the mid 15th century and inherited by his grandson, Thomas, in 1506. The ambitious Thomas Boleyn was created Earl of Wiltshire and Ormond by Henry VIII as a result of the King's infatuation with Thomas' daughter, Anne. Anne seemed to have inherited some of her father's concern for a better position. Not content with being the King's mistress, she refused to have anything to do with him unless he married her and made her Queen of England. She was granted her wish in 1533 and shortly afterwards gave birth to a daughter, Elizabeth, but she could not provide Henry with the male heir he so desperately wanted and she was beheaded three years later. Henry VIII also executed Anne's brother, and when her father died in 1538, he took possession of Hever. It was here that he sent Anne of Cleves, his fourth wife, after their divorce.

The house contains paintings of three of the Tudor Monarchs—Henry VII by Mabuse, Henry VIII by Holbein, and Elizabeth painted by Geevarts. A portrait of Anne Boleyn, by an unknown artist, which hangs in the long gallery, shows nothing to explain Henry's infatuation with her. Many people at the time pointed out that her only good features were her beautiful black eyes.

KNOLE PARK

Once owned by Archbishop Bourchier of Canterbury, Knole is a house of complicated architecture, but has great charm and character with its gables, towers, and long tiled roof. The interior is interesting, having seven courtyards corresponding to the days in the week, fifty two staircases for the weeks in the year, and three hundred and sixty five rooms for the days in

the year. Henry VIII said of Knole, "it standeth on a sound, perfect and wholesome ground; and if I should make abode here, as I surely mind to do now and then, I will live at Knole." This in fact, he did and the house remained a royal possession until Elizabeth I gave it to her cousin Thomas Sackville, subject to lease. In 1603 he bought the freehold and it has remained in the Sackville family ever since.

Thomas Sackville, who spent thousands of pounds on improving the house, was created 1st Earl of Dorset in 1604 and served as Lord Treasurer for Elizabeth and James I before he died in 1608.

In 1716 the Prince of Wales, later George I, visited Knole when Lionel Cranfield Sackville was in residence. Lionel was later promoted from Earl to Duke of Dorset. Now a National Trust property, Knole House is open to the public on certain days during the year.

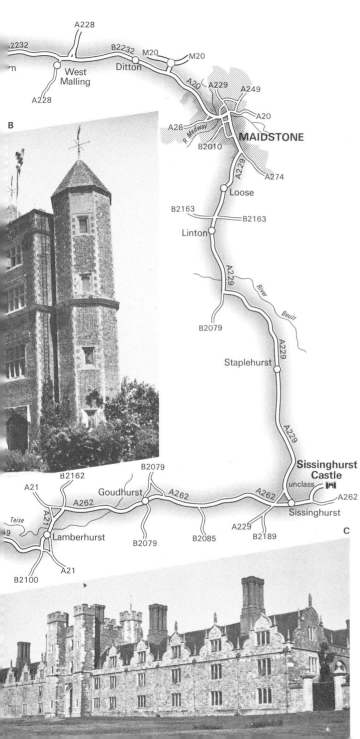

4 miles north west of Sevenoaks lies Chevening, the house of H.R.H. Prince Charles, The Prince of Wales. The gardens are open on one day in April every year.

MAIDSTONE

5 miles to the east of Maidstone (off the main route of this tour) stands Leeds Castle.

Formerly a Saxon castle, it was enlarged by the Normans, and became a royal residence during the reign of Edward I. On the understanding that it was still the property of his wife, Edward gave the castle to Lord Badlesmere, but while he was away from home, his constable would not allow the Queen on to the property. Some of her men were killed and as a result the King besieged the castle, banished Badlesmere, and executed the over-zealous constable.

Richard II was imprisoned here for a while and so was Elizabeth when she was princess and ruled by her half-sister Mary Tudor. Henry VI came to the castle in 1431 when his aunt was on trial as a witch and a traitor. She was sentenced to life imprisonment to be spent in Leeds Castle. The castle, open once a year under the National Gardens scheme, is said to have Anne Boleyn's shoes among its contents.

SISSINGHURST CASTLE

Even before Sir John Baker built his large family house at Sissinghurst, the place was visited by royalty, in the person of Edward I in 1305.

Sir John Baker held a variety of positions under the Tudors, Henry VIII, Edward VI and Queen Mary I who came to the house at the end of August, 1557. Sir John was an ardent Catholic who, during the reign of Queen Mary, took an active part in the persecution of Protestants, but he escaped retribution by dying soon after Elizabeth, the Protestant Queen, came to the throne. Queen

Elizabeth was a guest of Sir Richard Baker at Sissinghurst on August 15th, 16th and 17th, 1573. The castle was later destroyed and all that can now be seen are the moat and the soaring, brick gatehouse. The enchanting gardens were the creation of Vita Sackville-West.

A Penshurst Place, the birthplace of Sir Philip Sydney
B The Tudor tower of Sissinghurst Castle
C Knole Place, where Henry VIII once lived
D Hever Castle, where Anne Boleyn spent her childhood
E Catherine of Aragon once lived at Leeds Castle

GREENWICH

The Queen's House,
Greenwich, designed by Inigo Jones,
and completed in 1635. It now houses the
National Maritime Museum

The colonnades at
either side of the Queen's House
were a later addition, and afford a fine view
of Greenwich Park

Long famous for its park, hospital and observatory, Greenwich was once the site of Queen Elizabeth I's favourite palace. A pleasant, highly individual riverside town, it is appropriate that the National Maritime Museum should exist here in buildings created for royalty. The land by the river has belonged to the crown since 1414. Greenwich Palace was started here by Henry V's brother, the Duke of Gloucester, who built Bella Court, the finest house of its time in England, here in 1426–34. After his downfall, Queen Margaret of Anjou installed herself here, made a number of improvements and changed its name to Placentia. In 1485, Henry VII renamed it Greenwich Palace. Henry VIII was born here, and the palace was one of his favourite residences. Mary and Elizabeth I were also born here, and during her reign, many of the chief royal functions were held here. James I was often here, and he gave it to his consort Queen Anne of Denmark, who made a number of extensions. Charles I subsequently gave the palace to his queen, and she employed Inigo Jones to build the Queen's House (now the National Maritime Museum). By the time Charles II came to the throne, Greenwich Palace by the river was derelict, and he pulled it down, at the same time enlarging the Queen's House and the gardens. William and Mary donated all the buildings to the Navy for a hospital, which was built by Christopher Wren. The painted hall in what is now the Royal Naval College shows a number of scenes of royal occasions at Greenwich. The Queen's House subsequently became the National Maritime Museum, and contains Mary II's Shallop (a light, open boat) of 1689, and a state barge built for the Prince of Wales in 1732. Excavations beneath the riverside lawns

The Royal Naval College, Greenwich occupies buildings designed by Sir Christopher Wren as a naval hospital. The change took place in 1873

have revealed remains of Bella Court and Placentia Palace. There have been many royal associations with Greenwich, although the palace was not used much after the time of William and Mary. However, George I landed in Greenwich on his way from Hanover to claim the British crown. Greenwich was also the location chosen by Queen Elizabeth II to knight Francis Chichester after his voyage round the world.

The Royal Park

Behind the museum rises Greenwich Park, the oldest royal park. It was first enclosed by Duke Humphrey, but Charles II employed the famous French landscape-gardener of Louis XIV, Le Notre, to lay out this fine park. Especially notable are the avenues of Spanish chestnuts and the hawthorns. A famous tree in the park is Queen Elizabeth's Oak, now merely a hollow stump of a tree which died in the 1870s. Legend has it that Henry VIII danced with Anne Boleyn under this tree.

On the hill in the centre of the park is Flamsteed House, which used to house the Royal Observatory before it moved to Herstmonceux Castle, Sussex. Outside the Observatory is the meridian stone marking the zero of longitude, together with a barometer and a standard measure of length.

On the west side of the park is Ranger's House, which used to be the residence of Queen Caroline when she was Ranger of the Park. In the north west corner of the park is a statue of William IV, removed here from the City of London. In the town of Greenwich, the Church of St Alfege, rebuilt by Hawksmoor in 1712–14 and restored after extensive bomb damage, was the church in which Henry VIII was baptized.

The beautifully-restored Ranger's House in Greenwich Park. It used to be the residence of Queen Caroline when she was Ranger of the Park

By London's River

WOOLWICH

The home of Woolwich Arsenal, the dockyard here used to be the major Royal Dockyard until superseded by Devonport in 1869. It was founded in the 15th century and the ships "Great Harry" and "Royal Sovereign" were built here. All the old dockyard has been built over with a variety of military and industrial buildings.

DARTFORD

Although it is a busy industrial and commercial centre, Dartford has a long and royal history. However, there is little left which can be seen. Edward III founded a Dominican Friary here, which was taken over by Henry VIII at the Dissolution. He lived in the house with Anne of Cleves, who died there in 1557, and Elizabeth I also lived there for a time. A few remains of the Friary can be seen in Victoria Road and Kingsfield Terrace.

GRAVESEND

At the time of Richard II the people of Gravesend were granted the royal privilege of being the only people allowed to transport passengers from Gravesend to London by water. This privilege was continued into Elizabethan times and brought prosperity to the town. In 1539, faced with the danger of invasion, Henry VIII ordered blockhouses to be built here and at Tilbury across the river, but these no longer exist. Tilbury itself has many interesting royal associations. The fort was constructed by Henry VIII and was improved and extended for Charles II. Elizabeth I carried out an impressive review of her troops here at the camp established to resist the Spanish Armada.

ROCHESTER

This city was first inhabited by Belgic people before the Roman invasion, and has had a long and stormy history involving many of England's kings and queens. It was constantly under threat from the Danes and King Alfred built ships in the Medway to repel them. The Norman Conquest led to the building of the castle and subsequently the cathedral. The medieval years saw continued battles in the city. These stormy times eventually gave way to a more peaceful period during which visits to the city were made by Henry VIII, Elizabeth I and Charles II.

The castle is a fine example of Norman military building. William the Conqueror ordered its construction, but it was not completed until 1126. In 1215 King John seized the castle from rebellious barons, at which time the south east turret was destroyed. Simon de Montfort captured the city in 1264 and besieged the castle. From this point on, the castle was allowed to fall into disrepair although Edward III took steps to maintain it. In the 19th century the castle grounds were turned into a pleasant garden. Considerable portions of the outer walls still stand,

as does the keep, the best surviving structure of its kind in the country.

The cathedral is one of the most interesting in England. It was first built in 1130, but because of a series of fires had to be rebuilt during the period from 1179 to 1240. It was badly damaged during the Civil War by parliamentarian soldiers and heavily restored in the 19th century. On the west door are figures, said to be of Henry I and his Queen Matilda, but

A

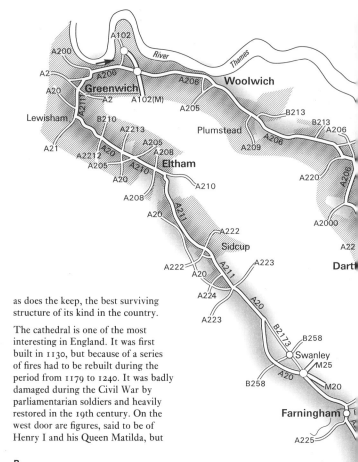

B

they were badly mutilated by parliamentarian soldiers in the Civil War.

There are several other buildings in the city which have royal associations. One of these is Satis House, to the south of the castle, where Queen Elizabeth I was entertained in 1573. She expressed her gratitude in the one word "satis", which became the name of the house. Next door to it is Old Hall, a Tudor building where Henry VIII probably met Anne of Cleves on her arrival in England. The Guildhall, built in 1687, contains portraits of William III and Queen Anne in the panelled council chamber. The Corn Exchange was renamed the Queen's Hall in honour of Queen Elizabeth II's visit in 1961, and the Old Corn Exchange was called Prince's Hall in honour of Prince Philip. Eastgate House, now a museum, was purchased by the corporation as a memorial of Queen Victoria's Jubilee. Restoration House is traditionally where Charles II stayed on his return to England in 1660. In one of the half timbered houses just off the high street James II was imprisoned for four days after his abdication.

Just north of Rochester is Chatham, the home of the Royal Dockyard built by Queen Elizabeth I in 1588. It was enlarged by Charles I and Charles II

C

and became Britain's principal naval station. The River Medway was invaded by the Dutch fleet in 1667 and many warships were burned. As a result a series of riverside forts were built, and these were strengthened in 1807 against a threat of a Napoleonic invasion.

COBHAM

Just south of the village is Cobham Hall, now a girls' school and only occasionally open to the public. It is a very large Elizabethan brick building with Jacobean additions. In the reign of James I Lord Cobham was accused of treason, and the estate, confiscated by the King, was given to the Darnley family, blood relations of Mary, Queen of Scots. This family still owns the property.

FARNINGHAM

Four miles south of Farningham is Lullingstone Castle, a fortified Tudor manor house with some 18th century additions. The gateway which remains dates from the reign of Henry VII. Henry VIII and Queen Anne were both visitors here.

ELTHAM

Eltham is principally interesting for the remains of Eltham Palace, initially the home of the Bishop of Durham. It was given to the crown and became the favourite Christmas residence of monarchs from Henry III to Henry VIII. It was the scene of splendid banquets, tournaments, hunting parties, even the meeting place of Parliament. Henry VII made many improvements to the palace, and Henry VIII built a new chapel and made numerous additions, converting the palace to the most up to date and comfortable of all royal residences. However, with the rise of Greenwich in royal favour, Eltham became more neglected. After Charles I's execution it was confiscated by Parliament and sold. Rebuilding started in the 1930s. The chief relic is the Banqueting Hall with its very fine hammer-beam roof, and there is also a medieval bridge over the moat.

A The Norman keep of Rochester Castle
B The magnificent west door of Rochester Cathedral
C Cobham Hall, dating back to the 16th century

Eleanor Crosses

Eleanor of Castille married Edward I in 1255 and lived with him devotedly for thirty-six years. She was crowned with him on the day of his coronation. Her touching love for him is exemplified by the story of her drawing poison from a wound he suffered in Palestine with lips "anointed with the virtue of lovely affection", as a contemporary writer put it.

When Edward was travelling to Scotland in 1291, his cherished wife was taken ill and died at Harby. He halted his journey there to pay his deeply felt respects to her. Her body was embalmed, and the internal parts laid in Lincoln Cathedral. The body was conveyed to Westminster in a slow and mournful procession, which aroused sincere sympathy from the English people. At every stopping place, Edward perpetuated the memory of his dead queen by erecting a beautiful Gothic cross. Originally there were twelve crosses, but now only three remain. They are at Geddington in Northamptonshire, Hardingstone (1½m south of Northampton) and Waltham. The last-named cross, probably the most beautiful, has been extensively restored.

The final cross in the journey was at Charing in London (then a village). The original no longer exists, having been replaced by a new Eleanor Cross erected in 1863. Her final resting place was the Chapel of St Edward the Confessor in Westminster Abbey.

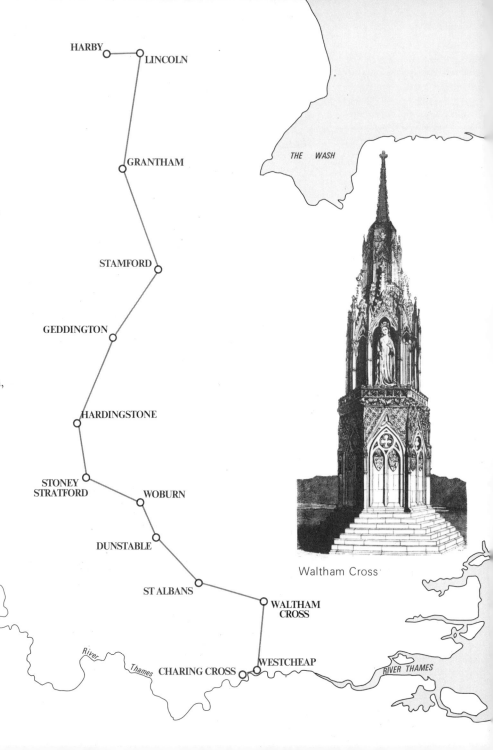

Waltham Cross

Royal London

The Tower of London

The Tower has always been a focal point in British history. It has been a fortress, a royal residence and a state prison. It was started by William the Conqueror to impress the people of London, and was greatly expanded by Henry IV into a massive citadel. It has seen the imprisonment of kings and princes; the secret murders of the little princes in the tower; two of Henry VIII's marriage ceremonies and the beheading of two of his wives, Anne Boleyn and Catherine Howard; and the torture and executions of a stream of traitors.

When William the Conqueror came to London, work was started on the square keep, the White Tower, which still stands, substantially in its original design. It was not a large castle until it was extended by Henry III who built the inner wall with its towers, and the outer wall facing the river. Edward I built the remainder of the outer wall and the western section of the inner wall with the Beauchamp Tower. The Bloody Tower and the Cradle Tower were built in the 14th century. Henry VIII rebuilt St Peter's Chapel and added the outer bastions on the north side. In the 19th century, several towers were restored and the barracks for the garrison built. No trace survives of the palace which stood to the south of the White Tower, and was demolished by Cromwell. Every monarch until James I (except Elizabeth I) used it as a royal residence, although Charles II was the last king to observe the custom of spending the night before his coronation here. Richard II signed his abdication here in 1399. Henry VI is believed to have been murdered here in 1471 (in the

The White Tower, the original Norman keep, is the oldest part of the Tower of London

Traitors' Gate, the entrance for many prisoners to the Tower

The finale of the Ceremony of the Keys

Wakefield Tower). The Duke of Clarence, (Edward IV's brother) was murdered here in 1478, as were the little princes, Edward V and his brother the Duke of York; Henry VIII married Catherine of Aragon and Anne Boleyn here, and Anne Boleyn was later executed (1536) as was Henry's fifth queen, Catherine Howard (1542). Lady Jane Grey was imprisoned and executed here during Mary's reign and Elizabeth I (later queen) was also imprisoned here for a while. The White Tower contains a magnificent collection of arms and armour, including many pieces worn by English kings. It also contains St John's Chapel, closely associated with the Order of the Bath.

The Waterloo Barracks (West Wing) house the collection of the Crown Jewels, which include those used in the coronation ceremonies, the famous Koh-i-Noor diamond, and examples of Maundy money.

A brass plate on Tower Green marks the site of the scaffold, and several of those beheaded are buried in the Chapel Royal of St Peter ad Vincula.

The Bloody Tower was the prison of many famous traitors, and up a winding staircase is the room in which the little princes are supposed to have been smothered. The Queen's House (not open) is the residence of the Governor, the Major of the Tower; it was built in Henry VIII's reign and was the last prison of Anne Boleyn.

On *Tower Green* can be seen the ravens, protected by the crown under a Raven Master. They may be a relic of the Royal Menagerie, which used to be kept in the Lion Tower.

The Royal Mint used to be situated on Tower Hill until 1968, when it was moved to Llantrisant near Cardiff.

Tower Wharf, through an opening in the wall to the east of Traitors' Gate, is the site of salutes by the Honourable Artillery Company. 62 guns are fired on the anniversaries of the birth, accession and coronation of the sovereign, and 41 on the birth of a prince or princess and other royal occasions. The Ceremony of the Keys takes place here every night. (see page 86).

Westminster Abbey

The premier church of England, Westminster Abbey may be the most beautiful and historic church in the country. It has been intimately associated with many centuries of English history, and every English monarch. Elizabeth I made it a "royal peculiar" which means that it is not subject to the Archbishop of Canterbury, or to the Bishop of London, but only to the sovereign.

In the 8th century, Benedictine monks built an abbey on what was then Thorney Island in the Thames. It subsequently became a royal residence, and was splendidly restored by Edward the Confessor. Harold was the first king to be crowned here, and every sovereign since has continued this tradition (except Edward V and Edward VIII). In 1245, Henry III rebuilt the entire church in the magnificent style it is today. From then until George IV's time, it was the royal burial church. In 1503, the Lady Chapel was pulled down to make way for the glorious Chapel of

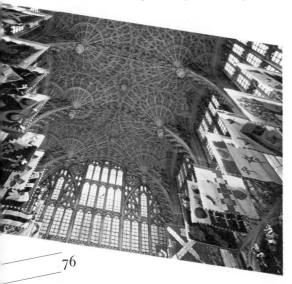

Henry VII. In the Nave, on the south west pier, hangs the oldest known portrait of any English king, Richard II.

The Altar Sanctuary contains the tomb of Anne of Cleves, fourth wife of Henry VIII, and is the scene of coronations. The Chapel of St Edward the Confessor is the most sacred part of the church. In the middle stands the saint's mutilated shrine. It was originally a golden shrine, but much of it was taken at the Dissolution. The south side of the Chapel contains the tombs of Edward III and his wife, Philippa of Hainault, with statuettes of his children. Next to it is the highly decorated tomb of Richard II, and his first wife Anne of Bohemia. At the west end of the Chapel is the Coronation Chair, enclosing the Stone of Scone, used in every coronation. Next to it are the State Sword and Shield of Edward III. On the north side is the very plain tomb of Edward I, and the more elaborate tombs of Henry III, and Eleanor of Castille, wife of Edward I. Farther to the east, the Chapel of Henry VII is the best example in the country of Tudor Gothic architecture. It was begun as a shrine for the saintly Henry VI, and in 1725 it became the chapel of the Order of the Bath. The tall canopied tomb in the centre of the north aisle is the tomb of Elizabeth I and her sister Mary I. At the east end of this aisle are contained in a sarcophagus the bones of the little princes, Edward V and Richard, Duke of York, who were murdered in the Tower. Nearby are the tombs of the children of James I. On each side of the chapel are the impressive carved stalls of the Knights of the Bath, and, at the west end, the naval sword of George VI, with which he conferred the Order.

George II, Queen Caroline and members of his family are buried under the floor between the door and the altar. The grave of Edward VI is below the altar. Henry VII's tomb, a magnificent

The roof of the Chapel of Henry VII, with its intricate fan-vaulting, is one of the best of its kind in Britain

The shrine of Edward the Confessor

monument, is just behind the altar, and James I is buried in the same vault. In the south aisle is the tomb of Mary, Queen of Scots, originally buried in Peterborough Cathedral, but moved here by James I. Also on this side is the vault containing the remains of Charles II, Mary II, William III, Queen Anne and her husband, Prince George of Denmark.

The Norman Undercroft, on the east side of the cloisters, houses a museum illustrating the history of the abbey. It contains the life-like effigies of monarchs which were carried at their funerals. They include Edward III, Henry VII, Elizabeth I, Charles II, William III, Mary II and Queen Anne. Also in the museum are the royal writ and seal of Edward the Confessor and William I, the sword of Henry V, and the ring said to have been given by Elizabeth I to the Earl of Essex (but intercepted by the Countess of Nottingham and returned). In the Jerusalem Chamber, Henry IV died while praying at the shrine of Edward the Confessor.

Houses of Parliament

Known as the New Palace of Westminster, it incorporates Westminster Hall and St Stephen's Hall. It was built by Sir Charles Barry in 1840–50 and contains the House of Commons, the House of Lords and the dwellings of various parliamentary officials. The façade facing the river is decorated with the statues and arms of British sovereigns from William I to Victoria. Earlier kings are seen on the north front. Ascending the Royal Staircase, the Royal Gallery, through which the sovereign passes when going to the House of Lords, is hung with royal portraits, and contains gilt statues of English monarchs. In the Prince's chamber are portraits of the Tudor sovereigns and a white marble statue of Queen Victoria. The House of Lords contains, at the south end, raised on a dais, the ornate throne, with the Woolsack in front of it. Over the doors of the Peers' lobby are the arms of the royal lines of England, with the initial letters of each monarch carved below. In the Central lobby are statues of the Plantagenet kings and queens, and in the ceiling, glass mosaics of royal emblems. The House of Commons meets in a new chamber, opened in 1950.

ST STEPHEN'S HALL

The meeting place of the House of Commons from 1547 until the fire in 1834, this lofty vaulted chamber stands on the exact site of the royal chapel of St. Stephen, founded by Edward I and completed by Edward III. In the angles of the hall are figures of the early Norman kings. An excellent view of Westminster Hall is obtained from St Stephen's Porch.

WESTMINSTER HALL

One of the most historic buildings in London, it was originally built by William II in 1097. It is one of the largest timber-roofed buildings in Europe, the splendid hammerbeam roof being added by Richard II in 1394–1402. The hall was the scene of the forced abdication of Edward II in 1327, the deposition of Richard II in 1399, and Charles I's condemnation in 1649. From Stephen to George IV, it was the custom for the King to give a feast here, prior to his coronation. A tablet on the east wall marks the door through which Charles I entered in 1641 to arrest the five Members of Parliament. No monarch entered the House of Commons from that time until 1950. From the 13th century the chief English law courts sat here, but since the 19th century it has been used for the lying-in-state of monarchs and eminent statesmen.

Sir Charles Barry's Palace of Westminster, facing the River Thames

Buckingham Palace, The Queen's London residence

BUCKINGHAM PALACE

Formerly known as Buckingham House, it was built in 1703, and bought by George III in 1762. Nash altered and remodelled it for George IV in 1825, when its name was changed to Buckingham Palace. It was not much used until Queen Victoria came to the throne in 1837, when the court was moved here. It has been the London home of the monarch ever since. The west wing is largely as Nash designed it. The east wing was added in 1847 and the whole east façade re-designed in 1913. The interior of the palace with many splendid rooms is not open, the Royal Family living in the north wing. Edward VII was born here and died here. Charles, Prince of Wales, was born here in 1948, Prince Andrew in 1960 and Prince Edward in 1964. In the palace gardens is one of the mulberry trees planted by James I to encourage the silk industry. When the sovereign is in residence, the royal standard is flown. Every day in the forecourt at 11.30 am the ceremony of the Changing of the Guard is carried out by the Brigade of Guards.

Queen's Gallery used to be the private chapel of the palace. It was damaged during the Second World War, but rebuilt in 1962 and opened to show a selection of paintings and other works of art from the royal collections.

Royal Mews displays a collection of state coaches and houses the Queen's horses. The Coronation Coach was made in 1762 for George III. The coach used for the state opening of Parliament is the Irish State Coach bought in 1852 for Queen Victoria. The Glass State Coach is used for royal weddings and was bought in 1910 by George V. In the old Carriage House is a frieze showing the Coronation of William IV.

KENSINGTON PALACE

William III bought the house in 1689 and commissioned Wren to alter and improve it. The south wing is the best surviving part of his work. It was enlarged by Kent for George I, and was the principal private royal residence until George II died here in 1760. Mary II, William III, Queen Anne and George II all died here. Queen Victoria was born here and lived in the palace until she became Queen. Mary, the queen of George V, was born here in 1867. It is now the residence of Princess Margaret.

The State Apartments include rooms by Wren and Kent, extensively hung with royal portraits. The rooms where Queen Victoria lived are full of mementoes of her. In other rooms are collections of royal wedding dresses and the coronation robes of George V and Queen Mary.

KENSINGTON GARDENS

Although close to Hyde Park, these Gardens are completely different in character. When William III made Kensington Palace his home, the original gardens consisted of twenty-six acres taken from Hyde Park. Queen Anne, George I and George II increased them to their present size. However, their present character is due to Caroline, wife of George II, who laid out the Round Pond and Broad Walk and also planned the formation of the Serpentine. The gardens contain a statue of Queen Victoria by her daughter, Princess Louise, and one of William III, given to Edward VII in 1907 by William II of Germany. The sunken garden is a particularly attractive area. The Pumping Station, at the head of the Long Water, is said to have been designed by Prince Albert.

HYDE PARK

At the Dissolution of the monasteries, Henry VIII seized Hyde Park from the monks of Westminster and converted it into a royal

The magnificent horses and livery in the Royal Mews at Buckingham Palace

Kensington Palace, the residence of Princess Margaret

Kensington Gardens

hunting park. Elizabeth I also enjoyed hunting here and introduced ceremonies of military manoeuvres, which still take place on special occasions. James I opened the park to the public, and it became a fashionable resort under Charles I. He laid out the Ring, a circular chine and racecourse which proved very popular. Charles II re-stocked the park with deer. In William III's reign the park became very much less safe due to the activities of footpads, so an early form of road lighting was introduced. Probably the grandest occasion to take place in the park was the Great Exhibition of 1851 with the Crystal Palace, which was subsequently moved to Sydenham and later burned down.

ST JAMES'S PALACE

The original palace was started by Henry VIII in 1531, and, after the destruction of Whitehall Palace, was the official London residence of the sovereign. Foreign ambassadors are still appointed to the Court of St James. The Gatehouse facing St James's Street is the main remnant of the Tudor building, with carving over the doors of the initials of Henry VIII and Anne Boleyn. The Chapel Royal was originally built by Henry VIII, but was much altered in 1837. However, the ceiling by Holbein is original. Several royal marriages have been solemnized here, including those of William III and Mary II, Queen Anne, George IV, Queen Victoria and George V. Every year on 6th January (the Festival of Epiphany) at Holy Communion in this Chapel, an offering of gold, frankincense and myrrh is made on behalf of the Queen by two of Her Majesty's Gentleman Ushers. In Friary Court, the new sovereign is proclaimed from the balcony by the Heralds. Charles II, who was born here, made some additions to the palace, commissioning Wren to add some state apartments facing the park. James II, Mary II, Queen Anne and George IV were all born here. George IV employed Nash to restore and redecorate the palace, but Queen Victoria moved the court to Buckingham Palace when she came to the throne. It is now used largely for "grace and favour" establishments.

The Gatehouse of St. James's Palace

York House is on the north side of Ambassador's Court. It was occupied by the Duke of Windsor when Prince of Wales in 1919–30. It is now the residence of the Duke of Gloucester.

Clarence House was designed by Nash for William IV when he was Duke of Clarence. The interior was restored for Princess Elizabeth before her accession in 1952. Princess Anne was born here and it is now the home of Queen Elizabeth, the Queen Mother. A piper plays in the garden every morning when the Queen Mother is in residence.

Lancaster House, a massive palace, was originally built for the "grand old" Duke of York, and was acquired by the Duke of

Sutherland. Chopin played here before Queen Victoria in 1848. It is now a Government Hospitality Centre.

Marlborough House was built by Wren for the Duke of Marlborough, and was later occupied by Leopold I and Queen Adelaide. In 1850 it became the official residence of the Prince of Wales. George V was born here and after he became King, it became the home of Queen Alexandra, Edward VII's widow. On the garden wall in Marlborough Road is a memorial to Queen Alexandra, and on the wall in the Mall is a plaque to Queen Mary. In the State Dining Room is a collection of royal portraits. The house is now the Commonwealth Centre.

The Queen's Chapel was designed by Inigo Jones in 1623, initially for the Infanta Maria of Spain, and subsequently for Henrietta Maria, queen of Charles I. George III was married here in 1761. The chapel is notable for its royal pews.

ST JAMES'S PARK

The oldest of London's Royal Parks, it was drained by Henry VIII in 1532, before he built his new palace there. He converted it into a deer park. James I set up a menagerie of exotic animals in it, and Charles I made a few minor improvements to it. It was through St James's Park that Charles I walked to his execution at Whitehall Palace in 1649. Charles II completely

re-designed the park in the manner of Versailles, and it became a very popular recreational park with the King himself frequently walking in it. He founded an aviary near Birdcage Walk. When George IV came to the throne, he had Nash completely re-design the park along English lines, creating the lake, the plantations and the walks which exist today.

GREEN PARK

At one time a violent place (Queen Mary's troops fought an artillery battle here), it was used by Charles II for royal picnics, and he built a snow house and an ice house here. He frequently walked on the hill, giving it the name Constitution Hill. In 1730, Caroline, wife of George II, had Queen's Walk prepared for the pleasure of the royal family. The Broad Walk running up to Piccadilly was part of the design for the Queen Victoria memorial. Green Park has seen its share of violence including an assassination attempt on Queen Victoria on Constitution Hill.

REGENT'S PARK

Appropriated by Henry VIII as a hunting forest, it was once known as Marylebone Park. In 1811 the Prince Regent acquired the land and planned to build a palace in the centre. This was never carried out, although Nash laid out a superb series of terraces. For a time, Mrs Fitzherbert, the wife of the Prince Regent, lived in one of the terraces. The Broad Walk leads to the Zoological Gardens founded in 1826. Within the inner circle are Queen Mary's Gardens, with a full and very pretty rosery. George V approved its name in honour of his Queen.

St. James's Park

Clarence House, the home of Queen Elizabeth, the Queen Mother

ADMIRALTY ARCH, The Mall, SW1
It was designed by Sir Aston Webb in 1910 as part of the National Memorial to Queen Victoria.

BANQUETING HOUSE, Whitehall, SW1
The main survival of Whitehall Palace, it was built by Inigo Jones in 1619-22. The main hall contains beautiful ceiling paintings by Rubens, designed for Charles I. Charles I was, ironically, executed in 1649 on a scaffold just outside the house, and a bust over the entrance in the staircase annexe marks the approximate site of the window through which he stepped. The weathercock at the north end of the roof was placed there in 1686 by James II to indicate whether or not the wind was favourable for the Prince of Orange.

BRITISH MUSEUM,
Great Russell Street, WC1
Founded in 1753, the museum was presented with the Royal Library by George II. In 1823, George IV donated his father's splendid library, and this can be seen in the King's Library. Among its many treasures with royal associations are original copies of Magna Carta; a manual of Prayers, believed to have been used by Lady Jane Grey on the scaffold; part of the diary of Edward VI; a description of the execution of Mary, Queen of Scots; Cromwell's report of the Battle of Naseby; the state sword of Edward V as Prince of Wales; wall paintings from St Stephen's Chapel, Westminster; and the signet ring of Mary, Queen of Scots.

CHAPEL OF THE SAVOY, Strand, WC2
After the sacking of the Savoy Palace, Henry VII built a chapel here in 1505, but it was almost completely destroyed by fire in 1864. Queen Victoria restored it, and it is the private

Rubens' beautiful ceiling in the Banqueting House, Whitehall

The carefully restored buildings of Charterhouse

chapel of the monarch as part of the Duchy of Lancaster. It is also Chapel of the Royal Victorian Order, of which the Queen is Sovereign, and the stalls of the knights are emblazoned with their arms. The royal pews are at the west end. Windows commemorate George VI, Queen Mary and the Duke of Kent. The ancient ceremony of beating the bounds of the Liberty of the Savoy takes place in July.

CHARTERHOUSE,
Charterhouse Square, EC1
Founded in the 14th century as a monastery, Charterhouse was turned into a mansion in 1545 by Lord North and extended by Thomas Howard, Duke of Norfolk. Elizabeth I paid several visits here, and James I was entertained here before his coronation in 1603. It subsequently became a hospital and, later, a great public school (now in Godalming, Surrey). It suffered bomb damage, but has been carefully restored.

CHELSEA
The manor of Chelsea was acquired by Henry VIII in 1536, and he built a palatial manor house in which Elizabeth I spent some time before she was Queen, and where Anne of Cleves died in 1557. After the Restoration, Chelsea was very popular with Charles II and his court. Until 1829 King's Road used to be a royal way from Hampton Court to St James's.

The Royal Hospital, Chelsea was founded by Charles II for veteran soldiers and was designed by Wren in 1682-92. The in-pensioners wear a uniform dating from the time of the Duke of Marlborough. A very special occasion in the hospital is Founder's Day (or Oak Apple Day), 29th May, Charles II's birthday. On that day, the bronze statue of Charles II by Grinling Gibbons in Figure Court is decked with oak boughs to commemorate the King's escape after the Battle of Worcester by hiding in an oak tree.

The pensioners wear special tricorn hats on this day and receive double rations. From Founder's Day on through the summer they exchange their dark blue winter coats for summer ones. The panelled Great Hall contains a collection of royal portraits and a very large equestrian portrait of Charles II. The Governor's House also contains some fine royal portraits.

Chelsea Old Church, restored after bomb damage, was originally built in the 12th century. The north (Lawrence) chapel is thought to have been the scene of the secret marriage between Henry VIII and Jane Seymour several days before their official marriage.

CROSBY HALL, Cheyne Walk, SW3

In the 15th century, it was a sumptuous mansion in Bishopsgate, occupied by the Duke of Gloucester, later Richard III. It was "of stone and timber, very large and beautiful, and the highest at that time in London". Fire

destroyed it in the 17th century, with the exception of the magnificent Great Hall, which was skilfully removed and re-erected in Roper's Gardens, Chelsea. It is now a college hall of the British Federation of University Women.

COLLEGE OF ARMS, Queen Victoria Street, EC4

The present 17th century building replaces the one destroyed in the Great Fire of 1666. It is the seat of the Office of Arms, first incorporated by Richard III in 1485, and given a new charter together with this site by Mary I in 1555.

DUTCH CHURCH, Throgmorton Street, EC3

A modern church built on this historic site contains a window depicting Edward VI, who in 1550 assigned the original church to Protestant refugees. It became the church of London's Dutch community.

GUILDHALL, EC2

The Hall of the Corporation of the City of London, the Guildhall is the seat of municipal government in the City, and a major centre for civic occasions. It was built in 1411–25, but was severely damaged in the Great Fire, and again in the Blitz. It was partly restored in 1954, and new extensions are being built. The hall is used for banquets and receptions, particularly for visiting royalty and State officials. It used to be the case that a banquet was given here for the Queen when she returned from an overseas tour, but this is no longer so. A magnificent banquet was given, however, for the Queen's Silver Wedding Anniversary. The hall was formerly used for important trials, and Lady Jane Grey was condemned here. The library contains a fine collection of manuscripts, prints and works on all aspects of London, and also has a statue of Charles II.

MARBLE ARCH, W1

Close to the historic execution site of Tyburn, it was originally designed in 1828 by Nash for the new Buckingham Palace. However, it was found to be too narrow for the state coach and was moved to its present site in 1850.

NATIONAL PORTRAIT GALLERY, Trafalgar Square, WC2

This collection was founded in 1856 and illustrates British history and culture by means of portraits of the eminent men and women of the periods. There are a great many portraits of kings and queens, the medieval monarchs being on the second floor landing. Different historical periods are collected in different rooms, with sections on the Tudors, the Elizabethan period, the Jacobean court, Charles I and the Commonwealth, the Restoration court, the later Stuarts, and men of the nineteenth and twentieth centuries.

ROYAL EXCHANGE, EC3

The first Royal Exchange was built by Sir Thomas Gresham in 1569, and so delighted Elizabeth I that she gave it its present name. It was destroyed in the Fire of London in 1666. The present building dates from 1844 and its courtyard contains large paintings of episodes of London's history and statues of Elizabeth I, Charles II, Victoria and Prince Albert.

ST MARTIN'S IN THE FIELDS,
Trafalgar Square, WC2

This is the parish church of Buckingham Palace. It was built during 1721–6 by James Gibbs on the site of a previous church built for Henry VIII. Charles II was christened here, and Nell Gwynn was buried in the churchyard before it gave way to Duncannon Street. George I was the first church warden and his arms appear in the chancel arch as well as in the pediment above the portico. The Royal Box is to the north of the chancel.

ST PAUL'S CATHEDRAL, EC4

Sir Christopher Wren's masterpiece is the largest and most famous city church, and the parish church of the British Commonwealth.

It was completed in 1710 and has recently been skilfully cleaned. The Great Tom bell is tolled if one of the royal family dies. There are no royal memorials in the cathedral, although there is a statue of Queen Anne outside. An inscription on the pavement behind it records that Queen Victoria prayed here on her Diamond Jubilee.

ROYAL MONUMENTS

George VI; Carlton House Terrace

At the end of the Terrace, at the top of a flight of steps, facing Carlton Gardens, the National Memorial to George VI was created in bronze by William McMillan in 1955. The King is wearing the robes used in the ceremonies of the Knights of the Garter.

George V; Westminster Abbey Environs

In front of the chapter house and facing the House of Lords, the statue was erected in 1947 by Sir W Reid Dick and Sir Giles Scott.

Edward VII; Waterloo Place

On south side of Pall Mall, the National Memorial to Edward VII consists of an equestrian statue by Sir Bertram MacKennal.

Queen Victoria and Edward VII (as Prince of Wales); Temple Bar

Near the east end of the Law Courts and the foot of Chancery Lane, the Temple Bar consists of statues of Queen Victoria and Edward VII as Prince of Wales. It marks the boundary between Westminster and the City.

St Paul's Cathedral

St Martin's in the Fields

Statue of George III, Trafalgar Square

Statue of George VI, Carlton House Terrace

When the Queen visits the City on State occasions, the custom is still observed of asking permission to pass the Temple Bar. The Lord Mayor of London surrenders the Sword of State. It is returned to him and carried before the Queen as a symbol that he is responsible for her protection in the City. The existing Memorial was set up in 1880 by J E Boehm, when the original gateway was moved to Theobalds Park.

Queen Victoria; Kensington Palace Gardens
In the private gardens on the south side stands a statue by Princess Louise.

Albert Memorial; Kensington
The national monument was designed by Sir G Gilbert Scott, and the statue of the prince is by Foley. The pedestal is decorated with marble reliefs of men of letters and artists, as well as allegorical groups.

Queen Victoria; Blackfriars Bridge
Situated at north end of the bridge.

Queen Victoria; Buckingham Palace
In the centre of the circus in front of Buckingham Palace is the Queen Victoria Memorial. Designed by Sir Aston Webb and sculpted by Sir Thomas Brock, it consists of the seated figure of Queen Victoria in white marble, crowned with a gilded bronze figure of Victory with Courage and Constancy at her feet and surrounded by water. There are other allegorical groups round the sides.

William IV; Greenwich Park
In the north west corner of the park, the statue was removed here from King William Street in the City.

George IV; Trafalgar Square
An equestrian statue by Chantreay, it is situated in the north east corner of Trafalgar Square. It was originally intended to top Marble Arch outside Buckingham Palace.

George III; Pall Mall
At the east end of Pall Mall at the junction of Pall Mall East and Cockspur Street is a bronze equestrian statue by M C Wyatt (1936).

George II; Golden Square
In the centre of the square (which is to the east of Regent Street), a statue of George II in Roman costume by John van Nost (1753).

George II; Royal Naval College, Greenwich
In the Grand Square, a statue by Rysbrack.

George I; St George's Church, Bloomsbury
On top of the steeple, a statue which was a butt for the wits of the period.

Queen Anne; Queen Anne's Gate
Outside No 13 Queen Anne's Gate is a contemporary statue (probably by Francis Bird), of Queen Anne in ceremonial robes. It was originally intended for the portico of St Mary-le-Strand.

William III; St James's Square
In the centre of the square is a bronze equestrian statue by John Bacon the Younger (1808).

William III; Kensington Palace Gardens
To the south of the palace, the statue was presented to Edward VII by William II of Germany in 1907.

James II; National Gallery
On the grass in front of the National Gallery is a bronze statue of James II in Roman costume by Grinling Gibbons.

Charles I; Charing Cross
The equestrian statue of Charles I by Hubert Le Sileur was cast in 1633, and set up in 1675 after the Restoration. It faces down Whitehall to the scene of Charles I's execution. On 30th January, the anniversary of the king's death, the statue is hung with wreaths by his admirers.

Elizabeth I; St Dunstan in the West, Fleet Street
Over the east porch of the church is a contemporary (1586) statue of Elizabeth I.

Richard I; Westminster, Old Palace Yard
A bronze equestrian statue by Marochetti (1860) facing the House of Lords.

Changing of the Guard

Buckingham Palace, every day, 11.30 am.
Normally carried out by the Brigade of Guards, the Queen's colour is trooped from St James's Palace to Buckingham Palace, where the old Guard joins the old Palace Guard. The new Guard, with a band, marches from either Chelsea Barracks or Wellington Barracks to Buckingham Palace, where they form up facing the old Guard. The officers of the old and new Guards advance and touch hands to symbolize the exchange of the keys, and the changing of the Guard. The sentries are relieved, and the old Guard then returns to barracks. The new Guard for St James's Palace and Clarence House leaves finally. When the Queen is in residence at Buckingham Palace there is a Guard of four sentries, otherwise only two. When she is at Windsor Castle, another Changing of the Guard ceremony takes place there at 10.00 am.

The Ceremony of the Keys

Tower of London, every night, 9.40 pm. (prior permission required). This ceremony has taken place every night for the last 700 years. The Chief Warder of the Yeoman Warders (Beefeaters) with his Escort locks the West Gate, Middle and Byward Towers, then returns to the Bloody Tower Archway where he is challenged by the sentry. Having received permission to pass through the archway, the party forms up facing the Main Guard of the Tower. After they present arms, the Chief Warder cries "God preserve Queen Elizabeth". At 10.00 pm, the bugler sounds the Last Post, and the Chief Warder takes the keys to the Resident Governor in the Queen's House.

Royal Maundy

Westminster Abbey, Maundy Thursday, 11.30 a.m. This ceremony was the first public

The Changing of the Guard at Buckingham Palace

ceremony carried out by Queen Elizabeth II after her accession. Until 1754 the ceremony involved the sovereign in washing the feet of the poor, but since then, specially minted Maundy money has been distributed. Maundy money is on view in the Tower of London with the Crown Jewels.

Trooping the Colour

Horse Guards' Parade, Whitehall, Queen's official birthday (second Saturday in June), 11.15 am.
The Queen always takes part in this ceremony in which, after a regiment of Foot Guards is trooped before her at Buckingham Palace, she rides to Horse Guards' Parade where she inspects the assembled Brigade of Guards. This is followed by the Trooping Ceremony, and the Queen then takes the Salute as the Guards march past to the music of massed bands. Finally, the Queen returns to Buckingham Palace at the head of her Guards.

Royal Epiphany Gifts

Chapel Royal, St James's Palace, 6 January, 11.30 am.
At the Holy Communion service on the Festival of the Epiphany, gifts of gold, frankincense and myrrh are made on the Queen's behalf by two of Her Majesty's Gentlemen Ushers. The Yeomen of the Guard are also present.

Entry into the City of London

Temple Bar, occasional.
When the sovereign enters the City of London she is met at the City boundary, Temple Bar, by the Lord Mayor. The Sword and Mace are reversed, and the City's Pearl Sword is held out for the Queen to touch. Receiving it back, the Lord Mayor bears it before the sovereign, after which the royal party enters the city.

State Opening of Parliament

Houses of Parliament, November, midday.
At the start of each Parliamentary session, and after a General Election, a glittering State ceremony takes place, dating back to 1523. The Queen travels in the Irish State Coach from Buckingham Palace to the Houses of Parliament where she is greeted by a salute from the King's Troop, Royal Horse Artillery, and met by the Earl Marshal, the Lord Great Chamberlain, the Lord High Chancellor, the Lord Privy Seal and the Lord President of the Council. In the Robing Room, she dons the royal robes and crown, and, to the sound of trumpets from the Heralds, moves to the Throne. Black Rod summons the Speaker and members of the House of Commons, and the Lord Chancellor then hands the Queen the Speech outlining the Government's forthcoming proposals. A few hours before the State opening, the Yeomen of the Guard carry out the ceremony of searching the vaults of the Houses of Parliament and they notify the Queen that all is well. This tradition dates from the Gunpowder Plot of 1605.

Royal Salutes

Hyde Park and the Tower of London, occasional.
On a number of royal occasions, salutes are fired at Hyde Park (41 guns) and the Tower of

London (62 guns). These occasions are:

6 February—the anniversary of the Queen's accession

21 April—the Queen's true birthday

2 June—the anniversary of the Queen's coronation

10 June—Prince Philip's birthday

14 June—the Queen's official birthday

4 August—the Queen Mother's birthday

Charles I Wreath Laying

30th January 1649 was the date Charles I was executed. Every year a number of ceremonies take place in London to honour that event. An act of devotion is held outside the Whitehall Banqueting House at 11.20 am and a wreath is hung under the bust of the King. At 12.15 pm, High Mass is held at St Mary-le-Strand. Another service is held on the Saturday nearest to this date in St Martin's-in-the-Fields at 11.30 am, followed by the laying of a wreath on the equestrian statue of Charles I in Whitehall. Yet another wreath-laying ceremony takes place at 11.00 am on 30th January at the King's Statue at Charing Cross.

Charles II—Founders Day

Royal Hospital, Chelsea, 29 May, 10.45 am. (ticket-holders only). The anniversary of Charles's escape after the Battle of Worcester is celebrated by the Chelsea Pensioners of the Royal Hospital Chelsea. For details see description of Royal Hospital, Chelsea, page 82.

Swan-Upping

River Thames, July.

All the swans on the River Thames belong to the Queen, or to the Dyers or Vintners companies. Once a year, the Queen's Swan-master and the Swanmasters of the Dyers and Vintners dressed in ceremonial costume and working from gaily decorated boats, mark all the cygnets on the river between London Bridge and Henley-on-Thames. The Royal cygnets are left unmarked.

The impressive ranks of the Brigade of Guards at the Trooping of the Colour

The pensioners at the Royal Hospital, Chelsea wear special tricorn hats on Founder's Day

WINDSOR

The Royal Borough of Windsor is chiefly famous for its superb castle, which has been the home of royalty for nearly nine centuries. Much of the town's history has been linked to the fortunes of the castle, but it has also been influenced by the Forest of Windsor, which at one time occupied a vast area, extending as far as Hungerford. Hunting in this forest was a popular pursuit with many kings, but little trace of it now remains.

Windsor Castle

This beautiful castle occupies a central place in the life of the present Royal Family, indeed the family name is the House and Family of Windsor. They all spend a considerable amount of time here, and the castle is used on State occasions and for royal functions.

There has been a castle here since the time of William the Conqueror, when Windsor presented an excellent site for the protection

St George's Chapel, Windsor, one of the most sumptuous pieces of Gothic architecture in the country. It is the spiritual home of the Order of the Garter

A distant view of Windsor Castle shows the coherence of Wyatville's architecture

of the west side of London. However, nothing remains of his building. The earliest surviving parts of the castle date from the time of Henry II, although there are not many of these. Henry III had the task of rebuilding parts of the castle because during the unpopular reign of King John the castle had been besieged and severely damaged. The Curfew Tower dates from this time. Little further building was done for the next 100 years until Edward III pulled down the old castle and raised the Round Tower, the Norman Gateway and two other towers. Edward III's other major contribution to Windsor was to make it the spiritual home of the Order of the Garter which he founded in 1348. He enlarged the chapel here to accommodate the knights of the Order of the Garter. However, the condition of the chapel deteriorated over the years, and in 1472, Edward IV replaced it with the noble St George's Chapel. He also built the charming Horseshoe Cloister, in which the choirmen and vergers now live. St George's Chapel was, however, not completed by Edward IV, the nave being built by Henry VII and the choir roof set by Henry VIII. Elizabeth I was very fond of the castle, and built the North Terrace looking over Home Park towards Eton. Charles

II was very attracted to Windsor, hoping to convert it into the British equivalent of Versailles. To this end he created the three mile Long Walk. He carried out a great deal of restoration in the castle, commissioning the Italian artist Verrio to paint many of the ceilings in the Royal Apartments. Charles's successors were, however, not so interested in the castle, and it was not until the time of George IV that renovation started in earnest. George commissioned Jeffrey Wyatville to undertake extensive restoration of the castle, and after sixteen years, he succeeded in almost completely altering its appearance, creating the castle we know today. He saw the castle as a composite building, and worked to create a unity and this can be seen best from a distance. He built the Grand Corridor, and the Waterloo Chamber to commemorate the defeat of Napoleon. Most of Wyatville's building has stood the tests of time and few alterations have been made since then. A number of improvements were made to the State Apartments by King George V and Queen Mary, and the present Royal Family have continued to modernise the apartments.

Windsor Castle has occupied an important place in the lives of most British monarchs

Henry VIII's Gateway is the entrance to the Lower Ward of Windsor Castle from Castle Hill

from William I to Elizabeth II. It is full of memories and mementoes of events great and small, majestic and private, which help to fill English history with living people. For William I it was the castle he rested in after a day's hunting in the local forests. For King John, it was where he spent the humiliating days when he had to seal Magna Carta at Runnymede. Henry VIII commemorated Catherine of Aragon here, although he soon divorced her. During the Civil War, Windsor was a parliamentarian stronghold, and indeed Charles I was a prisoner here for a few days before his execution in London. His body was brought back here and buried in St George's

Chapel. Queen Anne was here when news came of the Duke of Marlborough's victory at Blenheim, for which the nation gave him Blenheim Palace. In Queen Victoria's time the castle acquired its central place in the life of the British monarchy. She was happy here with her husband until his death, but after that the castle became a gloomy place. Edward VII livened it up, and George V and Queen Mary carried out many improvements. During the Second World War, it was a secure home for George VI and his family, and in the present days it is a much loved residence for Queen Elizabeth II and Prince Philip.

There are a great many items of interest in the castle, but we give here the principal ones.

St George's Chapel is a magnificent example of 16th century Gothic architecture and is the chapel of the Order of the Garter. It contains the tombs of Henry VI, Edward IV, Henry VIII and Jane Seymour, Charles I, Edward VII and Queen Alexandra, George V and Queen Mary, and George VI in the memorial chapel named for him. The Royal pews can be seen and the Sovereign's stall is marked by the Royal Standard. Along the length of the nave hang the arms of the Knights of the Garter, and the window compartments contain figures of kings and saints.

Albert Memorial Chapel is at the east end of St George's and was originally built by Henry VII for Henry VI. Queen Victoria restored it in memory of Prince Albert. Beneath the chapel are buried George III, Queen Charlotte, George IV and William IV

The State Apartments open from the North Terrace. They are used mainly for royal functions and are full of an enormous variety of paintings, furniture and other treasures. The Waterloo Chamber, St George's Hall, the Queen's Presence Chamber, the Queen's Audience Chamber, Charles II's Dining Room, the Queen's Drawing Room and The Grand Reception Room are particularly fine. Queen Mary's Dolls House can also be seen. It is a scale model, with running water, in which every detail is correct and all the moving parts work. Occasionally items are made for it by the present Royal Family.

The Round Tower dates from 1170, and has an excellent view.

The Town was made a Royal Borough in 1922. A memorial to George V can be seen on the corner of Thames Street, and at Castle Hill is a statue of Queen Victoria. The Guildhall contains statues of Queen Anne and Prince George of Denmark, and has many royal portraits. Home Park adjoins Windsor Castle on the north and east sides and contains Frogmore House and Royal Mausoleum where Queen Victoria and Prince Albert are buried. This, together with Frogmore Gardens, is open to the public on one day a year. Windsor Great Park lies to the south, and three miles down the long walk, planned by Charles II, stands an enormous bronze statue of George III.

Through Royal Berkshire

ASCOT

The road to Ascot traverses Windsor Great Park, on the far side of which on the B3022, lies Windsor Safari Park. At one time, George I had a hunting lodge there. Ascot is chiefly known for its racecourse. This was laid out by Queen Anne, and every year in June, the Royal Ascot Races take place. These are important horse races in their own right, and they have become extremely fashionable. The Royal Family usually drives up the course in State, with their horses in their regalia, and with outriders of the master and huntsmen of the Royal Buckhounds.

WOKINGHAM

The history of Wokingham dates back to at least Saxon times. In the Elizabethan era, there was a thriving silk industry here, and in the old church hangs a wooden panel with the arms of Queen Elizabeth I. Other items of royal interest in the town are the portraits of kings and queens to be found in the town hall in the market place.

READING

The largest town in Berkshire, it has had a long history of association with the British monarchy. Most of the early connections centre round the abbey, which used to be one of the greatest and most powerful in the land, but is now in ruins. It is situated in Forbury Gardens, which were once the outer courtyard of the abbey. It was founded in 1121 by Henry I while he was still mourning the loss of his son drowned at sea; the king was buried here. It was consecrated by Thomas Becket during the reign of Henry II. Edward IV announced his

marriage here. However, in 1539 during the reign of Henry VIII, the great monastery was dissolved, and the Abbot hanged outside his own gateway. This gateway is now the abbey museum and contains some stones from the 13th century chapel of St Edmund as well as oil paintings depicting the history of the abbey. From this time until the reign of Charles I, the abbey became a royal palace, and Henry VIII, Edward VI, Mary Tudor and Elizabeth I all came here. Of the ruins, the shape of the Chapter House is best preserved, and the site of the burial of Henry I is marked by a tablet as well as a granite cross memorial. Also buried in the abbey were Henry I's second wife, Henry II's eldest son and Henry III's mother. Reading museum also contains some relics of the abbey.

The Church of St Lawrence, the municipal church of Reading, has associations with Elizabeth I. She came to Reading several times and used to worship in the church. In 1575 a special seat was made for her in the chancel. A window in the tower depicts Henry I, Henry VII and Charles I. The church was used as a barracks during the Civil War, a period during which the town suffered badly, changing hands from royalist to parliamentarian several times. Years later, in 1688, James II's troops met the army of William of Orange in the town, and were defeated.

Caversham is now almost absorbed into the borough of Reading, but it too has had an interesting history of royal associations. Charles I was kept prisoner at Caversham House in the Civil War. Before that, Caversham was in royalist hands until they were defeated on the bridge by the parliamentarians. Between the bridges is an island where Henry II came to witness a duel between Robert de Montfort and Henry of Essex who had been accused of cowardice.

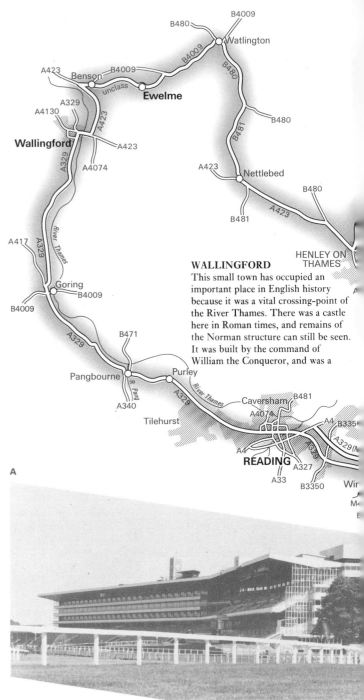

WALLINGFORD

This small town has occupied an important place in English history because it was a vital crossing-point of the River Thames. There was a castle here in Roman times, and remains of the Norman structure can still be seen. It was built by the command of William the Conqueror, and was a refuge for Queen Matilda during her war with King Stephen. She found safety here after she escaped from Oxford. The town's involvement in the disputes over the monarchy in the 12th century, led to the Treaty of Wallingford which gave Henry II the

crown. During the Civil War, the town held out for Charles I, but after his downfall, the roundheads demolished the castle, which up until then had been used as a prison.

EWELME

A peaceful little village lying in the Chilterns, it was created by Alice, Duchess of Suffolk. She built the almshouses, school and church which still remain as fine examples of 15th

century craftsmanship. She was the granddaughter of Geoffrey Chaucer, and lived in the manor house in great style. She was responsible for guarding Margaret of Anjou when she was brought to England to marry Henry VI. In later years Henry VIII came

here to spend his honeymoon with Catherine Howard. Elizabeth I came here too, as a girl and, later, on a royal progress. Prince Rupert also lived here. Little remains of that great palace, except some fragments incorporated into the present manor house.

The perpendicular church is of great interest. It contains the tomb of Alice, Duchess of Suffolk who died in 1475. The font cover is very striking, and just above it, a carved head is thought to represent Edward III. Ironically, Ewelme might have had even closer connections with the English monarchy. The son of the Duchess of Suffolk was with Richard III at Bosworth Field. There, Richard named him as his heir, but the battle went against them, and the Tudors became the kings of England.

MAIDENHEAD

A popular riverside resort, Maidenhead has had a number of connections with the English monarchy. Henry VIII's fourth wife, Anne of Cleves, lived in the town, in a house near the war memorial in St Ives Road. Charles I, while a captive in Caversham House at the end of the Civil War, came to the Greyhound Inn which used to stand half-way down the High Street. The parliamentarian General Fairfax had allowed him to see his children, and the town put on a great show when the king arrived, with bells ringing and flowers in the street.

ETON

Lying in the shadow of Windsor Castle, Eton, the home of the famous school has provided the nation with great men for over 500 years. It was founded by Henry VI in 1440, and his statue stands in the centre of School

Yard. The Long Room, which at one time was the teaching hall, contains the busts of famous Etonians and patrons, among them George III, William IV, Queen Victoria and Prince Albert. The oldest buildings in the College are in Cloister Court, the Hall containing a small organ which was built for George III, and portraits of Henry VI and George III. The library contains a number of treasures with royal associations, such as deeds with the seals of King John and William II, and Mary Tudor's Book of Hours. The best known building, however, is the Old Chapel, one of the finest works of architecture in the country. Inside is a statue of Henry VI in white marble, holding a model of the chapel.

HAMPTON COURT

Hampton Court has been called the loveliest palace in Europe. It was the home of kings and queens for over 200 years and has been the scene of the grand entertainments and the tragic personal disasters which make up the history of Britain and its monarchs.

Henry VIII and his wives

It was first built by Thomas Wolsey, Lord Chancellor in the reign of Henry VIII. He made it the finest, most extravagant palace in Europe, and it was greatly admired by many foreign kings and princes. He gave this palace to Henry VIII at a time when his own position was in question, but it did not delay his eventual downfall. At the time Henry was trying to obtain a divorce from Catherine of Aragon who was not able to bear him a male heir. He moved into Hampton Court with Anne Boleyn, his new love, even though they were not yet married. He carried out many alterations to Wolsey's palace, adding a new library and the magnificent Great Hall which still remains. He was a keen player of tennis (a game which survives now only in the unusual form of "real tennis") and had a tennis court built here. It is still in existence and is the oldest one in England. All Henry's tempestuous marriages took place against the background of Hampton Court, and Anne of Cleves visited the palace for a few days while waiting for her divorce. The lives of Jane Seymour and Catherine Howard were especially tragic here, and it is said that they both still haunt the Queen's apartments. The last two years of Henry's life were almost entirely spent at Hampton Court, where he was very ill, although only 53, and extremely fat. His successor, Edward VI, was young and not very strong, and the palace saw scenes of great turbulence while his Protectors quarrelled and plotted.

The Great West Gatehouse of Hampton Court Palace. In the centre of the gateway, below the oriel window, is a panel carved with the arms of Henry VIII

The heyday of the palace

Mary Tudor spent her honeymoon at Hampton Court with Philip II of Spain. It was not a happy marriage, made much sadder by Mary's mistaken belief during 1555 that she was pregnant. An heir to the throne was announced although no birth had taken place— the queen was suffering from dropsy. She died in 1558 and was succeeded by her sister Elizabeth, who had in fact been imprisoned by her in the Water Gallery here at Hampton Court. In spite of these unhappy memories, Elizabeth frequently visited the palace for festivities or to hunt in the parks. Her first visit was a secret one to meet James Hamilton, a possible husband. She made few structural alterations to the fabric of the palace, but took an active interest in the gardens, adding plants brought to her from the New World by Hawkins, Raleigh and Drake.

The bright, festive atmosphere here changed completely when James I came to the throne in 1603. The court was filled with Scotsmen, several of them the King's favourites. The most important event which took place here at this time was the commissioning of the new Authorised Version of the English Bible, which was announced after the conference between the Church of England and the Puritans. Charles I lived here with his French wife Henrietta Maria, and during this time several violent marital quarrels took place because he did not want her to have so many French retainers. One of these quarrels resulted in great commotion and breaking of windows, and the retainers were removed. Charles' life here, however, was sharply disrupted at the start of the Civil War, when he had to get away from London to Nottingham. During the Civil War, the palace was ill-treated by the parliamentarian soldiers, but after Charles' capture following the battle of Naseby, he was brought back here as a prisoner. He was, in fact, given considerable freedom of movement in the palace and the parks, and in November 1647, he managed to escape. He was subsequently re-captured and ultimately executed.

The Queen's Apartments at the east end of Hampton Court, seen from the Great Fountain

Restoration and improvement

In the period that followed, Hampton Court was sold and became the property of Oliver Cromwell, who lived here happily, although with less than the previous regal grandeur, for

Fountain Court was part of the extension to the original palace carried out for William III by Sir Christopher Wren

the rest of his life. When Charles II was restored to the throne, he was delighted with Hampton Court and had it redecorated and refurnished. He arrived at the palace in great state for his honeymoon with Catherine of Braganza, although his several mistresses, one of them brought in to live here, made this marriage a stormy one. Charles had been very impressed by the lovely gardens at Versailles, and he was determined to adopt similar landscaping at Hampton Court. During his reign and that of William III, the gardens were laid out in the impressive form they have today.

William III and Mary II had major influences on the shape of Hampton Court. When they first saw it they decided it was the ideal place in which to live, and commissioned Christopher Wren to make a grand palace here, a Versailles on the banks of the River Thames. All Henry VIII's State Apartments were demolished, and, in their place, Fountain Court, the South Front containing the King's State Apartments, and the East Front and Queen's State Apartments were built. Mary II loved the gardens and made many alterations. She was responsible

for many of the ornamental iron grilles and gates which were designed by Tijou. William created the famous Maze later in his life after Mary had died. The plans for rebuilding the entire palace proceeded no further because of lack of money, which leaves an interesting mixture of Wren's newer buildings and the older Tudor ones. William III was killed at Hampton Court in a riding accident when his horse stumbled over a molehill. Anne, succeeding William, was not able to keep up the new building work, although she had Wren redecorate the Tudor Chapel and Grinling Gibbons install the carved wooden reredos.

George I and George II both lived in the Palace for short periods, and George II was the last British sovereign to do so. After his death it became a series of 'grace and favour' residences, although William IV worked hard on restoring it in order to attract paying visitors. Queen Victoria carried out further restoration and increased its attractions for the public. Today it can be seen as a grand palace, filled with priceless paintings, tapestries and furniture, set in glorious gardens, and filled with echoes of great scenes in English history.

Thames-side meadows

BUSHY PARK

Bushy park was used by Henry VIII for hunting, and today contains a fine collection of old trees, particularly the mile-long chestnut avenue. This avenue leads to Bushy House, which used to be occupied by the rangers of the park, among whom was William IV while Duke of Clarence.

RUNNYMEDE

A meadow by the side of the Thames, Runnymede is universally known as the site of the sealing of Magna Carta. King John was an unpopular Monarch, and the church and the barons rebelled against him. He was forced to make peace with them in 1215 by sealing Magna Carta. The charter was dated 15th June 1215, and only four copies still exist. A memorial to Magna Carta and a facsimile of the document stand at the foot of Cooper's Hill.

FROGMORE

A small estate to the south of Home Park, Frogmore was originally bought for the crown by Henry VIII. Queen Charlotte, wife of George III, found it a congenial retreat from court life, and created the lovely gardens. Queen Victoria was very fond of Frogmore. When her beloved Albert died, his body was interred in the mausoleum here, and so was Victoria's, forty years later. The house itself continued to be used by the Royal Family, and the children of King George V spent a good deal of time here. The house, mausoleum and gardens are open to the public on only one day a year at Whitsun.

WINDSOR

Full details of the historic castle and town are given on page 89.

COLNBROOK

Several kings and queens have passed through this village. King John is thought to have stopped at King John's Castle on his way to Runnymede. Edward III met the Black Prince here, bringing his prisoner the King of France. Elizabeth I, while a prisoner in Mary Tudor's reign, stopped in Colnbrook when she was being brought from Woodstock to Hampton Court. Charles I stayed here during the Civil War.

BRENTFORD

Brentford has seen two important battles. The first, in 1016, was between the armies of Edmund Ironside and Canute, and the second was during the Civil War in 1642, when Prince Rupert for the royalists, surprised a small parliamentary garrison and defeated them.

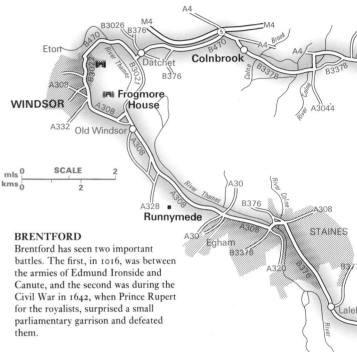

A

B

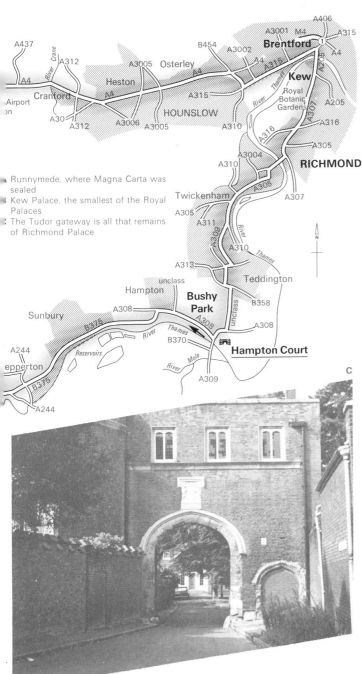

On the map:

Runnymede, where Magna Carta was sealed

Kew Palace, the smallest of the Royal Palaces

The Tudor gateway is all that remains of Richmond Palace

Syon House, between Brentford and Isleworth stands on the site of the Syon Monastery founded by Henry V. Protector Somerset converted it into a splendid palace and laid out the grounds. James I later gave it to the Earl of Northumberland and his son employed Inigo Jones to restore it. Queen Anne lived here for a while before she came to the throne. The gardens were landscaped by Capability Brown. Syon Park also houses the London Transport Collection of old buses, trams, locomotives etc, and exhibits of the world of motoring.

KEW

Until 1841 the Royal Botanical Gardens were owned by the Royal Family. Princess Augusta started a botanical garden in 1759 when she lived in Kew House (since disappeared). George III was also interested in the garden when he lived in Richmond Lodge (also no longer standing). The original area was enlarged in 1897 when Queen Victoria donated the Queen's Cottage grounds in commemoration of her Diamond Jubilee. The strongest link with the Royal Family is probably the series of ten Queen's Beasts, replicas of the stone beasts which stood in front of the window of Westminster Abbey during the coronation of Queen Elizabeth II. They stand at the foot of Palm House terrace facing the pond. In the south-west corner of the gardens are the Queen's Cottage and Grounds. These have been kept in a semi-wild condition, and are traversed by a single cindered path. The Queen's Cottage is a romantic old thatched house, probably built by George III in 1760, and used in Queen Victoria's reign as a shooting box and a summer house for picnics. It is not open.

Kew Palace, also known as the Dutch House, is situated near the northern end of Broad Walk. George III acquired it in 1781, and regularly used it as a residence from 1802. The Dukes of Kent and Clarence were married here in 1818 and Queen Charlotte died here. It is open and contains many historical documents, paintings and pieces of furniture.

RICHMOND

This Thames-side town has long had associations with royalty, and is a royal manor whose lord is the sovereign. A palace was first built here by Henry I in 1125, and was known as Shene Palace. Edward III died here, and Richard II had the palace demolished in remorse after the death of his wife. Henry V restored it but it was burned down in 1487. Henry VII rebuilt it and changed its name to Richmond Palace. It was an important and impressive palace, rivalled only by nearby Hampton Court. Henry VII and Elizabeth I died here, and it was the home of Charles I while Prince of Wales. After the execution of Charles I it was restored as a home for his widow Henrietta Maria. Its last royal resident was Prince James Edward Stuart, son of James II. The palace was pulled down in the 18th century, but the Old Gateway and Wardrobe survive.

In Richmond Park is situated White Lodge, now the home of the Royal Ballet School, but originally built as a royal residence in 1727. Queen Victoria, Edward VII, George V and Queen Mary all spent some time here, and the Duke of Windsor was born here in 1894. George VI and Queen Elizabeth spent their honeymoon here. An exhibition tracing the history of the house and its royal associations can be seen in the house which is open by appointment only. The royal connections with Richmond are perpetuated in the Thatched Cottage (not open), the home of Princess Alexandra and Angus Ogilvie.

WOBURN

Woburn Abbey has been in the family of the Duke of Bedford since it was given to John Russell under the terms of Henry VIII's will. The son of a merchant, John Russell had come to the court of Henry VII as an interpreter and continued in the service of the Crown as an envoy under Henry VIII, who made him a baron, and later under Edward VI. As a reward for his forty years of service he was created 1st Earl of Bedford. The gift of Woburn Abbey, however, was not greatly appreciated by the Earl. It had been badly damaged by fire before the Dissolution and the family already owned estates in the West Country as well as the family home at Chenies in Buckinghamshire.

Visit of Elizabeth I

Queen Elizabeth's decision to stay at the abbey in 1572 was not met with a great deal of enthusiasm either. The 2nd Earl, Francis Russell, was still living at Chenies and had to make special preparations for the visit. He wrote to Lord Burghley, one of the Queen's ministers, "I am now going to prepare for Her Majesty's coming to Woborne which shall be done in the best and hastiest manner I can. I trust your lordship will have in remembrance to provide help that her Majesty's tarrying be not above two nights and a daye, for so long tyme doe I prepare. I pray God the rowmes and

Woburn Abbey, the home of the Dukes of Bedford, is full of priceless treasures collected in the 18th and 19th centuries

lodging there may be to Her Majestie's contentacion for the tyme . . . " The abbey that Queen Elizabeth knew does not exist today, most of the present building being of 18th century origin. A part, however, can be dated to around 1630, notably the Grotto, a domed room with walls and ceiling decorated entirely with pieces of quartz and thousands of shells.

The 4th Earl brought his family to stay at Woburn to escape the Great Plague which was sweeping through the capital in 1665. Although at first they did not intend to remain after the threat of disease had subsided, they developed a great affection for the estate and began to transform the building into a magnificent Jacobean mansion.

Under the 4th and 5th Earls the estate continued to grow and they, along with the Dutch enginner Vermuyden, embarked upon a scheme to drain the Fenland. The project, which cost in the region of £100,000, made available several thousand acres of land for agricultural use.

Stuart times
Charles I was a visitor to Woburn on several occasions, but only once brought his wife, Queen Henrietta Maria. When he came during the Civil War, his wife had gone to France to escape the hostilities. The 5th Earl, at the beginning of the war, was in sympathy with Parliament, but later changed sides to support the royalists.

In 1683 the 5th Earl's eldest son, Lord William Russell, was executed for his part in the Rye House Plot to assassinate Charles II and his brother James. Ten years after his death, however, he was pardoned by William and Mary and a dukedom was conferred upon his father. The 1st Duke's grandson gambled excessively and proceeded to dissipate the huge family fortune, but when he died his brother inherited the title and estate and set about restoring its wealth and building the magnificent abbey which stands today. He employed the architect Henry Flitcroft, who designed the west front including the fourteen state apartments, and the stable block.

Queen Victoria's visit
The most recent royal visit was that of the newly-wed Queen Victoria and Prince Albert in 1841. The royal couple, both twenty-two years old at the time, stayed with the Duke and Duchess for three days. The Queen spent much of her time at Woburn driving in the park, and she wrote in her journal of Albert attempting to play tennis.

During their stay the Queen and her Prince Consort used the same bedroom as Charles I and Henrietta Maria nearly two hundred years earlier. The room, now called Queen Victoria's Bedroom, contains two portraits of her and is sumptuously decorated with silk hangings and an ornate gilded ceiling. Also named in honour of their visit are Queen Victoria's Dressing Room and Prince Albert's Dressing Room. The latter includes a number of etchings executed by the royal couple and given to the Duchess of Bedford who was a Lady in Waiting to the Queen.

The treasures of Woburn
The house contains many paintings and works of art valued at several million pounds. The China Room contains porcelain from Japan, China and England, together with Sèvres porcelain from France and Meissen from Germany. The Heirloom Vaults, previously used as wine cellars, house the world-famous Sèvres dinner service given by King Louis XV of France to Gertrude Leveson Gower. Her husband, the 4th Duke, had been instrumental in ending the Seven Years War by negotiating the Treaty of Paris. The dinner service, with 183 pieces, is displayed in a special pavilion, under the watchful gaze of a portrait of the donor, Louis XV. There is also a book room, a silver room, and a souvenir room with family portraits, including one of Elizabeth Sackville-West who was a bridesmaid to Queen Victoria and married the 9th Duke. There is a room dedicated to "The Flying Duchess", wife of the 11th Duke, who was famous as a record-breaking pilot. In 1937 she failed to return from one flight and parts of her plane were washed up during the next few weeks on the Norfolk coast. These pieces of the aircraft are on show in the room.

Another room is dedicated to the work of the artist Sir Joshua Reynolds, but the most famous room in the house is the Canaletto Room. The private dining room of the family, it has twenty-one views of Venice painted by Canaletto which are thought to have been purchased by the 4th Duke during his Grand Tour of Europe. The house also contains paintings by Rembrandt, Van Dyck, Cuyp, Gheeraerts, and the "Armada" portrait of Queen Elizabeth I by George Fower which has hung for more than two hundred years in the long gallery.

Agriculture has always been of great importance to the Dukes of Bedford, pioneered by the 5th Duke. He began the Bedfordshire Agricultural Society in 1801 and also the "Woburn Sheep Sheerings" which were, more accurately, a type of agricultural show. In 1876 the Woburn Experimental Farm, and later the Experimental Fruit Farm were set up to research into various methods of cultivation. The produce from the farm sold well at Covent Garden, which had also been a gift to the family from Henry VIII. The Market was sold by the then Duke of Bedford just before the First World War. Safari parks and wildlife reserves may appear to be modern innovations but the collection of birds and animals in Woburn Park began in the mid 19th century. The 10th and 11th Dukes were particularly interested in rare species and began to collect such creatures, notably Père David's Deer, at Woburn.

Great houses in the Chilterns

KNEBWORTH

Knebworth House, the ancestral home of the Lytton family, stands on the site of a Norman castle. In the late 13th century the castle belonged to one of the sons of King Edward I, and upon his death it passed to his son-in-law, Sir Walter Manny, one of the first Knights of the Garter. The basis of the present house was built around 1492 but it was subsequently altered, enlarged, partly demolished and rebuilt. The present house, which still retains a lot of its Tudor characteristics, has some beautiful oak panelling and carvings and an impressive collection of portraits. The Queen Elizabeth Chamber is where the Tudor Queen stayed on several occasions.

HATFIELD

The family home of the Cecils for over 350 years, Hatfield House was once the home of two of the Tudor monarchs. In the time before it became a royal residence, Edward III's second son was born there.

Henry VIII made the manor crown property and his son lived there until, after the death of his father, he became King Edward VI. When the young King died and Queen Mary came to the throne, Princess Elizabeth made Hatfield her home. She was arrested and sent to the Tower, charged by her half sister of approving the conspiracy of Sir Thomas Wyat, but she later returned to Hatfield and remained under house arrest until her accession to the throne in 1558.

The original manor that the Tudor monarchs knew so well is not the one we see today, although some parts still remain and are used as stables and other offices. The present house was built in 1611, that date being engraved on the tower at the centre of the building. It contains some fine portraits of royalty and noblemen, some of which were once owned by Elizabeth I. In King James's room there are paintings of George III and Queen Charlotte and a marble statue of James I.

The Library at Hatfield contains an impressive collection of state papers, manuscripts and other historical documents. One manuscript includes a miniature of Henry VII, another was sent by Henry VIII to the Pope. There are papers and letters referring to the divorce of Anne of Cleves, the Articles of Edward VI, matters concerning Mary of Scotland, and the heredity of Elizabeth I. The total collection numbers around thirteen thousand letters.

A The elaborate gateway at Hatfield House
B The west end of St Albans Cathedral
C The scanty remains of Berkhamsted Castle
D Entrance gateway to Ashridge Park

A

B

98

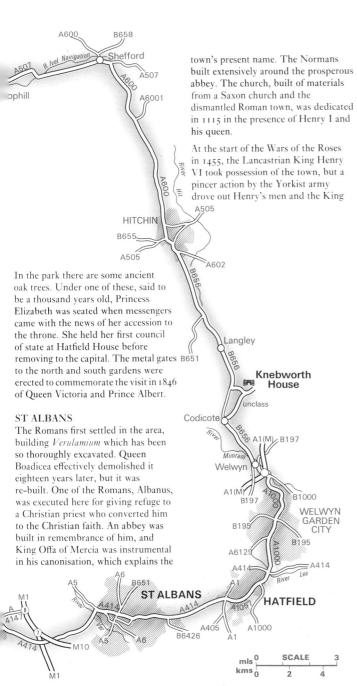

town's present name. The Normans built extensively around the prosperous abbey. The church, built of materials from a Saxon church and the dismantled Roman town, was dedicated in 1115 in the presence of Henry I and his queen.

At the start of the Wars of the Roses in 1455, the Lancastrian King Henry VI took possession of the town, but a pincer action by the Yorkist army drove out Henry's men and the King

In the park there are some ancient oak trees. Under one of these, said to be a thousand years old, Princess Elizabeth was seated when messengers came with the news of her accession to the throne. She held her first council of state at Hatfield House before removing to the capital. The metal gates to the north and south gardens were erected to commemorate the visit in 1846 of Queen Victoria and Prince Albert.

ST ALBANS

The Romans first settled in the area, building *Verulamium* which has been so thoroughly excavated. Queen Boadicea effectively demolished it eighteen years later, but it was re-built. One of the Romans, Albanus, was executed here for giving refuge to a Christian priest who converted him to the Christian faith. An abbey was built in remembrance of him, and King Offa of Mercia was instrumental in his canonisation, which explains the

was wounded at the Battle of St. Albans. He was taken by the Duke of York to the abbey before being imprisoned in the Tower. He later agreed to make the Duke of York his heir and was released. The King came to St. Albans with his queen twice in 1459 and again in 1461. By this time the war had been renewed because Queen Margaret objected to her son losing his entitlement to the throne as a result of Henry's promise to the Duke of York. The Yorkists were encamped at St. Albans when Henry's army came and this time the Lancastrians were the victors. After celebrating in the abbey, the royal family remained in the town for a few days until the news arrived that the Duke of York was again marching on the town, when they removed to safer quarters.

BERKHAMSTED

Berkhamsted House was constructed by Sir Edward Cary, using materials from the ruined castle given him by Queen Elizabeth I. It was here that Charles I spent part of his youth.

The old castle, foundations of which can still be seen, had a more illustrious history and was a royal residence on many occasions. The original Anglo Saxon castle was improved in the 11th century by the Earl of Moreton, half brother of William the Conqueror. William came here in 1066 after his success at the Battle of Hastings to receive the Saxon nobles who offered him the throne of England. Moreton's son had his estates confiscated by Henry I. He gave them to his Chancellor, Randulph, who rebuilt the castle and invited the King to visit him. After Randulph's death, the castle was eventually given to Thomas Becket. During the rebellion of the barons against King John, the French Dauphin, who came to support the uprising, laid siege to the castle in 1216. Later, Henry III gave the castle to his brother, Richard, and

upon his death it passed to his son Edmund who founded the nearby monastery at Ashridge.

The castle saw its best times when Edward III renovated it and used it as his main residence. He later gave it to his son, Edward, the Black Prince, who lived there amid great festivities for some time. Although the castle remained the property of the crown until the 16th century, it was never again used as a permanent residence but was visited by Richard II, Henry VI and Edward IV, whose mother lived there until her death. After this it was sadly neglected and fell into ruin.

ASHRIDGE PARK

A monastery was founded on the site of Ashridge House in the 13th century and it was here that King Edward I held a Parliament in 1290. After the Dissolution it became the property of the crown and it was here that Elizabeth was arrested in 1554 by order of her half-sister, Queen Mary. The building was demolished in 1800 and replaced with the present mansion, now used as a college.

D

AUDLEY END

The magnificent mansion of Audley End stands in beautiful parkland about one mile west of Saffron Walden. The Abbey of Walden, which used to stand on this site, was given to Sir Thomas Audley by Henry VIII in gratitude for his assistance with the Dissolution of the monasteries. He converted the Prior's house for himself, and, on his death, the house passed to the Howard family. Lord Thomas Howard, who figured prominently in the battle against the Spanish Armada, was made Baron Howard of Walden by Elizabeth I in 1597. He became a favourite of James I who made him Earl of Suffolk and Lord Chamberlain. In 1603, he started to build a new house at Audley End. It took 13 years and £200,000 to build, and the Earl of Suffolk had by this time been made Lord High Treasurer. James I is reputed to have said of the house that it was too much for a King but it might do very well for a Lord Treasurer.

Grand Mansion and Royal Palace
When it was complete, the mansion was enormous, very much bigger than the present house. Through the grand entrance gateway of four circular towers, were two square courtyards, one after the other. The main rooms in the principal courtyard were on the first floor, supported on columns above an open walkway. Beyond the hall was the inner courtyard, three sides of which remain and make up the house as it is today.

In 1618, after completion of the house, the Earl of Suffolk was convicted of embezzlement and lived on at Audley End in disgrace until his death in 1626. His successors lived quiet lives, even managing to avoid involvement in the Civil War. After the Restoration of King Charles II to the throne in 1660, the King became very attracted to the house, particularly

as he needed another palace. He eventually bought the house in 1669 and the Court was established here, the name being changed to New Palace. It was used intermittently by James II and William III, until, in 1701, when payments of the purchase money failed to be made, it reverted to its former owners, the Earls of Suffolk. Almost the only structural features of the house reflecting its royal occupants are the rainwater heads, which bear the royal cipher, in some cases of James II and in one case of William and Mary.

Demolition and restoration
The 7th Earl, in 1721, consulted the architect Vanbrugh for his advice on how to manage such a large house. He recommended demolishing three sides of the huge, impressive outer courtyard, leaving only the smaller, inner courtyard complete. He also carried out a good deal of restoration inside the house, sticking carefully to the Stuart style of the early 17th century. When the Suffolk line failed, the property passed into the hands of Lady

Portsmouth. She considered completely demolishing the house, but eventually restricted this demolition to the eastern range of buildings. She left the house to her nephew, who, in 1788 was created Baron Braybrooke. It was he who undertook the restoration of the house to the condition it has today and is said to have spent a total of £100,000 on the project.

The first thing he did was to rebuild and restore the eastern side of the building with a gallery and a first floor passage. He also employed Robert Adam to decorate the living quarters in the south wing, and Capability Brown to landscape the gardens. Much of the stonework on the exterior of the house was replaced, keeping carefully to the original style. The saloon and chapel were completely restyled, probably by Robert Adam in 1786, in "Strawberry Hill" Gothic style. Lord Braybrooke's son continued with the embellishment of the house, and he also interchanged the ground floor and first floor apartments in the south wing. The library was

The splendid Jacobean house of Audley End, at one time a royal palace

built during this time, between 1820 and 1825. No other major improvements were made after this date, and, following the death of the 7th Lord Braybrooke in 1941, the house became the property of the nation.

The Interior

The lobby, at the north of the hall, contains some of the original, early 17th century work, particularly the wooden screen, and also an engraving by Winstanley of the Royal Palace of 1676. The south end of the hall contains the enormous fireplace displaying the arms of the 7th Earl of Suffolk. Along the length of the hall, hanging from the ornate beams are the colourful, if slightly faded, banners representing the different families who have owned Audley

End. Among the portraits in the hall and on the staircase, are those of Charles II, William III, Mary II and a full length portrait of Edward VI. An interesting item in the stair well is a vellum patent, dated Greenwich, May 1634, which is a grant of an augmentation of arms by Charles I to the Earl of Stirling. The Saloon contains a great deal of the work done in 1785, but the ceiling is earlier and is of great interest, lending the Saloon the name of the Fish Room. The Drawing Room is filled with some magnificent 18th century French furniture, while the Library and South Library are sumptuous rooms displaying the large book collections of the Braybrookes, all in their distinctive bindings.. In the Dining Room, the chimney

pieces carry the arms of the kings who owned Audley End in the 17th century. This room also contains a good portrait of George II and a small one of Mary II.

The Neville Room contains a portrait of Queen Charlotte which is a companion to the portrait of George III on the hall staircase. The chapel, recently redecorated, is a fine example of late 18th century Gothic architecture with painted glass windows. One of the finest rooms in the house is the Painted Drawing Room, largely the work of Robert Adam. In the vestibule is a copy of a self portrait of Van Dyke with a sunflower, this being considered an emblem of royal favour.

The Gardens

When the house was restored in the 18th century, great attention was also paid to the landscaping of the gardens. The River Cam flows through the park, and Capability Brown reshaped the river and landscaped the grounds in front of the house. Several of the elegant buildings in the garden were designed by Robert Adam, including the Adam Bridge, the Ionic Temple built to commemorate the ending of the Seven Years War and the Temple of Concord which commemorates George III's recovery from his first attack of insanity.

The Great Hall at Audley End, retaining from the original house the 17th century porches. The banners represent the different families who have owned the house

The enormous fireplace in the Great Hall, displaying the arms of the 7th Earl of Suffolk

Cambridge and the Fens

SAWSTON

Sawston Hall stands in the centre of the village. Little is known of its early history, but in 1553, the owners gave shelter to Mary Tudor who had been kept in poverty by her father for failing to renounce her religious faith. The Duke of Northumberland, hoping to see Mary behind bars, sent her a bogus note that the King wished to see her. Mary set out for London, not knowing that Lady Jane Grey had been proclaimed Queen on the death of Edward VI. During her journey, she learned the true state of affairs, and at once returned to Sawston Hall where she was offered hospitality by the Huddlestons, who were devout Catholics. By the morning, the great hall was surrounded by a hostile force, but Mary escaped in disguise. The hall was burnt down, but Mary helped build another one which was erected between 1557 and 1584.

CAMBRIDGE

The beautiful city of Cambridge is bounded on the west and north by the river Cam. During the 12th century churches and abbeys were built, and scholars from Oxford arrived in the city and established the nucleus of the university. During the next two centuries, twelve colleges were established, including King's and Queen's which were founded by Royalty.

King's College was founded in 1441 by Henry VI, who began work on the chapel which was completed by Henry VIII. The beautiful fan vaulted ceiling was completed in the 16th century, and the chapel also contains a wooden screen on which are carved the initials of Henry VIII and Anne

Boleyn. The picturesque Queen's College was founded in 1448 under the patronage of Margaret of Anjou, wife of Henry VI, and refounded by Elizabeth, wife of Edward IV in 1465.

Trinity College was founded by Henry VIII in 1546, and is built on the site of King's Hall, founded in 1336 by Edward III, and Michaelhouse, dating back to 1317. The Great Gateway, forming the entrance to Great Court from Trinity Street, carries the 14th century arms of Edward III and his sons, and, on the east face, a statue of Henry VIII. On the other side of the gate are statues of James I, his wife Anne of Denmark, and their son who became Charles I. On the south side of Great Court is the Queen's gate which has a statue of Elizabeth I. Edward VII, George VI (as Albert, Duke of York) and Prince Charles all attended Trinity College. Christ's College (1505) and St John's College (1511) were

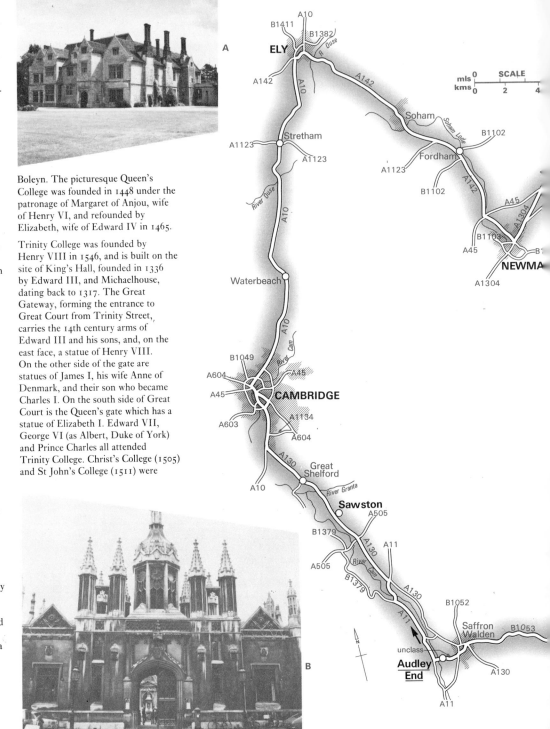

both founded by the mother of Henry VII, Lady Margaret Beaufort, Countess of Richmond.

ELY

The Isle of Ely, in the midst of the Fens, on which the city of Ely stands, was the place occupied by Hereward the Wake, "Last of the English" in his stand against the Norman invaders.

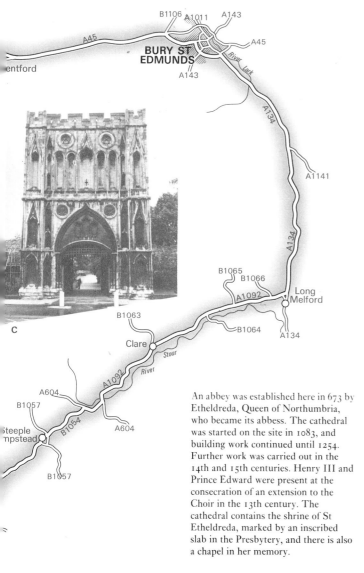

C

An abbey was established here in 673 by Etheldreda, Queen of Northumbria, who became its abbess. The cathedral was started on the site in 1083, and building work continued until 1254. Further work was carried out in the 14th and 15th centuries. Henry III and Prince Edward were present at the consecration of an extension to the Choir in the 13th century. The cathedral contains the shrine of St Etheldreda, marked by an inscribed slab in the Presbytery, and there is also a chapel in her memory.

NEWMARKET

A famous place in the horse-racing world, Newmarket grew from the village of Exning, 2 miles north west. Exning was the home of the ruling family of the Kingdom of East Anglia, and St Etheldreda was born there in 630. A plague there resulted in the market being transferred to Newmarket. First mention of the town goes back to 1226, and its first association with horse racing stems from 1605, when James I stopped on his way from Theobalds to Thetford. He very much liked the area, and visited it regularly between 1607 and 1625. Races were arranged for his visits, and in 1634, a race for a gold cup took place. Charles I visited the town every year, and he was here when he received the ultimatum precipitating the Civil War. After the Restoration, the sport of kings was resumed by Charles II, who also visited the town every year, often taking part in races himself. In 1683, a serious fire swept through the town destroying many buildings, and causing the royal party to leave the recently built Palace. This unexpected move foiled the plot hatched in Rye House to assassinate the King.

The royal family continued to take an interest in racing at Newmarket, maintaining a royal stables here. The first three Georges showed little interest in the sport, but the Prince Regent was very enthusiastic. In Queen Victoria's reign, the Royal Palace was broken up and sold, but Edward VII, as Prince of Wales, had a long association with the town. King George VI attended meetings here, and Queen Elizabeth II has horses training here.

Part of the Old Palace still exists in the High Street, as does a house which belonged to Nell Gwynne.

BURY ST EDMUNDS

This market town takes its name from King Edmund, once patron saint of

D

A Sawston Hall, refuge of Mary Tudor
B The entrance gateway to King's College, Cambridge
C Abbey gateway, Bury St Edmunds
D The King's School, Ely

England. Its motto is "Shrine of a King, Cradle of the Law", and this reflects its important place in English history. The young King Edmund was brutally killed by Danish invaders, and was buried at Hoxne. After 33 years, the body was moved to the monastery here, where it became a shrine. It was paid homage by Edward the Confessor, who made the last mile of the pilgrimage on foot. The monastery had become an abbey and grew in importance due to the presence of the famous shrine.

A great many visits were made to the abbey by England's monarchs, including Henry III, Edward I and Queen Eleanor, Queen Isabella, wife of Edward II, and Henry VI, who held a Parliament here in 1446. The last important ceremony to take place in the abbey was the funeral of Mary Tudor, sister of Henry VIII, and grandmother of Lady Jane Grey. At the Dissolution, her body was re-interred in St Mary's Church, to which, in 1881, Queen Victoria gave the Queen's Window portraying the story of Mary's life. The marble stone round her tomb was given by Edward VII.

NEWBURY

At one time Newbury had a strong and important castle, all trace of which has now disappeared save for some stonework incorporated into a much later building.

Boy hostage

The castle saw one of its most historic moments during the civil strife between King Stephen and Matilda. John Marshall held the castle for Matilda, but it was eventually captured by Stephen after a two month siege in 1153. During the siege the garrison of the castle had asked for a truce in which to consult with Matilda. Stephen agreed to this, but as a surety demanded a hostage. The hostage was John Marshall's fourth son, William, a boy of five or six. John Marshall apparently cared little for his son, for under cover of the truce he set about strengthening the defences of Newbury. When he learned of this Stephen was enraged and determined to hang young William, although he eventually spared the boy. Later it was suggested that William be catapulted over the castle ramparts, but Stephen refused. The boy grew up to become one of the great men of the kingdom.

In 1200 King John visited the town accompanied by his natural son Geoffrey. John took Newbury into his own hands in 1204 and bestowed it upon Robert FitzRoger. Legend has it that whilst on the run from the barons John took refuge in the house of an old spinning woman at Newbury. This prompted him to look upon Newbury in a kindly light. He is thought to have founded St Bartholomew's Hospital. In 1215 he granted the town a statute fair which was held every year up until 1939.

Jack O'Newbury

Henry VIII granted the town to Anne Boleyn and Jane Seymour in turn. One of Newbury's most famous characters, Jack O'Newbury, mustered a force of men to assist Henry at the Battle of Flodden in 1513. As a reward for his services Henry was determined to bestow a knighthood upon him. With this in mind Henry and Catherine of Aragon came to visit him at his home in Northbrook Street. Jack, a cloth-maker by trade, was too modest to accept such an accolade and declined the honour. On the side of Wilson's Gown shop there is a plaque commemorating the King and Queen's stay. The oriel window of the room where the Queen slept still remains.

Edward VI granted the town to his sister Elizabeth who later became queen. She made her first visit here in 1568 and gave the town its first surviving charter in 1596. Elizabeth restored the revenues of Donnington Hospital in 1570, and with the Earl of Nottingham she refounded the almshouses as the Hospital of Queen Elizabeth in 1602, from which time the present buildings date. The gilded arms of the Queen are preserved above the doorway. The

Remains of Donnington Castle, Newbury, include the 14th century gatehouse. The castle was heavily involved in the Civil War

town was given by James I to his queen, Anne of Denmark. They both visited the town in 1603. In 1627 Charles I granted the lordship and rights to the mayor and corporation in return for a quit rent.

The Battles of Newbury

During the English Civil War of 1642–5 Newbury and nearby Donnington Castle were the scene of much action. Donnington Castle, of which only the massive gatehouse remains, was granted a licence to crenellate in 1386. Edward VI stayed here in 1552, and Queen Elizabeth I granted it to the Earl of Nottingham in 1600 as a reward for Armada services.

At the start of the Civil War Donnington was owned by one John Parker, who opposed the King, but it was soon taken by the royalists. On the evening of 19th September 1643, the royalist army arrived in Newbury just ahead of the parliamentary forces. At a council of war that night Prince Rupert, Charles' principal lieutenant, strongly advised against becoming involved in any engagement with the enemy on the following day, but he was overruled. During the battle which ensued on the 20th the royalists suffered heavy losses. It was pouring with rain that day, both sides were thoroughly dispirited, and by the end of the day neither side had the upper hand. On the next day the parliamentary forces, commanded by Lord Essex, marched off towards London unopposed by the King's infantry, who had run out of ammunition. The King put a garrison at Donnington castle and withdrew.

Donnington, under the command of John Boys, withheld a lengthy siege during the summer of 1644, during which time much damage was done to the castle by cannon fire. In the end Charles took an army to Newbury, raised the siege and knighted John Boys. An informer told Parliament that the King's army at Newbury was under strength, so a large force was mustered and arrived at Thatcham on 25th October 1644. The royalist army calmly fell back into Newbury town, then drew their main forces up on Speen Heath, partly under the protection of Donnington Castle. They intended to hold out either until the arrival of Prince Rupert, or until the parliamentary army withdrew. On the 27th the roundheads, commanded by Cromwell, Waller, Essex and Manchester, launched a two pronged attack. Victory should have gone to Parliament, but Manchester, who was attacking the King's outpost at Shaw House, made a tactical error. The fighting continued all day and into the night, but the results were indecisive. The King watched the progress of the fighting from Donnington, and later withdrew to join Rupert, who was approaching from the west. During that night, the main royalist army withdrew towards Oxford, leaving the King's cannon at Donnington Castle.

On the 9th November the King, Rupert, and the royalist army arrived to relieve the castle and collect the cannon, meeting with little opposition. The castle continued to hold out for the King, and only surrendered on the express orders of Charles when he was close to defeat. The garrison marched out of the castle with colours flying in April 1646.

Newbury is situated on the River Kennet and the Kennet and Avon Canal

Civil War in Hampshire

BASING

Entered from the village's main street are the scant remains of Basing House. It was already important during the reign of Edward I, who stayed here in 1285. The estate passed to the Paulet family during the reign of Henry VII and Sir William Paulet, treasurer to King Henry VIII, turned Basing House into a palace. Sir William was a most extraordinary man, holding positions of great power during the reigns of four monarchs, and was created 1st Marquess of Winchester by Edward VI. He entertained Elizabeth I at his palace (it was then the largest privately owned dwelling in Britain) in 1569.

She was so impressed by the house and its owner that she declared, only half jokingly: "By my troth, if my Lord Treasurer were but a young man, I could find it in my heart to love him for a husband before any man in Europe". The 1st Marquess died in 1572 and was buried in Basing Church. Elizabeth I visited the house again in 1601 and stayed for 13 days. Her stay proved so expensive that much of the house had to be pulled down as an economy measure.

At the outbreak of the Civil War in 1642 John, the 5th Marquess of Winchester, fortified Basing House for the King. On 31st July 1643 the garrison was strengthened by 100 musketeers from Oxford, and later 150 more were added. Basing House was a sore thorn in the side of the parliamentary forces, for it commanded the western road, a great trade route to London.

In November 1643, General Waller with an army of 7,000 men attempted

A

to take the house by storm. This they failed to do and eventually retired to Farnham. During the summer and autumn of 1644 the house was besieged for a total of 24 weeks. A plot to surrender the house was devised, a brother of the Marquess, Lord Edward Paulet being one of the ringleaders. The plot was discovered and the conspirators hung, all except for Lord Edward who was forced to act as hangman.

As the winter set in conditions became intolerable for the parliamentary troops. Reluctantly, on 19th November, they began to withdraw. In September 1645 the siege was once more resumed. This time the roundhead troops were commanded by Colonel Dalbier, a Dutch engineer who intended to reduce the house to rubble with the use of cannon. By October a force of 7,000 parliamentary troops were ready to storm the house, and Oliver Cromwell was to lead the attack. The number of defenders was now reduced, by desertion, illness, and death to 300.

On 14th October, Dalbier's bombardment having made two breaches in the defences, the final assault began. Cromwell's troops poured into the house, and within an hour it was all over. Cromwell gave orders that the house should be

"utterly slighted and dismantled". The Marquess was taken prisoner and sent to the Tower, but was subsequently allowed to go into exile.

Basing House today retains little of its former glory. Of the palace or "New House" only foundations remain, but the mighty earthworks of the Old House still stand, as do some of the outer walls, portions still displaying clear signs of the siege.

ODIHAM

Odiham's connection with royalty is centred upon the castle, which in fact is not in the town at all but is situated 1m west by the old Basingstoke Canal.

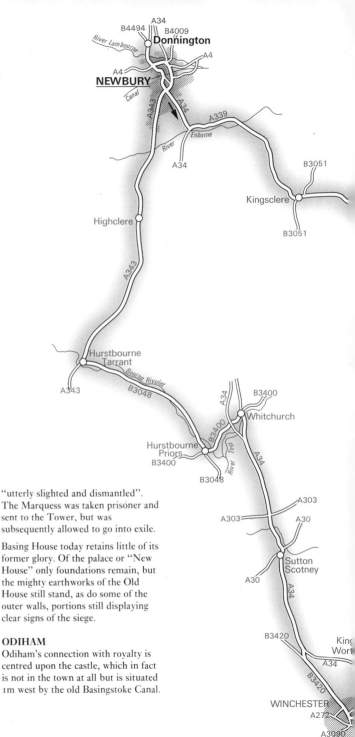

Here King John stayed, for only a few days, before he journeyed to Windsor and signed Magna Carta at Runnymede. David Bruce, King of Scots was imprisoned here for eleven years after the Battle of Neville's Cross. Simon de Montfort also came here, in the days of the barons' war, with Prince Edward. All that remains of the castle is the much battered flint keep.

ALTON

The town has frequently been visited by monarchy, some of whom were simply passing through and some of whom came to hunt in the surrounding countryside. When Henry I succeeded to the throne in 1100 his brother Robert rebelled against him. Soon, however, peace was restored and the treaty was signed at Alton. The name Normandy Street is believed to commemorate this. King John visited the town in 1204 and again in 1217. Charles I, Charles II, and James II all passed through the town.

The parish church of St Laurence has some interesting pillar paintings including one that is thought to depict Henry VI. During the Civil War the church was the scene of an heroic stand by Colonel Boles and 80 men against the forces of Parliament. Boles died in the pulpit. When Charles I heard of his death he said "Bring me a mourning staff; I have lost my best officer". The church still bears scars of the fight.

Royalty have paid several visits to Treloar Hospital at Alton. The Duke of Kent opened one of the buildings, and Princess Margaret was here in 1959. In 1967 Princess Alexandra opened the Florence Treloar School at Holybourne.

NEW ALRESFORD

Three miles north of New Alresford is The Grange, Northington. Once the home of the Prince of Wales, later George IV, it is a daunting building, standing like a Grecian temple overlooking a lake and a large wooded park, all now sadly overgrown. The Prince of Wales leased the Grange as a hunting lodge for one year in 1795 at a total cost of £2,100. At the end of this period, so the story goes, he commissioned his own architect to carry out £600 worth of repairs and then installed three sisters. The house was originally designed in the 17th century by Inigo Jones. Later, in the 19th century, it was altered, enlarged and encompassed by a portico with great Grecian columns. The house is not open to the public.

A The Garrison Gateway, Basing House
B The 16th century dovecote, Basing House
C King John's Castle, Odiham
D The church of St Laurence, Alton

OXFORD

View of Christ Church, Oxford, from the college gardens. In the centre of the picture is the Great Hall

The first settlement in Oxford was in Saxon times when Frideswide, a king's daughter who died in 735, fled here from an unwelcome suitor and founded a nunnery. Fragments of her shrine are in the cathedral. The first mention of the city's name occurs in the Anglo Saxon Chronicle in the year 912, a copy of which can be seen in the Bodleian Library. King Athelstan established a mint here in 925, and Canute held a council of Saxons and Danes here. William the Conqueror built the Castle, of which only a Norman tower, the crypt and the mound remain. In 1130, Henry I built Beaumont Palace which used to be where the bus station now stands. This palace was used by Stephen when he besieged Queen Matilda in Oxford Castle. She managed to escape, and fled at night over the frozen river to the safety of Abingdon.

The University is born
Henry II lived in Oxford, and his sons were born here—Richard Coeur de Lion in 1157, and John in 1166. Henry was a scholarly man and was instrumental in the growth of Oxford as a seat of learning. In his feud against Thomas Becket, who was exiled in France, Henry ordered that all scholars studying abroad should return home. Many of them settled in Oxford, and tried to recreate the life they knew at continental universities. The hostile attitude of many of the townsfolk caused numbers of students to move to Cambridge. Temporary harmony had been reached between the two factions by 1214, when a formal agreement marked the official founding of the university.

Magna Carta was sealed by King John in 1215, but Henry III tried to ignore its implications. In 1258 at Oxford, Parliament met the King to enforce the charter in the Provisions of Oxford which established parliamentary control in the country. In the Civil War, the University supported the King, although the town was more in favour of Parliament. Charles made the city his headquarters in 1642, moving into Christ Church. For four years the city was enmeshed in the turmoil of war until it surrendered in 1646 to Fairfax. After the Restoration, times in the university city returned to normal. The industrial and commercial aspects of the town developed and today the city is a thriving academic and commercial centre, enriched in recent years by some attractive modern architecture built to cater for the expansion of the university.

Tour of the city
Oxford is so full of places of interest which have royal connections that this brief description of selected items follows a path starting at the south of the city and ending on Magdalen Bridge. No distinction is made between university and other buildings.

Christ Church was founded under the name of Cardinal College by Wolsey in 1525 on the site of St Frideswide's Priory. A great deal of money was spent on the college by the Cardinal, until he fell from power in 1529. Henry VIII re-founded it in 1532, but it was suppressed at the Dissolution and Christ Church founded in its place. The Hall, built by Wolsey, is one of the finest in England, and was the scene of a play acted out before Elizabeth I in 1566. It contains portraits of Wolsey, Henry VIII, and Elizabeth I. James I and Charles I were also entertained here, and Charles I located his headquarters here during the Civil War. Tom Tower, the entrance to the college, houses a statue of Queen Anne.

Among the many distinguished men produced by the college was King Edward VII. *The Cathedral* is hidden behind the east side of Tom Quad in Christ Church. Originally St Frideswide's Priory, it was rebuilt in 1004 by Ethelred II, and later substantially modified by Wolsey. St Frideswide's shrine is situated between the Lady Chapel and the Choir and was made in 1289.

The *Ashmolean Museum* contains important art and archaeological collections, perhaps its most

Jesus College

Magdalen College, from Magdalen Bridge. On the right of the picture, across the River Cherwell, is Addison's Walk

famous treasure being the Alfred Jewel. The Medieval Room also houses a number of other Saxon and Viking antiquities. The Tradescant Room contains several items connected with royalty, such as the spurs worn by Charles I and chairs given by Charles II. Portraits in the museum include those of Charles II and James II.

St John's College was founded in 1555. The library contains a portrait of Charles I, made up from minute script of the Psalms. Statues of Charles I and Henrietta Maria are on the gate towers. Archbishop Laud's library also contains prayer books belonging to Edward VI and James I. *Balliol College* is one of the oldest colleges of the university, and dates from 1266. It was endowed by John de Balliol, father of a Scottish king. Most of the present buildings are Victorian, although the original gates have been restored. *Jesus College* was nominally founded by Elizabeth I, and the Hall contains several royal portraits, including Elizabeth I, Charles I and Charles II. In the Common Room there is a very fine portrait of Elizabeth I.

The main university library is the *Bodleian Library*. It is the oldest and one of the most important in the world, having been founded in 1602. It contains the library of Duke Humphrey, brother of Henry V, which holds some of the rarest manuscripts. Exhibitions held in the New Bodleian Library display many items with royal interest, including the Confirmation of Magna Carta by Edward I, a school book of Edward VI, letters from Elizabeth I, Charles I and Oliver Cromwell, and the Anglo Saxon Chronicle.

All Souls is a graduate college and was founded in the memory of Henry V and the men who died at Agincourt. A statue of the founder, Henry VI, can be seen over the gateway. The Chapel is a superb building, and the glass depicts numerous kings of England with particular emphasis on Henry V.

Queens' College, next door, was founded by the chaplain to Queen Philippa and favoured by her and other queens of England. On the High Street front there is a statue of Queen Charlotte, wife of George II, and the Hall and Senior Common Room contain a great many portraits of English kings and queens. Henry V is reputed to have stayed in the college. Around the library, a row of statues of benefactors includes that of Queen Philippa, and she is also represented inside the library.

University College, opposite Queens', is one of the oldest in the university, and claims to have been founded by King Alfred. The gateways display statues of Queen Anne, James II and Queen Mary II. *Oriel College* was at one time known as the King's College, and was refounded in 1326 by Edward II. It contains a statue of its founder, and one which is of either James I or Charles I. *Merton College* claims to be the oldest college in Oxford, and is certainly the oldest residential college. It was used during the Civil War by Henrietta Maria, who had rooms in the Fellows' Quadrangle, and later by Charles II and his queen when they fled here during the plague. The college also has a statue of Henry III over the gatehouse.

Magdalen College is one of the most famous colleges in Oxford as well as one of the richest. It has always enjoyed great royal favour, although during the Civil War, in common with most other colleges, it had to make great sacrifices for the King. Among its members were Prince Henry, eldest son of James I, and Prince Rupert, the royalist commander in the Civil War. Among the portraits in the Hall are those of Henry VIII, Charles I and Henrietta Maria. On the Founder's Tower is a statue of Edward IV. Across the road from the college are the *Botanic Gardens*, the oldest of their kind in England. The gateway contains figures of Charles I and Charles II.

The Vale of Aylesbury

WOODSTOCK

At the time when the great forests of the kingdom were set aside for the monarch to hunt in, a royal palace was built here by Henry I. It was here that Henry II kept his mistress Rosamund. The Black Prince was born here, and Mary Tudor had Elizabeth imprisoned in the palace for 11 months. James I came here for the hunting, but during the Civil War the palace was destoryed and left as a ruin. When the magnificent Blenheim Palace was built, the architect, Vanbrugh, wanted to retain the ruin as part of the landscape, but the Duchess of Marlborough insisted that it was demolished.

In 1704 John Churchill, Duke of Marlborough, was given the royal manor of Woodstock by Queen Anne in gratitude for his famous victory over the French and the Bavarians at Blenheim. Sir John Vanbrugh was commissioned to design Blenheim Palace in 1705, the enormous palace taking 17 years to build and costing £300,000. It was not finished until after the Duke's death. The grounds were laid out by Capability Brown, who created the artificial lake from the River Glyme.

An old custom, kept up every year on the anniversary of the battle, is for the duke to present to the monarch at Windsor a blue silk banner as the rent for the property. The house contains a wonderful collection of china, pictures and furnishings and in the chapel is the elaborate marble tomb of the first Duke and Duchess, Sarah, who was such a powerful figure at the court of Queen Anne. The enormous grounds are exquisitely landscaped with an artificial lake and water gardens, and contain a column, 134 feet high, in honour of the victor of Blenheim. The groups of trees around the column form the plan of the battle.

Perhaps the most famous son of the Churchill family was Winston, grandson of the 7th Duke. He was born at Blenheim in 1874, and spent most of his school holidays here. He also spent his honeymoon here, and when he died in 1965 he was buried in Bladon churchyard, in the south eastern part of the grounds, and within sight of the palace.

AYLESBURY

Aylesbury is a charming town, with a tree-lined market place, overlooked by a Victorian clock tower, and possessing many narrow cobbled streets preserving much of the character of medieval England. Its history goes back to well before the 6th century, but its royal associations began in 921 when Edward the Elder was surprised by the Danes and in the ensuing conflict lost many of his men.

Aylesbury's greatest days, however, were undoubtedly during the Civil War. One of the three bronze statues in the market place is of John Hampden, the man responsible for sparking off the troubles which forced Charles I to war.

When the Civil War broke out, Aylesbury was a centre of unrest, with its inhabitants strongly in opposition to the crown. On 1st November 1642, Prince Rupert passed by the town on his way to London, and decided to make a surprise attack. The Battle of Aylesbury followed. Sir William Balfour, however, quickly came to the rescue of the town bringing with him 1500 men, and soon forced Prince Rupert to flee to Oxford.

In a field near Holman Bridge, the alleged site of the battle, 200 skeletons

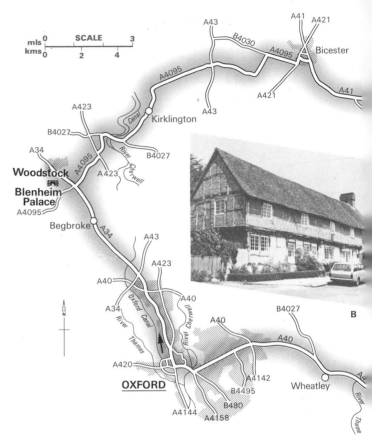

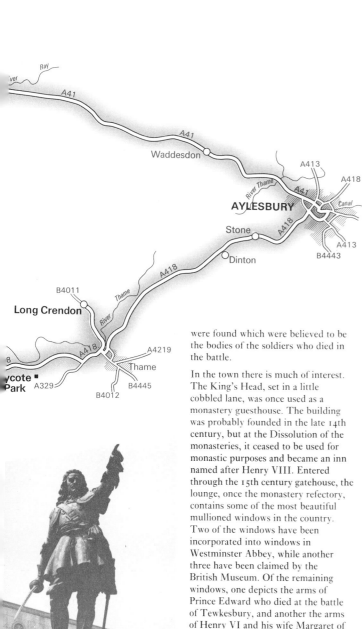

In a corner of the lounge stands an old chair, reputed to be the chair which Cromwell used when he was staying at the inn in 1651.

The museum in Church Street contains a great deal of material related to the history of the county, as well as a bed and confessional chair, relics of Louis XVIII's stay in exile at Hartwell House nearby.

RYCOTE PARK

Three miles south west of Thame is Rycote Park, where a 15th century chapel, a fragmented turret and some outbuildings are all that remain of a magnificent mansion which once stood within these grounds. The chapel is rich in Jacobean woodwork with a beautifully carved pulpit, altar rail and musicians' gallery as well as a royal pew with a domed canopy which was constructed during the 17th century for Charles I who often came to worship here.

In the north west corner of the grounds, set by a lake and surrounded by trees, are the remains of the manor house which was probably built during the early part of the 16th century by Henry VIII's treasurer, Sir John Heron. In 1542 the house passed to Sir John Williams, later Lord Williams, and it was during this period that Princess Elizabeth, guarded by Sir

Henry Bedingfield, was brought here and imprisoned, en route for Woodstock. Elizabeth always referred to Bedingfield as her gaoler, but she came to have great respect for Lord Williams, because of the kindness he showed her during the period she was held captive. In later years, after she had come to the throne, she twice came to visit Lord Williams. The house was destroyed by fire in 1745.

LONG CRENDON

The village of Long Crendon was once a centre for lacemaking and is rich in 16th and 17th century timbered houses. The most important building in the village is the 15th century Catherine's Court House, given by Henry VIII to Catherine of Aragon. The building is long and low, and its brick and timbered front with five bays, four of which make up one long room, hangs over the whitewashed ground floor. Inside the house, which was one of the first to be acquired by the National Trust, there are many exposed beams.

were found which were believed to be the bodies of the soldiers who died in the battle.

In the town there is much of interest. The King's Head, set in a little cobbled lane, was once used as a monastery guesthouse. The building was probably founded in the late 14th century, but at the Dissolution of the monasteries, it ceased to be used for monastic purposes and became an inn named after Henry VIII. Entered through the 15th century gatehouse, the lounge, once the monastery refectory, contains some of the most beautiful mullioned windows in the country. Two of the windows have been incorporated into windows in Westminster Abbey, while another three have been claimed by the British Museum. Of the remaining windows, one depicts the arms of Prince Edward who died at the battle of Tewkesbury, and another the arms of Henry VI and his wife Margaret of Anjou, probably designed to commemorate their marriage in 1445.

A Blenheim Palace, one of the largest mansions in England
B The Court House, Long Crendon, given to Catherine of Aragon
C Statue of John Hampden in Aylesbury. He was an opponent of Charles I
D Sir John Vanbrugh's architecture at Blenheim Palace, home of the Duke of Marlborough

Vanished Palaces

Carlton House

Carlton House, the lavish London home of George IV when Prince of Wales, used to stand where Carlton House Terrace stands today. He was given the house in 1783, and immediately spent a fortune on altering and enlarging it. When the Prince Regent became King, he moved to Buckingham House, and in 1826 Carlton House was demolished.

Holland House

All that survives of this great 17th century house is the east wing; the remainder was destroyed by incendiary bombs in 1941. It was the centre of the sparkling literary and political world of the Whigs, and for a time, William and Mary lived here.

Nonsuch Palace

Henry VIII built this splendid mansion, which had turrets, minarets, clocks, curious chimneys and was more ornate than any other palace of the time. Charles II eventually gave it to his mistress, Barbara Villiers, but she pulled it down. Finds from the excavations are exhibited in the Bourne Hall Cultural Centre, Spring Street, Ewell.

Oatlands, Weybridge

Never a very large palace, the former house at Oatlands was acquired by Henry VIII in 1537 and converted at some expense. Elizabeth I used the house occasionally, and James I settled the house on Anne of Denmark. Charles I's queen, Henrietta Maria, used the house at times until the Civil War, and returned to it afterwards.

Richmond Palace

The Palace of Shene, the forerunner of Richmond Palace, was first occupied by Henry I in 1125, and was the scene of Edward III's death in 1377. Richard II demolished it but it was rebuilt by Henry V and his successors. It was destroyed by fire in 1498 while Henry VII and his family were staying here. Henry VII

The sumptuous interior of Carlton House, once the home of George IV as Prince of Wales

Nonsuch Palace in 1568, one of the most ornate houses ever built in England

built a new and magnificent palace here, changing its name to Richmond. Elizabeth I found it her favourite residence and eventually died here. It then became more and more dilapidated and crumbled away leaving only the lodge. The old Gateway and an 18th century reconstruction of the Wardrobe survive.

Somerset House

The present building of Somerset House stands on the site of a once-splendid royal palace. It was built by Lord Protector Somerset, and was forfeited to the crown upon his execution in 1552. Elizabeth I lived here for a while during Mary I's reign, but did not use the house much when she became Queen. In James I's reign the palace came to life again; he gave it to Anne of Denmark and renamed it Denmark House. It subsequently passed to Charles I's queen, Henrietta Maria. After she left it, the palace was closed for the next sixteen years until it was used for the lying in state of Oliver Cromwell in 1658. After the Civil War ended, Henrietta Maria started re-building the palace into a superb waterside palazza, but in George III's reign it was demolished.

Theobalds

This manor house at Waltham Cross has completely disappeared, and the present mansion, Old Palace House, was built in 1768. The original house was acquired by Henry Cecil in 1564, and he spent an enormous sum on enlarging it. It eventually comprised two large courts with a Great Gallery and elaborate gardens, and became one of the most ambitious architectural developments of Elizabeth's reign. During the Civil War it fell into considerable disrepair, and when Charles II came to the throne, it was sold. Nothing remains of the palace now, although the park gateway is the original archway from Temple Bar in the City.

Westminster Palace

This was the premier royal palace from the reign of Edward the Confessor until Henry VIII. William II built Westminster Hall and Henry IV was especially fond of the palace, building the Painted Chamber. In 1512 nearly

The medieval palace at Westminster, of which very little now remains

all of it was destroyed by fire, and it was never rebuilt as a royal residence, although Parliament still met in Westminster Hall. Another fire in 1834 burned the whole palace to the ground, except for Westminster Hall, the Jewel Tower, the chapel crypt and part of the cloisters, and the new House of Commons was built on the site.

Whitehall Palace

Originally York Place, the home of the Archbishop of York, it was seized by Henry VIII from Wolsey when he fell from favour. Henry rebuilt much of the old house and it became the sovereign's principal residence for the next 150 years. Henry VIII died here, and Elizabeth, James I and Charles I all conducted great festivities here. Charles I was executed in 1649 in front of the Banqueting Hall. Oliver Cromwell died here in 1658. In 1698, the palace was accidentally burned to the ground. The Banqueting House is the chief relic of the palace. The weathercock at the north end was placed there by James II to show whether the wind was favourable to William of Orange.

Woodstock

The royal palace of Woodstock has completely disappeared, but was once a favourite hunting lodge and palace. It was built by Henry I and was much frequented by him and by Henry II. "Fair Rosamund", the mistress of Henry II, lived here in seclusion, away from his jealous queen, and is supposed to have been murdered here by her. Edward, the Black Prince, son of Edward III, was born here. Elizabeth I, while a princess, was confined here by her half-sister, Mary, in 1554. The palace later fell into disrepair, and Queen Anne gave it to the Duke of Marlborough when he was given Blenheim. Vanbrugh, the architect of Blenheim Palace, wanted to keep the ruin as part of the landscape of the grounds, but Sarah, the Duchess, insisted that it should be destroyed.

WORCESTER

Worcester was fortified in the late 9th century as part of a defensive scheme by Ethelfleda, "The Lady of Mercia", daughter of Alfred the Great, and her husband Ethelred, Duke of Mercia. It was the first of around thirty towns to be treated by them in this way, and an earthen wall and possibly a wooden palisade were erected.

In the 12th century Worcester figured in the struggle between Stephen and Matilda, daughter of Henry I, who were rival claimants for the throne of England. In 1139, Stephen, on a state visit to Worcester, offered his royal ring at the cathedral's high altar. The ring was restored to him on the next day by the monks, who were then praised by the King for their devotion to him. In 1140 Matilda landed in England to press her claim to the throne. Towards the end of the year she attacked the city, which was held by the recently created Earl of Worcester, Waleran de Beaumont, and much of it was burnt to the ground. Ten years later the city suffered a similar fate, but this time at the hands of King Stephen. The Earl had changed his allegiance and was this time defending the city for Matilda. Stephen attacked and the city was reduced to ashes for a second time.

Henry II, who succeeded Stephen, undertook a second crowning at Worcester. Although Henry was Matilda's son, Stephen had agreed to make him his heir after the death of his own son. The first royal council to be held at Worcester took place during Henry II's reign, at Easter in 1158.

The King's homage
King John, who came to the throne in 1199, was particularly fond of Worcester. He is known to have paid eleven visits to the city during the course of his reign, the first being

The Choir of Worcester Cathedral, looking east towards the Lady Chapel. It is a fine example of Early English architecture, and was built between 1220 and 1260

Easter 1200. In 1207 he arranged for the monks' cloister to be rebuilt, and paid homage at the shrine of St Wulstan, a former Bishop of Worcester, who had been canonised. John's final wish was to be buried in Worcester Cathedral between the shrines of St Oswald and St Wulstan, and so in 1216, his body was brought here for burial. An important celebration marked the occasion of the re-dedication of the cathedral choir in 1218, which was attended by the young King Henry III, only eleven years old at that time, when St Wulstan's body was solemnly placed in a new shrine.

The barons' revolt against Henry III began in 1263 with the taking of Worcester, and Henry together with his son, the future Edward I, were held prisoner here on 13th December of the following year. In 1265, following his escape from Hereford, Prince Edward made Worcester the base from which he carried out his expedition to Kenilworth, where he seized the banners of Simon de Montfort's son, and from where also he marched to Evesham for the final battle of that war. Edward was again to use Worcester as his headquarters later in his life. From here he conducted his operations against the Welsh under the leadership of Llywelyn the Last, grandson of Llywelyn the Great, and Prince of Wales.

The last known royal council to be held at Worcester was under Edward I towards the end of 1294, when he paid homage at the tomb of his grandfather, King John. He again visited the city the following summer to offer thanksgiving at the shrines of St Wulstan and St Oswald for his prayers of deliverance from a further Welsh revolt being answered. The last important royal ceremony to take place in Worcester Cathedral was the funeral of the young Prince Arthur, Henry VII's eldest son, who died in 1502 at the age of 16. Prince Arthur's Chantry was erected by his father in 1504, in memory of his son, on the south side of the chancel. It is the last great work of Perpendicular Gothic carving prior to the Reformation.

Elizabeth I visited Worcester on one of her royal progresses in 1575. She is claimed to have addressed the people of the town from the gallery of Trinity House, which has since been known locally as Queen Elizabeth's House.

Royalist stronghold
It was for its adherance to the King's cause in the Civil War that Worcester earned its memorable motto 'Civitas in Bello et Pace Fidelis'—'The faithful city in war and in peace'. One of the first battles of the Civil War took place near Worcester. It was known as the Battle of Powick Bridge and took place on

23rd September 1642. It was little more than a skirmish, but was of great importance to the early fortunes of the royalist cause (see also Shrewsbury on page 126). Apart from a short time following this battle the city was held throughout the first Civil War for the royalists. Charles I spent a week here in June 1644 to rally support and gather supplies. In 1646, at the end of the first Civil War, Worcester endured a two months' siege. It finally surrendered on 22nd July, the last city defending the royalist cause to do so.

Charles II followed his proclamation as King at Scone on 1st January 1651 by moving south with an army of Scots later in that year. He made his stand at Worcester, where he was also proclaimed King, this time of Great Britain, Ireland and France. Charles is supposed to have set up his headquarters at Rowland Berkeley's house, afterwards known as King Charles' House. Over the doorway are inscribed the words 'Love God, Honor ye King'.

Although Charles had gained the support of Worcester and turned out the small parliamentarian garrison with comparative ease, he failed to recruit the help he had needed from the surrounding region. When Cromwell's force of 30,000 arrived, the King could muster an army of only 16,000 with which to oppose him. Cromwell's plans to encircle Worcester were carefully executed, and were aided by a beam of the destroyed bridge at Upton that had been left across the Severn. At other points Cromwell built bridges of boats across the rivers Teme and Severn. Charles watched most of the operations from the cathedral tower, but ventured out in the early stages to encourage his troops against the forces advancing from the west. But his reserve cavalry failed to charge at the crucial moment and the parliamentarians' advance on the city went unchecked. Charles, who had returned to the safety of the cathedral tower, saw that Cromwell's central forces were weakened, and also saw this as his last chance for victory. He joined the battle behind the Duke of Hamilton,

King Charles' House, Worcester where King Charles II took refuge after his defeat at the Battle of Worcester

The tomb of King John in Worcester Cathedral, the effigy being of Purbeck marble. It is the oldest royal effigy in England

but Cromwell himself arrived on the scene with more reinforcements and turned his army's retreat to a counter-attack. Charles' forces were thrown back towards the city, and the Duke of Hamilton was mortally wounded. Charles retreated to Berkeley's house and eventually escaped through the back doorway.

From this point onwards in history, Worcester's importance to the fortunes of the royal family fades. Several monarchs, however, have visited the city since that time. James II came in 1689 but when he went to visit a new Roman Catholic chapel the Mayor and Corporation, who disapproved of his adherence to the Catholic faith, refused to accompany him. George III attended the Three Choirs Festival here in 1788, and portraits at the Guildhall of the King and his queen commemorate this. The entrance to the Guildhall is flanked by statues of Charles I and Charles II and above is a statue of Queen Anne. Queen Elizabeth II paid a visit on 23rd–24th April 1957.

Rivers and Hills

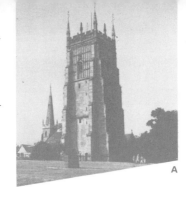

A

EVESHAM

The battle of Evesham, which took place on 4th August 1265, ended the barons' revolt. Prince Edward, Henry III's son, had returned to Worcester from a partially successful expedition to Kenilworth against Simon de Montfort's son, to learn that de Montfort himself had slipped past him and was marching towards Evesham. Edward immediately began a pursuit. After the opposing forces had come into contact the battle was delayed by a violent thunderstorm. When, after midday, the first blows were struck, the Prince had skilfully divided his force into two. De Montfort's forces were trapped by these two arms of men on the one side and by the River Avon on the other, with the result that several thousands perished.

Henry III, de Montfort's prisoner, had been dressed in an ordinary suit of armour so that he would not be recognised, and only escaped death at the hands of his son's forces by crying out that he was the King. De Montfort was killed during the battle and his body, minus head and hands, was buried in the abbey at Evesham. An obelisk in the gardens of the abbey ruins commemorates the battle, and a plaque the burial place of Simon de Montfort.

WINCHCOMBE

During the 8th and 9th centuries, there was a royal residence here, King Offa of Mercia making it one of his most important centres and founding a nunnery.

Sudeley Castle, or Royal Sudeley as it is known, lies less than a mile to the south of Winchcombe. It became the last home of Catherine Parr in 1547 when, as the widow of Henry VIII, she married her former sweetheart Lord Seymour. She died the following year, however, and is buried in the castle chapel. Catherine of Aragon, Henry VIII's first wife, also stayed here, and an altar cloth in Winchcombe church is said to be largely her work. During the Civil War the castle fell into parliamentary hands and Catherine Parr's tomb was destroyed. The present canopied tomb was the work of Sir Gilbert Scott in the 19th century.

CHELTENHAM

Cheltenham became a fashionable place for society following the visit of George III with his family, Queen Charlotte and the three princesses in 1788. They stayed at Bayshill Lodge, the home of Lord Faulconberg, for five weeks. The royal visit was considered a great success, although the spa waters failed to cure the King's complaint.

TEWKESBURY

After Henry VI had been imprisoned in the Tower by Edward IV, Henry's wife, Margaret of Anjou, and their son Edward, rightful heir to the throne, continued the struggle which led to the battle of Tewkesbury on 4th May 1471. The Queen's forces, tired from their march from Bristol, were overwhelmed by those of Edward IV, and the ferocity of the battle is recalled today by the name of the battlefield: Bloody Meadow. Following the battle the young Prince Edward was brutally murdered. His body was buried in Tewkesbury Abbey and a plaque recalls the traditional place of his burial.

GLOUCESTER

Gloucester first achieved prominence under the Saxons. Ethelfleda, 'The

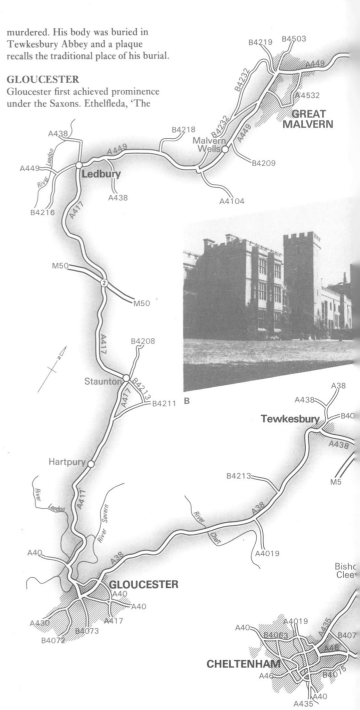

B

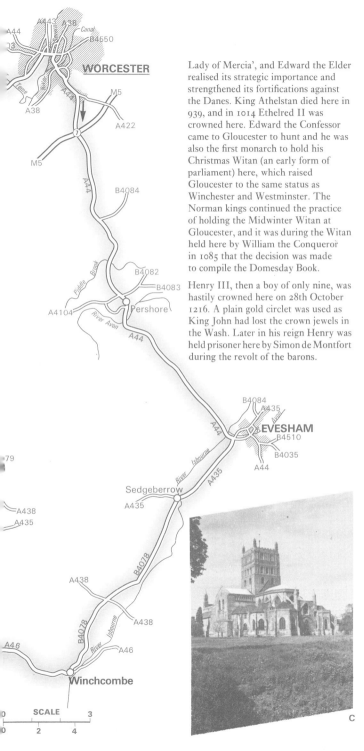

WORCESTER

Lady of Mercia', and Edward the Elder realised its strategic importance and strengthened its fortifications against the Danes. King Athelstan died here in 939, and in 1014 Ethelred II was crowned here. Edward the Confessor came to Gloucester to hunt and he was also the first monarch to hold his Christmas Witan (an early form of parliament) here, which raised Gloucester to the same status as Winchester and Westminster. The Norman kings continued the practice of holding the Midwinter Witan at Gloucester, and it was during the Witan held here by William the Conqueror in 1085 that the decision was made to compile the Domesday Book.

Henry III, then a boy of only nine, was hastily crowned here on 28th October 1216. A plain gold circlet was used as King John had lost the crown jewels in the Wash. Later in his reign Henry was held prisoner here by Simon de Montfort during the revolt of the barons.

Edward II was buried at Gloucester after his brutal murder at Berkeley Castle. In later years the martyr's tomb was venerated, and one of the pilgrims was Henry V. Also in the cathedral is the tomb of William the Conqueror's eldest son, Robert, Duke of Normandy.

In the first Civil War Gloucester proved to be the turning point in the fortunes of the King. Charles I, after his victory at Bristol in 1643, decided to secure his hold on the west by taking Gloucester. On 10th August he made camp outside the city and demanded the city's allegiance. The garrison, although only numbering about 1,500 replied defiantly and retreated inside the city walls. During the ensuing siege, which lasted for about a month, Gloucester was reduced to the point of starvation. Eventually the town was relieved by the arrival of the Earl of Essex.

LEDBURY

A Civil War skirmish took place here in April 1645, when Prince Rupert, marching from Hereford to Shrewsbury, turned to make a surprise attack on a force of 1,000 men under the command of General Massey, who had taken the town. The battle resulted in a royalist victory. Prince Rupert escaped unhurt, although, according to one

account, five bullets pierced his clothes and struck his armour and he fought hand to hand with General Massey.

GREAT MALVERN

The importance of this spa was greatly increased by the visit in 1830 of the eleven-year old Princess Victoria with her mother, the Duchess of Kent. The Priory Church contains a window in its north aisle in honour of Queen Victoria's Jubilee. It depicts the news of her accession being delivered to her, her coronation, and Jubilee service. Another window situated in the North transept portrays Prince Arthur, eldest son of Henry VII.

Malvern Chase was formerly a royal forest. It was taken into royal ownership at the instigation of Matilda, the Queen of William the Conqueror, as part of her revenge against Brictric Meawe, a Saxon lord and holder of the forest who had once rejected her affections. Brictric himself was seized and died a prisoner at Winchester. The forest then remained a favourite hunting ground, particularly of King John, until the time of Edward I when he gave it as part of his daughter's dowry to Gilbert de Clare. It again passed into the ownership of the king after the death in battle of Richard, Earl of Warwick, who had become its owner by marriage. From this time until the time of Charles I the royal forest was gradually reduced, either through royal gift or the monarch's need to raise funds.

A The Perpendicular bell tower of Evesham Abbey, with the tomb of Simon de Montfort in the foreground
B Sudeley Castle, associated with two of Henry VIII's wives
C The magnificent Abbey Church at Tewkesbury
D The effigy of King Edward II above his tomb in Gloucester Cathedral

C   D

COMPTON WYNYATES

Compton Wynyates has often been described as the perfect picture book Tudor mansion. It is the home of the Marquess of Northampton and has been in the same family, by the direct male line of the Comptons, since the 13th century. The house is situated in a hollow, which would suggest that it was built in peaceful times, even the battlements being added at a later date. Built on the site of an earlier dwelling, the present house was begun in the 15th century by Edmund Compton, using brick, an expensive building material at the time, but salvaged from the ruins of Fulbrook Castle, near Warwick.

Edmund's son, William, was only eleven years old when his father died and he was placed under the protection of the King. Henry VII made him a page to the two year old Prince Henry who was to become the much-married Henry VIII. Henry and William became great friends as they grew up together and when Henry became King he showered William with titles and property, thus sealing the good fortunes of the Compton family. For his part, William served his ruler well, particularly at the Battle of Tournai in France in 1512 for which he was made a Knight of the Garter.

An intricate design
Despite its peaceful setting the house at Compton Wynyates reflects the uncertainty of Tudor times, with its secret passages, staircases and hiding places. Apart from the usual intrigues which surrounded any monarch and his courtiers, there were the religious problems following Henry's break with Rome, Mary's return to Catholicism, and Elizabeth's reversion, once again, to the Protestant doctrine. Many people were martyred for their beliefs, and many more were cruelly persecuted. Others preferred to conform outwardly to preserve their freedom, while keeping priests secretly in their homes. The Priest's Room at Compton Wynyates is a fine example of the strategems resorted to. It has three exits, two of them leading to roomy hiding places, and the third into a council chamber with a number of different exits.

The irregular design of the house was, in fact, carefully planned by its builder, as was the use of brick in an area which normally used stone. The four wings were built round a quadrangle, facing south west in a hollow. That in itself was unusual, for it was generally thought at the time that a house should face east and west. A striking feature of the house is its exotically twisted chimneys which rise irregularly above the battlements. In its original state, the house had two moats, the outer one having a drawbridge and a portcullis. Its walls were four feet thick, but its many windows show that it was never intended to be a fortress.

Tudor days
The house contains much evidence of Henry VIII's frequent visits, sometimes accompanied

The appearance of the house at Compton Wynyates has a pleasing irregularity, softened by the use of red brick

The entrance porch to Compton Wynyates carries the Royal Coat of Arms of Henry VIII, a frequent visitor to the house

by his first wife, Catherine of Aragon. The royal coat of arms carved above the entrance porch is rather weather-beaten, but the crown supported by a greyhound and a dragon can be clearly seen. The inscription reads "Dom Rex Henricus Octav", My Lord King Henry the Eighth. Also on the exterior walls are the Arms of Catherine of Aragon, and the Tudor badge. Henry VIII's Bedroom, inside the house, with its ornately carved four poster bed, displays his arms once again, together with those of Catherine of Aragon, in the windows. The ceiling, dating from around 1630, also includes his royal monogram, as well as those of Elizabeth I, James I and Charles I. The portrait of Henry in the room is a copy of one by Holbein.

During Elizabeth's reign, William's grandson, Henry, was also in favour. The Queen visited the house in August 1572, and greatly enjoyed the few days she spent here. Her chief minister, Lord Burghley, wrote, "Surely the entertainment is very great".

Seventeen years later, near the end of Elizabeth's reign, Henry's son, William, inherited the title. He wanted to marry the daughter of Sir John Spencer, Lord Mayor of London, but her father did not think the boy good enough. Undeterred, William smuggled the girl out of the house in a baker's basket, but her father, in his anger, disinherited her. The Queen intervened to calm Sir John, and eventually the families were re-united.

Civil War Vandalism

Spencer, their son, was also loyal to the King, becoming Master of the Robes to Charles I. At the outbreak of Civil War, he and his sons fought bravely for the royalist cause, and Compton Wynyates became a centre for wounded soldiers. Spencer was killed during the war, at the Battle of Hopton Heath. In 1644, the house was captured by Parliament, and used to billet troops. Part of the south wing of the house is still known as 'The Barracks'.

The family tried to recapture the house, with the aid of royalist troops, but, in spite of heavy fighting, were unsuccessful. They did eventually get the house back, however, on payment of a £20,000 fine and a promise to fill in the moat and destroy the battlements. During the parliamentary occupation of the house all the deer in the park were killed, the church was destroyed and all the family monuments were thrown into the moat.

Spencer's sixth son, Henry, became Bishop of London. He signed the invitation to William of Orange to come and assume the English throne; he also rode before William and Mary when they went to Oxford, and he subsequently crowned them.

Saved from destruction

Although the house had been preserved intact through the ravages of war, it was nearly demolished during the 18th century. An extra wing had been added on the east side of the house. John Compton, Lord Northampton, however, was a heavy gambler, and had also been recklessly extravagant in a parliamentary election in Northampton in 1768. He sold the contents of the house to pay for his debts, went abroad, and ordered that the house be pulled down. Fortunately for posterity, his agent, John Berrill, disregarded his instructions, merely bricking up the windows because of window tax.

The family returned in 1835, to find the house in reasonable repair. They altered the east front and re-modelled the staircase in Gothic style. Subsequent marquesses have continued to improve and furnish the house to bring it to its present superb condition.

Inside the house, the Big Hall with its minstrels' gallery contains a carved representation of the Battle of Tournai. The original timbered ceiling dates from the time of Henry VII. The Dining Room is full of portraits of the illustrious members of the Compton family, as well as an illuminated document which is a royal grant of arms from 1512. Henry VIII's Bedroom and the Priest's Room are of great interest, and the Chapel contains a reminder of the times of the Civil War, the broken glass from the original stained glass window. One panel in the Chapel is carved with a row of seven crowned kings. Services in the Chapel could be watched from the Chapel Drawing Room, through open mullions.

Compton Church was completely destroyed during the Civil War, and was rebuilt in 1665. The family memorials were recovered from the moat, where the parliamentarian soldiers had thrown them, and are on display in a somewhat mutilated condition. The banner and helmet used to hang in St George's Chapel, Windsor, when the 5th Marquess was a Knight of the Garter. On the top of the hill to the south of the house stands Compton Pike, one of a country-wide network of beacons to warn of the landing of the Spaniards at the time of the Armada.

The Cockpit of England

EDGEHILL

This peaceful hill in the Cotswolds was the scene of the first battle of the Civil War, which turned out to be no victory for either side. Following the battle, a fateful decision by Charles I led to a prolonging of the war, resulting in his losing his crown and his life.

Charles, having raised his standard at Nottingham at the start of the war, had moved to Chester, collecting troops. His cavalry commander, the brilliant Prince Rupert of the Rhine, had gone on to Worcester, where he had defeated a small parliamentary force. The roundhead commander, the inexperienced Earl of Essex, was retreating from Worcester, and Charles blocked him at Edgehill.

The two sides were drawn up on the morning of 23rd October 1642, the royalists looking down on the parliamentary forces in the valley. There had been no warfare in England for the past 150 years, and both sides were inexperienced. The first move

A

B

was made by the royalists who started an hour-long burst of cannon fire. This was followed by a charge led by Prince Rupert, which completely dispersed the enemy horsemen. Joined by the reserve cavalry, Prince Rupert chased the stragglers down the road to Warwick. Without his cavalry, the battle in the centre of the field turned against the King, and he was on the point of retreating when the cavalry returned. They re-took the royal standard which had been captured, and both sides retired exhausted.

Each side lost about 2,500 men, and each side claimed a victory. The King had the advantage, however, that the road to London lay open before him. His folly was that he did not press this advantage, but retired to Oxford.

The battlefield is private property, but is marked by a small monument beside the B4451. Edgehill Tower Inn affords a good view of the battlefield.

WROXTON

An Augustinian Priory once existed on the site of Wroxton Abbey and some of the foundations of the original building have been excavated in the grounds. Sir William Pope built the abbey and once entertained King James I there.

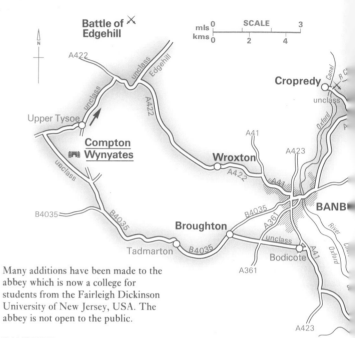

Many additions have been made to the abbey which is now a college for students from the Fairleigh Dickinson University of New Jersey, USA. The abbey is not open to the public.

BANBURY

The famous Banbury Cross was erected in 1859 to commemorate the marriage of Queen Victoria to Prince Albert. In 1914, carved figures of Queen Victoria, Edward VII and George V were added. Banbury town hall houses paintings of Prince Rupert, and the Young Pretender, Prince Charles Edward Stuart.

CROPREDY

Over 18 months after the Battle of Edgehill, Charles was again involved in a battle with Parliament in this area. His headquarters were still in Oxford, but his forces were depleted due to action in the West Country. He had had to withdraw his troops from Abingdon, and this was soon captured by Parliament. Before long, the roundheads were able to surround Oxford, and Charles decided to leave the city. He was pursued by the parliamentary commanders Essex and Waller, but after some days, Essex went off to relieve Lyme, leaving Waller to attack the King. Charles then decided to return to Oxford. He moved first to Woodstock, then to Buckingham and Banbury, and was marching north towards Daventry, with Waller on the other side of the River Cherwell. Charles sent a force ahead to hold the bridge at Cropredy, and Waller, seeing a gap in the enemy forces, attacked. He was out-manoeuvred by the King, however, and his forces were captured at Cropredy Bridge. This royalist victory ensured that Oxford was safe, and Charles shortly pursued Essex into the West Country. The battle is commemorated by a small monument on the bridge.

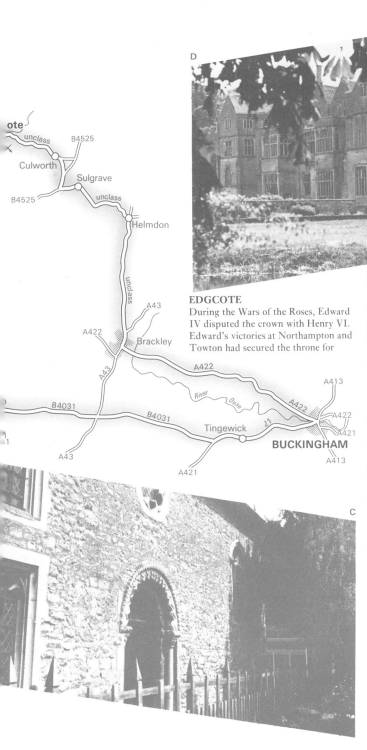

EDGCOTE

During the Wars of the Roses, Edward IV disputed the crown with Henry VI. Edward's victories at Northampton and Towton had secured the throne for him, but he depended heavily on the Earl of Warwick, the "Kingmaker". Edward forfeited that assistance when he announced that his daughter was to marry Charles of Burgundy, jeopardising England's relationship with France. Warwick now turned against the King. He allied himself with a Yorkshire rebellion led by Robin of Redesdale, and ordered him to stop the King, then at Nottingham, from reaching London. Edward called for reinforcements from the Earl of Pembroke. On their way to intercept the men of Robin of Redesdale, Pembroke's men were surprised one morning by the rebel army who occupied three hills around their position. At a disadvantage, they tried to take each hill in turn, but eventually were beaten back. Then, just when Pembroke seemed to be gaining the upper hand, a surprise attack by another of Warwick's forces from behind completely overwhelmed them, and Pembroke was killed. This temporarily gave the Lancastrians the upper hand in the war.

BUCKINGHAM

In the 9th century, Alfred the Great divided the country into shires and made Buckingham the county town of Buckinghamshire. With recent development, however, Aylesbury has taken over as the administrative centre. In August 1578 Queen Elizabeth I visited the town. There are some very old buildings, notably Castle House where Catherine of Aragon was entertained in 1514. In the same house Charles I presided over a council of war in 1644, at the height of the Civil War. Later, after the siege of Hillesdon House, Oliver Cromwell directed operations from the house opposite. Down the hill, close to the market place, is the oldest building in Buckingham. The little Norman chantry became a classroom of the school which Edward VI founded, and is now the property of the National Trust.

BROUGHTON

The medieval castle at Broughton was built in 1306. It has remained in the hands of its present owners, the Saye and Sele family for 500 years. Its most famous ancestor was William Fiennes, who was an ally of John Hampden's in his opposition to King Charles I's levy of Ship Money. When the Civil War broke out, he was arrested by the King for refusing to sign an oath of loyalty. He and his sons fought at the Battle of Edgehill in 1642, and a sword used in this battle is on display in the castle. After the battle, the castle was occupied by Prince Rupert and his troops for a while.

At the Restoration, Charles II made William Fiennes Lord Privy Seal, and a Lord Privy Seal bag can be seen in the castle. Also on view is a painting of Charles II returning to England in 1660.

A The battlefield at Edgcote
B The Banbury Cross, erected in 1859 in place of the original which was destroyed in 1602
C The Norman doorway of the Chantry House in Buckingham
D Broughton Castle, which was much involved in the Civil War

WARWICK

This ancient county town of Warwickshire was founded in AD 914 by Ethelfleda, the daughter of King Alfred the Great. Also known as the "Lady of Mercia", she was entrusted with the fortification of the north west midlands by her brother King Edward the Elder. The Danes had invaded much of the eastern part of the country and the King and his sister made every effort to prevent any extension of the Danish boundaries, eventually driving them back and retrieving some of their territories. Ethelfleda is said to have constructed the mound which carries her name and stands in the grounds of Warwick Castle.

The Norman era left its mark on Warwick when William the Conqueror ordered that a new castle be built on the site of the Saxon fortifications. He had also decided that this was a wise location for the development of defences. The first Earl of Warwick, Henry de Newburgh, was given the title by King William Rufus, the Conqueror's son. Later the title passed to the Beauchamp family. A son of this family, Richard Beauchamp, served Henry V in France, and was visited later by the King at Warwick. His tomb, along with those of many other Earls of Warwick, can be seen in St. Mary's Church.

The Kingmaker

On the death of the last of the Beauchamp line, the title passed to the husband of Anne Beauchamp. Perhaps the most famous of all the Earls of Warwick, Richard Neville, was better known as "The Kingmaker". In a small way he was a king himself, being given the titles of Duke of Warwick and King of the Isle of Wight by Henry VI. The Duke later became a friend and ally of the Yorkist King Edward IV, but he was ill-rewarded by the petulant King for his service. On one occasion the King had grossly maligned Warwick and acted deliberately against his advice, so, seeking

Warwick Castle still retains most of its original 14th century walls, towers and hall. It has seen very little action, coming under fire for only three days during the Civil War

The River Avon gave Warwick a good defensive position, and its castle has been continuously inhabited up to the present day. It contains a superb collection of art treasures

revenge, the Duke secretly married his daughter to the King's brother, the Duke of Clarence. This made Clarence potentially more wealthy than the King, who at that time had no heir other than his brother. At the same time, Warwick initiated a Lancastrian uprising, drawing the King into battle, and after the Yorkist defeat, Edward was taken to Warwick Castle. He was imprisoned there until he gave assurances to the Duke that he would in future act in a more responsible manner. On the death of Richard Neville at the Battle of Barnet the title reverted back to an Earldom which was inherited by his son-in-law, the Duke of Clarence. He met an unfortunate end by drowning in a vat of wine and the estate passed to Richard of Gloucester who later became King Richard III.

King Richard began to build a fort at the castle which was never completed, but the Bear Tower which exists today was a part of its construction and is said to have contained a bear pit. The Duke of Clarence had a son who should have inherited the estate, but he was imprisoned by Richard and later by Henry VII, eventually being executed on fabricated evidence. For sixty years there was no Earl of Warwick until Henry VIII bestowed the title on the unworthy John Dudley who later tried to prevent Henry's eldest daughter, Mary, from becoming Queen.

Lady Jane Grey

There was a reluctance in Tudor times to accept a woman on the throne of England, so when the sickly boy King, Edward VI seemed likely to die, Dudley wanted him to make "the heirs male of Lady Jane Grey" the next in line, rather than Edward's sister, Mary. Lady Jane was Dudley's daughter-in-law and to press his case he stressed the point that Mary was a devout Catholic and would alienate the French. The Protestant King was persuaded by Dudley's forceful personality, but it became apparent that the King would die before Lady Jane could produce any male heir. Dudley had the wording of Edward's order changed to read "Lady Jane *and* her heirs male", which, of course, invalidated the objection to a female heir to the throne. For his inconsistency and forgery Dudley was executed along with the unfortunate Lady Jane Grey by Queen Mary. His son, Ambrose, was given back the title by Queen Elizabeth, who visited him at Warwick Castle on her way to Kenilworth. In preparation for her visit Ambrose built a hunting lodge for the Queen in Castle Park. Despite his three marriages, Ambrose Dudley died without an heir and the title died with him for a while.

The castle, but not the title, was given by James I to Sir Fulke Greville who, at the same time, was made Baron Brooke of Beauchamp Court. It was he who transformed the building from a cold castle into a comfortable residence. He was stabbed to death by a servant who suspected that he had been omitted from the Baron's will, and the estate was inherited by Greville's cousin, Robert. During the Civil War Robert supported Cromwell, taking part in the Battle of Edgehill, and the castle was besieged by the royalists for a time. When Robert was killed at Lichfield, the castle was given to a supporter of the King who refurbished the State Apartments.

Castle treasures
There are many fine paintings in the castle, including a portrait of Henry VIII and Anne Boleyn by Holbein and another of Queen Elizabeth I in her coronation robes which can be seen in the Great Hall. The daughter of James I, Queen Elizabeth of Bohemia, is portrayed with her family, also in the Great Hall. In the Cedar Drawing Room is Van Dyck's portrait of Charles I. This artist also began a portrait of Charles's wife, Henrietta Maria, but it was completed by Reynolds. There are portraits by Phillips and Richardson of some 18th century members of the royal family, and one of Prince Rupert, the nephew of Charles I.

Other relics of the past include a lead bust of Charles I and a travelling truck belonging to Queen Anne which can be seen in Queen Anne's bedroom along with the bed she once owned and a portrait of her painted by Kneller. There is a fine collection of armour including

the helmet worn by Oliver Cromwell and a death mask of him together with some pieces of armour belonging to Edward, the Black Prince.

Leycester Hospital
Another building of historical interest in Warwick is the Leycester Hospital, founded by Robert Dudley, Earl of Leicester. He acquired the buildings and then approached Queen Elizabeth, who, it is generally thought, was in love with the Earl. She granted a charter, with the details to be drawn up by Dudley, and he stated that the home should be open to a Master and twelve brethren who were retired soldiers. The ex-servicemen were to be selected from residents of Warwick, Stratford, Kenilworth, Wotton-under-Edge and Arlingham, the idea being to give an incentive

to the men of these towns to join the army. The hospital still has residents who have retired from the three services. They act as guides to visitors and, on special occasions, wear the Tudor style robes and hats with silver badges made in 1571. In the banqueting hall at the hospital visitors can see the chair in which James I sat when he was entertained in 1617 by Sir Fulke Greville.

Edward the Confessor founded Warwick School and a statue of that monarch can be seen in the grounds. It was founded for a second time by Henry VIII.

The tomb of Robert Dudley, Earl of Leicester in St Mary's Church, Warwick. He was a favourite of Queen Elizabeth I, and founded the Leycester Hospital in Warwick

The medieval Midlands

A

KENILWORTH

Even though it is now in ruins, the castle at Kenilworth is an impressive sight with its mellow red sandstone walls rising out of the surrounding green pastures. It was at one time the only lake castle in England, making it one of the most impregnable fortresses in the country. Originally given to Geoffrey de Clinton by Henry I, it became the residence of King John in 1212. During his four year stay at the castle King John constructed Lunns Tower and the Water Tower. When Henry III was on the throne, he gave the castle to his sister, Eleanor, transferring it to joint ownership on her marriage to Simon de Montfort. De Montfort led the barons in their rebellion against the King, defeating him at the Battle of Lewes and imprisoning his brother Richard and younger son, Edmund at Kenilworth.

The Earl of Lancaster imprisoned King Edward II at Kenilworth following the plotting of the Queen and her lover, Mortimer. Edward III's

fourth son, John of Gaunt, married the Earl's daughter and took up residence at Kenilworth where he built the magnificent banqueting hall. His son usurped the throne by murdering Richard II and became King Henry IV. He frequently lived at Kenilworth, as did his son, Henry V. Henry VIII had the castle extended, but no trace of this building work remains.

There are few large buildings in England that do not boast of a visit by Queen Elizabeth I, but none could have entertained her on such a grand scale as Kenilworth. She visited the man she loved, Robert Dudley, Earl of Leicester, on several occasions but the most splendid visit was in July 1575 when the Queen spent seventeen days merrymaking at the castle. The Earl spent around £60,000 on preparations and £1,000 a day on the festivities. Never again would the castle see such times. A royalist stronghold during the Civil War, it was taken by Cromwell after heavy cannon fire had broken through the walls. Cromwell gave the property to Colonel Hawkesworth who let it fall into ruins. Charles II gave the demolished castle to Lord Clarendon and it remained with his family until 1937 when Sir John Siddeley bought it and donated it to the nation.

COVENTRY

The city of Coventry has changed drastically since Lady Godiva made her memorable journey through the town. It is now a modern industrial city which had to be extensively re-built following one of the worst air raids of the Second World War. The old cathedral was ruined beyond repair and its empty shell now stands beside the modern cathedral. Edward, the Black Prince was Lord of the Manor of Cheylesmore in Coventry in the 14th century, and took considerable interest in the city. His effigy in stone can be seen in the Council House, together with those of

Edward the Confessor, Leofric the Earl of Mercia and his wife, the famous Lady Godiva.

Although St. Mary's Guildhall was also bombed, it has since been carefully restored and the historic treasures contained in the Great Hall were undamaged. The Black Prince is depicted in the stained glass of the east window, and his plume of

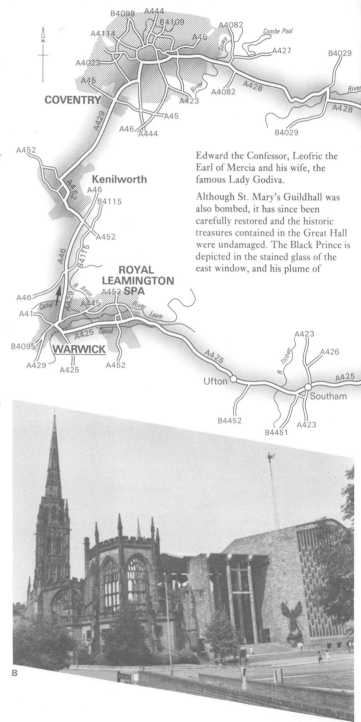

B

It was in this Great Hall that Henry VII held his council, first in 1487 and again in 1500 when he and his wife were entertained with great pomp and ceremony. They were made Brother and Sister of the Trinity Guild during this visit. Below the

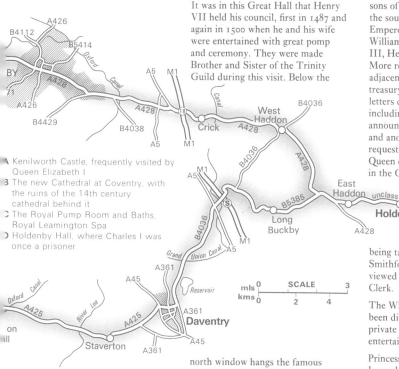

A Kenilworth Castle, frequently visited by Queen Elizabeth I

B The new Cathedral at Coventry, with the ruins of the 14th century cathedral behind it

C The Royal Pump Room and Baths, Royal Leamington Spa

D Holdenby Hall, where Charles I was once a prisoner

feathers is included in a tapestry. There is a panel which tells, in Latin, of the Prince's involvement with Coventry and of his victory over the King of Bohemia; a portrait of him hangs on the wall of the Hall.

north window hangs the famous Coventry Tapestry commemorating the visit of Henry VII and his Queen Elizabeth of York in 1500.

Also in the Great Hall are portraits of Edward II's wife, Richard II, and two

sons of Henry IV. The stained glass of the south window portrays the Emperor Constantine, King Arthur, William I, Richard I, Henry III, Edward III, Henry IV, Henry V and Henry VI. More royal portraits hang in the adjacent Mayoresses' Parlour. The treasury at the Guildhall contains letters connected with Queen Elizabeth including one from Anne Boleyn announcing the birth of her daughter, and another from Elizabeth herself requesting the safe keeping of Mary, Queen of Scots, who was imprisoned in the Guildhall Tower in 1569, after

being taken from the Black Bull Inn in Smithford Street. The letters can be viewed by arrangement with the Town Clerk.

The White Friars monastery, having been disbanded, was turned into a private mansion by John Hales who entertained Elizabeth I there in 1565.

Princess Elizabeth, daughter of James I, was brought to Coventry in 1605 to the safety of The Elizabethan House in Old Palace Yard. It was the time of the Gunpowder Plot, and it was thought that the conspirators would try to seize Elizabeth and put her on the throne of England.

HOLDENBY

There was once a very large and grandiose house on the site of Holdenby Hall, built by Sir Christopher Hatton, a favourite of Queen Elizabeth I. He also re-built the village and created an enormous deer park. It became a royal residence in 1608 when Sir Christopher's heir sold the estate to James I. Charles I was kept under house arrest here during the Civil War, and after his death, the house was bought by a

parliamentary captain who proceeded to pull most of the building down. A small part was kept for use as a farmhouse, and two arches of the original house can still be seen in the grounds.

The property reverted to the Crown at the Restoration and was later sold to the Duke of Marlborough, whose heirs enlarged the building again. The present house was visited by Edward, Prince of Wales before he became Edward VII, when he was met by two thousand horsemen.

DAVENTRY

Daventry was a prosperous market town when, in 1383, the sixteen year old King Richard II paid it a visit. Queen Elizabeth I granted a Charter of Incorporation to the town in 1576, as did James I in 1606, and Charles II in 1674. Charles I brought his army to Daventry in 1645 during the Civil War, staying for six nights at the Wheat Sheaf Inn while preparing his troops for the Battle of Naseby, in which he was defeated.

ROYAL LEAMINGTON SPA

Leamington Spa was granted permission to prefix its name with "Royal" by Queen Victoria, who visited the town in 1838. Her statue can be seen in front of the Town Hall. The Adelaide Bridge, over the River Leam, was built in 1839 to commemorate a visit by Queen Adelaide.

SHREWSBURY

Tradition states that Shrewsbury, whose original name was *Scrobbyrig*, was founded by Offa, King of Mercia in the 8th century. This is disputed by those who claim that the Scrob in the old name was an 11th century Norman who arrived before the Conquest. What is certain is that a castle was begun here in about 1080 by Roger de Montgomery. The fortifications were strengthened by Robert de Belesme, who eventually had to surrender the castle to Henry II. The present castle, which is open to the public, dates mainly from the time of Edward I's campaigns against the Welsh. During Edward's reign the first Parliament in history to include the commons was summoned at Shrewsbury.

The Battle of Shrewsbury

A bank now stands on the site where Prince Dafydd ap Gruffydd, brother of Llywelyn the Last, was executed in 1283. It was here also that the body of Harry Hotspur was exposed for three days after he had been killed at the Battle of Shrewsbury in 1403. The battle took place four miles north of Shrewsbury at a spot now called Battlefield. The church of St Mary Magdalene was founded here by Henry IV to commemorate the fallen, and the crests of the victors are displayed inside the church. In July 1403 Prince Henry ("Hal" as Shakespeare called him) was encamped at Shrewsbury with a small army. He was joined on the 20th July by his father, Henry IV, in order that their combined forces should prevent Hotspur joining up with the Welsh rebel Owain Glyndwr.

Hotspur was the son of Henry Percy, Earl of Northumberland, who was head of the most powerful family in the north of England. Although Percy had helped Henry to depose Richard II there was no love lost between them, and when Henry refused to give aid to Percy in his feud against Glyndwr Percy did a complete about-turn and joined up with the Welsh rebels. Upon hearing that Hotspur was marching from Chester to join his father and Glyndwr with an army of 10,000 men, Henry and Hal drew up their forces. Before the fighting began the Abbot of Shrewsbury tried to arrange a truce, but to no avail, and the King's army began to advance. Both sides were armed with longbows and Hotspur's bowmen soon brought the royal advance to a halt. Henry's army began to retreat, but soon stopped and faced the enemy, whereupon hand-to-hand fighting began. Hotspur, with some 30 knights, tried to hack his way through the King's men and get at Henry, but before this could happen Henry was persuaded to leave the field. Meanwhile Prince Hal's army was overcoming its opponents and began to attack Hotspur's force from the rear. Suddenly, from the centre of the turmoil, it was cried that Hotspur had been killed by an arrow. This immediately caused his army to fall into confusion and they were easily driven away. Today the site of the battle is mostly in private ownership.

One of Shrewsbury's best preserved half-timbered houses, on Wyle Cop, is called Henry Tudor's House. This was where, in 1485, Henry VII lodged while on his way to the Battle of Bosworth. A few houses away is the house where Mary Tudor stayed in 1525.

Henry Tudor's House, Shrewsbury, where Henry VII lodged prior to the Battle of Bosworth

Shrewsbury School was founded by Edward VI in 1552; the old buildings in Castle Gates which housed the school date from 1598. They now contain the town's library, art gallery, and natural history museum.

Charles I in Shrewsbury

During the Civil War Shrewsbury was an important royalist stronghold. Charles I arrived in the town in September 1642 where it was said that a force of 5,000 men were mustering for him. Prince Rupert, greatest of all the royalist generals, was also at Shrewsbury, and it was nearby that he gained his first victory over the parliamentary forces. In reality the fight, which took place near the village of Powick on 23rd September, was little more than a skirmish, but it made Rupert a hero and caused his name to be spoken with fear in parliamentary circles.

During his time at Shrewsbury, Charles I appeared happy and relaxed; he was surrounded by his closest allies and by a strong army and there was little doubt in anyone's mind that victory would soon be his. He left the town on several occasions in order to rally support for the royalist cause, and was, for instance, welcomed by many when he rode into Chester. There were setbacks, however; Manchester was still held by Parliament, and the Earl of Cumberland proved a poor, though willing, leader of the royalists in the north. By and large the king remained untroubled and his army at Shrewsbury was daily being swelled by men from the Welsh Marches. Prince Rupert lost no time in drilling the new recruits, and was helped by the arrival of a veteran soldier—the Earl of Forth. Surrounded by his cronies, many of whom were extreme Catholics, Charles was seen to smile more than he had done for years. Men of moderate views became troubled by the thought that if Charles did achieve total victory over Parliament the prospects might not be pleasant.

Shrewsbury continued to be a royalist centre throughout most of the war, and was used by both Rupert and Prince Maurice to recruit troops from Wales. Its loss to the parliamentary side in 1645 was a bitter blow to the royalist cause. In February of 1645 Prince Maurice was called away from the town and it was left in the command of the governor, Sir Michael Ernle. He was unwell and neglected his duties. By this time the townsfolk of Shrewsbury were tired of the undisciplined royalist troops. After Maurice's departure two traitors showed Colonel Mytton, parliamentary commander in Shropshire, a gap in the town's defences. At four o'clock in the morning the parliamentary troops rushed through the breach and took the royalists completely by surprise. Sir Michael Ernle was killed in a last minute bid to rally his men. The royalists surrendered, and all the arms and provisions in Shrewsbury were lost. The houses where Charles and Rupert lodged may still be seen. Charles II offered to make the town into a city but the "proud Salopians" declined.

Ireland's Mansion, Shrewsbury, built in around 1575 by Robert Ireland, a wool merchant. This is one of Shrewsbury's grandest buildings

Shropshire heritage

MUCH WENLOCK

A nunnery was founded at Much Wenlock in the 7th century by St Milburga, but this was destroyed by the Danes in about 896. This foundation was restored as a college for secular cannons by a close friend of Edward the Confessor, Earl Leofric and his famous wife Lady Godiva. After the Norman Conquest it was re-founded as a Cluniac priory by one of William's strongest supporters, Roger de Montgomery. The priory ruins are open to the public. The efforts of a succession of able priors ensured that many royal privileges and favours were bestowed upon Wenlock town. The Quincentenary of its Charter of Incorporation was celebrated in 1968. Although Edward IV's charter incorporated the town "for ever" the borough of Wenlock ceased to exist in 1966 and it became a Rural Borough—the first of its kind.

Charles I lunched at the Raven Inn on his way to Bridgnorth in 1642. The King was also at Tickwood Hall, which is 2½ miles from the town, in order to enlist money and men for the royalist cause.

BRIDGNORTH

Ethelred, 10th century hermit brother of King Athelstan, is said to have had his retreat in the sandstone cave here called the Hermitage, which is open to the public. The keep of Bridgnorth Castle, which leans a remarkable 15 degrees from the vertical, was built on the orders of Henry II between 1168 and 1189. The castle was originally a pre-Conquest structure and was rebuilt by Robert de Belesme between 1098 and 1101. In 1102 it was taken over by Henry I and given by him to Hugh de Mortimer. Henry II reclaimed the building in 1155 and made it a royal castle.

Charles I stayed at Bridgnorth in 1642, and the castle was held by the royalists for most of the war. Eventually parliamentary forces took the castle and drove the royalists into the town, where they made St Leonard's Church their ammunition store. A parliamentary cannon scored a direct hit on the church, causing an explosion and subsequent fire which destroyed most of High Town.

BEWDLEY

Tickenhill House at Bewdley incorporates parts of a palace built by Henry VII for his eldest son, Arthur. As the heir to the throne and eldest son, Arthur was automatically created Prince of Wales, and he was the only such Prince actually to rule his principality, which he did from Ludlow and from Tickenhill. It was no coincidence that Arthur was named after the most potent of all Welsh heroes, the half-legendary King Arthur, for Henry was more than conscious of his own Welsh ancestry and upbringing. Leland, the greatest historian of the time, described Tickenhill as a "fayre mannour". Arthur died in 1502, and the throne eventually went to his brother Henry. Arthur had announced his betrothal to Catherine of Aragon from Tickenhill. He could not have known that Catherine was to become the wife of Henry and that the collapse of their marriage would lead to the Reformation.

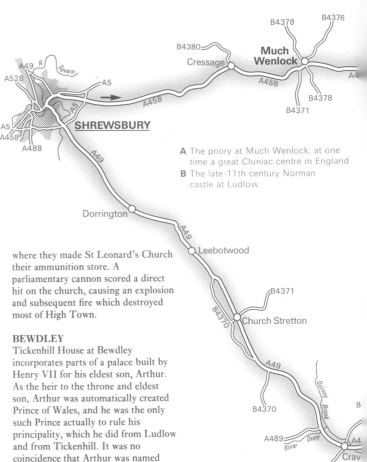

A The priory at Much Wenlock, at one time a great Cluniac centre in England
B The late-11th century Norman castle at Ludlow

Mary, daughter of Henry VII, lived at Tickenhill for a while, and it was whilst staying here that Charles I learnt of the crushing defeat of his forces at Marston Moor. The present house, which was largely built in 1738, is under private ownership.

MORTIMER'S CROSS

The battle which took place here on 2nd February 1461 was one of the many in which the Yorkists and

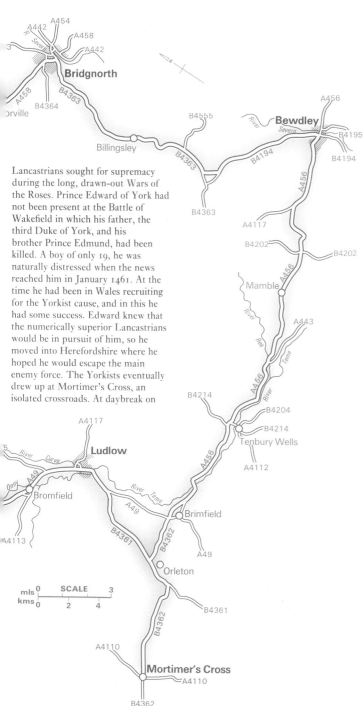

Lancastrians sought for supremacy during the long, drawn-out Wars of the Roses. Prince Edward of York had not been present at the Battle of Wakefield in which his father, the third Duke of York, and his brother Prince Edmund, had been killed. A boy of only 19, he was naturally distressed when the news reached him in January 1461. At the time he had been in Wales recruiting for the Yorkist cause, and in this he had some success. Edward knew that the numerically superior Lancastrians would be in pursuit of him, so moved into Herefordshire where he hoped he would escape the main enemy force. The Yorkists eventually drew up at Mortimer's Cross, an isolated crossroads. At daybreak on

2nd February, the Lancastrians, under the command of the Earl of Pembroke approached from the west. An attack by the Earl of Ormonde broke the Yorkist right flank, but an attack upon Edward's group by the Earl of Pembroke failed and was driven back. Ormonde, returning to help Pembroke, found him defeated and waited upon peace terms. The final Lancastrian attack was led by Owen Tudor. His force attempted to outflank Edward, but was cut in two by Edward's left flank. The Lancastrians retired in disorder, and Owen Tudor was captured, to be executed later in Hereford market place. The whole battle site can be viewed from the bridge 200 yards east of the crossroads and a monument to the battle stands outside the Monument Inn.

LUDLOW

Roger de Lacy founded the castle at Ludlow in about 1080. At the time it was a frontier post, built to keep the war-like Welsh under control. After de Lacy had rebelled against William Rufus and was exiled, the castle became crown property. Before this, however, Roger had laid out the town of Ludlow on a rigid grid plan. Henry I granted the castle to Payne FitzJohn who was killed by the Welsh in 1136. The castle then passed to Sir Joyce de Dinan. In 1138 the castle was captured by the allies of Queen Matilda, and Stephen laid siege to it. By 1166 the castle once more belonged to a de Lacy, but from 1181 to 1190 it was under royal control.

Roger Mortimer owned the castle in the 14th century, and it was this man who not only became the lover of Edward II's wife, Isabella, but was instrumental in the death of that unfortunate king at Berkeley Castle. Eventually Mortimer was captured by Edward III and subsequently executed at Tyburn.

Ludlow was the headquarters of Richard, Duke of York, when, during

the Wars of the Roses, he made his bid for the English Throne. After the Battle of Ludford Bridge both town and castle were sacked by victorious Lancastrians. Richard's son, Edward, eventually became King Edward IV and bestowed much honour and many privileges on Ludlow. Until 1483 Edward's two sons lived at Ludlow Castle. After their father's death they were taken to the Tower of London and murdered, and have since come to be known as the "Princes in the Tower."

During Tudor times Ludlow became a place of great importance. Arthur, the Prince of Wales, watched over his principality from here, and spent his honeymoon with Catherine of Aragon at the castle. After his death, his heart was buried in St Laurence's Church. The future Henry VIII lived at Ludlow, and sent his daughter, Mary, to live here. The end of the Tudor period brought about a rapid decline in Ludlow's importance. During the Civil War it was held for the royalists, and was one of the last places to surrender. Much careful restoration work has been carried out on the castle, which is open to the public, and the town itself may justifiably be described as one of the most beautiful in England.

The country divided

The causes of the War

Charles I came to the throne in 1625. He was a proud, dignified, hard-working man, but with no understanding of human nature and devoid of tact. From the start of his reign, relations with Parliament were difficult. Several times he dissolved Parliament, and governed for quite long periods without them, and during all this time he gradually became less popular in the country. This was partly because of the heavy taxes he imposed, but also for religious reasons due to suspicions that he favoured Roman Catholicism. Matters came to a head when, after Charles had tried to arrest several members of Parliament at Westminster, Parliament removed the control of the army from the King. On 22nd August 1642, Charles called on his subjects to support him, and raised his standard at Nottingham. From this time until the formation of the Protectorate in 1651, the country was enveloped in Civil War.

The progress of the War

The War was not initially expected to last very long, but in the event it was fought from 1642–1646, there was a second phase in 1648 which ended in the trial and execution of the King, and there was a third phase in 1649–51 during which Charles II attempted to regain the throne. Charles intended to move from Nottingham to Worcester, and from there to march to London to claim his capital. The parliamentarians set out to intercept him, and the first major battle of the war was fought at *Edgehill*. This ended as a victory for the King, and the royalists held the upper hand for the first nine months of the war. Charles made his headquarters at Oxford, the royalists had

victories at *Chalgrove Field* and *Roundway Down*, and they took Bristol. In 1643, Prince Rupert, the royalist commander, cut off the parliamentarians from London, and there was a battle at *Newbury*, which ended as a parliamentarian victory and marked a turning point in the war. During 1644, the allegiance of the country was almost equally divided between royalist and parliamentarian. A move against Charles at Oxford led to the battle of *Cropredy Bridge*, near Banbury, which ended in victory for the King, allowing him to move back to Oxford. Charles gained his greatest victory of the war when he led his army into royalist Devon. A parliamentarian army was drawn up at *Lostwithiel* in Cornwall, but their morale was low and the leadership poor, and they surrendered easily. At this point in time royalist troops were besieged in York, and Prince Rupert went up there to relieve them. Battle was drawn outside the city at *Marston Moor*, and resulted in a royalist defeat, assuring the reputation of Oliver Cromwell. The King's men were, by now, very tired, and moved to *Newbury*. The battle, which took place there on 27th October, was inconclusive, and Charles withdrew to Oxford.

The parliamentary commanders realized that a fresh impetus was necessary, while Charles felt he should try and cement his support in the West Country. In June 1645, Charles moved his army north from Oxford to Market Harborough, but parliamentary forces had pursued him, and they met at the battle of *Naseby*. This inflicted severe damage on the

royalist forces and their morale, and the following months saw increasing parliamentarian inroads into royalist strongholds. Charles' final battle was at *Rowton Heath*, near Chester, where he was again defeated. He finally surrendered some eight months later to a Scots army, and they handed him over to Parliament. Charles was initially very reluctant to come to any form of settlement, although Cromwell was anxious to do so. This continued prevarication caused a split to develop between Parliament and the army, which led to the army seizing custody of the King. His intrigues while he was a prisoner helped bring about a renewed phase of hostilities. He, himself, managed to escape and flee to the Isle of Wight, where he made secret agreements with the Scots in exchange for which they promised to restore him to the throne. The failure of Parliament to make an agreement with the King led to a series of royalist uprisings in different parts of the country. The parliamentary forces were much better organized now and succeeded in crushing these rebellions. After this second phase of the Civil War had ended, negotiations with the King were re-opened, but Parliament was eventually convinced that Charles had to be deposed and on 27th January 1649, he was tried and condemned to death.

Charles II and the Third Civil War

After the execution of Charles I, his son, 19 year old Charles, Prince of Wales, was in Holland. He decided to attempt to regain the throne, and enlisted the help of the Scots. Cromwell led an army north to capture Edinburgh and suppress the Scots, and on 3rd September 1650, he defeated them at the Battle of *Dunbar*, although the Scots army was twice the size of his own. Charles escaped from this battle and attempted to revive royalist support both in Scotland and in England. Cromwell finally caught up with him at *Worcester* and surrounded him. Charles managed to escape, and after a series of romantic adventures, reached France. He did not return to England until after the death of Cromwell, when he was restored to the throne.

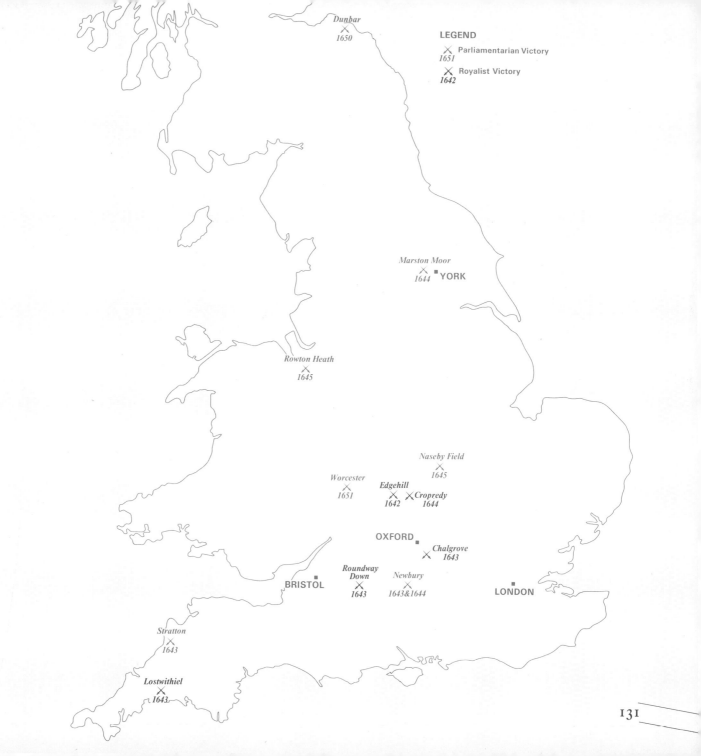

Dunbar
1650

LEGEND
✗ Parliamentarian Victory
1651
✗ Royalist Victory
1642

Marston Moor
1644 ■ YORK

Rowton Heath
1645

Naseby Field
1645

Worcester
1651

Edgehill
1642 ✗ Cropredy
1644

OXFORD ■

Chalgrove
1643

Roundway
Down
1643

Newbury
1643 & 1644

BRISTOL ■

LONDON ■

Stratton
1643

Lostwithiel
1643

LEICESTER

The history of Leicester dates back to pre-Roman times. The oldest remains still standing are Jewry Wall, a stretch of wall some 73 feet long and more than 20 feet high. It dates from 130, and is believed to have been part of the forum. The Jewry Wall Museum contains much of interest from prehistoric and Roman times, and near by in Blackfriars Street a beautiful mosaic floor may be seen.

Simon de Montfort

William the Conqueror, recognising that Leicester occupied an important strategic position and was also in need of defence, built a castle overlooking the River Soar. During the years 1108 to 1118, the Earl of Leicester built three more castles and inherited two more. This so alarmed Henry II that he ordered them all to be destroyed. During the 13th century the castle passed to Simon de Montfort, brother-in-law to Henry III who was Earl of Leicester from 1231 to his death in the Battle of Evesham in 1265. De Montfort led the opposition to Henry III's extravagance in his foreign policies, and his incompetence at home. The group of barons involved finally formed an alternative government which ruled Britain for almost two years from 1258. Eventually de Montfort's supporters deserted him and he was finally slain in battle. However de Montfort is remembered for his role in creating the first English Parliament. In the castle, he rebuilt the Great Hall and used the nearby church of St Mary de Castro as his chapel. During his spell of power, the castle saw great pomp and ceremony, and entertained several regal visitors.

A Victorian clock tower which stands near the market square serves as a monument to de Montfort. He left no heirs, so the castle passed to the son of Henry III, Edmund Crouchback, so called because he always

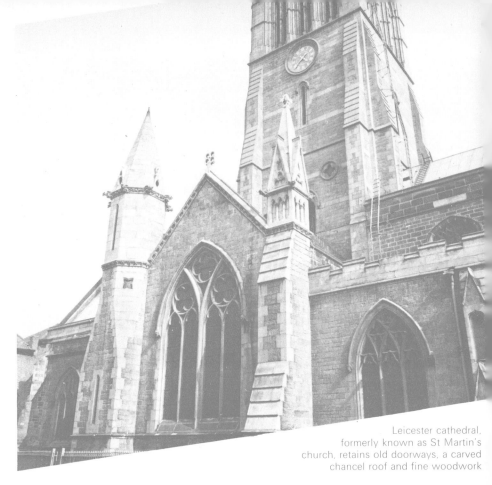

Leicester cathedral, formerly known as St Martin's church, retains old doorways, a carved chancel roof and fine woodwork

carried the sign of the cross on the back of his armour. Edmund and his successors owned numbers of forts and large areas of land, all of which later became known as the Duchy of Lancaster. Edmund Crouchback's son Henry was responsible for founding Trinity Hospital and almshouses. The hospital, with its own small chapel where Mary Bohun, wife of Henry Bolingbroke and mother of Henry V, is reputed to lie buried, still functions charitably to this day. The building is reached through the old Turret gateway and is set in a large enclosed area known as Newarke or New Work, adjoining the castle precincts. The hospital has been generously endowed by monarchs through

the ages. In 1776, the building was restored at a cost of £1,600, towards which George III contributed £600. It contains some interesting relics, including armour formerly worn by the town watch, a nutmeg grater owned by Queen Elizabeth dated 1579, and the Duke of Lancaster's porridge pot.

The last days of Richard III

In the 14th century the castle passed to John of Gaunt, son of Edward III and father of Henry IV, and during this time it reached the peak of its splendour and saw many royal guests. In 1385, and again in 1390, Richard II and his queen visited Leicester Castle, while Edwards I,

II and III are also known to have stayed here. After the death of John of Gaunt, the castle fell into decline and by the time Richard III rode into the town before the Battle of Bosworth Field of 1485, the building was thought unsuitable for such a noble visitor and he stayed near by in the Blue Boar Inn. The inn no longer exists, but a plaque over the shops in Blue Boar Street commemorates the King's stay. After a few nights in the city, on the morning of 22nd August 1485, the King set out for battle mounted on a large white horse.

Fighting valiantly against Henry Tudor, and deserted by his allies, Richard III died on the battlefield. His body was brought back to Leicester, and after being exposed for two days was buried in the church of Greyfriars. At the Dissolution of the monasteries, the King's body was unearthed from its grave and flung into the river Soar. Later it was retrieved and reburied at a site near Bow Bridge, which spans the river. The bridge, which was rebuilt in the last century, bears a plaque commemorating King Richard's burial.

During the Civil War, Leicester was constantly under siege, occupied first by the royalists and latterly by the parliamentarians. In 1645 Prince Rupert fired his cannons at the castle walls until, after three days, the town surrendered. By this time the castle had become a total ruin, and was sold in parts by Charles I to raise funds for his war. Most of the remaining great hall was dismantled in 1715 to make way for the present-day assize courts. Inside the court building the roof beams are those of John of Gaunt's country home, while outside, some steps lead down to the old castle dungeons.

Other places of interest

The church of St Mary de Castro still bears the scars of the siege of Leicester—the southern walls of the churchyard are punctured by holes made by cannon shot in Prince Rupert's determined attack of 1645. Opposite the old Jewry Wall is the Guildhall, one of the oldest buildings in Leicester, parts of it dating back to the 14th century. A building full of

Richard III was killed at the Battle of Bosworth Field, and his body was brought back to Leicester for burial

The plaque on Bow Bridge commemorates the final burial place of Richard III

interest, it now houses the city museum. In the mayor's parlour is a chair, said to have been used by Prince Rupert after he had captured the city.

The Blue Boar Inn is not the only inn to have featured in Leicester's history. The Angel, which once stood in Cheapside, and of which only the gateway, Angelgate, remains, was where Mary, Queen of Scots stayed on her way to execution at Fotheringhay. Charles I stayed here, and Oliver Cromwell, when he visited Leicester, stayed either at the Angel or at the old Guildhall.

The abbey ruins at the north end of the town are of great interest, although only the boundary walls and the restored foundations remain. Once one of the wealthiest abbeys in the country, kings and princes were entertained in its hall. In 1530, Cardinal Wolsey, stripped of his power, came here to die. His tomb is now lost, but a stone memorial slab serves as a reminder that he was buried here. A mansion named Cavendish House was built on the site of the old monastic building, using some of the stone from the abbey itself. Charles I stayed here after the surrender of the city to Prince Rupert, but before the King left, he forced the inhabitants to pay £2,000 as a punishment for their part in the rebellion and then ordered his soldiers to burn the building down. In 1882 the abbey grounds were transformed into the city park opened by Edward, Prince of Wales, and his wife Alexandra.

Defeat of the King

OAKHAM

Domesday Book records that the town of Oakham was once the property of Anglo Saxon queens, and that after the death of Queen Edith, wife of Edward the Confessor in 1075, the castle passed to William the Conqueror. All that remains of the castle now is the great banqueting hall, probably built about 1190, its walls lined from floor to ceiling with horseshoes of every size and shape, given by royalty and peers throughout the ages. The custom of giving a horseshoe, or leaving sufficient funds for a horseshoe to be cast, probably stems from the time that the Conqueror's farrier lived in the town. The earliest horseshoe mounted on the walls is reputed to have been given by Elizabeth I, while perhaps the most recent one was given by our Queen Elizabeth II on her tour of the county in May 1967. Others have been given by George IV, Queen Victoria, King George VI, the Duke of Windsor and Prince Philip. Originally the horseshoes were nailed

to the outside of the castle doors, but more recently they have been brought inside.

5½ miles east of Oakham is Empingham, once the scene of a minor skirmish during the Wars of the Roses. On 12th March 1470, while on his way to suppress an uprising in Lincolnshire, Edward IV was waylaid by a group of Lancastrian supporters. The King acted quickly, killing many and forcing the rest to retreat. In their haste to escape unscathed the rebels shed their coats, and the battle became known as Losecoat Field.

ROCKINGHAM

Rockingham Castle was built by William the Conqueror and was used by many monarchs for hunting in Rockingham Forest and also as a place to hold council. At the end of the 12th century, Richard I summoned a council meeting on the outskirts of Rockingham Forest, meeting King William of Scotland and making arrangements for his forthcoming crusade. Before he left, he granted the castle to his queen, Berengaria, but on his death, King John seized the castle and converted it into a hunting lodge for himself and his Queen Isabella. Inside the great hall of Rockingham Castle is the chest left here by King John in 1216 before he died. As the years passed and monarchs had less

time to spend hunting in Rockingham, the castle fell into a state of neglect. Edward I was the first King to carry out substantial improvements, and during the 13th century he built the great hall, and made the square Norman gate towers circular. During the 14th and 15th centuries Rockingham was frequented by the queens Philippa (Edward III's wife), Anne, and Margaret of Anjou (Queen of Henry VI). The kings who made visits here were Edward II, who fortified the castle in 1323; Edward III

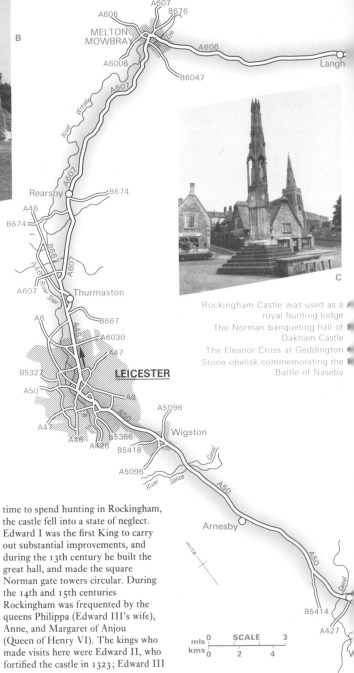

Rockingham Castle was used as a royal hunting lodge
The Norman banqueting hall of Oakham Castle
The Eleanor Cross at Geddington
Stone obelisk commemorating the Battle of Naseby

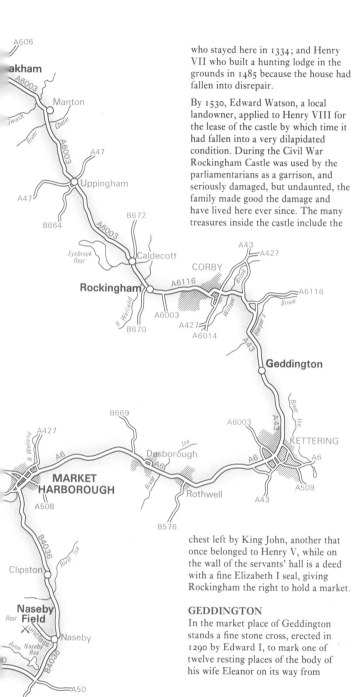

who stayed here in 1334; and Henry VII who built a hunting lodge in the grounds in 1485 because the house had fallen into disrepair.

By 1530, Edward Watson, a local landowner, applied to Henry VIII for the lease of the castle by which time it had fallen into a very dilapidated condition. During the Civil War Rockingham Castle was used by the parliamentarians as a garrison, and seriously damaged, but undaunted, the family made good the damage and have lived here ever since. The many treasures inside the castle include the chest left by King John, another that once belonged to Henry V, while on the wall of the servants' hall is a deed with a fine Elizabeth I seal, giving Rockingham the right to hold a market.

GEDDINGTON

In the market place of Geddington stands a fine stone cross, erected in 1290 by Edward I, to mark one of twelve resting places of the body of his wife Eleanor on its way from Harby in Nottinghamshire to Westminster Abbey. Of the original twelve crosses, only three remain; one at Northampton, one at Waltham and the finest of all at Geddington. At the top of the cross are three niche statues of the queen.

MARKET HARBOROUGH

The manor of Harborough was granted, in 1267, to Eleanor, Henry III's queen and subsequently to Queen Margaret, wife of Edward I and then to Isabel, Edward II's queen.

During the Civil War Market Harborough was plundered by Prince Rupert, and twice used by King Charles I as his headquarters in 1645. On 13th June 1645, the King held a council of war here before setting off for the disastrous Battle of Naseby. After the battle, Cromwell marched to Market Harborough, occupied the town, and wrote to Parliament from here announcing his victory.

NASEBY

Just outside the village of Naseby, on 14th June 1645, the decisive battle of the Civil War took place. Parliament had recently formed the New Model Army, and they had set out to attack King Charles' headquarters at Oxford. In order to draw them off, Charles had moved to Leicester, and the parliamentarians caught up with him at Naseby.

Charles had drawn up his men on one ridge, and Parliament drew up their forces on another, three-quarters of a mile distant. 7,000 cavaliers faced twice that number of untried, but disciplined men of the New Model Army. Prince Rupert attacked first, sweeping Colonel Ireton's cavalry before him and putting them to flight. The royalists in the centre of the battle were fighting with similar determination, and it seemed as though the roundheads would be defeated. But Cromwell timed his cavalry attack very well and succeeded in surrounding the King's men on three sides. They fought bravely, but it was hopeless. Although Rupert and his cavalry had returned from chasing Ireton's cavalry, it was clear that the royalists had lost the battle, and Charles rode away towards Leicester leaving his infantry to die where they stood. In the end, more than 4,000 were either captured or killed. Cromwell and his army then pursued the King, and although they failed to catch him, they knew they had won a great victory.

Two monuments commemorate the battle. Outside the village, a small obelisk was erected in 1823 to mark the event, and there is another, more recent monument on the battlefield showing Cromwell's position before the start of hostilities. In the village church of All Saints can be seen the table at which some of Cromwell's soldiers dined on the eve of the battle, as well as some other battle relics.

D

SANDRINGHAM

Sandringham House, a private residence of the Royal Family. The estate was bought for Edward VII in 1861. The major improvements to the house were carried out from 1870

The house and estate at Sandringham were purchased for Edward, Prince of Wales, by his father, the Prince Consort, shortly before the Consort's death in 1861. The money (£220,000) came from the invested revenues of the Duchy of Cornwall which Albert had carefully controlled with the financial future of his eldest son in mind.

On 10th March 1863 Edward married Princess Alexandra of Denmark, and the royal couple paid their first visit to Sandringham on 28th March. The house had previously belonged to the Hon Charles Spencer Cowper and needed extensive improvements to make it a suitable home for the heir to the throne. Partly with this in mind Parliament increased the Prince's income by £50,000. Edward adhered to a strict social round and was usually at Sandringham during January and February. He was very proud of his estate and, every Sunday, an after-luncheon tour, with all the guests, was made of stables, kennels, gardens, stud farm, etc. This Sunday perambulation became a ritual, as did the Prince's arrival in church exactly half way through the service immediately before the sermon. The Prince himself demanded that the sermon be strictly limited to ten minutes.

Edwardian life and entertainment
Alterations were made to the house in 1867, and, on a much larger scale, in 1870. Edward was worried that the building's damp atmosphere might affect his wife's health, and, in any case, the house was soon found to be too small for the number of guests whom both Edward and Alexandra loved entertaining. The work carried out in 1870 from the plans of Albert Humbert virtually replaced the original structure with a red brick mansion. Further additions, including a ballroom and a new wing which was built after a serious fire in 1891, changed the house

so much that eventually only the billiard room incorporated parts of the original building.

Edward was a keen sportsman, and one of his main interests at Sandringham was the shooting. He enjoyed being in the open air as much as he did the actual bagging of game. The wish to use daylight as much as possible, and his desire that everyone should be punctual, led the Prince to adopt the habit of one of his neighbours in putting all the clocks at Sandringham forward by half an hour. "Sandringham Time" was kept until the reign of Edward VIII, who made its abolition his first act.

As well as vastly improving the quality of the shooting at Sandringham, Prince Edward did much to improve the appearance of the estate and built new cottages for his tenants. He was keenly interested in the living conditions of those at the bottom of the social scale, and in

1884 he was appointed a member of the Royal Commission on the Housing of the Working Classes.

Darker days
In October 1871 Edward became ill with typhoid fever which he had contracted whilst staying at Londesborough Lodge in Yorkshire. He came to Sandringham to fight the illness, and in December his condition became critical. The illness brought Queen Victoria on her first visit to the house, and on 11th December she was informed that the Prince must be expected to die during the night. The crisis passed, however, and the Prince improved slightly, spending the next 36 hours in a state of extreme delirium. On 14th December the fever ended and Edward slept peacefully. The news that the Prince would live was greeted rapturously by the British people, many of whom had, only a

few weeks previously, been bitterly angry at reports of the Prince's gambling activities on the Continent.

The Duke of Clarence, Edward's eldest son, died of pneumonia at Sandringham on the 14th of January 1892, and Edward and Alexandra spent the summer of 1892 in mourning at the house. Queen Victoria wrote of her son at this time: "Poor Bertie, his is not a nature made to bear sorrow, or a life without amusement and excitement, he gets bitter and irritable."

Edward was crowned King Edward VII on 9th August 1902. He made his last visit to Sandringham on 29th April 1910, where on the Sunday the traditional inspection of the estate was made. A strong east wind caused the King much discomfort and he returned to Buckingham Palace on 2nd May in a fragile state of health. He died peacefully on 6th May.

Post-Edwardian Sandringham
A cottage had been built as an annex to the main house by Albert Humbert. This small Victorian-Gothic house was given by the then Prince of Wales to his son George, Duke of York, in 1893. George married Princess May of Teck on 6th July 1893, and the couple not only spent their honeymoon at the cottage, but made it their permanent home for the next 33 years. How the tiny cottage accommodated not only the Duke and his wife and their six children, but also lords and ladies in waiting, tutors, nannies, various servants and guests was a mystery. The Duke once said that he supposed the servants slept in the trees.

The Duke, who became on his father's death George V, loved Sandringham just as much as his father had done. Alexandra stayed at the house and continued to take a very active interest in the running of the place until her death in 1925. George made his first Christmas Day broadcast to the nation from the house in 1932, and he eventually died at Sandringham in 1936.

Edward VIII entrusted the care of Sandringham to his brother George, who shared his father's

Sandringham was rebuilt in the Jacobean style, using red brick and stone. The porch, seen here, is most imposing

love of the estate and of the sporting activities which it afforded. When he became George VI he continued to visit the house frequently and re-organised the shooting. He died at Sandringham in 1952 after having been out with his gun on the previous day.

Today Sandringham is still used by the Royal Family as a private home away from the formality and pressure of public life. The grounds are sometimes open to the public and it is anticipated that parts of the house will be opened to public view in 1977.

Norfolk houses

SAXTHORPE

During the Civil War, East Anglia was the mainstay of the parliamentary cause. Oliver Cromwell, who eventually became Lord Protector of England after having refused the crown, was himself an East Anglian. One of the places associated with him is Mannington Hall which stands 2 miles north east of the village of Saxthorpe.

BLICKLING HALL

After the Norman Conquest, the manor of Blickling, which had belonged to King Harold, was given by William the Conqueror to his chaplain, Herfast, whom he created Bishop of Thetford. During the reign of Edward III that part of the manor upon which Blickling Hall now stands passed into the hands of Sir Nicholas Dagworth, who became Captain of Aquitaine and a trusted servant of Richard II.

Sir John Fastolf bought Blickling in 1431 and became patron to Geoffrey Boleyn, whose father lived at Sall. Geoffrey made such a success of his life in London that he became Lord Mayor and was knighted, subsequently purchasing the house on which Blickling Hall was to stand. Geoffrey's grandson, Sir Thomas, attained even greater heights than his grandfather had, and his daughter Anne was married to Henry VIII. It has been said that Anne stayed at Blickling, but there is no evidence to support this. Sir Thomas died shortly after his daughter was executed in 1536 and the Boleyn family fell into obscurity.

In 1616 the manor was purchased by Sir Henry Hobart, and it was he who built the existing Blickling Hall. Charles II and his wife were entertained at the hall in 1671 by Lord Hobart, who had previously sat in Cromwell's upper House. During his stay the King knighted Lord Hobart's son. The hall was bequeathed to the National Trust in 1940. It contains, beside much else of interest, many portraits of English monarchs, and, in the hall, life sized reliefs of Anne Boleyn and her daughter Elizabeth I.

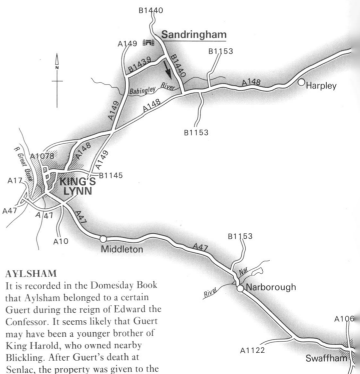

AYLSHAM

It is recorded in the Domesday Book that Aylsham belonged to a certain Guert during the reign of Edward the Confessor. It seems likely that Guert may have been a younger brother of King Harold, who owned nearby Blickling. After Guert's death at Senlac, the property was given to the Earl of Norfolk, but later it was acquired by William the Conqueror after the Earl had rebelled against him. In the 14th century the manor belonged to John of Gaunt, the father of Henry IV, and it is said that John founded the parish church.

During the Civil War, Aylsham was royalist, or at least, opposed to parliamentary taxes, in a predominantly parliamentary area. This led, in 1643, to a demonstration by some of the inhabitants which was quashed by a detachment of the Norwich trained bands. One of the leaders of this tiny disturbance, Edward Colfer, later joined the King at Oxford.

SALL

Standing alone and almost unused in the heart of the Norfolk countryside, this superb church is an essential stopping place for anyone who loves beautiful objects. It also has a definite, but in one respect controversial, connection with royalty.

Amongst the wealthy families who contributed to the building of the church were the Boleyns, who had risen, over several generations, from being farmers to titled gentry. It was Geoffrey Boleyn who began the increase in the family fortunes. He was

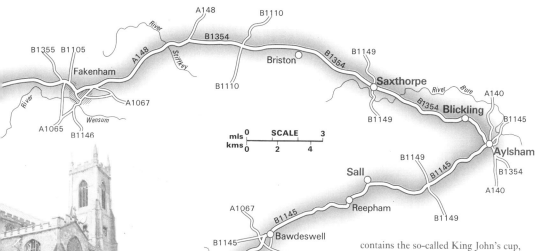

Map labels: River, A148, B1110, B1354, B1355, B1105, Fakenham, A148, Stiffkey, Briston, B1149, B1354, Saxthorpe, River, Bure, A1067, Wensum, River, A1065, B1146, B1110, Saxthorpe, Blickling, B1149, A140, B1149, B1145, Aylsham, B1354, SCALE, mls, kms, Sall, B1149, A140, A1067, B1145, Bawdeswell, B1145, A1067, River, B1147, Wensum, B1110, Swanton Morley, East Dereham, B1147, A47, River Wensum, A47, B1135, A1075, Reepham

C

patronized by Sir John Fastolf, of Blickling Hall, and eventually became Lord Mayor of London. His great-grand-daughter, Anne, became wife to Henry VIII and mother of the future Queen Elizabeth I. The controversy arises from the fact that local tradition asserts that after her execution Anne was buried in Sall Church. There is no evidence to support the story, and it is more commonly said that she was buried in the Tower of London. Whatever the truth of the matter, little excuse is needed to visit Sall Church which is one of Norfolk's greatest treasures.

KING'S LYNN

King John is the monarch most closely associated with King's Lynn. It was shortly after having been given a sumptuous banquet here in October 1215 that the King died. After the feast John left the town and began to cross the Fens. Travelling with him were the crown jewels and a great amount of treasure. It was decided to send the baggage train containing all this wealth by a short cut, but the tide took the convoy by surprise and everything was lost. John continued on his journey and eventually reached Newark Castle where he died, it is said, of a surfeit of lampreys which he had consumed whilst at King's Lynn.

There are several reminders of King John in the town. The Guildhall contains the so-called King John's cup, which in fact dates from 1340. Also in the Guildhall is King John's sword, which may in fact have been presented to the town by the King in 1204. Fisher Fleet, a narrow creek near the Wash, is said to have been presented to the fishermen of Lynn by King John, as is St Nicholas Chapel which stands in St Ann's Street.

During the Civil War King's Lynn was one of the few places in East Anglia to declare for the King, and it was the only place in Norfolk to experience bloodshed and gunfire. The casualties were few, however, for although the town withstood a siege little damage was done by it and a surrender was eventually agreed upon specifically to avoid death and injury. A statue of King Charles I may be seen on Bank House in King's Staithe Square, and the Customs House in King Street is adorned with a statue of Charles II.

5 miles north east of King's Lynn is Castle Rising. When the castle was first built it was set on the sea-shore, but it now stands 2 miles inland. William the Conqueror gave the lands first to his half-brother Odo and later to Stephen de Albini. It was his son, William de Albini, who began the castle. William married the widowed queen of Henry I. After the dreadful murder of Edward II, his widow Isabella, the "She Wolf of France", continued to wield an unhealthy influence in the reign of Edward III. In October 1330 both Isabella and Mortimer were overthrown, and it is said that Isabella was imprisoned at Castle Rising.

Of the castle, only the keep and some foundations remain, the structure having fallen into ruin by the 15th century.

Norwich lies 13 miles south of Aylsham, and a detour there should be considered. Norwich has been in existence since 850 and the town's name appears on coins minted for Athelstan. By the Norman Conquest it was one of the largest boroughs in the kingdom, and William I built a large castle there. Its prosperity grew, and it acquired charters in 1194 and 1256. After a rising of the people against the church, Henry III visited the city to punish them. The people were subsequently involved in two more uprisings in the 14th and 16th centuries. In 1578, Queen Elizabeth visited the city and stayed at the Maid's Head Hotel. The city is full of places of interest, particularly the castle and the cathedral.

A Blickling Hall, a fine, brick-red Jacobean house

B The 15th century church of Saints Peter and Paul, Sall

C The well-preserved Norman keep of Castle Rising

FOTHERINGHAY

Once a prosperous market town, Fotheringhay is now a small sleepy village with only a single street and a church which, though impressive, is only half the building it once was.

The church

At the end of the 14th century, Edmund, a son of King Edward III, built a choir on to the church and later additions were made in the form of cloisters and college buildings. Edmund's son, Edward Duke of York, was buried here after being killed at Agincourt and his body laid in state at Westminster. Another Duke of York, Richard Plantagenet, was finally laid to rest at Fotheringhay. He had been killed at the Battle of Wakefield during the Wars of the Roses and the victorious Queen Margaret ordered that his head be cut off and displayed at York. His body and that of his murdered son were buried at Pontefract, but another son, Edward, became King and ordered the removal of the bodies to Fotheringhay. After the long procession from Yorkshire, the coffins were met by the King and Queen and were interred in one grave close to that of Edward in the choir. The King, Edward IV, gave the pulpit to the church. The font in the church bears the badge of Richard III, who was born in the castle and baptised there. When Queen Elizabeth I visited the castle she was appalled to find the buildings of the choir, college and cloisters of the church in ruins and the graves of her ancestors neglected. She had the coffins removed to tombs in the church where wooden plaques were erected in their memory.

There is a house in the village known as the "New Inn" which is thought to have been built by Edward IV. It was used on several occasions as lodgings for visitors for whom there was no room at the castle, including

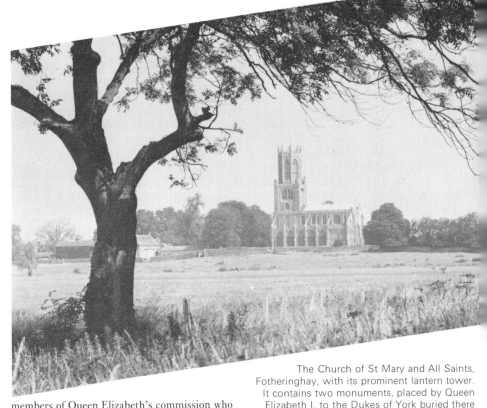

The Church of St Mary and All Saints, Fotheringhay, with its prominent lantern tower. It contains two monuments, placed by Queen Elizabeth I, to the Dukes of York buried there

members of Queen Elizabeth's commission who came to try Mary, Queen of Scots, for treason.

The castle

The castle which once stood at Fotheringhay was a large and impressive building protected by two stretches of water, the wide moat and the River Nene. The exact architecture of the building is unknown as no records exist, but a great deal is known of its history and the people who lived there over the centuries. Some believed that the castle held some sort of curse for the occupants, and certainly many met with great misfortune. There was Mary of Valence who became a widow on her wedding day and spent the rest of her life at the castle in solitude; the unfortunate members of the House of York including Richard III who was born here, who met such violent deaths, and Mary, Queen of Scots, whose life was ended at the castle.

Some happier owners of the castle were Elizabeth of York, who was given the property by her husband, King Henry VII, and Catherine of Aragon, who was very fond of the castle and spent a large sum of money on it. However, her affection for the castle changed when her husband Henry VIII expressed his intention to confine her there after their divorce. She vowed that she would not go to Fotheringhay "unless bound with cart-ropes and carried thither".

Mary, Queen of Scots

The troubled life of Mary, Queen of Scots, began when Elizabeth first came to the English throne. Mary questioned her legitimacy and tried to claim the crown for herself, but her attempt failed and she married the Dauphin and later became Queen of France as well as

Scotland. She remained in France until the death of her husband, when she returned to Scotland, and married Lord Darnley.

When her husband was murdered and she married Bothwell, she was soon forced to abdicate the throne of Scotland in favour of her son. She fled to England where once again she became a threat to Elizabeth's security. The Queen was afraid that Mary would be supported by the English Catholics in another bid for the throne and so Mary was kept constantly in confinement in various castles in country, coming finally to Fotheringhay.

Trial and execution

Elizabeth was reluctant to have Mary killed, but the threat of a Spanish invasion forced her to agree with her advisers that some action must be taken. The Queen appointed commissioners who came to Fotheringhay to try Mary for treason and, against tremendous difficulties, the Queen of Scots conducted her own defence. She was unwell at the time, the damp climate of the fen country causing her to suffer from rheumatism and neuralgia, and she was denied the use of the papers and the help of the people who would have supported her case.

The prosecution was unscrupulous and the witnesses unreliable, after having been tortured for their statements. Some refused to perjure themselves in court, but their written testimonies were allowed as evidence. There was never any hope of Mary's acquittal and the death sentence was finally passed, but her life was spared for a time following an appeal from her brother-in-law, the King of France. The threat from Spain was now becoming imminent, however, and after some days of uncertainty, Elizabeth had no alternative but to sign the death warrant.

The execution was to take place at Fotheringhay and was kept a closely guarded secret until a few hours before the event. Even the executioner travelled in disguise with the axe concealed in his baggage. Mary knew nothing of the plans for her death until the Earls of Kent and Shrewsbury came to her with the news that she had but twelve hours to live. She received the news with the same quiet dignity which she had shown throughout the whole episode and even said that she would be glad to be taken from a life which held nothing but misery for her. During the evening Mary distributed items of her clothing and jewellery to her faithful servants and wrote a letter to the King of France. She was refused the comfort of her own Catholic priest and so prayed alone.

Executions in Tudor times were very ceremonious occasions attended by as many spectators as the location would allow. On this occasion, however, Elizabeth had ordered that it should not take place in the open, but that the scaffold should be erected in the banqueting hall. In the morning, Mary was taken down the grand staircase in procession with a few of her attendants to the hall, where a few hundred privileged spectators were standing around the walls. After she had said her farewells to the weeping servants she turned to the executioner and, as was the custom, forgave him for the action he was about to take. She laid her head on the block and was saying her last prayer as the axe fell, but the executioner, overcome by the occasion, had to strike twice before the deed was properly done. While the severed head was raised on a velvet cushion to the window for the benefit of the crowds gathered outside, Lord Talbot rode with great haste to London to tell the Queen that her rival was dead.

Mary's embalmed body and head were kept in a lead coffin at Fotheringhay for six months before her son, King James of Scotland, obtained Elizabeth's permission for his mother to receive a proper Christian burial. So it was that in the middle of one August night in 1587, the remains of the Queen of Scots began their journey to Peterborough Cathedral. When James succeeded Elizabeth to the throne of England he gave the castle at Fotheringhay to three of his courtiers and they allowed it to fall into disrepair. Some years later the inheritor decided that too much expense would be involved in restoring the castle and decided to sell not only the land, but also the building. The magnificent castle was demolished stone by stone and its masonry dispersed to Conington Castle, Oundle, Fineshade and other places. Some 233 years later a man digging out the foundations of the castle uncovered a dirty piece of metal which, when cleaned, was found to be the ring given to Mary by her second husband, Lord Darnley. It was assumed that it fell from her finger at the execution and was swept into a corner with the sawdust from the floor. All that now remains at Fotheringhay to remind visitors of the ill fated visitor are the Milk Thistles which still grow profusely around the site of the castle, thought to have been scattered by the Queen, or her servants, during her captivity within the walls. It is interesting that the same thistles have been found growing around every one of Mary's former residences.

The New Inn, Fotheringhay, a 15th century house, in which stayed many of the members of the commission who tried and condemned Mary, Queen of Scots, in Fotheringhay Castle

The country of Oliver Cromwell

PETERBOROUGH

The original buildings of the Cathedral at Peterborough were constructed in the late 12th and early 13th centuries on the site of a monastery founded by King Penda of Mercia. He had embraced the Christian faith in order to marry the daughter of the King of Northumbria. In 1234 the Abbot, Robert of Sutton, entertained King Henry III, but the two men later found themselves on opposing sides during the siege of Northampton, for which the Abbot paid heavily in a series of fines. At the end of that century the Abbot was Godfrey of Croyland who was called the "Courtier Abbot" for his extravagant standard of living. At enormous expense he entertained King Edward I and his wife, Queen Eleanor. Their son, Edward II, is depicted in the form of a

stone figure in the gable of the entrance to the Bishop's Palace. Edward III and his wife, Philippa of Hainault, visited Peterborough twice between 1327 and 1338 and their son, the Black Prince, spent eight days at the monastery with his two sisters.

There are reminders of Tudor times in the city. The initials of King Henry VII and Tudor badges are carved in stone above the gate of the Dean's House. Henry VIII's first wife, Catherine of Aragon, whom he divorced in favour of Anne Boleyn, is buried in Peterborough Cathedral. Henry, who was delighted by the news of her death, ordered that the funeral should not be a ceremony befitting a queen, but something much simpler for the "Princess Dowager". The people of the Fens, however, had developed a great affection for the former queen who had spent her last years at the nearby Kimbolton Castle and they ignored the King's wishes. Hundreds of mourners followed the procession, more joining as the journey progressed. They were met at the cathedral by three bishops and six abbots and inside the building as

A

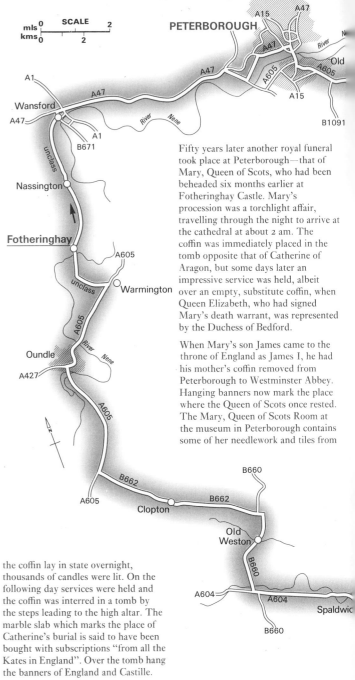

Fifty years later another royal funeral took place at Peterborough—that of Mary, Queen of Scots, who had been beheaded six months earlier at Fotheringhay Castle. Mary's procession was a torchlight affair, travelling through the night to arrive at the cathedral at about 2 am. The coffin was immediately placed in the tomb opposite that of Catherine of Aragon, but some days later an impressive service was held, albeit over an empty, substitute coffin, when Queen Elizabeth, who had signed Mary's death warrant, was represented by the Duchess of Bedford.

When Mary's son James came to the throne of England as James I, he had his mother's coffin removed from Peterborough to Westminster Abbey. Hanging banners now mark the place where the Queen of Scots once rested. The Mary, Queen of Scots Room at the museum in Peterborough contains some of her needlework and tiles from

the coffin lay in state overnight, thousands of candles were lit. On the following day services were held and the coffin was interred in a tomb by the steps leading to the high altar. The marble slab which marks the place of Catherine's burial is said to have been bought with subscriptions "from all the Kates in England". Over the tomb hang the banners of England and Castille.

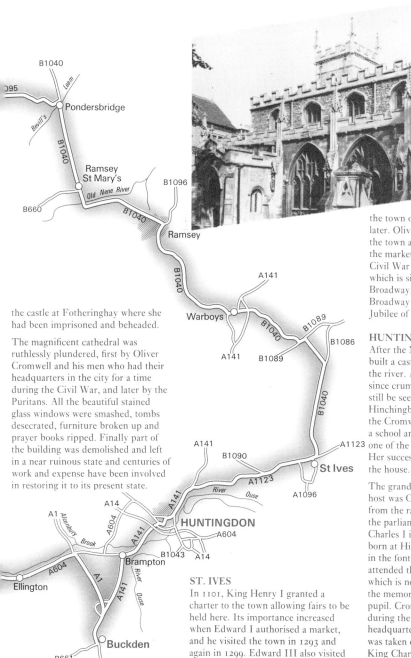

B

C

the castle at Fotheringhay where she had been imprisoned and beheaded.

The magnificent cathedral was ruthlessly plundered, first by Oliver Cromwell and his men who had their headquarters in the city for a time during the Civil War, and later by the Puritans. All the beautiful stained glass windows were smashed, tombs desecrated, furniture broken up and prayer books ripped. Finally part of the building was demolished and left in a near ruinous state and centuries of work and expense have been involved in restoring it to its present state.

ST. IVES

In 1101, King Henry I granted a charter to the town allowing fairs to be held here. Its importance increased when Edward I authorised a market, and he visited the town in 1293 and again in 1299. Edward III also visited

the town on two occasions, forty years later. Oliver Cromwell once lived in the town and a statue of him stands in the market place. There are several Civil War relics in the Norris Museum which is situated in The Waits Broadway. The fountain in the Broadway commemorates the Diamond Jubilee of Queen Victoria.

HUNTINGDON

After the Norman Conquest, William I built a castle at Huntingdon to guard the river. Although the walls have long since crumbled, the earthworks can still be seen quite clearly. Hinchingbrooke House was the seat of the Cromwell family before it became a school and Queen Elizabeth visited one of the Cromwells there in 1546. Her successor, James I, also came to the house.

The grandson of Queen Elizabeth's host was Oliver Cromwell who rose from the rank of captain to command the parliamentarian army against King Charles I in the Civil War. He was born at Hinchingbrooke and baptised in the font of All Saints Church. He attended the town's grammar school which is now a museum dedicated to the memory of its illustrious former pupil. Cromwell returned to the town during the Civil War to set up his headquarters at the Falcon Inn, which was taken over after his departure by King Charles for the same purpose.

BUCKDEN

Catherine of Aragon, the divorced first wife of Henry VIII, was a prisoner at Buckden Palace, the residence of the Bishops of Lincoln, for a time. She was then taken to Kimbolton Castle where she spent her last years. A large part of the building is now in ruins, but some of the buildings have been renovated and are occupied by Friars.

A The dramatic West Front of Peterborough Cathedral
B All Saints Church, Huntingdon, where Oliver Cromwell was baptised
C Hinchingbrooke House, Huntington, birthplace of Oliver Cromwell
D Buckden Palace, where Catherine of Aragon was once imprisoned

D

143

STAFFORD

Stafford's recorded connections with royalty begin in the 9th century when Alfred the Great drew up a treaty with the Danes at Wedmore. The Danes had arrived in the area in 874 and had caused havoc until Alfred's treaty, signed in 878, confined them to what was to become the northern part of Staffordshire.

The Danes remained quiet until 910 when they left the confines of the Danelaw, forcing the then King, Edward the Elder, to do battle against them. Edward's sister Ethelfleda played an important role during this period. Known as the "Lady of the Mercians" she built a chain of wooden fortifications, two of which were at Stafford, to defend the boundaries against further Danish encroachment. Once peace had been restored the town of Stafford began to grow up around one of Ethelfleda's fortresses. By the time Edward the Elder's son Athelstan had become King the town was well established and had a royal mint which remained in existence for 250 years.

Assault by the Conqueror

At the time of the Conquest the Midlands and north of England were only nominally subdued by the Normans and were constantly in rebellion against the new overlords. Consequently, in 1068, William found it necessary to conduct a campaign against the insurgents himself. He marched north and quashed the uprising with little difficulty. However in the following year the troubles began again and William determined to end the rebellion completely.

William proved what a ruthless leader he could be and laid the whole north country waste, including the towns of York, Chester and Stafford. As a final mark of his supreme authority he reinforced all Ethelfleda's forts in stone. By now the people were thoroughly

The ancient High House in Greengate Street, Stafford, where Charles I and Prince Rupert stayed during the Civil War (above and opposite)

cowed, and the strengthening of the fort at Stafford was an unnecessary measure. The castle, never used, had fallen into ruins by 1086 and was not restored until 1101 when William's son Henry I faced another rebellion.

William the Conqueror, after he had taken what he wanted, divided the remainder of the shire of Stafford amongst four of his followers. One of these was Robert, the son of William's standard bearer, who took the name of Stafford. Although the original castle founded by Ethelfleda in 913 and rebuilt by the Conqueror has long since disappeared, the ruins of a castle still to be seen on the northern outskirts of Stafford are those of the stronghold given by William to Robert de Stafford.

The Staffords were a prosperous and respected family and rebuilt the castle in 1350. When the 5th Earl married the grand-daughter of Edward III in 1444, and the 6th Earl was subsequently created Duke of Buckingham, the family fortunes reached their peak. After this things became less successful. In 1483 the 2nd Duke was beheaded for rebelling against Richard III and in 1521 the 3rd Duke was executed by Henry VIII for a variety of trumped-up reasons, but in reality because the Stafford family stood as a distant threat to the throne.

In 1485 Henry Tudor passed through Stafford on his way to the Battle of Bosworth Field, where he was victorious against Richard III and subsequently became Henry VII.

Parliamentarian conquest

During the Civil War the people of Stafford did not rush to support either the royalist or the parliamentarian side, and in November 1642 a meeting was held in Stafford to try and keep the county quiet. Charles I marched through the town on a recruiting campaign *en route* for Shrewsbury; the legend says that Prince Rupert burnt the houses of all those living in this area who refused to join the royalist forces. By the end of 1642, the royalists had complete control of Stafford. Feelings within the county were mixed, and in February 1643 a half-hearted siege was made on Stafford by the parliamentarians and their local supporters, and this was shortly followed up by a full-scale attack. On the night of the 16th May the parliamentarians crept into the town while everyone was asleep, and, because of the negligence of the royalists, were able to take the town without the loss of a single life.

Stafford Castle held out longer than the town, under the direction of Lady Stafford, an elderly lady with a will of iron. The castle hung on grimly until 22nd December 1643, when everyone was forced to abandon the fort, which was subsequently demolished by the parliamentarians. The existing ruins date mainly from 1817 when Sir George Jerningham rebuilt part of the old fort; these restorations and some of the ancient ruins are on view to the public.

In the town are some fine old buildings, including the four storeyed High House in Greengate Street, a black and white structure built in 1555. This was where Charles I and Prince Rupert lodged in 1642 while campaigning for more recruits to join royalist forces. From the gardens of the High House Prince Rupert allegedly tested his pistol marksmanship on the weathervane of the nearby parish church. It seems he hit the target twice, and the weathervane had to be replaced.

The outskirts of the town

1 mile west of Stafford is Tixall Hall where Mary, Queen of Scots was lured and held captive for 17 days while Walsingham examined her papers at Chartley Castle hoping to find fresh evidence of treason. Of the original mansion now only the old gatehouse remains—the rest of the stone was used to build the church of St John at Stafford.

Just outside Stafford is the area known as Cannock Chase, once a great hunting ground kept solely for the use of the Norman kings. It was patrolled by an army of guards, and anyone caught poaching or trespassing was subject to the severest of penalties. Within this area, which extended between Lichfield and Stafford, there once stood a hermitage endowed by King Stephen, but which was later taken over by Cistercian monks and became known as Radmore Abbey.

The Cistercians' time here, however, was soon ended, for, constantly worried by the forest guards, the monks applied to Henry II on his coronation day in December 1154 for help. The King listened to their plea and gave them some land in Warwickshire in exchange for Radmore Abbey which he converted into a hunting lodge. At Castle Hill near Hednesford, the highest point in Cannock Chase, may be seen the foundations of a Norman tower, all that remains today of Henry's hunting lodge.

Charles II's hiding places

CHARTLEY CASTLE

The first castle at Chartley was built in 1220 by the Earl of Chester. It passed into the hands of the de Ferrars family, and was involved in disputes with Henry III during the barons' rebellion against him. It was formerly an immense structure, with five huge towers, walls that were five feet thick, and a large keep. By the 15th century, however, the fort had been abandoned, and Chartley Hall was built near by. Some crumbling stonework is all that now remains of the castle.

Queen Elizabeth I visited the Hall in 1575, and enjoyed herself greatly. Ten years later, Mary, Queen of Scots was brought here by order of Elizabeth, and held captive until September 1586, when she was taken to Fotheringhay and executed. Mary was involved in a number of unsuccessful intrigues while she was here. Unfortunately for her, her letters, which were smuggled in and out of the house in a beer barrel, were intercepted by Elizabeth's agent Walsingham. Some of these letters were to her friend Babington, who was involved in a plot to murder Queen Elizabeth. This provided the evidence needed to send Mary for trial.

In 1781, Chartley Hall was burnt down, the existing grey stone house being built during the 19th century. It is not open to the public.

MOSELEY OLD HALL

The Hall was built in 1600, and, as was the case with many large houses erected at that time, it was equipped with a secret hiding place or priest-hole. Charles II had reason to be grateful for the priest-hole at Moseley when he stayed at the hall in 1651 after the defeat of his army at Worcester. He arrived on 8th September after having hidden at nearby Boscobel House, and he was warned as he lay resting, that soldiers were coming. Immediately Charles was hidden away in the priest-hole. That night Charles left Moseley on the next part of his escape route to the Continent. Visitors may enter the hall through the Orchard Door, which Charles used, and ascend the stairs to the King's Room where the bed in which the monarch slept is preserved,

A

B

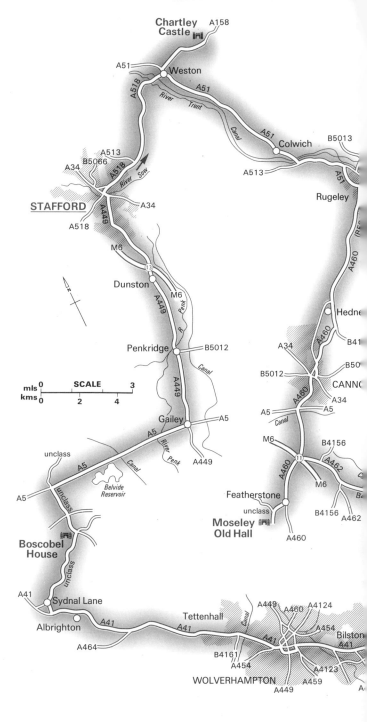

and where may be seen the famous hiding place.

RUSHALL

During the Civil War, Rushall Hall, near Walsall, was owned by Edward Leigh, who held out firmly against the royalist cause. The Hall was attacked by Prince Rupert in spring, 1643. Leigh and his wife withstood the attack bravely, but the determined assaults of the royalist forces compelled them to abandon their home. For a short period the royalists made Rushall their headquarters, and during this time, Henrietta Maria, queen of Charles I, arrived here bringing her reinforcements. However, on 22nd May 1644, the parliamentarians arrived, bringing with them Roaring Meg, a great cannon, with which they bombarded the Hall until the royalists were forced to surrender. Some of the cannonballs embedded in the walls of the 14th century remains of the Hall are still to be seen. The Hall was dismantled in 1646.

ASTON HALL

This beautiful building stands on the outskirts of Birmingham. Begun in 1618 and completed in the 1630s, it remains largely unchanged. During the Civil War King Charles sent 40 royalist soldiers to defend the house.

Before long, however, the house was besieged by 1,200 parliamentarians armed with cannons, and in the face of such odds the royalists surrendered. Two cannon balls, relics of the siege, are exhibited on the landing. The hall, which is open to the public, contains a room occupied by Charles I in 1642 as well as many fine architectural details and a children's museum.

BOSCOBEL HOUSE

On 3rd September 1651 the hopes of Charles II were crushed when his army was soundly beaten at the Battle of Worcester. In order to escape, Charles decided to make for London. Riding with Charles' party was a Mr Giffard who owned a house called Boscobel which lay deep in Brewood Forest, and it was suggested that Charles should seek shelter there. Charles agreed and the party immediately made for Whiteladies, a house which also belonged to Giffard and which stood about a mile away from Boscobel. Charles was fitted out with a disguise, but in view of the imminent danger of the arrival of enemy search parties, Charles was quickly bundled out of the house and spent what remained of the night and the whole of the following day in a nearby wood. By the time evening arrived, Charles had changed his plans. He had decided to escape into Wales, and he intended to make the journey that night. Charles and his guide hoped to reach Madeley, a house owned by a Catholic, which lay about nine miles west, but the journey, made on foot, was most unpleasant.

Eventually they reached Madeley, only to be told that escape into Wales was hopeless; every bridge across the Severn was guarded, and the whole area was crawling with parliamentary troops. The next night Charles returned to Boscobel. Another royalist, Colonel Carlis, was at Boscobel hoping to avoid capture, and both he and Charles spent that day hiding in an oak tree. It was as well that they did for a thorough search was made of the whole of the area. The Royal Oak that stands on the site today is a descendant of the original tree.

At dusk the two men descended from the tree and entered Boscobel House for a meal. Charles spent the night cramped into a hiding place between two walls. This royal hiding-hole may still be seen.

D

A The ruins of Chartley Castle
B Elizabethan Moseley Old Hall
C Boscobel House, hiding place of Charles II
D Royal Oak at Boscobel

C

Map

55
kenall eath
A461 ● **Rushall**
434
A454
B4151
A34
A461
WALSALL
Great Barr A4041
-54
A34
A461 A4031 M6 7 M6
A4041 Canal A453
A4040
A34
Wednesbury **Aston** 6
A41 M6
Canal A4040 M6
A4031 M5 A34
A461 A41 A38(M)
98 A41 A41 **BIRMINGHAM**
1
WEST BROMWICH
M5 A4031

DERBY

The City of Derby, well known today for the Rolls-Royce company and Royal Crown Derby pottery, was a thriving town in Saxon times, where coins were minted for kings Athelstan and Edgar. In the 10th century the Danes occupied parts of Derbyshire, and were allowed to do so as long as they recognised Alfred as their King. In 912 they revolted against Edward the Elder with the aid of a force from Wales, but they were defeated and took refuge in Derby. The King's sister marched on the town and attacked, killing the Welsh Prince and destroying the castle, of which no trace now remains.

Medieval unrest
The people of Derbyshire did not readily accept the Conquest of 1066 and frequently rebelled against the Norman King. Much of their property was confiscated by William, who retained parts for himself and distributed the rest among his noblemen.

For a time, because of this unrest, the town did not prosper, but in 1154 it was granted a charter to hold markets and merchants came from miles around to conduct their business transactions. King John granted the town the right to carry on the dyeing process, which it did for many years, and several mills for the textile industry grew up around the Derwent River.

The Royalist Cause
King Charles I passed through Derby in 1641, before the onset of the Civil War. He took lodgings for the night at a house in the Market Place and, during his stay, promoted Sir Francis Rodes and Sir John Curzon from knights to barons. He returned to Derby in the following year, the first of the war between the royalists and the parliamentarians, where he borrowed £300 and a supply of weapons from the Corporation before continuing his journey to Shrewsbury.

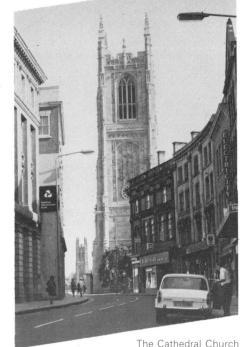

The Cathedral Church of All Saints, Derby. The west tower dates from the 16th century, and the cathedral houses the tomb of Bess of Hardwick

Although Derby was a strong royalist town, an army was raised in the county to support Parliament and they were joined in Derby by another roundhead regiment. The result was a royalist attack on the town, but it was delayed for so long that the roundheads had departed for Yorkshire before the King's men arrived and the whole exercise was rendered pointless.

When the government fell in 1659, the people of Derby gathered together in the Market Place and loudly demanded the restoration of the royal family. Two hundred and fifty dragoons were called in, but their leader managed to persuade the people to disperse quietly, avoiding a violent confrontation.

Some years later, when the Earl of Devonshire came to raise support for William of Orange against King James II, Derby was less inclined to commit itself to his cause.

The Young Pretender
In 1745 another threat to the throne occurred from the Scottish Prince Charles Edward. Although some of the inhabitants of Derby were sympathetic to his claims, they were extremely apprehensive when they received the news that the Young Pretender was marching towards their town. They raised two armies for the defence of the town, but the untrained and inadequately armed troops had little confidence and gave no real resistance to Bonnie Prince Charlie as he entered the town with his Highland army. Charles found accommodation in Exeter House in Full Street; it was demolished long ago and all that now remains is the oak panelling which clads the walls of a room in the public library. Charles' followers found lodgings around the town. These included not only the men who came to fight for him, but also the Lady Ogilvie who trailed after the handsome young Prince wherever he went. On the morning after his arrival, the Prince heard mass in the Church of All Saints, now the Cathedral of Derby.

During his stay, Charles discovered that certain people in Derby had made donations to the King and, obtaining a list of these subscribers, forced them to pay him a similar amount. He held some turbulent councils of war at Exeter House during his stay. His army consisted, in the main, of a variety of different clans and their chiefs, who had a long history of fighting among themselves. Although they united behind their Prince, their feuding continued within the ranks.

Meanwhile, the Duke of Cumberland had discovered the whereabouts of the Pretender and his army and was marching towards Derby to engage his enemy. The Prince took the only course of action open to him and retreated, leaving the town through the Friar Gate on his journey back to the Highlands.

The Market Place, Derby. Charles I stayed at a house in the Market Place during his march to Shrewsbury

Tour to Bosworth Field

STANFORD HALL

This fine 17th century mansion has been the seat of the Cave family for many generations, and is open to the public. Near by is Stanford Church, which contains tombs and monuments of the Cave family, including one to Sir Ambrose Cave, who was Elizabeth I's Chancellor to the Duchy of Lancaster. It is said that on one occasion when the Queen was dancing at court her garter slipped off and Sir Ambrose picked it up. Elizabeth refused to take it back, and Ambrose wore it on his left arm for the rest of his life. Two panels in the east window of the church depict Henry II and his Queen.

LOUGHBOROUGH

Hugh le Despenser inherited the Loughborough estate from the Earl of Chester and during the 13th century obtained charters from the Crown to hold fairs and markets in the village. However, le Despenser took the side of de Montfort in his rebellion against King Henry III in 1265 and was killed. The King gave his lands to Henry, Lord Beaumont, whose family held the property for some time.

The town was visited in 1387 by Richard II, the King who was later deposed and killed by the Lancastrian Henry IV. The Beaumonts supported his grandson, Henry VI during the Wars of the Roses, but when the victorious Edward IV came to the throne he took away their estates and gave them to Lord Hastings of Ashby-de-la-Zouch who was later beheaded for treason. The Great House beside the parish church in Loughborough was the place where Henry VII spent the night while visiting the town.

During the Civil War the town was royalist and King Charles I and his nephew, Prince Rupert, spent some time there.

BRADGATE PARK

The house, which was burnt down by the wife of the Earl of Stamford, was built by Thomas Grey, the Marquess of Dorset, when he found the family home at nearby Groby too small. His great granddaughter, Lady Jane Grey, was born in the house and spent the first fifteen years of her life there before her marriage to Lord Dudley. Not long after her marriage, King Edward VI died and, much to her horror, Lady Jane was pronounced Queen after a great deal of devious plotting by her father-in-law. Mary, true heir to the throne, gathered her followers about her and the downfall of the "Nine Days Queen" was soon brought about. Both Lady Jane and her husband were beheaded.

BOSWORTH FIELD

The Battle of Bosworth Field took place on 22nd August 1485, and finally put an end to the long Wars of the Roses between the Houses of Lancaster and York. Henry Tudor, nearest Lancastrian claimant to the throne, landed at Milford Haven from exile in Normandy. He made his way through Wales and the Midlands, finally camping his small army at Atherstone. In the meantime, King Richard III, hearing of the arrival of a rival claimant to the throne, set out from Nottingham. He paused for a while at Leicester, calling for reinforcements to be brought and sending scouts to discover the whereabouts of Henry. The King then made his way across the country and halted his army 2 miles south of Market Bosworth.

Lord Stanley led a regiment of the King's men, but Richard doubted his loyalty and so held hostage his son, Lord Strange. Nevertheless, Stanley secretly went to Henry's camp and, although he could not defect and cause the death of his son, he agreed to bide his time behind the King and take action for Henry when the opportunity arose. Although the King's army heavily outnumbered Henry's, Richard was killed in the battle and his men dispersed. Henry had reason to be grateful to Lord Stanley, and also to his brother, Sir William, who found the crown which had toppled from Richard's head and rolled under a thorn bush. It was on a nearby hill, now called Crown Hill, that the crown was placed on Henry Tudor's head, creating not only a new King, but a new dynasty. A small museum shows models, exhibitions and film shows,

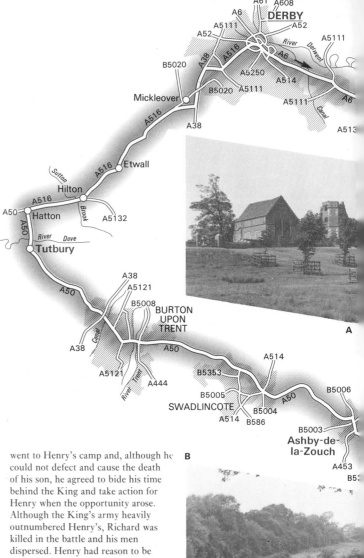

and visitors can see the battlefield and the well from which King Richard drank during the battle.

ASHBY-DE-LA-ZOUCH

The castle at Ashby-de-la-Zouch was formerly a Norman manor house and was extended by the first Baron Hastings. He had been given the estate by King Edward IV for the support of his private army on the Yorkist side during the Wars of the Roses. The Baron was later beheaded at the Tower of London after being denounced as a traitor by the Duke of Gloucester. Baron Hastings' grandson was created Earl of Huntingdon by King Henry VIII and he played some part in the trial of Anne Boleyn, Henry's second wife, who was beheaded after only three years as queen. Another Hastings was jailor to Mary, Queen of Scots, when she was imprisoned in the castle in 1569 on her way from Tutbury to Coventry, and again in 1586. James I visited his mother's former prison in 1617, and brought the whole of his court with him, which almost bankrupted the Earl.

In 1634 Charles I and his wife, Queen Henrietta Maria, came to the castle, and the King returned eleven years later during the Civil War. He stayed here for a few days to prepare for the Battle of Naseby and returned again after the battle to rest. The castle, under the command of the Earl's brother, Colonel Henry Hastings, withstood a siege by parliamentary troops for almost a year but was eventually forced to surrender, and the commander went into exile. He

joined Charles II in France, and at the Restoration, Charles created him Lord Loughborough. Much of the castle was destroyed by parliamentary troops, but remains include the tower and some of the domestic buildings.

TUTBURY

After the Norman invasion of 1066, Tutbury Castle was given to Henry de Ferrars by William the Conqueror, but it was destroyed a hundred years later by Henry II after William Ferrars' rebellion against the King. It was rebuilt in the 14th century, but the life of the new castle was a short one. Again, one of the Ferrars family took up arms against the King, this time Henry III, and the castle was torn down for a second time. Two years later, the King gave the property to his brother, the Earl of Lancaster, and it remained in his family for some time. When the Duke of Lancaster became King Henry IV in 1399, the castle became Crown property and was considerably enlarged with a self contained tower for fortification and defence.

By the time Mary, Queen of Scots, was imprisoned at Tutbury Castle it had fallen into disrepair and caused the Queen great discomfort during her stays. It was cold, with very little light, and extremely dank.

The ruins of Bradgate House, birthplace of Lady Jane Grey
The battlefield of Bosworth
Castle ruins, Ashby-de-la-Zouch

NOTTINGHAM

Nottingham is built above a honeycomb of underground caverns which may have been inhabited by Neolithic cave dwellers. There is no evidence of any permanent settlement here, however, before the 6th century when a community of Anglo Saxons made their home beside the River Trent at the edge of Sherwood Forest.

Occupation by the Danes

The Danish invasion had reached Nottingham in the 9th century, led by Halfdan and his brother, Ivan the Boneless. The town was in the Kingdom of Mercia and the ruler, Burghed, gathered an army with the aid of his brothers-in-law King Ethelred and the young Alfred, who later became King Alfred the Great. The expected battle did not take place, however, and a peace treaty was negotiated. The Danes withdrew to York and the army returned home.

The peace did not last long, and six years later the Danes took over a large portion of the country. Nottingham became one of the regional centres of Danelaw. Edward the Elder tried to regain the lands in Danelaw, and his son, Athelstan, carried on this endeavour. Both were in Nottingham, where Edward built a bridge across the River Trent and ordered the building of walls and ditches to protect the town in 920. Athelstan established the minting of coins in the town which continued until 1154. After the death of Athelstan, the Norse King of Dublin took Nottingham, but his occupation was short-lived and when he died two years later the town reverted to English rule.

After the Norman Conquest, William I visited Nottingham and chose the site for the castle. It was one of a series he had constructed at vantage points around the country to guard either coastal or river approaches. The castle at Nottingham was in an excellent position, high on a rock, making the construction of an artificial mound unnecessary. The Conqueror put his illegitimate son, William Peveril, in charge of the castle which was crown property for many years, and a settlement of Normans grew up around its walls who kept themselves separate from the English. This division was retained for many centuries. William Rufus, the Conqueror's son, also visited the town.

Stephen and Matilda

After the death of Henry I, the right of accession to the throne was disputed. Henry had wished for his daughter, Matilda, to become queen, but the barons would not be ruled by a woman and they supported Henry's sister's claim that her son, Stephen, should be king. Nottingham castle was being held for Stephen when Matilda's half-brother, the Earl of Gloucester attacked on her behalf. He found the castle impregnable and set fire to the town before retreating. After Stephen's arrest the castle was taken for Matilda, but a surprise attack deprived her of the stronghold. Her son, who later became Henry II, besieged the castle but was driven away when his opponents set fire to the town in which his men had found accommodation. He determined to return to the

The legend of Robin Hood, commemorated in the statue on Castle Green, is said to symbolise the feud which grew up between the Saxon townspeople of Nottingham and the Norman builders of the castle

town, which he did in happier circumstances after his accession to the throne in 1155. Henry rebuilt the castle in stone rather than wood and granted the town its first charter to hold a market. More charters followed from King John and Edward I, who instigated the holding of Goose fairs which are still held today. The importance of the markets authorised by these charters is reflected in the size of the market place—nearly six acres in all.

Defeat of Mortimer

When the Scots attempted to kidnap Edward II's queen in Yorkshire, she was sent to Nottingham for safety. Their marriage was not a happy one and some years later the Queen and her lover, the Earl of Mortimer, brought about the downfall of the King and ultimately his death. Her son, Edward III, was only a boy when he came to the throne and for some time was the puppet of his mother and Mortimer. They were openly living together by this time, to the disapproval of their subjects. In 1330, they took Edward to Nottingham, primarily to hold a parliament, but events turned out dramatically differently. The King was closely guarded in the fortress and in no position to take any action against his mother and her consort, but he had some faithful supporters outside who conspired to end the domination over Edward. The Deputy Constable of the castle was part of the plot and he led the King's men into the castle by a secret passage, now known as Mortimer's hole. Edward met them in the castle and together they captured the Earl. He was later executed and Queen Isabella was forced into retirement. Edward held his parliament in Nottingham on several occasions after that and made a number of alterations to the castle.

James I frequently hunted in Sherwood Forest and broke his journeys in Nottingham. The castle was in a poor state of repair by this time and he stayed at Thurland Hall, a mansion owned by Sir John Holles. Charles I brought his wife, Henrietta Maria, to Thurland Hall for a five day sojourn in 1634. To prepare for this visit every house in Nottingham was

Nottingham Castle, restored in the 19th century, stands on a 133 feet bluff. It houses the museum and art gallery

repainted and the streets cleared of refuse which was normally deposited there.

Civil War hostilities start

The town saw none of the hostilities which raged during the Wars of the Roses, but at the start of the Civil War, King Charles I came to the castle and raised his standard. The peace loving population were not interested in the quarrel with Parliament and only three hundred men rallied to the standard on Standard Hill. The parliamentarians were soon in possession of the castle which was besieged on many occasions by the royalists. After the King's men had fired on the castle from the tower of St. Nicholas' church, the church was demolished by the parliamentarians to prevent any recurrence. The castle was also destroyed at the end of the war, as were many

throughout the country, to render them useless to the supporters of the monarchy. In 1674 a mansion was built on the castle site by the Duke of Newcastle and four years later the church was replaced.

Industrialization

In the 18th century the town and its industries prospered and the Industrial Revolution saw such innovations as the stocking frame, the spinning jenny and a machine for making the famous Nottingham lace. The increase in prosperity brought an increase in the population, and living conditions among the working classes unfortunately became extremely unpleasant, with overcrowding and the resulting decline in health. The Luddite rebellion reached the town in 1811 and many machines in the mills were smashed. The workers rioted outside the castle.

Today, however, Nottingham has many varied industries and, is a developing modern city, which retains the links with its historic past.

The Castle by the Trent

MANSFIELD

A market town standing on the edge of Sherwood Forest, Mansfield has sometimes been a royal manor. Henry III granted a market charter in 1229 and later in the 14th century Richard II granted a fair. King's Mill is associated with the story of the 'Miller of Mansfield' who found Henry II wandering in the wood and entertained him with a pasty of venison which had been poached from the King's own property.

Hardwick Hall stands five miles north west of Mansfield. It is an Elizabethan mansion, built in the 16th century by the venerable Bess of Hardwick at the age of 70, a building which is famous for its many large windows, and a full length portrait of Mary, Queen of Scots.

CLIPSTONE

Five miles north east of Mansfield, in the beautiful area of the Dukeries and Sherwood Forest, are the ruins of King John's Palace which was a favourite hunting lodge used by King John. It was first enclosed by parkland by Henry II and later it was enjoyed by Edward I and Edward II. Edward III decided it was not big enough and

enlarged the lodge. It was also purported to be the meeting place of Richard I and Robin Hood. About one mile north west stands Parliament Oak, reputedly the place where Edward I held his parliament.

SOUTHWELL

Charles I stayed at the medieval King's Arms as it was known in 1646 (now the Saracen's Head) before surrendering to the Scots Commissioners. The town is noted for its Minster which has fine examples of Perpendicular, Norman and Early English architecture. The choir was built under the auspices of the archbishop and Henry III. Their heads are depicted in the carving on the corbels on the north side.

NEWARK-ON-TRENT

An ancient market town bordered on the north west by the River Trent, it stands at the intersection of the Fosse Way and Great North Road. The castle, now in ruins, has played a large part in the country's history. It was visited by Henry II in the 12th century, and was the scene of King John's death in 1216. Henry VII stayed in the castle in 1487, on his way to the Battle of Stoke Field. James I was very fond of the town, and stayed here when travelling to London for his coronation.

King Charles I passed through the town just before the start of the Civil War in order to confirm the people's loyalty. He was on his way to Nottingham to raise the standard,

marking the start of the war. The town was fortified in 1642 against a siege, and during the war sustained three sieges. Henrietta Maria, wife of Charles I, passed through the town in June 1643 breaking her journey to visit Lady Leake.

Parliamentary forces besieged the town in 1644, but it was relieved by Prince Rupert, King Charles I's nephew. After his defeat at the battle of Naseby, Charles I fled to Newark, where he surrendered to the Scots. At the end of the war, the townspeople were ordered

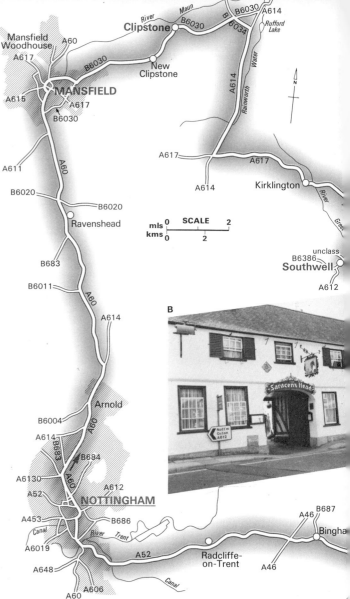

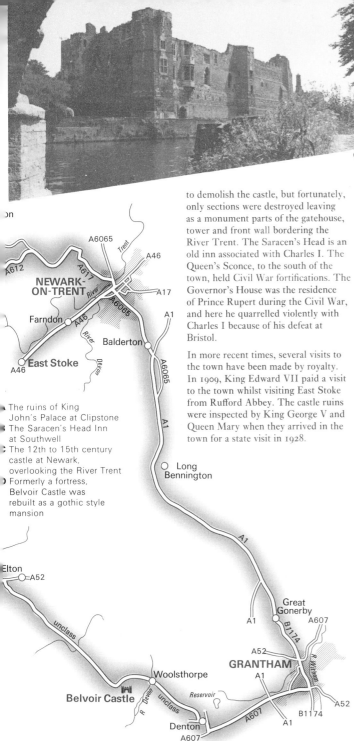

EAST STOKE

Situated just south of Newark between the main road and the River Trent is a 200 ft hill round the base of which the Battle of Stoke Field was fought. Henry VII, victor of Bosworth, ruled for about two years before trouble broke out in Ireland, the Earl of Lincoln proclaiming the youngster Lambert Simnel, King Edward VI. The Earl came over from Ireland in 1487 with about 9,000 troops, and met the superior forces of Henry VII here by the Fosse Way. After a three hour battle, Henry was victorious and captured the pretender Lambert Simnel.

GRANTHAM

The town of Grantham once belonged to Edith, wife of Edward the Confessor, and it was here that Edward I erected a cross to mark the resting place of the coffin containing his Queen Eleanor, on its way from Harby to Westminster Abbey. The cross was destroyed during the Civil War when the town was captured by Cromwell in 1643.

At the north end of the High Street, stands Grantham's famous medieval inn. It has a fine 15th century gateway, over which are carvings of the heads of Edward III and Queen Philippa. King John held court here in 1213, and the room is known as the King's Chamber. Here also in 1483 Richard III signed the death warrant of the Duke of Buckingham. King Charles I also stayed at the Inn in 1633 as, centuries later, did Edward VII when Prince of Wales. After Edward's visit the Inn became known as the Angel and Royal Hotel.

BELVOIR CASTLE

A castle was first built here in Norman times on land given by William the Conquerer. It was visited by King John, James I and Charles I. The castle was besieged for four months during the Civil War before surrendering, and Cromwell ordered its demolition. It was rebuilt in the 17th century, converted into a Gothic style castle in 1800, and was visited by the Prince Regent in 1813. It is rich in tapestries, paintings, armour and objets d'art.

to demolish the castle, but fortunately, only sections were destroyed leaving as a monument parts of the gatehouse, tower and front wall bordering the River Trent. The Saracen's Head is an old inn associated with Charles I. The Queen's Sconce, to the south of the town, held Civil War fortifications. The Governor's House was the residence of Prince Rupert during the Civil War, and here he quarrelled violently with Charles I because of his defeat at Bristol.

In more recent times, several visits to the town have been made by royalty. In 1909, King Edward VII paid a visit to the town whilst visiting East Stoke from Rufford Abbey. The castle ruins were inspected by King George V and Queen Mary when they arrived in the town for a state visit in 1928.

A The ruins of King John's Palace at Clipstone
B The Saracen's Head Inn at Southwell
C The 12th to 15th century castle at Newark, overlooking the River Trent
D Formerly a fortress, Belvoir Castle was rebuilt as a gothic style mansion

LINCOLN

The massive 14th century Eastern Gate is the entrance to Lincoln Castle, one of eight castles in Britain known to have been founded by William the Conqueror himself

The Romans took over the Iron Age hill fort at Lincoln for their garrison and re-named it *Lindum*. It stood at the junction of the Fosse Way and Ermine Street for the duration of the Roman occupation. After the departure of the Romans, Saxon invaders pillaged the town and the buildings fell into ruin, but it developed in later years as a Danish settlement. Coins were minted in the town, some of which have been discovered in Scandinavia.

Norman development

The Normans were the next to settle at Lincoln and William I, after his visit to the town, ordered that a huge castle be built on the hill-top. The walls enclosed several acres of land and it was recorded that a hundred and sixteen dwellings had to be torn down to make way for its construction. It was an unusual castle, having two mounds instead of one. The Norman keep, called Lucy's Tower, was built on one and the other includes the later addition of an observatory erected in Victorian times. King William also supported the building of the cathedral, an extension of the original church of St. Mary, by Bishop Bek and this too displaced many residents of the town. All those who lost their homes at the hands of the Norman builders were rehoused in new suburbs to the south of the hill.

The cathedral was demolished in the earthquake of 1185, but re-building was completed by around 1280 and the cathedral became the administrative centre of the diocese of Lincoln. It covered seven archdeaconries, twenty-five deaconries and the city contained forty-eight parish churches. A great bishop's palace was built to the south and other buildings grew up around the cathedral to house the clergymen.

Wars of succession

During the reign of King Stephen, the Empress Matilda came to England in a bid to seize the throne and she lived at Lincoln Castle for a time. She was driven out by the King, but later returned and in the ensuing battle Stephen was defeated and captured. Although Matilda was in a position to become queen, she alienated any support she had gained by her arrogance and was later forced to release the King. The enmity between the two continued for some years until Matilda left England to join her husband in Normandy.

The coronation of King Henry II took place at Westminster, and he was crowned for a second time at Lincoln. He granted several charters to the city and throughout the Middle Ages it prospered, becoming one of the principal centres of civilisation in the country. A flourishing textile industry developed, producing the famous Lincoln Green and Lincoln Scarlet.

Medieval associations

In 1200 King John came to the city on two occasions, the first time to receive the homage of William of Scotland and later to help carry the body of Bishop Hugh of Avalon to the cathedral. When the barons rose up in rebellion against King John they seized Lincoln Castle with the help of the French Dauphin, Prince Louis, who had come to support their uprising. Even after the death of King John, when most of the barons gave their allegiance to his son, the Dauphin again tried to enter the castle, but without success. The English army drove the rebels out after a running battle through the streets of Lincoln.

The Assize Court building
in Lincoln Castle grounds

The imposing bust of
George III in Lincoln Castle grounds

building are in evidence, but most of it dates from the 13th century with later additions, including the stained glass of the nave windows made by Victorian craftsmen.

The appearance of the castle was greatly altered in the 18th century when a jail was constructed in the enclosure, but it was only in use for about one hundred years and the Lincolnshire Archives Office now occupies the building. If the interior of the castle has been somewhat marred by the recent buildings, the castle walls still give superb views across the city, and of the cathedral.

The Stonebow gateway bears a carving of the arms of James I and an oak staircase leads up to the Guildhall above, both built in the late 15th and early 16th centuries. A room in the Guildhall contains the civic insignia which include three swords presented to the City by Richard II, Henry VII and Charles I.

A new shrine was erected to Bishop Hugh of Avalon eighty years after his burial and Edward I and his queen, Eleanor, were present when his body was removed. Ten years later, the Queen's body passed through Lincoln during the long funeral procession from Harby in Nottinghamshire to Westminster. Queen Eleanor was embalmed by the nuns of the priory of St Catherine just outside the city and one of the famous Eleanor crosses was erected. Only a fragment of the cross now remains, part of a female figure, which can be seen in the passage of the castle gateway.

In 1301 Edward I was in Lincoln to hold a Council opposing the claim of the Pope over the sovereignty of Scotland and when, fifteen years later, England was at war with Scotland, Edward II was provided with supplies from the city. Richard II also visited Lincoln when, in 1387, he presented the sword to the city which is now part of its civic insignia and gave permission for it to be carried before the mayor.

The Battle of Bosworth Field took place on 22nd August 1485 and resulted in Henry Tudor being crowned King Henry VII. He

came to Lincoln after his victory and spent three days giving thanks in the cathedral. His son, Henry VIII was also a visitor to the city when he brought his fifth wife, Catherine Howard, and both were the guests of Bishop Longland in 1541.

Changes since the Civil War

The city suffered considerably at the hands of both opposing armies during the Civil War. At the onset of the war Charles I received an ovation from the population of Lincoln when he came to the city, but it changed hands several times and was finally besieged by the Earl of Manchester for Oliver Cromwell. When the royalist defences collapsed in 1644, the parliamentary forces swept into the city, by which time the inhabitants had very little sympathy for either side. Had it not been for private quarrels between the individuals involved, the city would probably have remained totally neutral.

The cathedral is now one of the most impressive in the country with its three towers, once surmounted by spires, looking down over the whole of the city. Parts of the original Norman

Lincoln Cathedral is situated in one of the finest positions in England. It dates from the 11th to 15th centuries, and holds the best-preserved of only four copies of Magna Carta in the country

157

Sieges in Lincolnshire

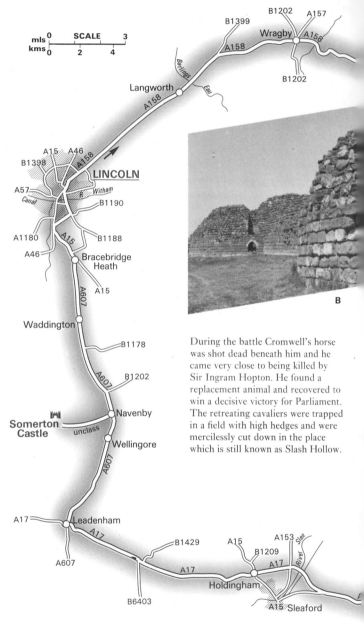

HORNCASTLE

The town of Horncastle derived its name from the horn-shaped piece of land on which it is built between the Rivers Bain and Waring. In Roman times it was a walled settlement and parts of the walls have been excavated and can be seen today. In later centuries a large proportion of the population came from the influx of Danish settlers who eventually numbered half the total population of Lincolnshire. With the coming of the Normans, Horncastle was the centre of one of the "Sokes" or estates into which the country was divided.

The Church of St. Mary contains a brass of Sir Lionel Dymoke, the Champion of England, whose descendants have retained the hereditary title. Their family seat is at nearby Scrivelsby Court. During the Civil War, Horncastle was occupied by parliamentary forces, but they left the town when news arrived of a large royalist force marching towards them from Lincoln. In the resulting confrontation at Winceby, Oliver Cromwell almost lost his life, but

recovered to win a resounding victory. Cromwell then travelled to Horncastle bringing with him the body of the man who had almost put an end to him, Sir Ingram Hopton, and made arrangements for his burial in St. Mary's Church. There is a house in West Street, bearing the name of Cromwell's House, but in actual fact it was in the house next door, which has since been demolished, that Oliver Cromwell resided during his stay in the town.

WINCEBY

During the second year of the Civil War small battles and sieges were taking place all over the country. Both the royalist and parliamentary armies were becoming more experienced and had learned that tactics were as important as enthusiasm. Bolingbroke Castle was being held for the King under siege from the Earl of Manchester, and a royalist force of 2,500 men advanced to relieve it. Manchester withdrew, to be joined by reinforcements led by Sir Thomas Fairfax and Colonel Oliver Cromwell and they were engaged at Winceby on 11th October 1643 by a combined royalist army.

During the battle Cromwell's horse was shot dead beneath him and he came very close to being killed by Sir Ingram Hopton. He found a replacement animal and recovered to win a decisive victory for Parliament. The retreating cavaliers were trapped in a field with high hedges and were mercilessly cut down in the place which is still known as Slash Hollow.

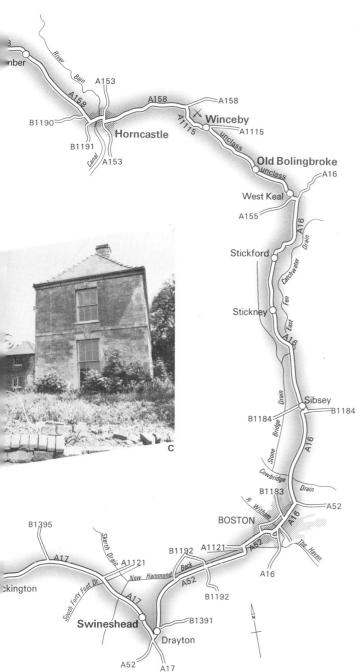

C

OLD BOLINGBROKE

Bolingbroke Castle was originally built by William de Roumare, the first Earl of Lincoln, on land given to him by King Henry I and it later passed to Edmund Plantagenet, brother of King Edward I. On his marriage to Blanche de Lacy, John of Gaunt became the owner of the castle at only nineteen years of age. The young Duke of Lancaster was the son of a king and the father of a king, but never a king himself. He and his bride were often visited at the castle by John's great friend Geoffrey Chaucer. On 3rd April 1367 a son was born to John and Blanche at Bolingbroke Castle who was later to become King Henry IV. He was the first king of England since the Norman invasion to be born and brought up in England by English parents. He grew up among the artistic and literary friends of his father to be a man of great culture.

He developed rather grand ideas of his own station in life, which led him to usurp the throne from Richard II in 1399. King Richard, formerly his friend, had banished Henry from the country in 1398, after a disagreement, and on the death of John of Gaunt, Richard took Bolingbroke for his own. Henry returned to the country with a small army to claim the lands which were rightfully his and his supporters forced the King to abdicate. Thus the estates became crown property until the Civil War. The royalist occupants were besieged by a parliamentary force and surrender was demanded, but when the aggressors were occupied at the Battle of Winceby, the inhabitants of the castle were able to get away. Cromwell's men returned to find the castle empty and they partly demolished it to prevent the return of their adversaries.

SWINESHEAD

The village of Swineshead no longer holds the markets once granted, but the ancient market cross remains as do the stocks once used to punish erring villagers. A Cistercian abbey was founded just outside the village in 1148, and King John rested there in 1216. While crossing the Wash he had been taken unawares by the advancing tides and the whole of his bags and baggage were lost, together with the crown and other treasures. The King consoled himself with large quantities of food and drink which proved too much for his constitution and he died at Newark-on-Trent just one week later. A farmhouse was built on the site of the abbey using the original masonry.

SOMERTON CASTLE

Just outside the village of Navenby are the ruins of the impressive Somerton Castle. The huge building was constructed around a quadrangle measuring 330ft by 180ft with a round tower at each corner. There were two moats and extensive outer fortifications. Built on the site of a Saxon fortress, the castle was crenellated by Bishop Bek, and given to King Edward I. It remained crown property for around three hundred years and was one of the places where King John of France was imprisoned with his son, Philip. They had been captured at the Battle of Poitiers by Edward, the Black Prince, and brought to this country for the purpose of being held to ransom. The sum raised in this way was the equivalent of nearly two million pounds.

A The battlefield at Winceby, where Oliver Cromwell defeated a royalist force during the Civil War
B The castle at Old Bolingbroke, where Henry IV spent his childhood
C This farmhouse in Swineshead incorporates parts of the old abbey, where King John came after losing the crown jewels in The Wash

Royal Land of Wales

Wales fought against domination by England up until the time of Edward I, who with his campaigns against the Welsh, and the string of mighty castles that he constructed, did much to subdue the country and bring it under the rule of the English crown. Trouble and rebellion continued sporadically, however, until the advent of Henry Tudor, Henry VII. Henry's Welsh ancestry and his introduction of Welshmen into court life did much to bring about a harmony between the two countries.

The following two pages highlight a selection of places throughout Wales which have special associations with royalty. The tour beginning on page 162 visits the places principally associated with royalty (both English and Welsh) in North Wales.

Aberffraw, Gwynedd (Anglesey)
Nothing now remains to show that this place was, between the 7th and 13th centuries, the capital of the kingdom of Gwynedd. Llywelyn the Great held court here as did his grandson, Llywelyn the Last.

Aberystwyth, Dyfed
The castle here was originally built by Edmund Crouchback, brother of Edward I. It was destroyed by the Welsh in 1282 and was subsequently rebuilt on the instructions of Edward I. Owain Glyndwr (who was descended from the royal houses of Wales) held the castle from 1403 to 1408. During the Civil War Charles I established a mint in the castle which produced coins from locally mined silver. The castle was eventually captured by parliamentary troops and destroyed.

Caerphilly, Mid Glamorgan
In the 13th century this part of Wales was ruled by Prince Gruffydd ap Rhys. Gilbert de Clare, Norman lord of Glamorgan, feared that Gruffydd, along with his ally Llywelyn the Last, would soon overrun his lands, so in order to prevent this he attacked and defeated Gruffydd in 1266. Work began on Caerphilly Castle in 1268, but it was destroyed by Llywelyn before it could be completed. In 1271 work was begun on the present castle; once more Llywelyn laid siege to it, but the intervention of Henry III brought a truce. Under cover of the truce, de Clare captured the castle and eventually drove Llywelyn from the area.

Edward II stayed briefly at the castle in 1326 whilst on the run from the nobles whom his wife Isabella had persuaded to rise against him.

Cardiff, South Glamorgan.
Cardiff was the capital of the kingdom of Morgannwg until the arrival of the Norman Robert Fitz Hamon who built a castle, the mound of which is crowned today by a later stone keep. In 1158 Prince Ifor ap Meurig of Senghennydd raided the castle and captured Fitz Hamon and his family.

Charles I came to Cardiff shortly after the Battle of Naseby in 1645; not long after he had left, the town was captured by Parliament. Cardiff was granted the status of a city in 1905 by Edward VII, and created capital of Wales in 1955 by Elizabeth II.

Carew, Dyfed
A magnificent cross here commemorates a Welsh prince. Dating from about 1035, it is inscribed: "The Cross of Maredudd son of Edwin". Maredudd was descended from Hywel Dda, one of Wales' great rulers, and ruled the kingdom of Deheubarth until his death in 1035.

The castle once belonged to Gerald de Windsor, who acquired it after his marriage to Princess Nest, the daughter of Prince Rhys, in 1095. Extensive changes were made to the castle in later years, especially by Sir John Perrot, who is reputed to have been a son of Henry VIII.

Carreg Cennen Castle, Dyfed
Without doubt one of Wales' most romantic ruins, Carreg Cennen commands impressive views of the Black Mountain. The castle, once one of the principal seats of the rulers of the kingdom of Deheubarth, fell to the forces of Edward I in 1277. It eventually passed to Henry Bolingbroke, the future Henry IV. At the end of the Wars of the Roses, the castle was given by Henry VII to Sir Rhys ap Thomas.

Castell-y-Bere, Gwynedd
At one time this ruined castle was one of the most important in Wales. A stronghold of the Welsh princes, it was held against the forces of Edward I by Llywelyn's brother Dafydd. Eventually Edward captured it and Dafydd fled, only to be captured later and executed at Shrewsbury.

Chirk Castle, Clwyd
Although much changed from the original castle founded by Edward I, the mighty corner towers still serve as a reminder of Chirk's former military purpose. During its long history the castle has had a succession of noble owners, including Thomas Seymour, husband of Queen Katherine Parr. In the castle's Tudor Room is a bed in which Charles I slept.

Cilgerran Castle, Dyfed
Tradition asserts that it was from here that Owain, son of the Prince of Powys, abducted the Princess Nest who was married to Gerald de Windsor. Later the castle was captured from the Normans by the Lord Rhys of Dinefwr. After Rhys' death in 1197 it was taken by the

Henry Tudor was born at Pembroke Castle in 1457

Normans, but was re-taken by Llywelyn the Great. In 1223 it was once more captured by the Normans and remained in the hands of the Marshall family until 1245. By the early 14th century it was in ruins but was re-fortified by Edward III. Henry VII granted the castle to the Vaughan family who seem to have allowed it to sink into honourable ruin.

Cilmery, Powys
A roadside obelisk here commemorates the fact that Llywelyn the Last, Prince of Wales, died near this spot in 1282. He had ridden south, after a victory over the English at Menai, to confer with some of his generals at Builth Wells. The English learned that the Prince was in the area and closed in, but in the end his death was a near-accident, for the English lancer who killed him, Stephen de Frankton, did not know who he was.

Denbigh Castle, Clwyd
Dafydd, brother of Llywelyn the Last, had his headquarters at Denbigh. After the defeat of the Welsh rebellion, Edward I gave the stronghold and accompanying lands to Henry de Lacy, Earl of Lincoln, who built the castle which stands today. Charles I is said to have spent three days at the castle during the Civil War.

Dolwyddelan Castle, Gwynedd
This castle was probably the birthplace of Llywelyn the Great. When he reached manhood, Llywelyn, by superb statesmanship, managed to unite all the petty princedoms of

Wales into one unit. He married King John's illegitimate daughter Joan, and strived to maintain a peace between Wales and England. At times it was difficult but Llywelyn managed eventually to achieve for Wales a greater independence and sense of unity than it had had before, or has had since. He died in 1240 at Aberconwy, a legend in his own lifetime.

Harlech Castle, Gwynedd
One of Edward I's great castles, Harlech stands as a symbol of England's domination of Wales. Its architect was Master James of St George, a genius of military planning. In 1294 the castle was besieged by Madog ap Llywelyn, who was related to the princes of North Wales. That siege failed, but another great Welsh nationalist, Owain Glyndwr, took the castle in 1404 and made it his capital for four years. It was re-taken by the English in 1408 and Owain's family was taken prisoner. Margaret of Anjou, wife of Henry VI, spent some time at the castle after her husband's capture at Northampton. During the Civil War it held out longer than any other castle, and did not eventually surrender until March 1647.

Machynlleth, Powys
Standing half-way down Maengwyn Street is the Owain Glyndwr Institute, where Owain held his parliament in 1404. He is thought to have been born in about 1354 and was related

to all the great royal houses of Wales. He was educated at Oxford and London, and even spent some time at the court of Richard II.

A series of misunderstandings and small grievances led Glyndwr to take up arms against a neighbour, and eventually against Henry IV. By 1402 he was the focus of all Welsh nationalism, and virtually the whole of Wales rose against the English overlords. He was proclaimed Prince of Wales, and it looked as if victory would be his, but the tide of fortune turned and by 1410 he was fighting a guerilla war from the fastnesses of Snowdonia. It is not known when or where Glyndwr died, or even if the free pardon offered to him by Henry V ever reached him. Glyndwr was without doubt, and still remains in the eyes of Welshmen, one of that proud country's greatest patriots.

Monmouth Castle, Gwent
The battered remains of Monmouth Castle seem modest of the fact that they witnessed the birth of a future English monarch, Henry V. Throughout its history it has been closely associated with great events; it belonged to Edward I, then to his brother, Edmund, Earl of Lancaster; it was confiscated from John of Gaunt by Richard II and was eventually taken back after John's son, Henry, had claimed the throne from Richard II.

Pembroke Castle, Dyfed
Henry Tudor, future King Henry VII of England, was born and brought up at Pembroke Castle. He was forced to go into exile at the age of 14, but returned to Wales in 1485, landing at Mill Bay near Dale, and marched through Wales to Bosworth where he defeated Richard III and claimed the throne for his own.

Rhuddlan Castle, Clwyd
Rhuddlan was a stronghold of the Welsh princes from at least the 11th century up until its capture by Edward I in 1277. Here in 1284 Edward I passed the Statute of Rhuddlan which confirmed his sovereignty over Wales. Here too, as a prisoner, came Richard II, on his way to Flint where he was forced to surrender the crown to Henry Bolingbroke.

CAERNARFON

Caernarfon Castle, looking down into the inner bailey, with the Menai Straits and the Isle of Anglesey in the background

The early history of Caernarfon is steeped in legend, and it does not enter documented history until the founding of a Roman fort in the 1st century AD. After the departure of the Roman legions the story is once more lost in the mists of time until the arrival of new invaders, the Normans. Hugh of Avranches, the first Norman Earl of Chester, built a motte-and-bailey castle at Caernarfon which was later used as a residence by two of Wales' greatest princes, Llywelyn the Great and his grandson Llywelyn the Last.

Welsh resistance

Ever since the Roman invaders the Welsh people had kept up a spirited resistance to any attempt to overrule their country, and they remained largely independent within their mountain and moorland fastnesses. By the 13th century Wales was felt to be an unbearable thorn in England's side and Edward I determined to subdue the country. Llywelyn the Last harried Edward's forces throughout 1282, but in December of that year Llywelyn was killed and the hopes of the Welsh people were dashed. Edward quickly overran north Wales, and work commenced on a series of mighty castles that were intended to dominate the Welsh people both physically and psychologically.

The Castle is built

The castle at Caernarfon, and the town walls, were begun in the summer of 1283, and Edward and Queen Eleanor stayed for over a month in specially prepared timber-framed buildings. The King and Queen returned to the castle in 1284, and it was then that Prince Edward was born. King Edward is said to have promised the Welsh nobility a "prince that was borne in Wales and could speake never a word of English". Prince Edward was not officially created Prince of Wales until 1301; since then the title has always been conferred upon the reigning monarch's eldest son.

In 1294 much of the castle and town wall was destroyed in an uprising led by Madog ap Llywelyn. Repair work was immediately set in hand, and by 1330 the castle stood much as it appears today. The castle remained garrisoned and held against the Welsh until 1485 when Henry Tudor, who came of Welsh stock, took the English throne. After that time it became less difficult for the Welsh-speaking population to make their way in the world. The advent of the Tudor dynasty, and the ensuing growth of trust and trade of all sorts between England and Wales, meant that Caernarfon, and all the other great Edwardian castles, were no longer needed. By 1538 the castle was in a very bad state of repair, except for its walls which continued to look as impregnable as ever. Not until the 1870s was restoration work begun, and this has continued to the present day.

Royal Investitures

It is chiefly as the scene of the two investitures of princes of Wales, in 1911 and especially in 1969, that Caernarfon is remembered. For the investiture of Prince Edward in 1911 much repair and restoration work was done to both town and castle. On the great day the place the Secretary of State for Wales. As the Letters were being read in Welsh Queen Elizabeth invested Charles with the insignia of the Principality of Wales and of the Earldom of Chester; these were: a sword, a coronet, a gold ring, and a gold rod. The Prince then paid homage to the Queen in these words: "I Charles, Prince of Wales, do become your liege man of life and limb and earthly worship, and faith and truth I will bear unto you to live and die against all manner of folks".

Prince Charles read his address to the people of Wales first in Welsh then in English, after which he was formally presented by the Queen to the people, who showed their approval by storms of cheers. An exhibition within the castle displays much that is of interest from the investiture ceremony.

The imposing bulk of Edward I's castle at Caernarfon qualifies it as probably the finest in Britain

The inner bailey of Caernarfon Castle, with the Eagle Tower in the background.

was teeming with dignitaries, soldiers and sailors and ordinary people. Upon his arrival at the castle Edward, then only 17, was escorted to his place by Lloyd George who, as Constable of the Castle, had been instrumental in much of the organisation of the event. The Royal Standard was run up upon the arrival of the King and the ceremony began. Winston Churchill, then Home Secretary, read the Letters Patent as George V invested his son. After the ceremony the new Prince of Wales was presented to thousands of cheering people.

For the investiture of Prince Charles on Tuesday 1st July 1969, the presence of television cameras meant that millions, not thousands as had been the case in 1911, of people could watch the ceremony. As for the 1911 ceremony, much preparation work was carried out, overseen by Lord Snowdon, the Constable of the Castle. The cost of the preparations was in the region of £200,000.

The Letters Patent were read first in English by the Home Secretary and then in Welsh by

North Wales castles

A

PENMYNYDD

Standing a little distance from Penmynydd village is Plas Penmynydd, once a small mansion and now restored as a farmhouse. It was here that Owen Tudor, founder of the great Tudor dynasty, was born. Owen fought for Henry V at Agincourt and in 1436 he married the King's widow, Katherine de Valois. The marriage was kept a secret for some years, but when it was eventually discovered Owen was thrown into Newgate Gaol and Katherine was sent to the Abbey of Bermondsey. Henry VI eventually pardoned Owen after Katherine's death, but he was executed after fighting for the Lancastrian cause at the Battle of Mortimer's Cross in 1461. Owen had several sons by Katherine and one of these, Edmund of Richmond, had a son called Henry who was born at Pembroke Castle in 1457. When he was 14 the young Henry Richmond was obliged to go into exile; he returned to Wales in 1485 and began a campaign which, after the Battle of Bosworth Field, led to his becoming King Henry VII of England.

BEAUMARIS

Edward I gave this place its name which is a corruption of the Norman-French *Beau Marais* which means fair marsh. The beautiful and imposing castle at Beaumaris was begun in 1295 as the culmination of the string of mighty fortresses which Edward built in order to subjugate the Welsh.

After Llywelyn the Last's death in 1282 it must have seemed that the fighting spirit of the Welsh would finally be crushed, but this was not so and in 1294 Madog ap Llywelyn led a revolt which numbered among its victories the destruction of the half completed Caernarfon Castle and the confinement of Edward within his own castle at Conwy. Eventually Edward crushed the revolt and decided that to totally pacify North Wales he needed another castle on the coast, and the northern end of the Menai Strait was the obvious place.

James of St George was the Master of the King's Works in Wales and it was he who was the architect of all the great Edwardian castles, including Beaumaris. James died before the castle was completed, but the work went on until the 1320s and even then not all of the architect's designs were brought to fruition. The castle never saw active service, and in fact it was never completed, but today it remains a superb example of medieval defensive construction.

ABER

Llywelyn the Last built a castle here, of which all that remains is the mound called Y Mwd. It was from here in 1272 that he defied the summons of Edward I to attend the English Parliament at Westminster.

CONWY

When Edward I's army arrived at Conwy in 1283 there were two groups of buildings on the site of what was to become one of Edward's greatest fortress towns in Wales. One of these was Aberconwy Abbey, in which lay the bones of Llywelyn the Great, and the other was the hall of the princes of North Wales. Subsequently the abbey was moved to Maenan.

Work on the castle and walled town was begun immediately, and by July 1283 a lawn had been laid for the enjoyment of Queen Eleanor. In charge of the building programme was

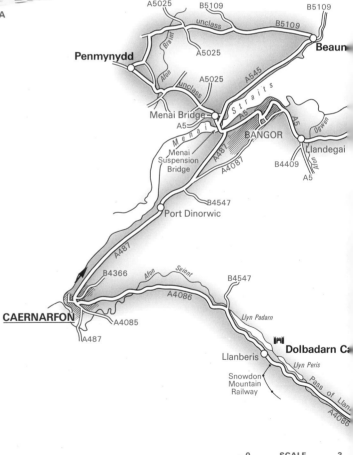

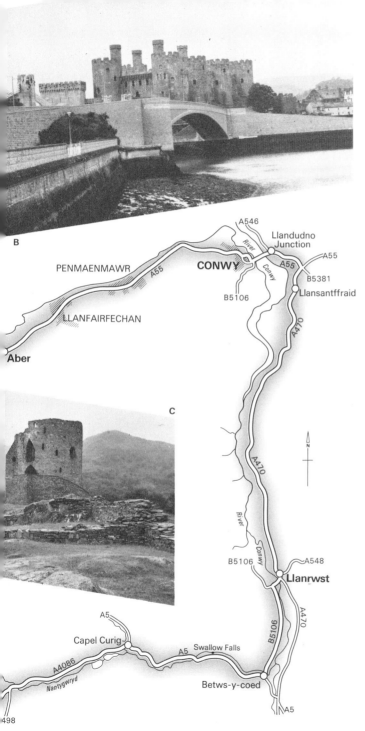

Edward's brilliant military architect Master James of St George, who, by November 1284 already had the task well in hand. It should be remembered that the building of these mighty fortresses, apart from costing a considerable fortune, involved the use of hundreds of labourers and tradesmen, some of whom were pressed into service from as far away as Somerset, Kent and Northumberland. By 1288 a substantial part of the work was finished, and is estimated to have cost the equivalent of one and a half million pounds. In 1294, during Madog ap Llywelyn's revolt, Edward and many of his followers were effectively besieged within Conwy. The attack was unsuccessful, however, and the defenders were eventually relieved by sea. The castle, which had become ruinous, was repaired and held for the King during the English Civil War, after which time it once more fell into disrepair.

LLANRWST

The stone coffin of Llywelyn ap Iorweth, one of Wales' most noble and enduring heroes, lies in the Gwydir Chapel here. Llywelyn was born by tradition at Dolwyddelan Castle (which stands off the A470 road between Betws-y-coed and Blaenau Ffestiniog). Descended from a long line of Welsh princes, Llyweln grew up to hold the title "Prince of Aberffraw and Lord of Snowdon". He managed by superb statecraft to consolidate all the petty princedoms into one unit which continually struggled against encroachment into Wales by the English. Because of his tremendous achievements he is usually referred to as Llywelyn Fawr, the Great. He died in 1240 and the coffin was originally placed at Aberconwy Abbey, which Llywelyn himself had founded. When Edward I moved the abbey to Maenan, the coffin was moved as well. The coffin found its final resting place at Llanrwst after Maenan Abbey had met its end at the Dissolution.

DOLBADARN CASTLE

This castle, watching over the entrance to the Llanberis Pass, was one of the strongholds of the 13th century princes of North Wales. It was built by Llywelyn Fawr "the Great" and based on the military architecture of his enemies, the English. Llywelyn died in 1240 and was succeeded by his son Dafydd, whose mother was Joan, daughter of King John. After Dafydd's death the leadership was taken by Llywelyn ap Gruffydd, grandson of Llywelyn Fawr. A treaty drawn up between the Welsh and the English in 1267 recognised Llywelyn, "the Last" as he came to be known, as the undisputed Prince of Wales. However Llywelyn's brother Owain was not in agreement with the decision and was consequently imprisoned in Dolbadarn Castle for 23 years.

When Edward I succeeded to the English throne in 1272 Llywelyn refused to pay homage to him, and Edward felt obliged to make his overlordship felt. In 1277 a peace treaty was signed which humiliated Llywelyn. At last, in 1282, an armed rebellion against Edward was begun by Llywelyn's brother Dafydd. Whilst riding to confer with his generals after a victory at Menai, Llywelyn was killed by an English lancer at Cilmery in Powys.

A Beaumaris Castle, the finest example of concentric fortification in Britain. However, its ingenious design was never put to the test, as it saw no war

B The approach to Conwy Castle from the west is guarded by three bridges, including Telford's famous suspension bridge. Conwy is one of the best-best-preserved of Edward I's walled towns

C The desolate remains of Dolbadarn Castle occupy what was once an important strategic position

CHESTER

Chester was once a Roman city known as *Deva*, a military centre which today still retains its entire 2 mile walled circuit following the path laid out by the Romans and still punctuated by some of the original towers and gateways. The Romans abandoned their fort during the 5th century and the city remained quiet until the 10th century, when Ethelfleda came to Chester. She extended the walls, and brought with her the relics of an important Mercian abbess who had died in the 8th century. She founded a church and dedicated it to the abbess, St Werburgh. During this time, Ethelred rebuilt virtually the whole city. Edgar the Peaceful became the first King of England in 973 when he was crowned in Bath. In Chester, eight vassal kings paid their homage to him by rowing him up the river Dee. The city flourished, set in a prosperous trading position on the Dee. Its own royal mint was set up in 970, proof of a flourishing community.

Norman Kings

Soon after the Norman Conquest, William I besieged Chester, realising it would make a useful base for his attacks on the Welsh. The city held out as long as possible, but eventually William was victorious and granted the city to his nephew, Hugh Lupus. This man was to play a very important role in the advancement of Chester. He constructed the castle, and the causeway or weir that provided power for the old mills which stood by the side of the Dee, and, in 1093, he transformed the church into an abbey for Benedictine monks.

In 1237 the last earl died, and the earldom reverted to the crown, whereupon Henry III took Chester as his royal fort and was responsible for giving the castle its stone walls and towers. The King declared that his eldest son Edward, the Black Prince, should also take

The Eastgate, Chester, the main entrance to the city. It was built in 1769 to replace the narrow medieval gateway, and the clock tower was erected in 1897 to commemorate Queen Victoria's Jubilee

the title of Earl of Chester. Up to the present day, it has continued to be the custom that the eldest son of the reigning monarch takes this as one of his titles. During the 13th and 14th centuries the city reached the peak of its life as a trading port, and merchants came from far and wide, bringing their goods to the old harbour of Chester paying tolls to the Earl of Derby at the Watergate (which still stands today). In the 14th century Richard II and the Earl of Salisbury were brought to Chester and imprisoned in the castle, as was Eleanor of

Gloucester, wife of the Duke of Gloucester, protector of the child King Henry VI. The castle originally built of wood and rebuilt in stone by Henry III retained its medieval appearance until 1789 when part of it was adapted to house the assize courts. Agricola's Tower, part of the 13th century structure, houses the museum of the Cheshire regiment as well as a delightful little chapel on the first floor, where James II once worshipped. Next to the assize courts are the County Hall offices opened by the Queen in 1957.

The corner of Eastgate Street and Bridge Street in Chester, showing the famous "Rows", consisting of a double tier of shops

Part of Chester's unique city wall

King Charles's defeat

At the northern end of the city walls is King Charles's Tower, where, on 24th September 1645, Charles I stood watching the closing phases of the battle against the parliamentarians which had started at Rowton Moor and which ended at the city walls. During the siege, Charles himself had a narrow escape when standing in the cathedral tower which his men were holding at the time. A bullet fired from the church of St John narrowly missed the King, hitting and killing the captain who stood next to him. The city withstood sieges over a period of two years during the troubles of the Civil War, but eventually Charles saw that his cause would fail and, after ordering the garrison to resist for a further ten days, he left over the River Dee taking most of his men with him. The city, noted for its stubborn resistance and firm in its support of the King, withstood the sieges until the following February when starvation forced them to surrender. The walls of the tower were slighted, but have since been restored to their original appearance, incorporating at the same time the Roman remains found underneath. Within the tower there is now a museum with relics and relief plans of the Civil War.

The City today

The Dee Bridge over which King Charles crossed, dates from very early times. It is mentioned in the Domesday Book and was probably first constructed in Roman times. It was of great importance in the middle ages during the troubles with the Welsh. The Grosvenor Bridge, opened by Queen Victoria in 1831, replaced the Dee Bridge as the main route to Wales. The Grosvenor, with a span of 200 ft, was an amazing feat of engineering, having then the largest span in the world. From Grosvenor Bridge, Grosvenor Road leads past the museum which houses a fine collection of Roman antiquities and coins minted in the city during Saxon and Norman times. Nearby in Castle Street is Gamul House where Charles I stayed during the siege of the city during the Civil War.

Following the course of the city walls, the visitor will arrive at the principal entrance to the city, Eastgate. The present gate was founded in 1769 replacing the medieval structure with its Roman foundations. Above the gateway is the clock tower erected in 1897 to commemorate the Diamond Jubilee of Queen Victoria. From Eastgate, and passing Chester's most important Roman remain, the amphitheatre (the largest of its kind in Britain), the visitor comes to the church of St John the Baptist, built in 1075 and used for ten years in Saxon times as the city cathedral. By the south wall of the churchyard is the Hermitage, an 18th century building erected on the site of a 13th century hermit's cell.

Chester is a perfect example of a fortified medieval city, world famous for its double storeyed shops in Watergate Street, known as the Rows. Northgate, in the north part of the city was once used as the city prison with a 30ft dungeon carved underground. The City Hall, opposite the cathedral, was opened in 1869 by Edward Prince of Wales, Earl of Chester, who later became King Edward VII. On either side of the main porch are carved illustrations depicting Chester's history.

Through Cheshire vales

ROWTON MOOR

At the beginning of 1645 the parliamentarians and the royalists met at Parliament for what proved to be fruitless peace talks to try and end the Civil War. In June of the same year the decisive battle of Naseby took place in which Charles I was hopelessly defeated, losing vast numbers of men.

After Naseby, Charles's only hope was to conquer Scotland. To this end, he arrived in Chester on 23rd September hotly pursued by Colonel Poyntz, a professional soldier with a vast army of men. Charles on the other hand had only 3,000 cavalry commanded by Sir Marmaduke Langdale. Using information learned from an intercepted letter, Langdale charged the parliamentarians from the side and put them to flight. Poyntz soon rallied his men and reversed the position just outside Rowton, causing the royalists to turn tail and head for the safety of Chester. There was great confusion, for the area around Rowton with its narrow lanes was most unsuitable for horses. The remainder of the battle took place in the city of Chester, with Charles a dismal onlooker from one of the city's towers. Three miles east of Chester, the suburb of Rowton lies, with only a modern inn by the name of Ye Old Trooper by the canal bridge to remind today's passer-by of the battle of Rowton Moor.

HALTON

Halton, in Runcorn New Town, clusters round its ruined castle, commanding spectacular views from the top of a hill. The castle was built by the 1st Baron Halton, Robert Nigel, soon after the Norman Conquest. During the reign of Henry II, the castle became, and

remains to this day, part of the Duchy of Lancaster. Later King John converted the fort into a hunting lodge for himself. In its prime, it was a circular structure protected by 20–30 ft sheer walls and nine great towers, two of which flank the main entrance gate. The castle was used at the time of Elizabeth I as a place of trial and gaol for offenders from the surrounding districts. During the Civil War, the fort was held by the royalists under Charles I, but was captured and partially demolished by the parliamentarians in 1646. Since that time it has stood as a ruin.

FARNDON

Edward the Elder died at Farndon on 17th July 924, a few days after settling boundary disputes that had come to a head in Chester. Edward was the effective ruler of the whole of England south of the Trent. The 14th century chapel at Farndon has been greatly restored and contains many treasures including a 17th century window dedicated to Sir Francis Gamul, a loyal attendant to Charles I during the fateful siege of Chester in 1645–6.

FLINT

Set on the River Dee, Flint Castle was one of eight built by Edward I during his conquest of Wales. Work started on the castle on 25th July 1277 and was completed three years later. The design is unique, the castle being incorporated into the town, with a great tower standing outside the main

curtain walls and connected by a drawbridge. The castle, which was surrounded by a great moat supplied by the sea, had walls 23 ft thick.

In 1282 the castle was unsuccessfully besieged by Llywelyn the Last, whose death shortly afterwards effectively

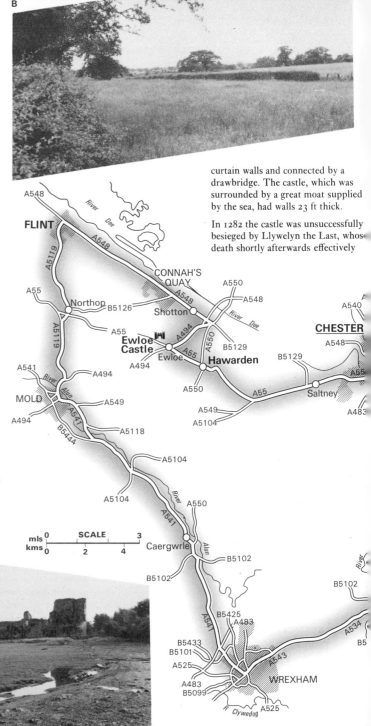

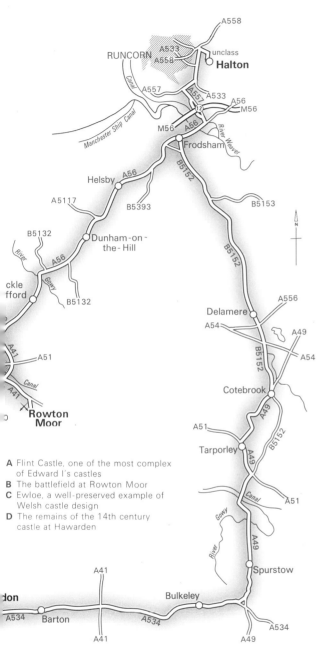

A Flint Castle, one of the most complex of Edward I's castles
B The battlefield at Rowton Moor
C Ewloe, a well-preserved example of Welsh castle design
D The remains of the 14th century castle at Hawarden

ended Welsh opposition to Edward I. In August 1399 Richard II was imprisoned at Flint Castle when news came to him of his forced abdication by Henry Bolingbroke. After saying mass in the castle chapel, Richard immediately left for London to sign the deeds of abdication, conceding his claim to the throne of England to Bolingbroke, who became Henry IV. The castle escaped troubles during the Wars of the Roses, but during the Civil War, the fort changed hands on a number of occasions. It was held by the royalists for Charles I and strongly besieged by the parliamentarians in 1646. The royalist occupants resisted defiantly but were eventually starved into submission, and forced to surrender. In 1652 the castle was destroyed, although considerable remains are still to be seen.

EWLOE

The castle at Ewloe is thought to have been built by the Welsh Prince, Llywelyn the Great, as a defence against the English. It is cleverly sited in a natural dip of the land, so that a visitor coming to Ewloe will not see the castle until he is actually upon it. The fort has never been of great historical importance, although there is a story that Henry II was encountered in this area by Welsh rebels. After the death of Llywelyn the Last, Ewloe lost much of its strategic importance. It is likely that the large earth mound that lies just to the south of the castle was built by Edward I's forces during their siege against Llywelyn.

HAWARDEN

Hawarden Castle was originally built by the Montalt family during the reign of Henry III to keep the Welsh at bay. The castle was taken from the Montalts by the Welsh Prince, Llywelyn, with the help of Simon de Montfort. After the de Montfort rebellion had been crushed the castle was taken by the English who restored it to the Montalt family. In 1282 the Welsh attacked again, capturing the castle and burning it to the ground. Edward I rebuilt it in stone. During the Civil War Hawarden remained in the hands of the royalists, but was captured briefly by the parliamentarians in 1643. Sir William Neale garrisoned the fort until 16th March 1646, when, after gaining permission from King Charles I, whom he had sheltered after the battle of Rowton Moor, the occupants of the castle were allowed to surrender honourably.

In 1647 Hawarden Castle, together with Flint and Rhuddlan, was almost completely destroyed. Now only the keep and part of the old walls remain to be seen. East of the castle ruins is the building constructed in 1752 which was the home of Mr Gladstone.

SHEFFIELD

Although much of Sheffield's history lies within the period of the Industrial Revolution, a major historical event took place here in the 9th century. The country was divided into several kingdoms, Sheffield being in the largest of these, Mercia. All this was to change, however, in the year 829 when King Ecgbert of Mercia came to Dore, then a separate village, but now a pretty suburb of Sheffield. As it was situated on the border between his kingdom and that of Northumbria, Ecgbert chose this place to receive the submission of the Northumbrian king.

A stone has been erected at Dore to commemorate the event and bears an inscription describing this significant occasion.

Sheffield, like Rome, is built on seven hills and encloses five valleys through which flow the rivers Sheaf, Porter, Loxley, Rivelin and Don. As none of these rivers was totally navigable from the sea, the settlement was not much troubled by invaders until the Danes settled more permanently in the country. Although the Danes lived fairly peacefully alongside the native inhabitants a few skirmishes did occur and on one occasion King Edmund found it necessary to bring his army to Sheffield. There was no major battle, a show of force being sufficient deterrent, and the Danes withdrew to live quietly within the community for a time. Edmund's son even gave some of them important appointments in the local government system of the time. Then further Danish invasions occurred and hostilities resumed in the area until the Dane, Canute, was appointed King of England in 1016.

The Medieval Town

After the Norman invasion, King William pardoned the Lord of the Manor of Hallam, Waltheof, who had supported King Harold, created him Earl of Huntingdon and gave him the hand of his niece Judith in marriage. Waltheof was nevertheless involved in a rebellion against the Norman King, but he was again forgiven. After a second revolt, however, he was captured and beheaded. His wife was allowed to keep the estates, which included Sheffield, until she also fell from favour and was deprived of her land. They were inherited by her son-in-law, the King of Scotland, who rented the manor of Sheffield to a Norman, Roger de Busli. A later tenant, William de Lovetot, built Sheffield Castle, around the beginning of the 12th century, on a piece of high land between the Sheaf and the Don. Under his family the town prospered, and they built a corn mill, a hospital, a bridge over the river and a parish church.

When, in 1266, Simon de Montfort instigated a rebellion against King Henry III, Sheffield supported the King and the town was attacked by the barons who burned the castle. The King afterwards gave permission for a stronger fortress to be built. During the reign of Richard I, Sheffield supported the King as opposed to his brother John.

Mary, Queen of Scots

When Mary, Queen of Scots, was forced to abdicate in favour of her son James, she fled to England hoping to find Queen Elizabeth I sympathetic to her. Instead she found that Elizabeth feared she would become a figurehead for the English Catholics who would try to put her on the throne. The rest of Mary's life was spent in close confinement in various castles throughout the country and fourteen years, almost a third of her lifetime, were spent in Sheffield. Most of Mary's imprisonment was in the Castle, but she was transferred to the Manor from time to time. The Turret House, standing beside the main building of the Manor, is thought to have been specially built to accommodate the exiled Queen. A stained glass window in Sheffield Cathedral portrays Mary, Queen of Scots, in the Manor Lodge.

The Castle in the Civil War

At the beginning of the Civil War, Sir John Gell took Sheffield Castle for parliament and, as there was no opposition to this move, left only a small regiment in residence. The following year, a large royalist army was reported to be advancing towards the town, and, knowing that they had no hope of holding out against them, the parliamentarians left before their adversaries arrived. In several battles in the area, the royalists were defeated, but the garrison at Sheffield remained staunch and refused to surrender. The roundheads tried several ways to take the almost impregnable castle, including a futile attempt to drain the moat which was fed by two rivers. Finally, they fired their massive cannon on the walls and the royalists were forced to surrender. After the war the castle was slighted and gradually dismantled to provide masonry for new building work.

The Industrial City

There was a tremendous population explosion in the 18th century, from 20,000 in 1750 to 135,000 by the middle of the 19th century when there were around 135 steel works in Sheffield and new methods of smelting were about to be introduced. The Abbeydale Industrial Hamlet, a working museum, shows how steel implements were made, and the cutlery industry is represented by a magnificent display in the Cutler's Hall. It is hard to imagine that any city could be transformed as Sheffield has been in the last few decades, much of it due to the implementation of the Clean Air Act. Horace Walpole once said that it was "one of the foulest towns in England in the most charming situation", and in fact even the residents at one time saw the pollution as a sign of prosperity. All that has now changed with the most stringent control over effluent, and the air is as pure as any in the country. The Victorian slums have all been replaced by an ambitious house building programme which has been recognised internationally as a major

The Town Hall, Sheffield, is a gabled Renaissance building, dating from the end of the 19th century. The tower is crowned with a 7 feet high statue of Vulcan

breakthrough in city redevelopment. In 1897, on 21st May, Queen Victoria came to Sheffield to open the impressive new Town Hall with its marble staircase and electric lighting throughout. She drove in procession through the decorated streets of the city with an escort of Life Guards and after the opening ceremony, she honoured the Mayor with the title of Lord Mayor, the Chief Cutler became a baron and the deputy Mayor was given a knighthood. Her statue can be seen outside the building which she opened. Her son, King Edward VII, is represented in the city by a statue in Fitzalan Square and a hospital which was named after him. The streets of Sheffield were again lined in 1913 when King George V and Queen Mary drove through to the cheering of the adults and the children waving flags. Twenty years later, the Duke of Kent, father of the present Duke, who was later killed in an air crash, made a tour of the factories in Sheffield and the Prince of Wales came also during those depression years to talk to the unemployed of the city. An extension to the University, known as the Arts Tower, was opened in 1965 by Queen Elizabeth the Queen Mother.

With Mary, Queen of Scots

CHATSWORTH

Magnificent Chatsworth House was built for the 4th Earl of Devonshire in 1687 on the site of the mansion belonging to his grandmother, the great Bess of Hardwick. This lady's fourth husband, the Earl of Shrewsbury, was the guardian of Mary, Queen of Scots, during her period of captivity at Chatsworth. Although Mary, Queen of Scots' apartments were demolished, they were replaced and the new rooms bear her name. The original windows of her rooms were re-housed in the west sub-corridor of the house and there is a portion of the garden known as Queen Mary's Bower, where she was allowed to stroll during her time at the house.

The 4th Earl who constructed the present house was instrumental in having William of Orange invited to assume the throne of England in 1689. For his loyalty, King William III created him 1st Duke of Devonshire and made a gift of the Dutch chandelier of 1694, which hangs in the State Dressing room. The gilt chandelier hanging over the Oak Staircase and Landing incorporating stag horns was also given by William III. It illuminates, among other paintings, a portrait of King George IV. The State Bedroom contains the bed in which King George II died in 1760, and two Chippendale chairs which were used by King George III and Queen Charlotte at their coronation.

The Orangery was added to the house in 1827 and contains the State Coach, built in 1890 which was last used at the coronation of Queen Elizabeth II in 1953. Next to the Orangery is the Sculpture Gallery which includes among its treasures an illuminated prayer book belonging to Henry VII. When King George V and Queen Mary visited Chatsworth in 1913, they were accommodated in rooms called the China Closet and the State Dressing Room. Both were originally designed as show rooms for exhibition pieces.

The house is surrounded by beautiful parkland, with a circumference of ten miles, made up of rolling hills and woods with the River Derwent running through it. The gardens were remodelled by Capability Brown with the later addition of the huge Emperor Fountain, supplied and pressurised from an artificial lake on a hill behind the house. This is the tallest fountain in Britain. Other attractions within the park are the farmyard with various breeds of animals, the forestry section and the woodland walk, which are open to the public at certain times. The hunting tower was part of the original Elizabethan structure.

HADDON HALL

This fine example of a fortified manor house dates in parts from Norman times and was extended by degrees until the early 17th century. It owes its excellent condition to the fact that it was never fought over. It was the home of the Vernon family from the 12th century until the male line ceased about three hundred years later when two daughters, Margaret and Dorothy were joint heiresses.

On the night of Margaret's marriage to the Earl of Derby, Dorothy eloped with her forbidden suitor, Sir John Manners, and after the death of her sister, Dorothy inherited

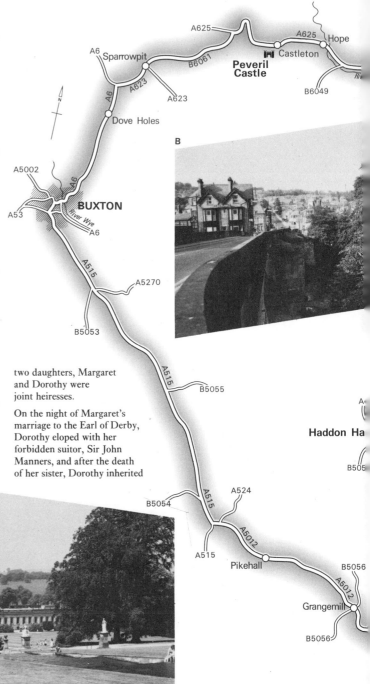

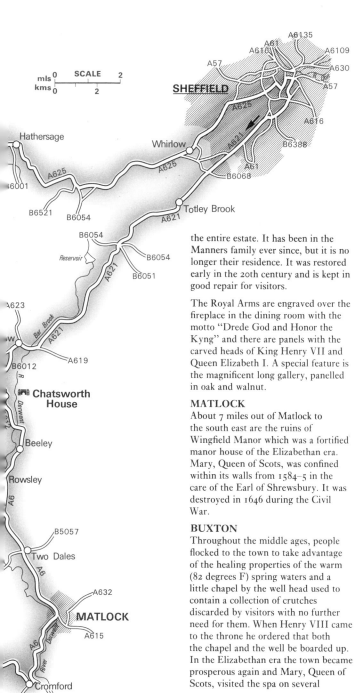

the entire estate. It has been in the Manners family ever since, but it is no longer their residence. It was restored early in the 20th century and is kept in good repair for visitors.

The Royal Arms are engraved over the fireplace in the dining room with the motto "Drede God and Honor the Kyng" and there are panels with the carved heads of King Henry VII and Queen Elizabeth I. A special feature is the magnificent long gallery, panelled in oak and walnut.

MATLOCK

About 7 miles out of Matlock to the south east are the ruins of Wingfield Manor which was a fortified manor house of the Elizabethan era. Mary, Queen of Scots, was confined within its walls from 1584–5 in the care of the Earl of Shrewsbury. It was destroyed in 1646 during the Civil War.

BUXTON

Throughout the middle ages, people flocked to the town to take advantage of the healing properties of the warm (82 degrees F) spring waters and a little chapel by the well head used to contain a collection of crutches discarded by visitors with no further need for them. When Henry VIII came to the throne he ordered that both the chapel and the well be boarded up. In the Elizabethan era the town became prosperous again and Mary, Queen of Scots, visited the spa on several

occasions. She was imprisoned at Tutbury Castle at the time, a dark and damp abode, and her health was failing considerably because of her inadequate living conditions. She pleaded with Queen Elizabeth I to be allowed to leave and finally the Queen granted permission for her to go to Buxton for a while. During her visits Mary stayed at Buxton Hall where she was closely guarded and allowed to see no one but her custodian.

The 18th century brought an increase in the popularity of all spa resorts. Buxton was no exception and a great deal of 18th century architecture is in evidence in the town. Princess Anne visited Buxton on 16th November 1972 to open the swimming pool in the Pavilion Gardens complex.

A popular attraction in Buxton every year in July is the Well Dressing Ceremony. The people of the town erect a flower mosaic of petals and leaves pressed into wet clay at the well head, there is a procession and a service is held at the site of the spring.

PEVERIL CASTLE

On a peak above the village of Castleton, Peveril Castle looks down over the valley. It was built by the Norman, William Peveril, an illegitimate son of William the Conqueror. When Peveril's grandson was forced into exile for murdering the Earl of Chester, Peveril Castle became crown property and was frequently used by subsequent monarchs as a hunting lodge. Henry II gave it to his younger son, later to become King John, but it fell into the hands of the powerful barons of the time, and the Earl of Derby had to take it by force for the King.

Henry III bestowed the estate on his son, Prince Edward, and it was later part of the dowry of the child bride Joan, sister of Edward III, on her marriage to the future King of Scotland, also a child. When the

Scottish alliance did not get the results Edward hoped for, he gave the lands at Castleton to his son, John of Gaunt, Duke of Lancaster, and it has remained a part of this Duchy ever since. The castle is now in ruins and overgrown, and can be reached by a path from the village.

A Chatsworth House, in a beautiful landscape by Capability Brown
B The River Derwent at Matlock is spanned by a 15th century bridge
C The 18th century Palladian Crescent at Buxton
D The small Norman keep of Peveril Castle, Castleton

173

YORK

The early history of the city is obscure until the Romans founded their city, *Eboracum*, here—the capital of the British Province. The first emperor to visit the city was Hadrian, and Constantine the Great was declared emperor here. The most substantial Roman building surviving is the Multangular Tower in the Museum Gardens. Further Roman antiquities can be seen in the Yorkshire Museum in the grounds of ruined St Mary's Abbey.

The Romans withdrew in 400, and York became the capital of the Kingdom of Northumbria, and at one time was one of the chief centres of learning in Europe. At the Norman Conquest, the city rebelled against William I, and he ravaged the city and built two castles. Of the first, only a mound, Baile Hill, remains on the west bank of the Ouse. The other, a wooden keep, was destroyed during the massacre of the Jews, and the stone Clifford's Tower erected in its place.

York Minster

When Edwin, King of Northumbria, was baptised, a wooden chapel was erected, and this was later replaced by a stone church. Further churches were built on the site until the 13th century, when work started on rebuilding and enlarging the then Norman church. The transformation to the present Minster took 250 years, spanning many different architectural styles. The transepts were the first to be rebuilt, followed by the nave, chapter house and vestibule. The choir was built in the 14th century, and the towers completed the building in the 15th century.

The glory of the Minster is its stained glass, which includes some of the earliest in England. The nave is exceptionally high and broad, and carries round its sides the painted stone shields of Edward II and the barons who held a

The famous West Front of York Minster. The cathedral is the largest Gothic church in England, and dates from the 13th century

parliament in York in 1309. The nave is separated from the choir by a Gothic rood screen with life-size sculptured statues of English kings from William I to Henry VI. All are originals except that of Henry VI which was replaced in the 19th century. The magnificence of the East Window can be seen from here, which is the largest sheet of medieval glass in the world. The north aisle of the choir contains the tomb of William of Hatfield, young son of King Edward III, who died at the age of eight. Indeed, Edward III was married to Princess Philippa of Hainault in the Minster in 1328. Other marriages which were solemnized here were those of Alexander II of Scotland to Joan, sister of Henry III in 1221, and Alexander III to Margaret, Henry III's daughter in 1251.

The chapter house, reached through the vestibule, is one of the loveliest parts of the Minster, and a superb example of the Decorated style. It contains beautiful glass in exquisite tracery, and suffered little from its restoration in 1845. The crypt lies down a staircase in the north choir aisle and houses some Roman paving and a portion of a Roman pillar. Near the foot of the steps is the traditional site of the well in which King Edwin was baptised.

In 1967 it was revealed that much of the structure of the Minster was in danger of collapse, and an extensive programme of restoration work started, during which it never closed. The total cost was over £2 million.

City walls

York's medieval city walls are almost as famous as the Minster. The earliest walls were built in Roman times by Severus, and a portion of this wall can be seen on the south side of Monk Bar. Most of the walls date from the time of Edward III, and their 3 mile circuit is one of the best examples in Europe of medieval fortification. There are four main gates, Monk Bar, the tallest; Bootham Bar; Micklegate Bar, the traditional Royal entrance to the city, used by Queen Elizabeth II when she visited York on the occasion of its 1,900th anniversary in 1971. Also at this gate was exposed the head of Richard of York in 1460, and the heads of Jacobite rebels in 1746. The fourth gate is Walmgate Bar, the only gate to retain its battlemented barbican. From many parts of the walls excellent views of the city and Minster can be obtained.

The King's Manor is in the grounds of St Mary's Abbey, and was originally the abbot's house. At the Dissolution, the house was assigned to the King's Council of the North. The stones of the abbey were used to extend the house into a Tudor palace. Only slight traces of this remain, most of it having been built by presidents of the Council during Elizabethan times and later. The main entrance has above it the arms and initials of James I who stayed here on his journey south from Scotland to be crowned King of England. Charles I stayed here more than once, and so

Medieval York had four main gates or bars. Bootham Bar guarded the road to the north

King's Manor, York. The former home of the Abbot of St Mary's Abbey, it was used as a centre for the Council of the North. It is now part of the University of York

did Charles II. The King's Council was dissolved in 1641, since when the building has passed through various hands before being beautifully restored and bought by the University of York.

York has had a lord mayor since the time of Richard II, who gave the city the sword which is still carried on state occasions. The Mansion House in St Helen's Square dates from 1725–6, and is built on the site of the old chapel of the Guild of St Christopher. Behind it, the Guildhall is one of the chief glories of York. Built on the river in 1447–53, it has been faithfully restored after the bomb damage of 1942. Its windows tell the story of York from Constantine's election to emperor up to the banquet given in 1850 for the Prince Consort. English kings shown in the window include Edgar, Edward III, Edward IV, Henry VII, James I and Charles I. In the little room overlooking the river, the Scots army was paid £200,000 for the help they gave Parliament in the Civil War against Charles I. Other reminders of the Civil War in York are the bust of the parliamentarian general, Sir Thomas Fairfax, in the City Art Gallery, and an

engraving of a portrait of Charles I. The city surrendered to Parliament after the Battle of Marston Moor in 1644.

St Mary's Abbey was once an important Benedictine monastery. It was founded by Stephen Lastingham in 1080, and enlarged by William II who laid the foundation stone. The extensive ruins date from the 11th and 13th centuries. In the grounds of the abbey is St Leonard's Hospital of which the ruins date from the 13th century. Originally attached to the Minster, it received its first endowment from King Athelstan, after the Battle of Brunanburgh in 937, which made him King of All England. He was the first man to issue one kind of money for the whole realm. The work of the hospital continued for 600 years. In Dean's Park near the Minster lies the Treasurer's House, formerly the home of the cathedral treasurer. Most of it dates from the 17th century, although parts are medieval. In 1900, Edward, Prince of Wales stayed here with his daughter, the Princess of Wales. The rooms they occupied are open to view.

Royal Trains

York also houses the National Railway Museum. The collection includes Queen Adelaide's Coach, built by the London and Birmingham Railway in 1842 for the widow of King William IV. It is an elaborate carriage which can be made up into a bed at night, furnished with gold plate in a body made by Hooper. The museum also contains Queen Victoria's favourite railway coach, built by the London and North Western Railway in 1869. Originally two separate coaches, it was later remounted on a single frame to give greater comfort. She used this train all her life, but after King Edward VII came to the throne, the railway were anxious to build something new. The King approved the construction of a new train, and two coaches were built for him and Queen Alexandra in 1903. These were very advanced forms of construction for their time, and are on show in the museum. The interiors were re-upholstered during King George V's reign.

Past moorland battlefields

STAMFORD BRIDGE

Stamford Bridge over the River Derwent was the scene of a famous battle in 1066. Less than one month before the Battle of Hastings, King Harold was faced with a force led by his rebellious brother, Tostig, supported by the King of Norway, Harold Hardrada. Harold set out from London, and, on 25th September, surprised the enemy resting at Stamford. Both Tostig and Harold Hardrada were killed, and the Norsemen were put to flight. A memorial stone near the old mill marks the scene of the battle which took place

about 400 yards upstream from the present bridge.

SELBY

It is believed that Henry I was born in Selby, the only son of William the Conqueror to be born in England. The town grew up around the abbey which dominates the market square. It was founded in 1069 by the monk Benedict, who felt himself inspired to come to Selby and set up a cell. The King gave him authority to establish a monastery, and the abbey eventually

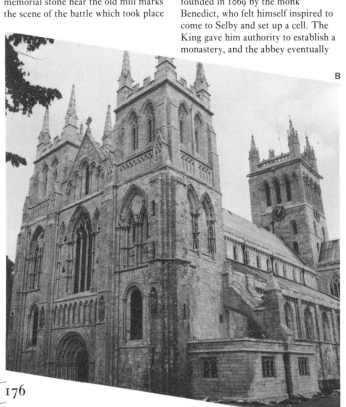

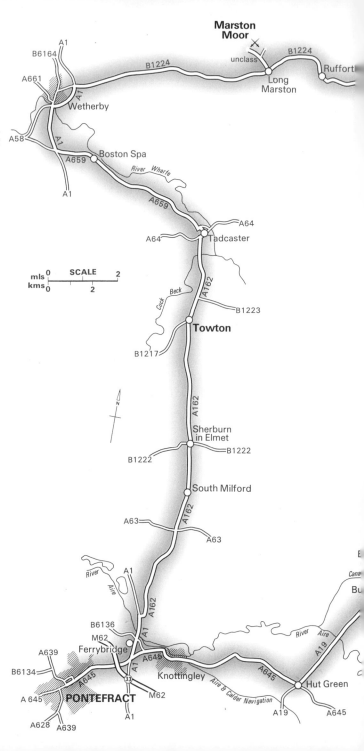

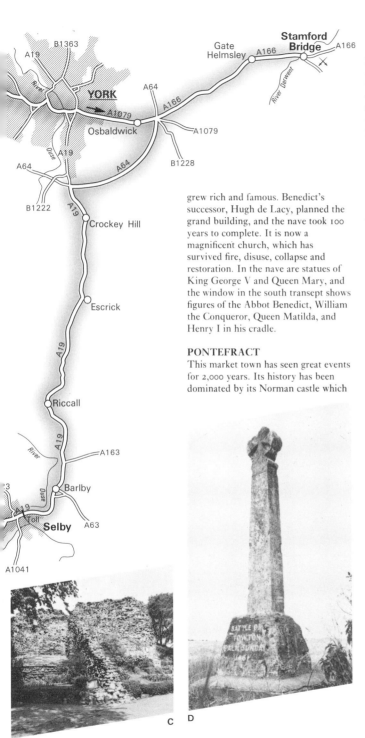

grew rich and famous. Benedict's successor, Hugh de Lacy, planned the grand building, and the nave took 100 years to complete. It is now a magnificent church, which has survived fire, disuse, collapse and restoration. In the nave are statues of King George V and Queen Mary, and the window in the south transept shows figures of the Abbot Benedict, William the Conqueror, Queen Matilda, and Henry I in his cradle.

PONTEFRACT

This market town has seen great events for 2,000 years. Its history has been dominated by its Norman castle which is now in ruins. There was probably a Saxon stronghold here, and William the Conqueror awarded the site to one of his captains, Ilbert de Lacy, to build a castle. For 250 years, de Lacy and his descendants worked on the castle, making it one of the strongest fortresses in England. The castle passed to John of Gaunt, fourth son of Edward III, who built the Queen's Tower and the King's Tower. When Edward III died, Richard II confiscated his estates and banished John of Gaunt's son. However, when Richard was forced to abdicate, he was imprisoned first in the Tower of London, and then in Pontefract Castle. He died here mysteriously in 1399, either murdered or starved to death. Subsequently, both James I of Scotland and the Duke of Orleans were kept prisoner here. In 1461, Edward IV came here on the eve of the Battle of Towton. In Tudor times, Henry VIII discovered the liaison between Catherine Howard and Thomas Culpeper here, which led to their deaths.

In the Civil War, Pontefract was a royalist stronghold, but was starved into submission. Soldiers who fell in the Civil War were buried in St Clement's Chapel in the castle. In 1648 the castle was demolished, a task which took only 10 weeks. One wall survives. In the Market Square is the pump given to the town by Elizabeth I, being the town's first public water supply.

TOWTON

The small town of Towton is famous for the largest battle of the Wars of the Roses in 1461. After the Lancastrian victory at St Albans, the Yorkist forces reorganised themselves and moved to face the 30,000 strong Lancastrian army at Towton. Thanks to a snowstorm, the Yorkists were able to rout the Lancastrians, although not without huge loss of life. Henry VI was ultimately captured and imprisoned in the Tower, and Edward IV was confirmed as King.

MARSTON MOOR

North of the road from Wetherby to York lies Marston Moor, the scene of a decisive parliamentary victory in the Civil War. In 1644 Parliament, in alliance with the Scottish army was besieging the Marquess of Newcastle in York. In June, Prince Rupert, with 12,000 troops set out to relieve the siege, and the parliamentary commanders decided to break off the siege, and concentrate their forces east of York on Marston Moor. Prince Rupert, by creating a diversion, was able to circle round the enemy forces and reach the outskirts of York to relieve the Marquess. Elated by his success, Rupert decided to stay and fight the parliamentarians at Marston Moor. During most of the day of 2nd July, the two sides faced each other on the Moor. At 7 in the evening, the parliamentary forces attacked, catching the royalists by surprise. It was a confused battle, in which Cromwell and Fairfax continually pressed their advantage, putting the royalists to flight. For the King, it was disastrous; he had lost 3,000 of his men and with them his control of the north.

The obelisk commemorating the battle is near Long Marston, and a good view of the battlefield can be obtained from Cromwell's Pump, reached by a footpath.

A Plaque marking the site of the Battle of Stamford Bridge
B The huge Norman Abbey at Selby
C Remains of the walls at Pontefract Castle
D The cross commemorating the Battle of Towton

DURHAM

The city of Durham sits on a peninsula, crowned by its cathedral and castle, and surrounded by the River Wear. In 995 the monks were chased out of their home at Chester-le-Street, taking with them the relics of Saint Cuthbert. Durham was a suitable site to refound their shrine, protected as it was, on three sides by water. By the year 998 the monks had already built the first part of the cathedral, but the troubles with the Danes and the Scots delayed its completion until 20 years later. The fort built by the monks was probably what William the Conqueror found when he arrived at Durham in 1069 looking for a suitable site for a castle which would serve as a base from which he could fight the Scots.

The Castle

In 1068, the northern rebellion broke out and the Earl of Northumberland arrived with 700 men to settle the troubles. The monks gathered their precious relics and fled to Lindisfarne (Holy Island). The following year, the Conqueror came to the city and decided to found his castle here, building it three years later while on a visit to the city to reaffirm to the people the privileges that had been granted to them by Canute. The castle contains much of interest. In the great hall there are some beautiful furniture and fine paintings, and the old kitchen boasts a huge fireplace. Through the ages the castle has welcomed many royal guests. Edward II dined here in 1322, and more recently, Princess Elizabeth visited here before she came to the throne.

The Bishop Princes

The Conqueror appointed the bishops of Durham as rulers of the area. This suited him and succeeding monarchs very well, since the position of bishop was not hereditary. The king could elect to the position whoever he pleased, and by endowing the cathedral and bishopric richly he could be assured of absolute loyalty. The Bishop Princes, as they became known, were inextricably involved with the monarchs of their time. They had absolute power and authority and were known for their ruthlessness. As well as administering a very large area, they were expected to raise and lead an army should it prove necessary, and were even sufficiently powerful to pass the death sentence on an offender, if they thought fit. William outlawed Bishop Ethelwain, and installed in his place Bishop Walcher, a highly respected man who laid the foundations of the reformed monastery. Its remains may still be seen incorporated into the south east corner of the cloisters. Walcher was murdered and was succeeded by William of St Carileph, who, with the aid of Duke Robert, conspired to overthrow William Rufus, and was immediately banished to Normandy. While in exile he made plans for improving the cathedral which he put into operation on his return to England. After his death, William Rufus waited three years before appointing his own favourite Bishop Flambard, the man who rebuilt the Conqueror's wooden castle in stone. Flambard did more for the improvement of Durham than any other bishop— he heightened the city walls, replaced the earthworks by stone, improved the cathedral and dug a moat.

By 1104, the monks felt that it was safe enough to return and to entomb the relics of St Cuthbert in his cathedral shrine. In a room that was once the monks' dormitory, and which now houses the library, are kept the other relics of St Cuthbert removed from his coffin, as well as a maniple given by King Athelstan when he visited the city in 934.

The Norman Cathedral at Durham, set on a high rock, and surrounded on three sides by the River Wear

In 1136 King Stephen took the castle and stayed here while negotiating with David, King of Scotland, to prevent the Scots from invading. Three years later the Treaty of Durham was signed. A relative of Stephen was set up as bishop, but his appointment was opposed by the Archbishop of Canterbury, and so Bishop Pudsey was appointed. He was ruling while Richard the Lionheart went off on his crusade, and when Richard returned, he discovered that the bishop had been handling a large and unaccountable sum of money. It transpired that Bishop Pudsey had collected the money for the ransom of the King and had spent it on the castle and the cathedral. Pudsey was succeeded by Bishop Philip, who, for his part in siding with King John against the Pope, was excommunicated, and when he died was buried in unconsecrated ground.

Bek, another important bishop, who took up his position in 1284, was responsible for building the fine great hall in 1296. Bek set out with Edward I and a great army of men against the Scots, but returned three years later without royal permission. Soon after that, Bek set off to Rome to answer charges against himself, again without permission from the King, and while he was away Edward I seized his power. In 1334 a bishop by the name of Richard de Buy took up his position in Durham. Once the tutor of Edward III, he later entertained the King and Queen here. De Buy was succeeded by Bishop Hatfield, tutor to the Black Prince, a man who played a prominent part in the Battle of Neville's Cross of 17th October, 1346 in which the Scots lost 1,500 men and King David II was taken prisoner. Today a cross marks the spot where one flank of the English army gathered.

Union between England and Scotland
Henry IV's nephew Robert Neville took up the position in 1437 and eleven years later he entertained Henry VI at Durham Castle—the King had come to make a pilgrimage to the shrine of St Cuthbert. Almost every bishop was involved with his monarch and Richard

Fox was no exception—he was instrumental in arranging the marriage between James IV of Scotland and Princess Margaret. Fox entertained Margaret at the castle when she was on her way to the wedding in Edinburgh. James I stopped at Durham on his way to London to take up the English crown and he was royally entertained here. He returned to Durham in 1617 and stayed for some time.

Charles I was another guest here in 1633, on his way to be crowned at Edinburgh. He made a tour of the town as well as visiting the shrine of St Cuthbert. Charles visited again in 1647, but this time flanked on either side by a guard, a prisoner of the Scots. During the Civil War the city was constantly besieged and was extensively damaged by the Scots after the battle of Dunbar in 1650. Scottish prisoners were held captive inside the cathedral where they destroyed the woodwork and wrecked the organs. While Cromwell was here, perhaps to check on his prisoners, he instructed that a college should be founded, but this was opposed by Oxford and Cambridge Universities and, later, by Charles II. Durham University, part of which occupies the castle, was eventually founded in 1832.

The City
By 1836, the power and authority of the Bishop Princes gradually dwindled and eventually passed to the crown. A sword given by George V serves as a reminder of the union that once existed so strongly and continues to this day between the church and the crown.

Next to St Nicholas' Church in the market place is the town hall with window portraits of Edward II astride a great white horse giving thanks to the citizens of Durham for rescuing his baggage train which he had left unattended while fighting against the Scots. Inside the building, the mayor's chamber contains portraits of Charles I and his queen Henrietta Maria. On the northern outskirts of the city, the County Hall which now administers the county of Durham was opened in 1963 by the Duke of Edinburgh.

Durham Castle dates from 1070. The buildings have been extensively restored, and are now used by the university

The Elvet Bridge over the River Wear is one of the oldest in Durham

Castles of the north

BISHOP AUCKLAND

The castle at Bishop Auckland began its life as a Norman manor house used by the Bishops of Durham as their residence. Some of the castle dates back to the 14th century while other parts are only 200 years old. The oldest part is the chapel built by Bishop Cosin who lies buried here. He decorated it lavishly, having converted it originally from a Norman hall. The room which was the library contains some beautiful oak panelling bearing the arms of Elizabeth I.

Charles I stayed here on three occasions, the first time as Prince of Wales, the second time as a guest of Bishop Morton on 31st May 1633 and the third occasion as a prisoner on 4th February 1647, before being taken to his execution.

HEIGHINGTON

Heighington is a picture postcard town, set on a hill, its buildings clustering round a large green. It is noted for its Norman church built around 1100.

To the south east is Walworth Castle, a great structure with two dominating towers. It was visited by James I on 14th April, 1603, while on his way to his coronation in London. He was lavishly entertained during his stay here. The castle was originally built by Thomas Jennison, the auditor general of Queen Elizabeth I. It was rebuilt in 1861 and now houses a boarding school.

RABY CASTLE

The 14th century Raby Castle was built by Sir John Neville. The Neville family were instrumental in getting Henry IV to the throne and Ralph, the son of John Neville, fought at Agincourt. Ralph married twice, and on the second occasion he married John of Gaunt's daughter. Of his 21 children, the youngest, Cecily, married Richard Plantagenet, Duke of York, and was mother to Edward IV and Richard III.

In the great Baron's Hall, some 136 ft long and overlooked by a minstrels' gallery, a meeting took place to plan the rising of the north which was intended to depose Elizabeth I and install Mary, Queen of Scots, on the throne of England. The plot was to take place on 13th November 1569, but failed and the Nevilles forfeited all their land to the crown. In 1626 Sir Henry Vane, a strong parliamentarian supporter bought it, and to this day the castle belongs to the Vane family.

It was extensively restored in the 18th century and is full of beautiful furniture and fine paintings. It also has an exhibition of horse drawn vehicles.

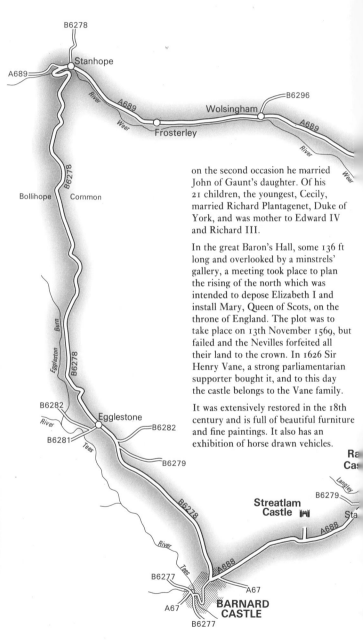

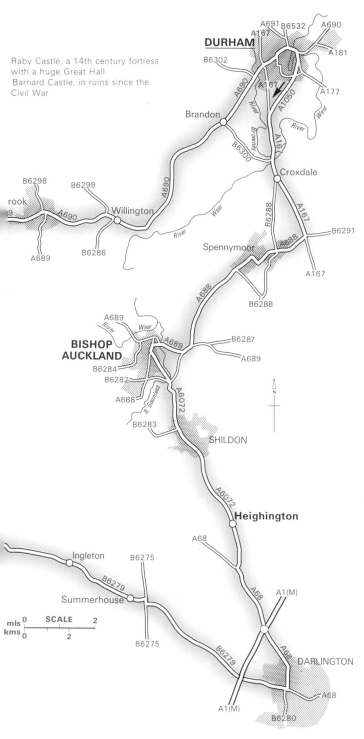

Raby Castle, a 14th century fortress
with a huge Great Hall
Barnard Castle, in ruins since the
Civil War

STREATLAM

Streatlam was once a castle built by
and belonging to the Balliol family,
one of whom was John Balliol
crowned King of Scotland in Scone in
1292. The castle fell into ruins and
was refaced in 1720. It was once the
seat of the Bowes and also the Bowes-
Lyon family. The Queen Mother,
a Bowes-Lyon before her marriage to
King George VI, was at one time a
frequent visitor here.

BARNARD CASTLE

Set on the banks of the River Tees,
Barnard Castle was built by Guy
Balliol on a site given him by William
Rufus in 1100—it was originally built
of wood but was rebuilt in stone by his
nephew Bernard Balliol. The town
evolved and grew up round Barnard
Castle. During the rising of the north,
the castle was in the hands of Charles,
Earl of Westmorland, a strong
supporter of Mary, Queen of Scots.
He was forced to leave the castle and

flee for his life, whereupon Sir George
Bowes garrisoned the castle for Queen
Elizabeth I. After withstanding an
11 day siege the castle surrendered,
although by this time the rebellion had
come to an end. The Vane family held
Barnard for the royalists during the
Civil War, when it was seriously
damaged and captured by the
parliamentarians.

Although looking rather shabby from
the outside, the castle retains much of
interest and is set in $6\frac{1}{2}$ acres of most
beautiful land. Balliol Tower can be
clearly seen for miles around, and
bears the arms of Richard III over
one of the windows.

About $1\frac{1}{2}$ miles from the castle,
standing in the market place, is the
little church of St Mary which has
pillar carvings of Edward IV and
Richard III, who married the daughter
of one of the owners of the castle and
who, when he lived here, was reputed
to have done much to improve it.

B

181

BAMBURGH

There has been a castle at Bamburgh since AD 547 when King Ida built his castle "huge and square" as described in Sir Walter Scott's *Marmion*. It looks out over Budle Bay towards the beautiful Holy Isle, Lindisfarne, and can be seen for miles around, towering above the small town on its high rock.

Early history
Bamburgh was the centre of Christian missionary work to the rest of the country, which was still pagan to a great extent and Aidan, a Celt, was canonised for his work in the Northumbrian church. When the Danes invaded our shores at the end of the 10th century, they plundered Bamburgh so terribly that it became no more than a ghost town until the Norman era. The Conqueror had a wooden castle erected and installed the Earl of Northumberland as his provincial governor. Almost thirty years after the Conquest, the Earl of Northumberland, Robert Mowbray, rebelled against the Conqueror's son, William Rufus. The King besieged Northumberland in Bamburgh Castle, but his father had made a strong fortress and William found it necessary to build a wooden structure which he called Malvoisin to isolate the castle. Mowbray escaped from the castle leaving his young wife in charge, but he was captured at his monastic retreat and threatened until he gave up the castle to the King.

War with the Scots
When hostilities began with the Scots across the border, Bamburgh Castle was rebuilt with stone walls rather than wooden ones to strengthen the fortifications and resist the attacks of the highlanders. King John was a visitor to Bamburgh, Henry III came some time later, and Edward III came to the castle after his victory at Halidon Hill to sign a treaty

Bamburgh Castle, although much restored in the 18th century, retains its prominent Norman keep

with the Scots. The Wars of the Roses brought bitter fighting in the struggle for the throne between the Houses of Lancaster and York. Bamburgh Castle was besieged twice in this long and drawn out war and was reduced to ruins by heavy cannon fire against its walls. In Elizabethan times the castle was given by the Queen to the Forster family, in whose hands it remained for several centuries. During the Civil War, when Parliament tried and finally succeeded in ousting the monarchy, the castle was taken for King Charles I by Sir Ralph Grey with his army of Scotsmen. With the royalists in occupation, the Earls of Northumberland and Warwick besieged the castle and ultimately repossessed it for parliament. Their cannon had again demolished the walls, injuring Grey who was later executed.

Restoration of the Castle
It was in the 18th century that the castle was extensively restored by Lord Crew, the Bishop of Durham, who had married into the Forster family. His wife, Dorothy was immortalised in Walter Besant's novel *Dorothy Forster*. The interior of the Norman edifice was

transformed to 18th century modernity and part of the building given over to a school for girls wishing to enter domestic service. The Bishop, and his successor at the castle, Dr John Sharp, were very aware of the needs of the poor in the community. A free surgery and dispensary were opened where they could receive treatment. They could bring their corn to be ground in the windmill which Crewe had erected, and storage was available in one of the towers. The old Norman keep was turned into a lighthouse to aid navigation at sea and, should a disaster occur, the victims of the wrecks could be housed within the castle. Bamburgh Castle has since been bought and completely restored and although it is still used as a residence it is open to the public at times. It contains many treasures, which include tapestries, portraits and a cradle which once belonged to Queen Anne.

The rock on which Bamburgh Castle stands is an outcrop of the Whin Sill

Border country

FLOORS CASTLE
Beside the River Tweed, just outside the town of Kelso, stands Floors Castle, home of the Duke of Roxburgh. It is one of Scotland's finest stately homes, surrounded by beautiful gardens and enclosed in a wall built by captive Frenchmen during the wars with Napoleon. James II of Scotland was killed here in 1460 when a cannon exploded and the place is now marked by a holly bush.

WARK
Before the unification of England, Wark was one of the most northerly towns of the Kingdom of Northumbria. After the Norman Conquest, William I put the country in the charge of the Earl of Northumberland, but he was killed at Wark by the invading Scottish King, Malcolm. The village was constantly being plundered by highlanders, so in the 12th century a huge castle was built to defend the borders. It held a key position for English forays into Scotland and Edward I was at Wark before his journey across the border. Edward II prepared his army at Wark before Bannockburn and Edward III was a visitor to the castle when he was entertained by the Countess of Salisbury.

Little remains of the fortress which was besieged a total of eleven times between 1136 and 1523.

FLODDEN FIELD
In the sixteenth century, France and Spain were in conflict. If either were victorious they would dominate Europe to the detriment of England's own power, so Henry VIII went to France to try to preserve a stalemate. Although Henry had made a treaty with his brother-in-law King James IV of Scotland, James also had a treaty with France and he decided that to attack England in Henry's absence would further the French cause in Europe. Henry had left but a small army in England and James had little respect for its leader, the Earl of Surrey, who was aged and so crippled with gout that he had to be driven to the battle in a carriage.

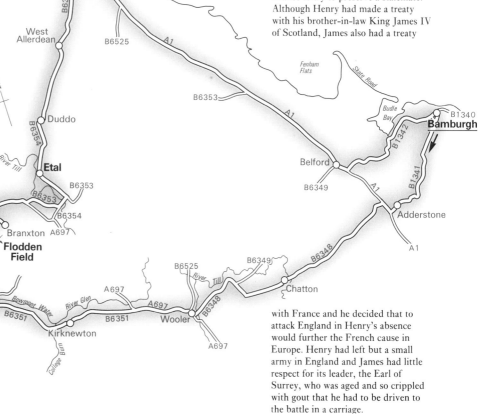

Floors Castle, near Kelso, was designed by Vanbrugh in the 18th century

183

A large Scots force had taken up position at Flodden Field on Branxton Moor. Somehow, the smaller English army managed to cross the River Till, circling round behind the Scots. James turned to face them, but the nature of his artillery prevented any sudden attacks, even though they had lit camp fires to make smoke thus hiding their movements from the enemy. While James advanced his main force towards Surrey and his son, his reinforcements were scattered by an English company, and another regiment attacked his flank with disastrous results. Finally the King of Scotland was killed and the 26,000 strong English army won a major victory over 40,000 Scotsmen. A monument has since been erected on the site of the battle.

A

ETAL

At the edge of the pretty village of Etal lie the ruins of Etal Castle, built by Sir Robert de Manners during the 14th century. Although it was a substantial building of some importance, it was destroyed by King James IV of Scotland in 1496 when he invaded England in support of the pretender, Perkin Warbeck.

In the mid 19th century the little church in the grounds of Etal House was donated to the village by Lady Augusta Fitzclarence as a memorial to her husband, a son of William IV.

BERWICK UPON TWEED

The most northerly town in England, Berwick, which stands at the mouth of the River Tweed, saw many troubled times when border skirmishes between England and Scotland were commonplace. The town changed hands between the two countries several times and the imposing fortifications around the town are still very much in evidence. A Scottish rebellion was quelled by Henry II, who was at Berwick Upon Tweed when the Scottish King William the Lion was brought to him in chains. As part of William's ransom, Berwick became part of England, but was returned to Scotland by Richard I in order to raise funds for his crusade. When his brother John came to the throne, he marched on Berwick and demolished the whole town.

In 1286 there was some rivalry over the accession to the throne of Scotland and the three parties agreed to put the problem before the English King Edward I for his decision. A committee of experts on the subject were assembled under the leadership of the King and took eighteen months to decide in favour of John Balliol as opposed to Robert Bruce, a decision which was announced in Berwick. Many Scots refused to abide by the ruling and as a result there was extensive fighting along the border for

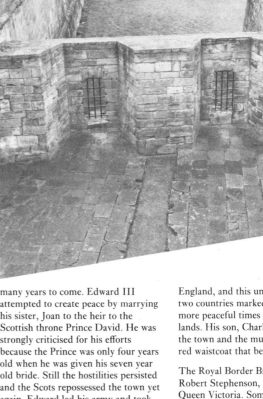

B

many years to come. Edward III attempted to create peace by marrying his sister, Joan to the heir to the Scottish throne Prince David. He was strongly criticised for his efforts because the Prince was only four years old when he was given his seven year old bride. Still the hostilities persisted and the Scots repossessed the town yet again. Edward led his army and took up position on Halidon Hill, which was surrounded by marshy ground. When the Scots advanced they were bogged down and from their vantage point high above, Edward's army cut them down where they stood. There is a monument to the battle on the hill.

James VI of Scotland made a triumphant entrance into Berwick at the beginning of his journey to London to be crowned James I of

England, and this unification of the two countries marked the advent of more peaceful times for the border lands. His son, Charles I, also visited the town and the museum contains a red waistcoat that belonged to him.

The Royal Border Bridge, built by Robert Stephenson, was opened by Queen Victoria. Some of the materials used were from the old castle, but parts of the great fortress are still very much in evidence together with the extensive walls which used to encircle the town.

A The monument on the site of the Battle of Flodden Field
B The Elizabethan town walls of Berwick Upon Tweed are the oldest of their period in Europe

The Kings and Queens of Scotland

Until the early eighteenth century, Scotland was a monarchy in its own right. However, it was never a stable monarchy, being constantly under pressure from the English and particularly prone to internal dissension and strife. Very few of the Scottish Kings died in their beds. Often, the heir to the throne was too young to rule, and for much of its history Scotland was governed by Regents. In 1603, James VI of Scotland became James I of England, but the Scottish kingdom remained separate until the 1707 Treaty of Union. When the English crown passed to the House of Hanover, there was considerable enthusiasm in Scotland for a restoration of the Stewart family to the throne, but all attempts were unsuccessful. It was only with Queen Victoria that the English sovereign came to be respected in Scotland, and the bonds of affection have grown stronger, right up to Queen Elizabeth II's time.

The Early Kings

Scotland was made up of four Kingdoms in the earliest days for which records are available, around the time of the Roman occupation. Following their nominal conversion to Christianity, a measure of unity was achieved in AD843, when Kenneth MacAlpin obtained the monarchy of Scotia. The Scottish system of succession was decided by tanistry, which meant that any mature male of the royal kindred was eligible for Kingship if he were the "stuff of Kings". He was nominated during the King's lifetime as second to the King. Kenneth MacAlpin established his seat of government at Scone, bringing there the Stone of Scone, the traditional seat for coronation. The land of Lothian continued to resist invasion for the

Kenneth MacAlpin	839–860
Donald I	860–863
Constantine II	863–877
Aedh	877–878
Eocha	878–889
Donald II	889–900
Constantine III	900–942
Malcolm I	942–954
Indulph	954–962
Duff	962–967
Colin	967–971
Kenneth II	971–995
Constantine IV	995–997
Kenneth III	997–1005
Malcolm II	1005–1034
Duncan I	1034–1040
Macbeth	1040–1057
Lulach	1057–1058
Malcolm II (Canmore)	1058–1093
Donald III (Bane)	1093–May 1094
Duncan II	May 1094–Nov 1094
Donald III (Bane)	Nov 1094–1097
Edgar	1098–1107
Alexander I	1107–1124
David I	1124–1153
Malcolm IV	1153–1165
William I	1165–1214
Alexander II	1214–1249
Alexander III	1249–1286
Margaret	1286–1290
John (Balliol)	1292–1296
Robert I (Bruce)	1306–1329
David II	1329–1371
Edward (Balliol)	Aug 1332–Dec 1332 periods 1333–1346
Robert II	1371–1390
Robert III	1390–1406
James I	1406–1437
James II	1437–1460
James III	1460–1488
James IV	1488–1513
James V	1513–1542
Mary Queen of Scots	1542–1567
James VI	1567–1603
James VI of Scotland and I of England	1603–1625

The Crown, Sceptre and Sword of State from the Scottish Regalia

following one and a half centuries, during which Kenneth MacAlpin was succeeded by fourteen kings, most of them obscure. In 1018 Malcolm II defeated the Angles at Carham on the Tweed, and annexed the Lothian territory. Malcolm reigned for nearly thirty years, and when he died he was succeeded by his grandson Duncan I, who was King of Strathclyde, thereby bringing about the union with Scotia and Lothian making a unity of Scotland, even though it did not then include the Western Isles or the Orkneys or Shetlands.

The tomb of Robert Bruce in Dunfermline Abbey

Stirling Castle, from where Robert Bruce defeated the forces of Edward II at Bannockburn

Duncan did not live long, and was killed by Macbeth in battle in 1040. Macbeth himself was later killed in battle by Duncan's elder son Malcolm, who also killed Lulach, Macbeth's successor. Malcolm II who was on the Scottish throne when William the Conqueror invaded England, married the beautiful and saintly Margaret. He promised loyalty to William, but was killed in 1093, when invading England. For thirty years after his death, Scotland was in turmoil, ruled by a succession of weak, insecure kings. In 1124 David, the ninth son of Malcolm, came to the throne and ruled for thirty eventful years, establishing considerable order in the country. The next king but one, William, concluded an agreement with France, the Auld Alliance, which dictated much of Scotland's subsequent history. Alexander III who came to the throne in 1249, had a peaceful and prosperous reign, brought abruptly to an end when he was killed in a riding accident. The heir to the throne was Margaret, infant daughter of the King of Norway, but when she died on the voyage from Norway, the succession to the throne was laid open. There were over a dozen claimants, and the choice among them was made by the English King, Edward I, who selected John Balliol. Before long, however, Edward invaded Scotland, deposing John Balliol, and taking the Stone of Scone to complete the conquest of Scotland.

The Wars of Independence
When John Balliol was deposed, Robert Bruce, his main rival for the throne, had himself crowned king at Scone, although the English conquest of Scotland kept him a fugitive for over a year. He was able to gather his forces and defeat the English at Loudon Hill in 1307, and this led Edward I to return to invade Scotland again. He died on the journey, allowing Bruce the opportunity of reasserting his position. Edward II of England took no action against Bruce until 1314, when he marched north to the relief of Stirling. Bruce was waiting for him, and in the Battle of Bannockburn which followed, the English were put to flight. After this the English released

their hold on Scotland, although for fourteen years the war raged in northern England. Bruce died in 1329, a national hero.

Robert Bruce's son, David, was only five years old when he was crowned, and the Earl of Moray was made Regent. The English wanted to get John Balliol's son Edward Balliol on the throne, and he was crowned at Scone. David was kept securely out of the country while this was going on, but his nephew was able to drive out the English, making it safe for him to return. David was not a strong King and preferred life in the English court, and on his death, the Scottish throne passed to his nephew Robert, who as Robert II was the first of the Stewart Kings.

The House of Stewart

Robert II had been a good Regent when his uncle David had been too young, but he was not a successful King. The land was rife with crime and border raids and the economy was in ruins. His successor Robert III was a cripple and he abdicated in 1399, and, for the next twenty-five years, Scotland was ruled by Regents. The heir to the throne, James, had been captured by pirates and was a prisoner of the English for the first eighteen years of his reign. In 1422, Henry V died, and the way was open for James to return to Scotland. He did so in 1424, and lost no time in restoring the lost power of the crown, and carrying out reforms. He was stabbed by his enemies in 1437 when his son was only six, so again there was a Regency. James II took control in 1449 at the age of nineteen, and for eleven years ruled wisely and well. He was killed in battle in 1460, when laying siege to Roxburgh during the Wars of the Roses. His son was nine, so again a Regent ruled. James III was not popular when he came to the throne, and in 1488 a group of conspirators tried to proclaim his son king in his place. In the Battle of Sauchieburn which followed, James III was thrown from his horse and mysteriously stabbed.

James IV was fifteen when he came to the throne, and a Regency existed for a short time. But James was an able and popular King,

The loch and the remains of the Royal Palace at Linlithgow

188

bringing to the war-torn country something of the civilization of the Renaissance. Magnificent palaces were created at Falkland, Linlithgow and Craigmillar. He made a serious attempt to come to terms with the Lords of the Isles, who regarded themselves as separate from Scotland and made treaties with the English. He tried different approaches, but only achieved a semblance of peace. He was on good terms with the English following his marriage to Margaret, sister of Henry VIII. But in Europe, France was under attack, and, abiding by the terms of the Auld Alliance, James IV declared war on England, and invaded. At the Battle of Flodden Field, the Scottish King was slain.

His son was only one year old, so again there was a succession of Regents until he was fourteen. Even then he was kept a prisoner until he managed to escape. During his reign James V tried hard to resist the attempts of Henry VIII to establish supremacy over Scotland and make it Protestant, but he was killed in battle in 1542. His only child was Mary, who became Queen of Scots. At the age of fifteen she married the Dauphin of France, but returned to Scotland in 1561 after his death. Her reign was a dramatic and tortuous one, ending with her abdication after the Battle of Carberry in 1567 (see page 196). Her infant son, James VI, was proclaimed King, and again Scotland was ruled by Regents. In 1583, James, who had been held captive in Ruthven Castle, managed to escape and proclaimed himself King at St Andrews. He became a shrewd political monarch who cultivated good relations with England. In 1603, Elizabeth I died, and he became King James I of England, from that point on leaving Scotland for England.

During James VI and I's reign and that of his successor Charles I, Scotland was governed from London. Charles I and Charles II both had support in Scotland, but this did not help them in their struggles for the English throne. In 1707 the Treaty of Union merged the Kingdom of Scotland with that of England, but for years there were many Jacobites in Scotland who felt that the Stewart line were the rightful heirs to the throne. The Old Pretender and the Young Pretender made romantic attempts to achieve this, but after 1766 their cause was effectively lost. In the years since then, Queen Victoria grew to love Scotland and her people, and the British monarchy during the twentieth century has established firmer and firmer links with the Scottish people.

The Royal Palace at Falkland (right) was very popular with the Stewart kings, especially during the reign of James V. The Chapel in the Palace is shown below

EDINBURGH

Edinburgh, capital of Scotland since it succeeded Perth in 1437 when it took James II's fancy, is steeped in the rich history of royal Scotland. Edinburgh itself was in ancient times a primitive fortress built by the Picts and was known as Duneadian. It was when the Northumbrian King Edwin rebuilt the castle in the 7th century that the town and fortress were re-named Edwinesburgh in his honour.

THE CASTLE

The Castle's origins are shrouded in antiquity but go back to at least the Bronze Age. It has been described as "the last port of defence for lost causes" and has been a refuge for Scottish sovereigns and a prison for their enemies.

Not until Malcolm III, last of the purely Gaelic kings, married Margaret, sister of Edgar Etheling, King-elect of England after Harold died at Hastings, and made it their residence, does its history become clear. Margaret, who was to become a saint for her piety and good work, had the chapel known as St Margaret's Chapel built in 1076 at the highest point of the castle rock. It is the only part of the castle to survive from this date. Queen Margaret died in the castle in 1093 on hearing the news that her husband and eldest son Edward had died after being surprised and ambushed on an unsuccessful raid on England. The castle was then besieged by Donald Ban, Malcolm's youngest brother who for three years ruled Scotland jointly with one of Malcolm and Margaret's surviving sons, Edmund. David I, youngest son of Malcolm and Margaret, resided in the castle for some time during his reign, which lasted from 1124 to 1153. In 1174 the castle was occupied by the English after Henry II had defeated William

Edinburgh Castle, 433 feet above sea level, overlooks the city

The Lion at Alnwick. It was again delivered into Scottish hands on the marriage of William The Lion to Ermadis de Beaumont in 1186.

Alexander III married Margaret, daughter of Henry III of England, here in 1252. King Alexander spent his last years in the castle and, after his death in 1286 followed shortly by that of his only daughter, Margaret of Norway, Scotland was plunged into the disputes over the succession. At that time the castle acted as a focus of loyalty for the Scottish people because it served as the treasury guarding the jewels of the Scottish kings, and housed the national records. In 1291–92 Edward I of England ordered the records and treasures to be delivered into his hands for safe-keeping until another king was found. This action was viewed with much suspicion by the Scots and many pieces of the royal regalia found their way into Edward's wardrobe at Westminster. When John Balliol became king they were never restored to the castle. Edward I visited the castle in 1291 and received homage from the Scots. After John Balliol was crowned in 1296,

the castle was besieged by the forces of Edward I and surrendered in eight days. It remained in English hands until 1313 when it was taken by the forces of Robert Bruce who commanded that the fortifications and buildings, except St Margaret's Chapel, be totally destroyed. It fell into English hands again during the minority of David II but was re-taken by him in 1341. During David II's reign the castle was considerably re-built and he added King David's Tower which took ten years to build. He died at the castle in 1371, and his successor Robert II granted the burgesses of Edinburgh the right to build houses within the castle walls for protection in times of war. Robert III resided here with his queen, Annabella, and his court.

Stewart times

During the minorities of the House of Stewart the castle was often used as a refuge. James II stayed here for a short while until his mother, Queen Joanna, smuggled him out to Stirling. It was after the young King James II returned to the castle, that on 24th November 1440 the famous "Black Dinner" occurred when William Earl of Douglas and his brother were invited to the castle then treacherously executed before the eyes of the 10 year old monarch. James II was an enthusiast of the new military art of gunnery and was responsible for the casting of the great cannon known as 'Mons Meg' which is still to be seen on the castle battlements. Unfortunately, the gun burst after firing a royal salute to Charles II in 1680.

James II was detained here during his minority by the castle's governor Sir Alexander Boyd and forced to approve a *coup d'etat* by the Boyds. He was again imprisoned here in 1482 by a group of noblemen who disapproved of his policies and his favouritism. It is said that James III's famous treasure, 'Black Kirst', which contained fabulous wealth, was held in King David's Tower in the castle. This was never proved, and when the castle was plundered by Cromwell in 1650 and the

Scottish national records were removed to Stirling, no mention was made of the treasure. Although no longer a royal palace in his reign, James IV stayed at the castle many times to attend Mass and watch John Borthwick, his master-gunner, casting cannon. He loved tournaments and participated in the ones that he organised in Edinburgh. It was under his instructions that the Great Hall was built in 1483 where the earliest Scottish Parliaments were supposed to have met.

Mary, Queen of Scots, first visited the castle in 1561 and the following year she took refuge at the castle after the murder of her secretary, Riccio. When her son, who was to become James VI (of Scotland) and I (of England), was born here in 1566 a salute was fired from the castle battlements. The Queen visited the castle again after the murder of her husband Darnley and she stayed here before her ill-fated marriage to Bothwell. Although large sums of money were spent on the upkeep of the castle during the reign of James VI and I, the castle ceased to be more than a fortress occasionally visited by the King. Charles I stayed at the castle for three nights before his coronation in

1633 and Charles II made an equally brief visit in 1650. After this no monarch visited the castle until George IV in the 19th century. Oliver Cromwell visited the castle in 1648 and took it in 1650 when the Scots proclaimed Charles II at the Mercat Cross. The Duke of Gordon held the castle for James II after the "Glorious Revolution" which put William III on the throne of England and he fought on until famine and disease forced him to capitulate. The Scottish regalia, the crown, the sceptre and the sword of state are displayed in the store vaulted Crown Room, which adjoins the royal apartments. The insignia, used in Scottish coronations since Robert Bruce, were hidden at the time of Cromwell's occupation, then stored in a wooden chest on the Act of Union in 1707. They were 're-discovered' in 1817 by a commission in which Sir Walter Scott participated. The crown, of unknown origin, was re-modelled in 1540 by James V and is made of Scottish gold.

ROYAL MILE

Most of the other buildings with which royalty has been connected are situated on or near the

Royal Mile, running between the castle and Holyroodhouse, down which kings and queens have travelled over the centuries.

ST. GILES

The High Kirk of St Giles, also known as St Giles Cathedral after Charles II elevated it to a cathedral, dominates the High Street on the Royal Mile. Its most famous minister was John Knox, and Charles I was crowned here in 1633. The beautiful Thistle Chapel, designed by Sir Robert Mortimer, is the Chapel of the Order of the Knights of the Thistle.

GREYFRIARS CHURCH

Greyfriars church houses the Martyr's Memorial which commemorates the severe reprisals imposed on the defeated Covenanters after the Battle of Bothwell Bridge. Twelve hundred prisoners endured outdoor confinement in the churchyard; two thirds were released after taking the Oath of Submission but the others accepted death by exposure, execution and transportation to the West Indies. Although the numbers of sufferers were relatively small and came from a limited area of Scotland the last years of Charles II's

The Tolbooth, Canongate, on the Royal Mile

White Horse Close on the Royal Mile

The West Door of the High Kirk of St Giles

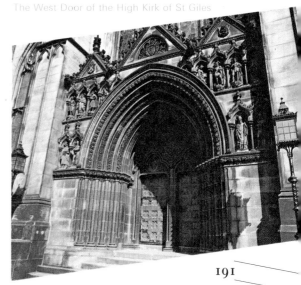

The Palace of Holyroodhouse, the official residence of the Queen when she is in Edinburgh

rule became known as "The Killing Time". The Earl of Morton, executed regent of Scotland during the minority of James VI, is buried in the churchyard.

THE MERCAT CROSS

The Mercat Cross stands by the west door of the High Kirk of St Giles and is part of an ancient shaft, restored in 1880, the old cross having been demolished in 1756. Traditionally, royal proclamations were heraldically spoken here, and these have included the news of the death of James IV at Flodden Field. In 1745, crowds gathered to hear Prince Charles Edward proclaim his father James VIII of Scotland and III of England.

RIDDLES COURT

"Macmorron's Lodgings" in the inner court were thought to be of such distinction that a banquet was held here in the spring of 1598, to entertain King James VI and Queen Anne of Denmark.

MORAY HOUSE

Charles I was a frequent visitor here, and Cromwell stayed on two occasions in the famous 17th century mansion, later part of Moray House School. The Treaty of Union between Scotland and England was signed in 1707 in the summer house in the garden of the mansion.

CANNON BALL HOUSE

A cannon ball is embedded in the gable of this house. It is traditionally thought to have been fired, from the castle, at the Palace of Holyroodhouse, when one end of the Royal Mile was held by anti-Jacobite forces and the other by the forces of Prince Charles Edward.

PARLIAMENT HOUSE

Seat of the Scottish Parliament from 1639 until the Treaty of Union in 1707 the buildings now house Scotland's supreme courts. The great south windows of Parliament Hall depict the inauguration of the Court of Session by King James V in 1532. In the centre of Parliament Square is an imposing equestrian statue of King Charles II.

QUEEN MARY'S BATH

A picturesque little building where Mary, Queen of Scots is popularly supposed to have bathed in white wine.

PALACE OF HOLYROODHOUSE

The palace, which lies at the opposite end of the Royal Mile from the castle, originates from the guesthouse of Holyrood Abbey. The abbey was dedicated by David I in 1128 to Christ's Rood or Cross because of what he believed to be a miraculous escape while hunting in the area. The ruins of the abbey lie to the north of the palace. Among those buried here are David II (1324–71), James II (1430–60), James V (1512–42) and Henry, Lord Darnley (1545–67). In 1688, a mob sacked the Catholic Chapel Royal at Holyrood and desecrated the tombs of some of the Stewart kings. Subsequently their bones were moved into a royal charnel house at the abbey.

James II was crowned at the abbey, thus breaking a tradition, originated by Kenneth MacAlpin, that Scottish kings were crowned at Scone. It was not until James IV's reign that the official palace was built beside the abbey. In 1543 the palace and the abbey were burned during an English invasion—only the church and the north west tower escaping destruction.

Mary, Queen of Scots, and her son James lived in the partly restored palace. She spent six tragic years of her reign here, during which time she had her famous interview with John Knox. On the floor of the audience chamber is a brass tablet marking the place where her secretary David Riccio's body was left after his murder in March 1566 by a gang of nobles led by the Earl of Morton and her husband Lord Darnley. Darnley himself was found strangled a year later in the ground of the house called Kirk O'Field. The house stood on the site of the present Edinburgh University and was blown up. Mary married Bothwell, who had been tried and acquitted of the murder of Darnley, at Holyrood in 1567.

The Music Room at the Palace of Holyroodhouse. All the State Apartments are rich with French and Flemish tapestries and 18th century furniture

Charles II, who was crowned here, was largely responsible for the building as it is today. He began re-building in 1671, designing it in the French style, partly a genuine relic of the "Auld Alliance" and partly as a result of his French tastes. James VII and II occupied the palace when as heir to the throne he resided in Scotland. After the fall of the House of Stewart, the palace remained largely unused except for a

brief occupation by Prince Charles Edward during the victorious part of his 1745 campaign, when he held a celebration ball here.

The picture gallery contains a remarkable collection of alleged portraits of ancient Scottish kings, painted by James de Will between 1684 and 1686 and purely his own invention. In 1822 George IV, the first king to visit Scotland for over a century, stayed at Holyroodhouse and attended a ball in full Highland dress, wearing pink silk tights. Years later, Edward VII lived here as Prince of Wales.

During the 20th century the palace has been in constant use and is the official residence of Queen Elizabeth II when in Edinburgh. The state apartments have French and Flemish tapestries and 18th century furniture which is particularly associated with Queen Victoria and her consort Albert who often stayed here. In Holyrood Park lies the extinct volcano known as Arthur's Seat. Queen Victoria was fond of the route round it which is now known as the Queens Drive.

SCOTTISH NATIONAL PORTRAIT GALLERY
In the gallery are fine portraits of the earlier Stewart kings.

ASSEMBLY ROOMS
The Assembly Rooms which are in George Street were built by public subscription and opened in 1787. George IV attended a reception held here in his honour.

REGISTER HOUSE
This lies at the east end of Princes Street and contains Scotland's national and historical records as well as legal documents. These date from the Charter of the Abbey of Melrose in 1137, continuing to the present day, and including one signed by our present Queen. There are also contemporary copies of the Declaration of Arbroath of 1320 and letters from Mary, Queen of Scots.

Fortresses in the Lothians

A

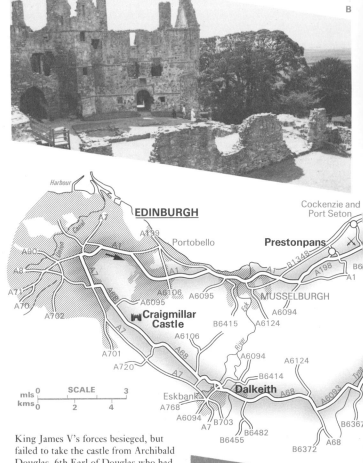

B

PRESTONPANS

The Battle of Prestonpans was fought on 20th September 1745 between the forces of Prince Charles Edward and an English army commanded by Sir John Cope. The victory by Charles was the high point of his success, but he failed to follow it up, waiting too long in Edinburgh hoping that Louis XV of France would be encouraged to send him reinforcements. Charles' army of highlanders was lightly armed with broad sword, dirk and a small circular shield called a targe. They had no mobile artillery, their cavalry numbered only about forty, and their main force was about 2,400. Cope's army of redcoats were armed with muskets with bayonet and included artillery manned by naval gunners. The actual battle lasted only ten minutes ending in a complete rout. Cope fled to Berwick-upon-Tweed, and on their march to England, the highlanders sang the ballad "Hey Johnnie Cope are ye walking yet".

At the onset of the battle Charles' army had the advantage of being able to overlook the opposing force, and outflank the English army. They charged with their backs to the sun, led by the Camerons, and the English with the sun in their eyes thought they were outnumbered and fled the field. Some 500 royal infantry and dragoons were killed and over 1,000 captured whilst the highlanders lost 30 killed and 70 wounded.

SETON

Seton Castle, built in 1790 by Robert Adam, stands on the site of the demolished Seton Palace. Mary, Queen of Scots, visited the palace with Lord Darnley in 1566 after the death of Riccio and again in 1567, this time

with Bothwell, after Darnley had been murdered. James VI and I and Charles I were entertained here by the Seton Family. The castle is not open to the public.

DIRLETON CASTLE

The beautiful sandstone ruins of the castle, not far from the village green of Dirleton, are some of the most picturesque in Scotland and rise from sheer rock in the midst of a lovely flower garden. The oldest parts, a group of towers, are thought to have been built in 1225 by John de Vaux, seneschal of the Queen Marie de Coucy. 15th to 17th century additions have also been made. In 1298 the castle was besieged by Edward I and captured, but was re-captured in 1311 by the forces of Robert Bruce. In 1650 it surrendered to Cromwell after strong resistance and was destroyed by General Lambert.

TANTALLON CASTLE

A castle has stood on this site since before 1300 under the name of 'Dentaloune'. The present structure, now an extensive ruin, commanding splendid views, was built in 1375 and was a Douglas stronghold for centuries. In October 1491, King James IV laid siege to the castle, obtaining guns from Linlithgow, when Lord Archibald Douglas, known as 'Bell-a-Cat' for his high-handed ways defied the King. In October 1528

King James V's forces besieged, but failed to take the castle from Archibald Douglas, 6th Earl of Douglas who had married the Queen Mother, Queen Margaret, Henry VIII of England's sister. The castle was held and was not surrendered to the King until May 1529 when Angus retired to England. In 1651 during the Cromwellian occupation it was attacked by General Monk, captured and dismantled.

HAILES CASTLE

The beautiful castle dates from before the Wars of Independence, and is in reality more of a fortified mansion house. It was built by the Earl of Dunbar in the 13th century, and in the

C

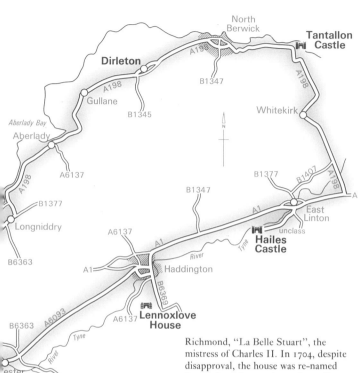

14th century it belonged to the Hepburn Family, who played an important part in history. James, 4th Earl of Bothwell, abducted and married Mary, Queen of Scots, and brought the Queen here in 1567 when they fled from Borthwick Castle. The castle was also heavily involved in the War of the Rough Wooing. In 1532 the castle was burned and in 1650 dismantled by Cromwell.

LENNOXLOVE

This charming house, formerly called Lethington, has belonged to the Maitland Family since the 14th century. Maitland of Lethington was Mary, Queen of Scots' secretary, and her death mask is in the hall of the house. In 1682, the house was sold to Frances, Duchess of Lennox and Richmond, "La Belle Stuart", the mistress of Charles II. In 1704, despite disapproval, the house was re-named Lennoxlove. It contains various gifts from Charles II, and is now the home of the Duke of Hamilton.

DALKEITH

Dalkeith Palace incorporates remnants of a 12th century castle and was largely re-built by Sir John Vanbrugh in 1700 for Anne, Duchess of Buccleuch and Monmouth, widow of the rebel Duke of Monmouth. James IV, James VI and Prince Charles Edward all visited the palace and Queen Victoria began her long period of devotion to Scotland by spending her first night at Dalkeith Palace as the guest of the then Duke and Duchess of Buccleuch in 1842.

CRAIGMILLAR CASTLE

This ruined fortress stands on the southern outskirts of Edinburgh, and because of its size, strength and proximity to the capital it became popular with the Stewart kings who enjoyed its comforts. James II youngest son of the Earl of Mar is said to have bled to death here in 1477. In 1544 the castle was burned and partially destroyed by an English force under Hertford but was still occupied. In 1566, Mary, Queen of Scots, fled here after her secretary Riccio's murder. It was also here that Argyll, Huntley, Bothwell, Maitland and Sir James Balfour signed the famous 'Band' which resulted in Lord Darnley's murder. It has never been proved that Queen Mary herself was directly involved in the plot but it is certain that she was living in the castle at the time that it was being planned. She spent her last night in the castle before being taken to imprisonment in Loch Leven Castle. On the nearby road to Dalkeith are some old houses known as Little France, where Mary's French attendants once lived. In the war following Mary's abdication the castle was garrisoned by Regent Mar against Edinburgh.

A Monument to the Battle of Prestonpans
B Dirleton Castle, in ruins since 1650
C Hailes Castle, formerly a fortified manor house
D Craigmillar Castle, associated with Mary, Queen of Scots
E Dalkeith Palace, rebuilt in the 16th century

195

Mary, Queen of Scots

Fairest and most tragic Queen

Mary is often presented as a naive and romantic woman, but the truth is that she was a courageous, astute and charming queen, who made a series of impetuous decisions which led inevitably to her downfall. She was born in 1542, but only eight days after her birth, her father died. She was contracted to the Dauphin of France in 1548, and spent many years in France. Sadly, he died in 1561, and the 19 year old widow returned to Scotland. She married Lord Darnley, but theirs was an unhappy marriage, and she relied considerably on one of her secretaries, the Italian Riccio. In 1566, Riccio was brutally murdered in her presence.

On 19th June, 1566, she gave birth to a son, who later became James VI of Scotland and James I of England. From this point on, her relationship with her husband Darnley was one of almost total estrangement. She was courted by Lord Bothwell, and in February 1567, the house in which Darnley was convalescing was blown up with extreme force. Curiously, the body of Darnley was found outside the house, and he had been strangled. No satisfactory explanation of this mystery has ever been found. Three months later Mary and Bothwell were married. Only one month later, as a result of strong opposition to the Queen's behaviour, the confederate lords raised an army against her, and she was defeated at the Battle of Carberry, captured, imprisoned and forced to abdicate in favour of her son, James VI.

After nine months' imprisonment in Lochleven Castle, she escaped, and in eleven glorious days managed to raise an army of 5–6,000 men at Hamilton. They were defeated at the Battle of Langside, and at that point Mary made the fatal decision to flee Scotland. She was never to return, and the rest of her life was spent in damp, dark, uncomfortable confinement in different country houses in England.

Eventually, Mary was trapped into an association with a plot to overthrow Elizabeth, and this led rapidly to her execution on 8th February 1587. Through the places associated with Mary, we can follow the course of her troubled life from birth to premature death.

THE REIGNING QUEEN

Falkland Palace
Mary was born on 8th December 1542. Her father was James V who, two weeks before Mary's birth, had been defeated by the English in the Battle of Solway Moss. He died on 14th December 1542 at the age of thirty.

Stirling Castle
At the tender age of nine months, Mary was crowned in the chapel of Stirling Castle on 9th September 1543. In 1566, she celebrated the baptism of her son, later to become James VI of Scotland and James I of England.

Holyrood Palace
Most of Mary's reign as ruler was spent in Holyrood Palace. Several years were spent in realistic intelligent politics, but with the murder of her secretary Riccio here on 9th March 1566, her connections with the place became more and more tragic. After the death of Darnley at Kirk O'Field, she was married to Bothwell here on 15th May 1567, but within 5 weeks she was here alone in disgrace after her defeat at the Battle of Carberry.

Edinburgh Castle
On 19th June 1566, she gave birth here to her son, James, who was to become James VI of Scotland and James I of England.

Dunbar Castle, Lothian
In 1566, after Riccio's murder, Mary and Darnley fled here from Seton. The following year she was brought here by Bothwell.

Jedburgh, Borders
In October 1566, Mary was in Jedburgh, administering justice. She knew of Bothwell's illness at Hermitage, ten miles away, and rode over there to see him. She made the journey there and back in one day, but this made her extremely ill and she was thought to be dying. The house is now known as Mary, Queen of Scots House, and exhibits a great many documents, portraits and other items related to Mary's life.

Kirk O'Field
This was a house on the outskirts of Edinburgh where Mary brought Darnley when he was ill from syphilis. At 2 o'clock in the morning on the night of 9th February 1567, there was an enormous explosion and the house was wrecked. Darnley's body was found in the grounds, strangled.

Borthwick Castle, Lothian
Mary's marriage to Bothwell provoked a great deal of disapproval, and in May 1567, shortly after their wedding, they were besieged in Borthwick Castle by the Earl of Morton.

Bothwell escaped, and Mary slipped out of the castle disguised as a boy.

Carberry, Lothian
Mary's army confronted that of her rebel lords on 15th June 1567 at Carberry. The army refused to stand and fight, and she was forced to surrender in disgrace.

RESISTANCE

Lochleven Castle, Tayside
After her defeat at the Battle of Carberry, Mary was taken to Lochleven and imprisoned. Her abdication was obtained and she remained a captive until 2nd May 1568. Then, with the help of a young member of the household, she managed a spectacular escape.

Cadzow Castle, Hamilton, Strathclyde
Mary had reached Hamilton by 3rd May 1568, and spent the next eleven days there. During that time she was able to muster a force of 5–6,000 men.

Langside, Glasgow, Strathclyde
Now known as Queen's Park, this is, today, a memorial to the battle which was fought here on 13th May 1568 in which Mary's forces were defeated. After the battle, Mary decided to flee to England, and from that point on her cause in Scotland was lost.

Dumfries, Dumfries and Galloway
Mary fled the 60 miles to Dumfries following the Battle of Langside, and after resting at Lord Herries' Castle at Corra, she went on to Terregles.

Dundrennan Abbey, Dumfries and Galloway
This is where Mary spent her last night on Scottish soil, before fleeing, in disguise, across the Solway Firth to England.

Carlisle, Cumbria
Mary reached Carlisle on 18th May 1568, where she was imprisoned in the Castle.

ROYAL MARTYR

Bolton Castle, Yorkshire
It was felt that Carlisle was not a very secure prison for Mary, so, on 13th July 1568, she was moved to Bolton.

Tutbury Castle, Staffordshire
In January 1569, Mary was housed in Tutbury Castle, but in November of that year, an attempt was made to free her and she was moved to Coventry and then to Sheffield. In January 1585, Mary was again imprisoned in Tutbury.

Sheffield, Yorkshire
Most of the 14 years in which Mary was held prisoner by the Earl of Shrewsbury were spent in Sheffield, at the Castle and at the Manor House.

Wingfield Manor, Derbyshire
Mary's imprisonment here was during the years 1584–5.

Chatsworth, Derbyshire
For short periods, Mary visited Chatsworth during her imprisonment.

Buxton, Derbyshire
When Chatsworth was being cleaned, Mary went to Buxton, where she took the waters.

Chartley, Staffordshire
Mary was moved here on 24th December 1585. She was caught up in a cleverly prepared trap set by Lord Walsingham. She allowed herself to be involved in a plot by Babington who intended to assassinate Elizabeth, and this proved her downfall.

Fotheringhay, Northamptonshire
Mary was brought from Chartley to Fotheringhay in 1586. She was tried in the Star Chamber and found guilty. Elizabeth signed her death warrant on 1st February 1587, and Mary was executed on 8th February.

Peterborough, Cambridgeshire
After her execution, Mary was buried in Peterborough Cathedral, but was later moved by James I and VI, her son, to Westminster Abbey where a splendid canopy was erected over the tomb.

STIRLING

The 15th century Portcullis Gateway of Stirling Castle, one of the older portions of the building. Most of the more sumptuous parts were added in the 16th century

Known as the Gateway to Scotland, Stirling was strategically important as the only link between the Highlands and Lowlands. In 1124, Alexander I died here and his brother David I, who succeeded him, often stayed at the castle. In 1147 he founded the nearby Abbey of Cambuskeneth, where James III and his queen are buried in front of the high altar. Queen Victoria unveiled a monument to their memory in 1864.

Struggles for the castle
The castle dominates the town both historically and physically, and has been the focal point of many savage battles between the Scots and English. During the War of Independence, the castle became the focus for military operations. Edward I took it without a fight in 1296, and the following year, William Wallace inflicted a defeat on the English at the battle of Stirling Bridge, and the castle was forced to capitulate to the victorious Scots. In 1304, and after a three month siege, it again surrendered to Edward, and for ten years remained under English control. After the Battle of Bannockburn, it surrendered to the forces of Robert Bruce, and his statue can be seen on the esplanade. When the Stewarts came to the throne the castle became a royal residence once more. James II was born here, and, in later years, he made the castle a dower house for his queen, Mary of Gueldres. At the time of his marriage, large tournaments and feasts took place here, but, three years later in 1452, a grimmer event took place. James summoned William, Earl of Douglas to reaffirm his allegiance, but when Douglas refused, a violent quarrel occurred, and James stabbed the Earl to death.

Royal Palace
In 1451 James III was born at the castle. When he succeeded to the throne, he founded the

Chapel Royal of Stirling and was responsible for many architectural improvements to the castle including the 125ft Parliament Hall. When he endowed the Chapel Royal with the revenues of Coldingham Priory in the Holmes and Hepburn Country the two families joined in an insurrection against him. He handed over the heir to the throne to Shaw of Sandie for his protection and marched north to quell the troubles. Shaw turned traitor and handed over the child to his enemies and when the King returned from the north he was refused entrance to Stirling. He was later killed at Sauchieburn.

James IV often visited Stirling, enjoying the hunting here and making many structural improvements. He welcomed many distinguished guests to the castle. After James IV's death at Flodden Field, the widowed Queen Margaret installed herself in the castle with her infant son.

James V, the last king of a Catholic Scotland, was crowned in the Chapel Royal at Stirling on 21st September, 1513. He spent much of his childhood here and later completed many of the palace buildings, improved the defences, and turned the castle into one the most sumptuous buildings of its kind in the land.

On 9th September, 1543, his infant daughter Mary, Queen of Scots, was crowned at the Church of the Holy Rood and for four years stayed at the castle with her mother. In 1566, Stirling was again selected to guard a Royal child, the two month old Prince James, who was baptised here in an elaborate ceremony. Darnley's House, which lies near the castle, is thought to have been a nursery for James. After Mary, Queen of Scots' abdication in 1567, the thirteen month old Prince was crowned James VI at the Church of the Holy Rood. The castle was attacked by rebellious lords in 1585, and the King, together with Montrose

Church of the
Holy Rood, Stirling, where
Mary, Queen of Scots and James VI were
crowned

Darnley's House, Stirling,
said to have been the nursery of James VI

and Crawford, locked themselves in and stayed there until they were assured that no harm would come to them if they surrendered.

Declining importance

James VI's eldest son, Prince Frederick Henry, was baptised in 1592 in the specially rebuilt Chapel Royal at an estimated cost of £100,000. He was the last Prince of Scotland to spend his childhood at Stirling, because, when James became King of England as well as of Scotland, the royal palace at Stirling declined in importance. Although James promised to return every three years he only made two visits during the rest of his reign. Charles I was not a frequent visitor either, for he spent only two nights here—in 1633, and Charles II paid an equally brief visit to the castle in 1650. The castle's importance grew again at the time of the Cromwellian occupation in 1651, when General Monk forced it to surrender, and garrisoned it with Englishmen. During the Jacobite rising of 1715, the castle was used by the English to prevent the Highland Jacobites from joining their lowland allies, and in 1745, it held out against the forces of Prince Charles Edward.

The Castle buildings

The castle is the finest example of Renaissance architecture in Scotland. When the Parliament Hall was built, a twisted passage was thrust under the lower storey of the 'Clunyie House' (Mint) and was the castle approach until the time of James VI. Beyond the 17th century Outer Gateway and the inner barrier with Queen Anne's initials on the keystone are the turreted Portcullis Gateway, curtain walls and flanking towers built by James III. The former height of these four imposing towers was equal to that of the Prince's Tower on the west of the wall. Here is the staircase leading to the school room where George Buchanan disciplined his wilful pupil, James VI.

The work carried out by James V has changed little since it was completed some four hundred years ago. Beyond the Portcullis are a lower and an upper square, and round the upper square are grouped the Great (or Parliament) Hall, the Palace, the King's Old Buildings and the Chapel Royal. The Palace apartments are grouped around the 'Lions Den' where, tradition says, the royal beasts were caged. James III and James IV certainly had lions, and James V may have kept one as a symbol of power. The Great Hall is in the process of being restored. At its south end was the raised dais reserved for royalty while opposite was the Minstrel or Trumpet Gallery. Below the castle battlements is the King's Park where Crichton kidnapped James II. Outside the castle, two places of interest are the Landmark and Mar's Wark.

The Landmark stands between the castle and the old town, and combines a multi-screen theatre and exhibition designed specifically to bring alive the history of the town. Mar's Wark is all that remains of the magnificent Renaissance palace built in 1570–2 by the Earl of Mar but never fully completed. James VI and his Queen lived in it until the castle was ready for their reception.

The ancient Scottish capital

DOUNE

Doune castle stands above the River Teith just east of the village. Although its exact building date is unknown, ancient records mention the castle being built as a royal palace in the late 14th century by Robert Stewart, Duke of Albany and Regent of Scotland in the reign of Robert III. It was confiscated by James I and used by his successors until 1528. Mary of Gueldres and Margaret of Denmark, the queens of James II and III, spent much of their widowhood here as did Margaret Tudor, wife of James IV. Mary, Queen of Scots, visited here with her son occasionally as the rooms known as "Queen Mary's Apartments" indicate. It was taken by Prince Charles Edward Stewart in 1745 and used to house prisoners taken after the battle of Falkirk in 1746.

DUNBLANE

The grand historic cathedral dominates the town. It was made a bishopric by Alexander I and the three Drummond sisters who were all poisoned in 1501 and who are commemorated in the cathedral were associated with James IV. The Queen Victoria School, built as a memorial to Queen Victoria and to soldiers and sailors killed in the Boer War, was opened by King Edward VII in 1908.

CASTLE CAMPBELL

The castle dates from the 15th century and was once known as Castle Gloume or Gloom. The Earl of Montrose tried to take the castle for Charles I in 1645 but failed, and in 1654 the castle was captured and destroyed by fire by Cromwell's troops under General Monk.

DUNFERMLINE

Dunfermline was the Scottish capital for six centuries and grew round the royal palace built by Malcolm III in 1070, about the time of his marriage to Margaret who founded the great abbey. She was buried in the abbey and a shrine was built at the east end of the church to hold her relics. A pilgrimage is held at Dunfermline each year in honour of Margaret about whom many legends have grown up over the years. Dunfermline remained the capital, its palace became a favourite abode of Scottish kings, and its abbey superseded Iona as their place of burial. Edgar, Alexander I, David I, Malcolm IV and Alexander III are all buried here, as well as Robert Bruce. The palace was the birth place of James I in 1394 and Charles I in 1600.

Edward I held court here during his second invasion and destroyed the abbey by fire. James IV often came to the royal palace before his ascendancy to the English throne.

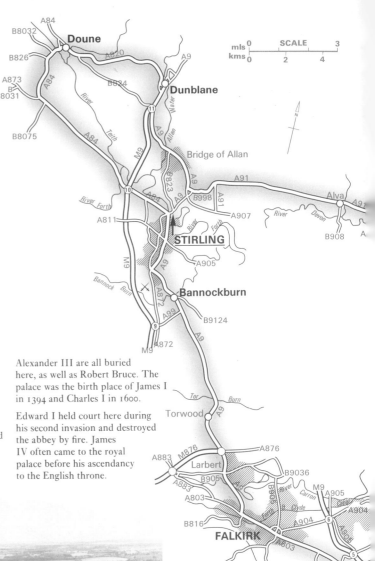

A   B

BLACKNESS

The village of Blackness was once a notable port and is dominated by the castle which stands on an outcrop of rock above it. It was taken by James II in 1452 and was part of the queen's jointure until 1465.

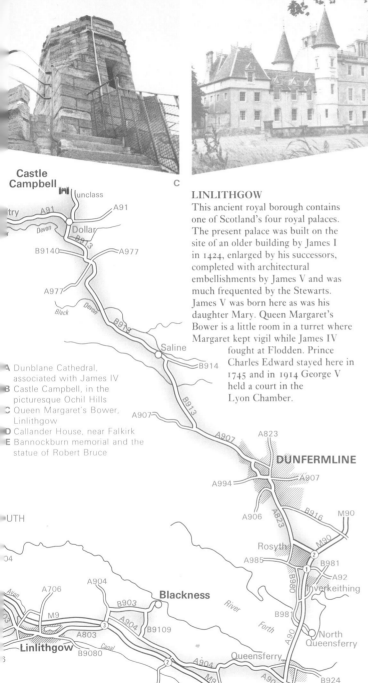

Castle
Campbell ⛨ C

A Dunblane Cathedral,
 associated with James IV
B Castle Campbell, in the
 picturesque Ochil Hills
C Queen Margaret's Bower,
 Linlithgow
D Callander House, near Falkirk
E Bannockburn memorial and the
 statue of Robert Bruce

D

LINLITHGOW

This ancient royal borough contains one of Scotland's four royal palaces. The present palace was built on the site of an older building by James I in 1424, enlarged by his successors, completed with architectural embellishments by James V and was much frequented by the Stewarts. James V was born here as was his daughter Mary. Queen Margaret's Bower is a little room in a turret where Margaret kept vigil while James IV fought at Flodden. Prince Charles Edward stayed here in 1745 and in 1914 George V held a court in the Lyon Chamber.

FALKIRK

The ancient town of Falkirk stands in a strategic position by the Firth of Forth. Two major battles were fought near here, the first in 1298, when William Wallace was defeated by great numbers of English under Edward I during the War of Independence. The Wallace Stone, a 10ft pillar on a hilltop, stands one mile south east of Callander Wood. The second battle took place in 1745 when Prince Charles Edward Stewart put to flight the Hanoverian forces under General Hawley after the Prince's retreat from Derby. A monument to this second battle is located in a recess in Greenbank Road. East of the town centre lies Callander House. Mary, Queen of Scots, was a frequent visitor to the house between 1562 and 1567. Oliver Cromwell besieged the house in 1650 and put its defenders to the sword after they broke an undertaking not to molest his troops.

BANNOCKBURN

The decisive battle of Bannockburn, fought on 24th June, 1314, established Robert Bruce on the throne of an independent Scotland after many years of English occupation. The battle was primarily fought for the possession of Stirling castle which was besieged by the Scots. Edward II marched north with an army of 22,000 to relieve it. Robert Bruce gathered a force of about 8,000 and took up a position in the New Park, effectively blocking the Falkirk—Stirling road. Edward's army was hemmed between two bogs and

Bruce's infantry inflicted heavy losses on the packed English knights. The Scots were trained to kill the horses first so that the heavy English knights would be helpless. Edward, wielding his battle axe, had his horse killed under him but was rescued by his bodyguard who took him to safety. When the King left the field the English army panicked and fled back through the Bannock where many were killed and trampled on. A memorial marks the battle site in the shape of a statue of Robert Bruce mounted on his charger, which was unveiled by H.M. the Queen in 1964.

South of the battlefield is Bannockburn House which was the headquarters of Prince Charles Edward Stewart on his retreat into Scotland in 1746. A little to the north west of Bannockburn is Sauchieburn where, in 1488, a battle was fought between James III and an army of insurgent nobles, amongst whom was James' son later to become James IV. James III fled the field but after being injured in a fall from his horse was stabbed to death by one of the rebels masquerading as a priest.

Near the Bannockburn monument, an information centre contains a historical exhibition, "The Forging of a Nation" which tells in sound and vision the story of the Scottish Wars of Independence culminating in the Battle of Bannockburn.

E

Bonnie Prince Charlie
The Young Pretender

In 1745, encouraged by the King of France, whose country was at war with England, a young prince, grandson of James II of England, attempted to recapture his lost throne. This young prince was Charles Edward Stuart, who became known as Bonnie Prince Charlie. His rebellion was foolhardy but highly romantic. For a while it threw King George II into panic, but it was eventually and remorselessly crushed, after which Prince Charlie spent five months on the run, helped by his many friends and by his own resources of courage, and finally escaped to Europe where he spent the rest of his days.

DIARY OF A REBELLION
1745

July 23, Eriskay. Charles set foot on Scottish soil for the first time.

July 25, Loch Nan Uamh. Charles landed on the mainland.

August 19, Glenfinnan. Proclaimed Regent, his standard was raised. Many Highland clansmen rallied to him.

September. Marched south to Perth and Edinburgh, where he was proclaimed King. He occupied Holyroodhouse and prepared his ragged army for the invasion of England.

September 21, Prestonpans. At a battle with the only Government army in Scotland, Charles' wild Highlanders put the English to flight.

November 8, River Esk. Charles crossed into England with less than 6,000 men.

November 15, Carlisle. A five-day siege was eventually won by the Prince.

November 27. Preston fell to the Jacobites.

November 29. Manchester fell.

December 4, Derby. Charles entered the town hoping to reach London before long. But English armies lay in wait for him and he withdrew after two days.

December 20, River Esk. The Jacobites re-crossed into Scotland.

1746

January 8, Stirling. The town fell to Charles, but the castle withstood his siege.

January 17, Falkirk. The Jacobites fell upon an English force in blinding rain, decimating them.

February 10, Ruthven. Prince Charles captured the barracks.

February 16, Moy. Government troops hunting Prince Charlie were defeated by a much smaller force of Highlanders.

February 20, Inverness. The town and castle surrendered to the Prince.

March, Fort Augustus. The town surrendered to the Prince. But at Fort William and Blair Castle sieges were unsuccessful.

April 16, Culloden. Fewer than 5,000 exhausted and hungry Jacobite men were defeated in a few hours by over 10,000 Government troops under the command of the Duke of Cumberland, whose pursuit of the withdrawing Highlanders was ruthless.

April 17, Invergarry Castle. Charles reached the empty castle after travelling all night and stayed for a few hours.

April 20, Loch Nan Uamh. After walking for days, Charles reached the place from where he started his rebellion.

April 26. The Prince and his companions set out into a gale, making for the Outer Hebrides.

April 27, Benbecula. After a stormy night, the party landed. For the next two months the Prince moved erratically up and down North and South Uist.

June 28, Over the sea to Skye. Disguised and in the company of the valiant Flora Macdonald, Charles crossed to Skye.

June 29, Kingsburgh. Flora arranged for Charles to be hidden in her relative's house.

June 30, Portree. Charles walked from Kingsburgh to the inn at Portree where he hoped to spend the night.

July 1. After taking leave of Flora, Charles set sail for Raasay.

July 3, Portree. It was discovered that the Prince had returned to Skye and was sleeping near Portree.

July 4, Elgol. After walking through the night, the Prince and his companion reached Elgol. That night he set sail for Mallaig.

July 10, Loch Nan Uamh. Charles decided to revisit his old friends here. During the next few days he lived in nearby caves to avoid detection.

August 6, Cannich. The Prince and his followers had reached the most northerly point of their wanderings.

August 14, Glen Garry. The Prince marched here in heavy rain and spent the night in the open.

August 30, Loch Ericht. The Prince met more loyal followers.

September 13. On hearing that French ships were in Loch Nan Uamh, Charles set out to reach them, marching by night.

September 19, Loch Nan Uamh. Bonnie Prince Charlie boarded the French ship "L'Heureux" and set sail for France. He never again returned to Scotland.

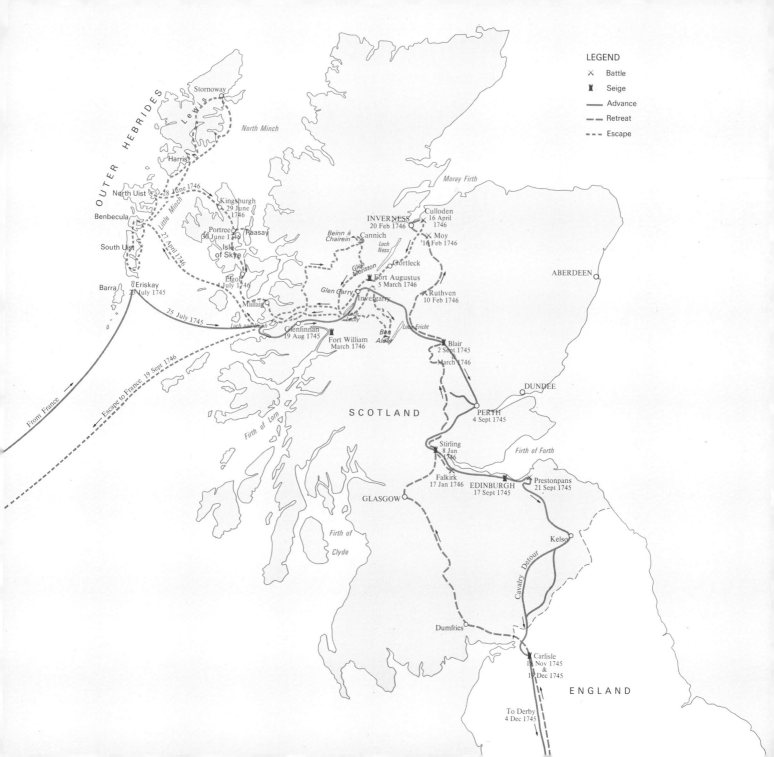

LEGEND

✗ Battle
♟ Seige
—— Advance
– – Retreat
· · · Escape

OUTER HEBRIDES

Stornoway

Lewis

North Minch

Harris

North Uist
28 June 1746
Kingsburgh
29 June
1746

Benbecula

Portree
30 June 1746
Raasay

Little Minch

South Uist

27 April 1746

Isle
of Skye

Barra

Eriskay
23 July 1745

Elgol
4 July 1746

Mallaig

25 July 1745

Loch nan Uamh

Glenfinnian
19 Aug 1745

Fort William
March 1746

Beinn á
Chairein
Cannich

Loch
Ness

Glen
Moriston

Gortleck

Glen Garry
Invergarry

Fort Augustus
5 March 1746

Loch
Lochy

Loch Fricht

Ben
Alder

INVERNESS
20 Feb 1746

Culloden
16 April
1746

✗ Moy
16 Feb 1746

ABERDEEN

✗ Ruthven
10 Feb 1746

Blair
2 Sept 1745

March 1746

DUNDEE

Moray Firth

From France

Escape to France 19 Sept 1746

Firth of Lorn

SCOTLAND

PERTH
4 Sept 1745

Stirling
8 Jan
1746

Falkirk
17 Jan 1746

GLASGOW

Firth of Forth

EDINBURGH
17 Sept 1745

Prestonpans
21 Sept 1745

Firth of
Clyde

Kelso

Cavalry Detour

Dumfries

Carlisle
15 Nov 1745
&
19 Dec 1745

ENGLAND

To Derby
4 Dec 1745

SCONE
PERTH

Scone, one of the most historic places in Scotland, was once the ancient capital of the Pictish kingdom. Kenneth MacAlpin, first of the kings of the House of Alpin, defeated the Picts here and made it his seat of government in about AD843. It was he who brought here the palladium of the Scots, the Stone of Destiny, which from its long residence here came to be called the 'Stone of Scone'.

The Legend of the Stone

By tradition the kings of Scots were ceremonially seated upon the sacred stone as part of the ritual of their inauguration. Identified with Jacob's pillow at Bethel and later the 'Stone of Destiny' at Tara in Ireland, it was thought to have been brought from the Holy Land to Ireland by the remote ancestors of the Scots, and from Ireland to Scotland by Fergus Mor mac Erc, the first king of the Scots, in about the year 500. Superstition credited the stone with the power to carry the rule of a Scottish king wherever it was placed and a Gaelic prophecy was said to have been carved on the stone in Latin which said:

Scots shall flourish strong and free
Unless proved false the prophecy;
That where the Scots shall yet be found
A Scot by princely right is crowned.

All Scottish kings were then crowned on the 'Stone of Scone', which is said to have stood on Moot Hill, in the grounds of the present palace, until 1296 when it was removed by Edward I after he defeated John Balliol. However, Edward's main reason for taking the stone was its symbolic power, and his flouting of the prophecy attached to it was eventually fulfilled when a Scottish king, James VI, was crowned as James I of England.

The Abbey

In 1054 the man who was to become Malcolm III defeated Macbeth in a battle at Scone.

The present palace at Scone was built between 1803 and 1805. and stands on the site of the previous historic palaces and the ancient abbey

In 1120 King Alexander I established a monastery here and in 1164 it was elevated to the status of an abbey. The site of the abbey is thought to have been towards the east end of the terrace on which the present palace is built. The abbey was sacked and burned by the reformers in 1559, the year in which John Knox preached his famous sermon from the pulpit of St John's Kirk in Perth, and by 1625 the abbey was a ruin.

The Palace

In 1581 the lands of Scone were made a temporal landship and were conferred on the Earl of Gowrie, but after the Gowrie Conspiracy in 1600 they were forfeited and made over to Sir David Murray of Gospetrie whose lineal decendant, the Earl of Mansfield, is still the owner. The present palace was started in 1803 and finished in 1805. 16th century needlework here includes bed hangings worked by Mary, Queen of Scots. Charles II was the last king to be crowned here—in 1651. The Old Pretender kept court here in 1716 and some 29 years later Prince Charles Edward slept here. Among the other historic events which took place here was the coronation of Robert the Bruce on a makeshift throne and crowned with a plain gold circlet, on Palm Sunday 1306. Edward Balliol invaded Scotland with English assistance and defeated David II in August 1332 at the Battle of Dupplin Moor near Perth and the following month was crowned at Scone. He was driven out of Scotland again by the end of the year and it is said he fled the country, 'one leg booted and the other naked'. Robert II, first king of the House of Stewart, was crowned here in February 1371.

PERTH

Capital of Scotland for a century until 1437,

St John's Kirk in Perth
is one of the city's few buildings
remaining from the medieval period. In 1559
John Knox preached here, and his sermon led
to widespread rioting and violence

the 'Fair City of Perth' is an ancient royal
burgh with a rich history. It was once called
St Johnstown, and St John's Kirk, one of the
noblest of the great Scottish burghal churches,
restored in the 15th century, is by far the
rarest of the city's relics, both in antiquity and
beauty. No substantial remains of other
historic buildings survive but their names are
perpetuated in the names of the streets and
lanes of the city—Charterhouse, Blackfriars,
Whitefriars, Greyfriars, Ponarium, Skinnergate.
Inscriptions and the like also abound: in the
North Port, where once stood the castle of
Perth, on the Waterworks, the place of
Cromwell's citadel. A token in the paving of the
High Street commemorates the old town cross.

The Medieval Kings
Although Perth was closely involved with
royalty since Kenneth MacAlpin made Scone
the capital of his kingdom the first king to be
closely associated with the city was Alexander
III, during whose reign Scotland acquired the
Western Isles from Norway by the Treaty of
Perth in 1266. After he was accidentally killed
in a fall his heart was removed and interred
within St John's Kirk. Perth was frequently a
royal residence in feudal times and parliaments
and general councils are known to have been
convened here from the time of Alexander I
(1106–7) until the death of Robert III (1406).
The city was overrun by the English on
several occasions and Edward I added
fortifications in 1298. Robert Bruce, however,
drove the English from the city and ordered the
fortifications to be destroyed.

The Royal Court
Perth was James I's favourite city and he held
his court and parliament here throughout his
reign. On 20th February 1437 the royal
lodgings of the former Blackfriars Monastery
were the scene of the brutal murder of James I
by a group of conspiritors led by the Earl of
Atholl. Despite the heroic efforts of Catherine
Douglas, one of the Queen's ladies, who put
her arm in the door in place of a stolen bar to
keep the murderers out, the king was trapped
in a vault beneath his bedchamber and stabbed
to death. James I was buried in the church of
the Charterhouse and in 1445 his queen, who
was wounded in her attempt to defend him,
was later buried beside him.

James II moved his court to Edinburgh and
Perth returned to a position of a strategic
stronghold, occasionally visited by royalty.
Margaret Tudor, sister of Henry VIII and wife
of James IV, was buried in the grounds of the
Chapter House, now the site of King James VI
Hospital. On 15th May 1559 John Knox made
his famous sermon in St John's Kirk after
which a mob sacked the abbey church at
Scone and effectively kindled the Reformation
in Scotland. James VI was imprisoned here in
1600 by the Gowries in their palace, which
stood on the site of the present County
Buildings.

The last days of the Stewarts
Charles I and Charles II both attended services
at St John's Kirk. During the last days of the
Stewart kings the city was held by Graham of
Montrose until Cromwell reduced it by siege in
1651 and placed a garrison there. In 1715 the
town was occupied by the Old Pretender who
was proclaimed King James VIII of Scotland
and III of England at the City Cross. It is said
that the 1745 rebellion was largely planned
during the Perth race meeting on South Inch.
With the arrival of Prince Charles Edward the
city became the operational centre, and he is
said to have attended services at St John's Kirk.

The Highland regiment, the Black Watch, has
long associations with the city. In 1947 Queen
Elizabeth the Queen Mother, who is their
Colonel-in-Chief, accepted the freedom of the
burgh on their behalf. Balhousie Castle is now
the regimental museum. The city's museum
and art gallery contain many interesting relics
including the stone of the old city cross.

Careful restoration work has been
carried out on many of Perth's
buildings. This waterworks dates
back to 1832

Palace for Scottish Kings

A

FALKLAND

The Royal Palace at Falkland is one of the loveliest in Scotland and is built on the site of an older castle of Falkland. The palace was a favourite haunt of the Stewart kings, used by them as a hunting palace, and it was probably started by James II. It was a popular seat of the Scottish court in the reign of James V and he was responsible for many of the improvements. Built in the Renaissance style, it has been described as 'the finest monument to the auld alliance'. James also had the tennis court built here, the second oldest royal tennis court in Britain.

James V died here on 14th December 1542, and on his deathbed uttered the famous prophecy concerning the crown of Scotland, 'It cam wi' a lass it will gang wi' a lass'. The room where he died has been specially decorated and furnished and is known as the King's Room. His daughter, Mary, Queen of Scots, used to hunt from the palace. Charles I and Charles II also visited here, the latter in 1650 giving new colours to the troops selected to guard him. This is now considered to have been the christening of the Scots Guards. The regiment has retained its connection with Falkland and in 1958 it mounted the guard when Queen Elizabeth II visited the town and the palace on the occasion of the quincentenary of the royal burgh.

The East Range of the palace was burned, apparently by accident, during occupation by Cromwell's troops in 1654. Beside the Palace Gatehouse is St Andrew's House which is typical of the dwellings occupied by courtiers and members of the Stewart household.

AUCHTERARDER

The barony of Auchterarder was a crown possession and the castle a royal residence. Today Auchterarder is one of the Royal Burghs of Scotland. The castle, traditionally a royal hunting seat, is just north of the town. It was a royal residence until Robert Bruce gave it, together with the freedom of the borough, to Sir William Montefact who then gave it as a dowry with his daughter Marie when she married Sir John Drummond. The castle then passed into the family ownership of the Earls of Perth.

Several major events in Scottish history occurred in and around the castle. When Edward I invaded Scotland in 1296, he spent a night here, and in May 1559 Mary of Lorraine, widow of James V, negotiated the Treaty of Perth from here. The terms of the treaty with John Knox gained the first State recognition of Protestantism in Scotland. The castle, of which only the keep and its surrounding moat survive, is not open to the public.

In 1716, after the Battle of Sherriffmuir, the Earl of Mar ordered the town of Auchterarder to be burnt to prevent shelter being taken by the Duke of Argyll and his troops; but it caused the local people such hardship that they would no longer agree to support the Jacobite cause.

DRUMMOND CASTLE

Drummond Castle stands about two miles to the north west of the village of Muthill. The keep at the castle, which dates from the 15th century, now contains an armoury. It stands apart from the modern mansion, well known for its pictures and fine gardens. It was besieged by Cromwell, destroyed in 1686, and partly garrisoned by Government troops in 1715. It was finally razed in 1745 by the Jacobite Duchess of Perth, so that Hanoverian troops could not make use of it.

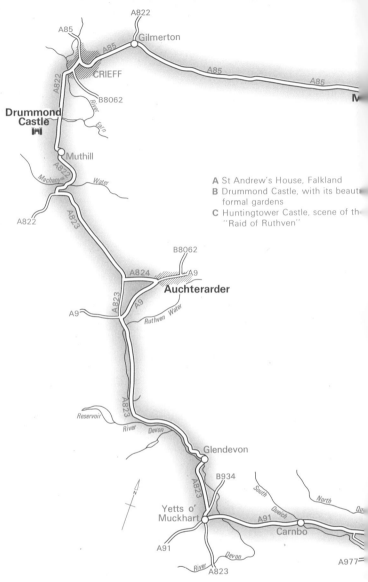

A St Andrew's House, Falkland
B Drummond Castle, with its beautiful formal gardens
C Huntingtower Castle, scene of the "Raid of Ruthven"

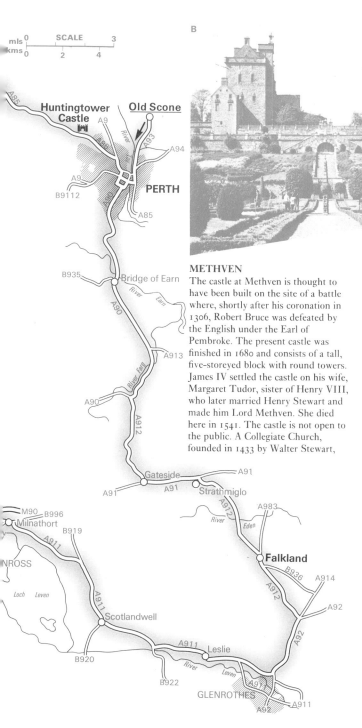

METHVEN

The castle at Methven is thought to have been built on the site of a battle where, shortly after his coronation in 1306, Robert Bruce was defeated by the English under the Earl of Pembroke. The present castle was finished in 1680 and consists of a tall, five-storeyed block with round towers. James IV settled the castle on his wife, Margaret Tudor, sister of Henry VIII, who later married Henry Stewart and made him Lord Methven. She died here in 1541. The castle is not open to the public. A Collegiate Church, founded in 1433 by Walter Stewart, Earl of Atholl, was situated in Methven. Only a fragment of the original building remains, but a surviving carved stone suggests that the church was added to by Margaret Tudor. Another battle was fought near here in 1644 when Montrose scored a victory over the Covenanters. The battle site lies south east of the town near Tibbermuir. The Covenanters were in their full strength of 6,000 men and Montrose had only about 2,000 Irish and Highlanders, yet he reduced his enemy to a rabble before entering Perth.

HUNTINGTOWER

Until 1600, Huntingtower Castle was known as Ruthven Castle and was the seat of the Ruthvens, a name often in the forefront of Scottish history. Sir William Ruthven was held hostage by the English for the ransom of James I and the son of the 1st Lord Ruthven was slain beside his King, James IV, at Flodden in 1513. Patrick, 3rd Lord Ruthven, as one of Darnley's supporters, took part in the murder of Riccio, favourite of Mary, Queen of Scots, in 1566. In 1581 William, the 4th Lord Ruthven, was made Earl of Gowrie, and in 1582, the castle was the scene of the 'Raid of Ruthven' when the sixteen year old King James VI was invited by the Earl of Gowrie to his hunting seat. He immediately found himself in the hands of Protestant nobles, including Gowrie and the Earl of Mar, who demanded the dismissal of James's favourites. The Master of Glamis barred the King's way when he tried to escape, and he was held for a year while the Ruthven conspiritors wielded power. Although the King at first forgave his captors, in 1585 he was persuaded to change his mind and the Earl of Gowrie was arrested and beheaded on 4th May. The 3rd and last Earl of Gowrie was killed in his town house in Perth, for an alleged attempt on the life of the King, and his body, together with that of his brother Alexander, was carried to Edinburgh. Here the Lords and Parliament pronounced 'Sentence and Doom' and annexed the title and estates to the crown. They also abolished the family surname of Ruthven and changed the name of the estate to Huntingtower.

The castle itself is a very fine castellated house of the 15th and 16th centuries and comprises two towers joined by lower buildings. The space between the buildings is known as 'maiden's leap', after the story of a daughter of the Ruthvens who leapt from one parapet to another in order to escape discovery in her lover's chamber. The castle has been considerably restored and has particularly fine painted wooden ceilings.

BRAEMAR BALMORAL

Braemar is a comparatively modern name for what used to be two villages (Castleton and Auchendryne) divided by the Clunie Water. The area has been a playground for kings, nobles and great men of the land since the dawn of Scottish history. The town is best known for its royal and ancient Highland Gathering, held on the first Saturday in September each year. Tradition has it that the originator of the Gathering was King Malcolm Canmore, who called the Clans to the Braes of Mar so that he might, by keen and fair contest, select his hardier soldiers and fleetest messengers. The modern Gathering dates from 1832 and was popularised by Queen Victoria when she visited it in 1848, showing a keen interest in the proceedings. The bestowal of royal patronage followed soon after, and the Queen became a generous contributor to its funds, a custom which she continued throughout her long lifetime.

The Gathering is held in the Princess Royal and Duke of Fife Memorial Park, named in response to the wish of Princess Arthur of Connaught. The present patron is Queen Elizabeth II, who often attends the Gatherings. Piping is the main attraction, with the athletic events culminating in the tossing of the caber. The arrival of the Queen and her party, who take their places in the Royal Pavilion in the afternoon, is the high point of the day.

Kindrochit Castle
On the east side of the Clunie, near the bridge, stand the ancient ruins of the royal castle of Kindrochit, strategically placed above a gorge and in a position to defend the ancient mountain passes of the area. Built in about 1390, when Robert II granted a licence to "our dear brother Malcolm de Drummond" to build a fortalice here, the site was already a hunting seat and the residence of Robert Bruce. The site's royal connection is said to date back as far as Malcolm Canmore. In 1390, one end of the old palace was pulled down and a massive stone tower built, the fifth largest in Scotland, of which only a fragment remains. For over a century the royal standard flew from the battlements, then, at the beginning of the 16th century the castle became derelict, and by the early 17th century had fallen into utter ruin.

Around Braemar
Braemar Castle, which stands on a hill above the Dee, is situated ½ mile north east of the town. It was built in 1628 by the Earl of Mar, John Erskine, who had it designed ostensibly as a hunting lodge, but intended actually as a sign of power to counteract the growing threat of the Farquharsons. In 1689, during the Claverhouse campaign, the castle was attacked and burnt by the celebrated "Black Colonel" John Farquharson of Invererey. It was repaired by the Government, and garrisoned by English troops after the rising of 1745. The castle still belongs to the Farquharsons of Invererey.

In the centre of Braemar stands the Meteorological Observatory, set up by Prince Albert in 1885. Although the observatory itself has given way to more modern equipment, meteorological observations have been made without a break in this, the second highest station in Scotland. 3½ miles west of Braemar stands Mar Lodge, set in a beautiful park and approached by Victoria Bridge which was opened by Queen Victoria in 1857. The foundation stone of this magnificent house was laid by the Queen in 1896, and the house became the home of her granddaughter Princess Louise, and later of Princess Arthur of Connaught. It is now a ski centre.

Braemar Castle, near which the standard was raised in support of the Old Pretender

BALMORAL CASTLE

Balmoral Castle, which lies in a curve of the river in Royal Deeside, is a private residence of Her Majesty the Queen and is used by the Royal Family as a summer holiday estate, a secluded spot where the Queen can retire with her family and enjoy privacy and a brief respite from the cares of state.

Majestic dwelling

The early medieval fortified manor on the site was a favourite hunting lodge of King Robert II. In 1390 Sir Malcolm Drummond was permitted to build a tower here, and the estate later passed into the hands of the Earls of Huntly. In 1484, a tax return was made for the estate, then known as "Bouchmorale", Gaelic for "majestic dwelling". The Gordons of Huntly held the castle until 1662, when they sold it to the Farquharsons of Invererey. They in turn were obliged to sell it as a bankrupt estate to the Earl of Fife in 1798, who let it in 1830 to Sir Robert Gordon. Sir Robert virtually created the Balmoral deer forest, and added a kitchen wing, public rooms, bedrooms and a turreted tower to the old castle. His creation was described as a "pretty little castle". It was here that, in about 1845, Sir James Clark, doctor to Queen Victoria, visited Sir Robert at a time when the royal family were holidaying at Ardverikie on Loch Laggan, where they were enduring "persistant rain and mist". On hearing glowing reports of Balmoral, the family obtained the tenancy on the estate in 1848 when Sir Robert died suddenly, and they occupied it as their summer retreat for the next four years. In 1852 Prince Albert bought the estate for £31,000 and engaged William Smith, city architect of Aberdeen, and son of John Smith who had rebuilt the castle for Sir Robert Gordon, to design Balmoral Castle as it appears today.

Royal home

The design, of which there is no doubt of Prince Albert's influence, is a typical castellated Scottish baronial mansion. The material is light grey Invergelder granite, quarried on the Balmoral estate. The hand-dressed granite work of the fabric is said to be the finest in Scotland. The dominating feature is a square tower rising to 80 feet surmounted by a turret with a circular stair, carrying the total height to over 100 feet. The rest of the building consists of two blocks connected by wings. From the main porch, the hall opens to the main corridor that runs along the centre of the building, and from which the grand staircase climbs to the Royal apartments on the first floor. The largest room, which measures 68 feet by 25 feet, is the vast ballroom, scene of several great assemblies and many a memorable ghillies ball. This room lies on a lower level than the rest of the building.

The dining-room, drawing-room, billiard-room and library are on the ground floor. The whole building was designed to house from 100 to 120 residents, and is situated against a magnificent background of wooded hills rising towards the mountains. The actual estate now extends to 24,000 acres, including Birkhall and Ballochbuie Forest.

Queen Victoria held an almost mystical love for the place, which she called "this dear paradise". She spent a part of every year here until her death, an example followed by successive sovereigns. Glen Gelder is south of the castle and leads to Balmoral Forest and the White Mounth group. This was the route taken by Queen Victoria and Prince Albert when they climbed Lochnager on ponies in 1848.

Balmoral Castle,
Highland residence of the Royal Family

Royal Deeside

CRATHIE

This little hamlet is the nearest populated place to Balmoral Castle, and is principally famous for the parish church attended by the Queen and her family during their residence on Deeside during the summer. The church was erected on the site of a plain, barn-like kirk which Queen Victoria unfailingly attended on her visits to Balmoral. It stands on a high bank just to the north side of the North Deeside road. The foundation of the present church was laid by Queen Victoria and it was opened in June 1895. It is cruciform in plan, and the royal pew and the royal porch are in the south transept. The church contains memorials to various members of the royal family, and the gates commemorate King George VI. On the opposite side of the road is the old churchyard of Crathie, where may be seen the tombstone erected by Queen Victoria to the memory of her faithful servant John Brown.

One mile east of the hamlet on the south side of the Dee the white tower of Abergeldie Castle can be seen above the trees. It was built in about 1550 by Gordon of Midmar, and is still in the possession of the Gordon family, although it has been leased by the royal family since 1848. It was besieged and eventually occupied by King William's troops under General MacKay in 1689. The castle, with 19th century additions, became the Highland home of Edward VII when Prince of Wales. It is not open to the public.

KILDRUMMY

This "noblest of the northern castles" is now an imposing ruin on the summit of the ridge above the main road, guarded on two sides by a ravine. It is the best surviving example of a 13th century stone courtyard castle in Scotland and the only one of its period that still retains a complete range of domestic buildings including hall, kitchen, solar and chapel. They all were part of the original design of Bishop Gilbert de Maravia, later to become St Gilbert, last saint of Scotland, who was King Alexander II's treasurer of the North. It was built on the pattern of the mighty Chateau de Coucy near Laon and at first consisted of an enormous semi-circular curtain wall defended by five projecting round towers, the largest of which is now known as the Snow Tower. The plans were altered to include a chapel which, with its three finely moulded windows, projects over the foundations of the curtain wall.

Before the castle was completed Scotland was overrun by Edward I of England who visited the area in 1296 and again in 1303. Kildrummy, under the Earl of Mar, became heavily involved in the struggle to put Bruce on the throne, and in 1306 the most famous event in the castle's story took place. After Bruce's defeat at the Battle of Methven in 1305, Sir

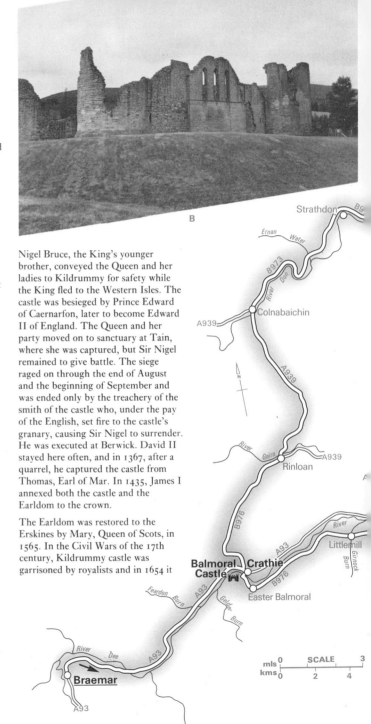

B

Nigel Bruce, the King's younger brother, conveyed the Queen and her ladies to Kildrummy for safety while the King fled to the Western Isles. The castle was besieged by Prince Edward of Caernarfon, later to become Edward II of England. The Queen and her party moved on to sanctuary at Tain, where she was captured, but Sir Nigel remained to give battle. The siege raged on through the end of August and the beginning of September and was ended only by the treachery of the smith of the castle who, under the pay of the English, set fire to the castle's granary, causing Sir Nigel to surrender. He was executed at Berwick. David II stayed here often, and in 1367, after a quarrel, he captured the castle from Thomas, Earl of Mar. In 1435, James I annexed both the castle and the Earldom to the crown.

The Earldom was restored to the Erskines by Mary, Queen of Scots, in 1565. In the Civil Wars of the 17th century, Kildrummy castle was garrisoned by royalists and in 1654 it

A

C

was captured for Cromwell. In 1690 it was burnt by the soldiers of Viscount Dundee, "Bonnie Dundee", rather than allow it to fall into the hands of William of Orange. Finally, in 1715 it became the headquarters from which the 10th Earl of Mar launched the Jacobite Rising of that year. After the collapse of the rising, the castle was dismantled by a tired, invading English army who threw down only one side of the building, leaving the rest complete.

ALFORD
This village on the south bank of the Don is chiefly famous for the Battle of Alford which was fought near the church, 2 miles west of the village centre. The battle took place on 2nd July 1645 at the height of Montrose's campaign for the cause of Charles I. Montrose routed the army of General Baillie, who was outnumbered and did not intend to give battle. For Montrose, the victory was somewhat soured by the death of his devoted friend and ally, Lord George Gordon.

DINNET
The village of Dinnet owes its existence to the coming of the Deeside railway in the middle of the last

century. On the largest islet of Loch Kinord stand the ruins of the Castle of Kinord, a medieval peel tower which played its part in a decisive period of Scottish history during the Wars of Independence. The English forces were defeated at the Battle of Culblean on 30th November, 1335, when the forces of Sir Andrew de Moray, Warden of Scotland, surprised and totally routed the English forces under the Earl of Atholl, who was slain in the battle. Part of the English force, under Sir Robert Menzies, took possession of the castle of Kinord as a refuge, but they were soon forced to capitulate. James IV visited the castle in 1504 and it was still in use in Covenanting times. It was finally destroyed in 1647. The ruins are not open to the public.

BALLATER
The Station Square of this busy little holiday resort on Royal Deeside was once familiar to many people in Britain as the scene of royal comings and goings. The railway has now closed but the town itself is still full of associations linking it with nearby

Balmoral. Victoria Barracks house the royal guard of honour during the summer when the Royal Family are in residence at Balmoral. The guard is chosen from the Scottish regiments in rotation. The Royal Bridge over the Dee was opened by Queen Victoria in 1885 and an interesting plaque commemorates the event. Ballater first became popular as a resort because of its proximity to Pannanich Wells, about 2 miles east. The wells flourished for many years and in 1870 Queen Victoria paid them a special visit. Although not now known as a spa, several of the springs can still be seen in the grounds of Pannanich Wells Hotel.

A Crathie Church, attended by the Royal Family when in residence at Balmoral
B Kildrummy Castle, a ruin with a stormy past
C The River Dee at Ballater, crossed by the Royal Bridge

Northern Ireland

BELFAST

It is only in relatively recent years that Belfast has assumed its present importance, mainly due to the industrial development of the 19th century. The town was originally founded in 1177 around an ancient fortress built to command a vulnerable part of the River Lagan. Belfast's fort was the scene of many battles in the next 300 years; the stronghold, alternating between Irish and English hands, was frequently destroyed and as frequently rebuilt. Edward Bruce was only one of many when he burnt the castle down in 1315. William III stayed here for one week on his way to the Battle of the Boyne. The castle was destroyed for the last time in 1708, being accidentally burnt down. Now Castle Place occupies a site just 300 yards from where the old fort stood. The new castle, built in 1870 by the Marquis of Donegal, stands on a different site at Cave Hill.

The memory of Queen Victoria is particularly strong in Belfast—it was she who finally conferred the title of city upon the town in 1888. **The City Hall**, which now houses the council chamber and other stately halls, contains seven stained glass windows depicting Ireland's history, while in the grounds there is a fine marble statue of Queen Victoria. In Chichester Street the **Albert Memorial Clock Tower**, the "Big Ben" of Ireland, towers 143ft above the ground and contains a niche statue of the Prince Consort facing the High Street. Queen Victoria founded Queen's University in 1849. It stands in the southern suburbs of the town, and houses, in addition to the college, an interesting museum which is open to the public.

About 4 miles from the city centre, near the village of Dundonald, is the **Parliament Building** and **Stormont Castle**. Parliament Building was erected in 1928–32 at a cost of £1,250,000, a gift from the British government, to contain the houses of parliament and certain ministries of the six counties. It was opened by the Prince of Wales, later Duke of Windsor, on 16th Nov 1932. The building, one of the finest in Northern Ireland, has a floor area of 5 acres and stands in a 300 acre park. One of the most spectacular features is the ¾ mile processional approach. **Stormont Castle** stands close to the Parliament Building and was once the official residence of the Prime Minister.

SCARVA, Co Down

On 13th July each year, Scarva House forms the backcloth for a mock battle held to commemorate the Battle of the Boyne in 1689. King William's supporters rallied here prior to the battle and each year the hawthorn topiary work shaped in the image of King William is decorated for the occasion.

ARMAGH, Co Armagh

About 2,000 years ago, the legendary Queen Macha, from whom the town derives its name, was said to have scratched on the ground with her brooch the outline of the palace she wished built. Today a hill and surrounding ditch about 2 miles outside the city centre are the only visible remains of **Navan Fort**, where Queen Macha herself is reputed to lie buried.

Of interest in Armagh, is the **Observatory**, founded in 1790, which contains several interesting instruments belonging to George III. Nearby, in College Hill, is **Royal School**, originally founded on a different site in 1608 by James I, and where the Duke of Wellington once took his lessons.

COOKSTOWN, Co Tyrone

Founded as a plantation town in the 17th century by a man named Alan Cook, Cookstown essentially consists of a 1½ mile long road. One mile south east of the town centre is **Springhill House**, built during the 17th century and looking rather like a dolls house. It contains some fine furniture as well as two interesting portraits of William III and Mary, presented by the King for services rendered. In the grounds there is a barn that houses a fine collection of old carriages, as well as a model traditional

Irish cottage with several rooms given over to a collection of ancient costumes.

Tullaghoge Fort lying 2½ miles south of Cookstown is where the inauguration of the ancient chieftains of Ulster took place. The last ceremony held there was in 1593, and in 1602, Queen Elizabeth I ordered that the inauguration stone should be destroyed. South east of Cookstown is **Killymoon Castle**, designed by Nash in the 19th century at a cost of £80,000. It was once owned by the Prince Regent, subsequently George IV, who won it at a game of cards.

ENNISKILLEN, Co Fermanagh

Set in the lakeland of Ireland, the country town of Enniskillen sits on an island in the River Erne. The ruling family of Fermanagh, the Maguires, made their base in Enniskillen during the 15th century, founding the beautiful castle and watergate. **Enniskillen Castle** provided the backcloth for many medieval sieges, as well as for the later 17th century troubles between James II and William III. In 1689 the castle served as the rallying point for all William III's supporters. The castle has been restored and now serves as a museum.

NEWTOWNSTEWART, Co Tyrone

On the outskirts of the town are the remains of an old **plantation castle**, built about 1618; James II twice stayed here while on his way to and from the siege of Derry and, after the second visit, commanded that the castle be dismantled and the town burnt down.

Four miles south west of Newtownstewart is **Baronscourt**, one of the most beautiful country mansions in Northern Ireland. Set in richly

Londonderry's
Bishop's Gate
commemorates William III

Carrickfergus Castle
is the finest example of Norman
defensive building in Ireland

landscaped gardens and surrounded by woodland, the house was designed in 1750 and has remained to this day the seat of the Abercorn family. The 4th Earl of Abercorn was aide to James II during his flight to France, and the anchor of the ship in which they sailed is preserved on the estate. The gardens of Baronscourt are open to the public every day of the week except Sunday, although the house is not.

LONDONDERRY, Co Derry

The ancient mile-long **city walls** of Londonderry were completed in 1618 at a cost of almost £11,000. They are 20 to 25ft high and from 14 to 37ft thick. The building of the wall was a move that paid off in later years, during the siege between William III and James II. Mounted on one of the bastions of the wall is Roaring Meg, a great cannon that featured strongly in the troubles of the 17th century. The four city gates are also standing, although the most imposing, **Bishopsgate**, is not the original but a triumphal arch built to commemorate

William III in 1789. Opposite Shipquay gate, is the **Guildhall**, which contains some fine stained glass windows depicting Ireland's history, as well as the mayor's chain and medal of office presented to the city by William III. Nearby is the **Cathedral of St Columb**, founded in 1615 by James I. It is noted for its peal of 13 bells, two of which were given by James I and five a gift of Charles I.

LARNE, Co Antrim

Fresh from the battles for Scottish Independence, and hoping to make himself king of Ireland, Edward Bruce landed near Larne on 25th May 1315. He brought with him a force of 6,000 men and started a three year campaign that eventually lost him both his cause and his life. The remains of **Olderfleet Castle** stand here, originally built and owned by the Bisset family who rallied strongly to Edward's cause. The castle formed the backcloth for most of Edward's stay here, and was subsequently confiscated by the British crown. In later years the castle passed through the hands of Queen

Elizabeth I to James I who returned it to the Irish. The castle was last occupied in 1641 by British forces.

CARRICKFERGUS, Co Antrim

The town of Carrickfergus is traditionally thought to have been named after the Ulster chieftain, Fergus MacErc, who, 2,000 years ago, became the first Irish king of Scotland and from whom the royal house of Scotland claims descent. Fergus was supposed to have drowned off the Irish coast, and the castle was built on the rocky peninsula off which he lost his life.

Carrickfergus Castle was completed in the early 13th century, the first of its kind in Ireland and certainly the finest. The castle which has been greatly restored by the Northern Ireland government, has an enormous keep and four huge defensive towers. The portcullis is still complete with ancient machinery, there are dungeons and a vast great hall—40ft by 38ft. It was here that King John slept during his visit to Ireland in 1210. In 1315, after a year-long siege, the castle was captured by Edward Bruce, backed up with reinforcements from his brother

Robert, King of Scotland. The triumph was short-lived and at the battle of Faughart in 1318, Edward lost both his cause and his life, relinquishing the castle into the hands of the English where it remained for the next 300 years. William III landed here on June 14th 1690, *en route* to the Battle of the Boyne. A great stone now marks the spot where he stepped ashore. In later years the castle was used as a prison and, until 1928, as English barracks. There is now an interesting museum, which together with the rest of the castle is open daily to the public.

The **Church of St Nicholas**, parts of which are as old as the castle, was greatly restored in 1640. The south and west windows originate from Dangon, the ancestral home of the Duke of Wellington which was sold in 1800 when the Duke's family fell on hard times. Remains of the old **town wall** can still be seen. The North gate, which spans the road, was restored in 1911 to mark the coronation of George V.

INDEX

Acknowledgments
The publishers wish to thank the following for their permission to use photographs. The details are arranged according to page number:

2, 3: Fox Photos; 6: Peter Grugeon; Camera Press; Paul Popper; 7: Patrick Lichfield; Camera Press; 8: H Fox; Camera Press; Keystone Press Agency; 9: Keystone Press Agency; 10: Associated Press; 11: Keystone Press Agency; Peter Grugeon; Camera Press; 12: Fox Photos; Copyright, The Sunday Times, London; 13: Patrick Lichfield; Camera Press; Keystone Press Agency; 14: Cecil Beaton; Camera Press; 15: British Tourist Authority; 16: Press Association; 17: Keystone Press Agency; Associated Press; 18: Camera Press; Paul Popper; 20-23: Anthony Martin; Outline Art Services; 28: by kind permission of the Rector of St Mary Redcliffe; 36, 37: by kind permission of the Trustees of the late Lord Berkeley; 45: by kind permission of the Dean and Chapter of Winchester Cathedral; 51: by kind permission of the Vicar of SS Thomas Parish Church, Newport; 60: by kind permission of the Dean and Chapter of Canterbury Cathedral; 74: Department of the Environment; 75: Department of the Environment; 76: by kind permission of the Dean and Chapter of Westminster; 79: British Tourist Authority; 82: Department of the Environment; 83: British Tourist Authority; 85: British Tourist Authority; 86: British Tourist Authority; 87: British Tourist Authority; 88: British Tourist Authority; 96: by kind permission of the Marquess of Tavistock and the Trustees of the Bedford Estates; 106: Robert Johnson; 114, 115: by kind permission of the Dean and Chapter of Worcester Cathedral; 117: by kind permission of the Dean and Chapter of Gloucester Cathedral; 118, 119: by kind permission of the Marquess of Northampton; 123: by kind permission of the Rector of St Mary's Church, Warwick; 136, 137: British Tourist Authority; 169: Royal Commission on Historical Monuments (England); 186: Crown Copyright; reproduced with the permission of the Controller of Her Majesty's Stationery Office; 187: The Scottish Tourist Board; 188: The Scottish Tourist Board; 189: The Scottish Tourist Board; 191: Paul Popper; British Tourist Authority; 192: Department of the Environment; 193: reproduced by Gracious permission of Her Majesty The Queen; 209: British Tourist Authority; 212, 213: Northern Ireland Tourist Board; Cover: British Tourist Authority.